Timf(

MW01253783

Advance Praise for Timfoolery

"Masterson is a great and ridiculous writer. He has a singular voice, one that always shocks me and makes me laugh. It's shocking he's not a huge writer, won't be a surprise if he becomes one."

James Frey

*Author of A Million Little Pieces, My Friend Leonard,
Bright Shiny Morning and Endgame: The Calling*

*

"Timber Masterson's stories dance madly along the line between truth and fiction, fun and addiction, trouble and affliction. His voice is unique, insistent and impossible to ignore. The man is a force to be reckoned with."

Shaughnessy Bishop-Stall

*Author of Down to This: Squalor and Splendour in a Big-City Shanty Town,
Ghosted and Mille Petites Falaises*

*

"In an age when some of our greatest creative geniuses – Phillip Seymour Hoffman and Robin Williams, amongst others – have succumbed to addiction, depression and their darker side, it is fascinating to pierce the mind of a talented young man with an impressive skill set with devils of his own. His writings provide insight into the creative mind and the challenges both internal and external that confront it."

Michael Levine
Chairman - Westwood Creative Artists
*

"Tim often publishes under the playful moniker of "Timber" Masterson. That moniker was well chosen, since his various musings, observations and confessions have always merited the cry that something major is hurtling forward. In a forest full of writers searching for their original voice, Tim has confidently found his."

Richard Horgan
Co-Editor - Adweek's Fishbowl NY

*

"Tim Masterson is a writer first and a junkie second (or third according to the title - I'm not sure what he does in between). As such, he manages to capture the absurdity of addiction from the perspective of an astute observer while simultaneously exposing the frenetic, and often-insane thought process used to justify active addiction. Through Tim's incredible gifts as a writer we get to see how absurdly funny addiction can be even when there is no fun being had."

Oran Canfield
Author of Long Past Stopping

*

"Crazed humor with soul and impact. Masterson makes you laugh even as he vivisects himself with razor sharp prose.

Frank Miles
Performer, Writer

*

Timber Masterson stories live on the borders, in the in-betweens, and are summarily thrust upon the reader, in media res, like a hot potato, as if to say, "Here, take this, I don't know what to do with it."

Mike Young
Editor - Noo Journal

*

"I've been looking after Mr. Masterson for over 25 years, and while I'm amazed that he got this done, I'm not the least bit surprised at how amazing it is."

Dr. Dave Greenberg
Toronto GP

*

T i m b e r   M a s t e r s o n

is a man on a mission. What's that mission,
you ask? Why, to poke and probe at the
quivering mass of strangeness that lurks just
below the surface of our personalities, the
Blob of our unconsciousness if you will, and
to try to get under its skin to see what makes
it tick. Or quiver. Or, well, whatever it is that
a Blob does.

Whether over the radio, on a film set, on
the page, Masterson deals strictly in the weird
and unexpected, specifically, the fantastical
space   between   reality   and   unreality,
imagination and delusion, fact and fiction. His
work   runs   the   full   gamut   of   the
electromagnetic spectrum, infecting you as
you affect it. Reading his stories is like
looking at old, grainy, black and white
photographs, faded by too much time spent
stuffed in shoe boxes in locked attics. The
images flicker in and out of transmission.
They could be of Minotaurs or mustachioed
street sausage vendors in Toronto. They
could sound like a papier-mâché Mel Tormé,
singing somewhere, off in the distance, in all
his velvety, foggy glory.

Secrets best kept secret often come
tumbling out of his stories like clowns out of
a clown car. The resulting effect is that of the
narrative, running far behind the secrets,
terribly out of breath and desperate to catch
up, cursing that free gym membership offer it
threw away last month, then finally stopping,

giving up, and drowning happily in a flood of seltzer water amidst a hailstorm of lemon meringue pies. This is not to say there's a preponderance of clowns in his stories, or any at all, for you coulrophobics out there. That was just to prepare your eyes for the burn.

Mike Young, Editor - Noo Journal

◆   ◆   ◆

The book tells the story of a decade that embraces the ennui of being broke and homeless in Los Angeles, jetting in and out of clinics and treatment centres, shelters, and AA meetings. This Outsider is at odds with dealers, doctors. with agendas, priests handing out redemption, creepy casting directors, and teachers with lessons too hard to learn. We encounter children at the door wanting only candy, getting more than they bargained for, enfeebled and enraged landlords complex, girlfriends turned escorts and Kafkaesque rabbits that rescue.

An addict with a life-saving charm, the protagonist pulls scams, crashes social events, and impersonates employees - whatever it takes to impress, to ingratiate and to get the next fix. His refuge is the interior world of drug-induced fantasies poised on the precipice of a fall into real memory and the imminent loss and waste, the spectral accompaniment to the addled life of addiction; a phantasmagoria of layered symbolism and imagery in the production of a unique vision somewhere this side of reality. Part Odyssey, part Fear and Loathing, this is a modern day voyage into the heart of darkness of isolation, a Gen-X coming-of-age tale while shaking it rough on the mean streets.

Spurning the usual gloom and doom of the addiction-recovery genre, this book vibrates with a manic and surreal energy and an astonishing facility with language, pushing it into the realm of narrative's most extreme and playful possibilities.

This novel may be the first example of a self-crafted magical realism rooted in North American popular culture, one in the tradition of Kubla Khan.

These meditations in the tradition of Coleridge unfold in a theatre of the absurd, forging a kind of William Burroughs situation-comedy-of-club-kids, driven through the narrator's world to a place where the reader wonders if it's truly happening in the present or is a wished for kaleidoscopic dream state.

This page intentionally left blank.

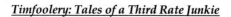

This page just kind of BECAME blank at will.

And this one, we don't have any idea what happened.

Timfoolery:
Tales
of a
Third
Rate
Junkie

by

TIMBER MASTERSON

☪

All this and more by special arrangement with
Routledge & Kegan Ltd., London,
a nifty and buxom firm that also hems dresses
and takes in riding gear.

Alternate Titles Proposed For This Paperback:

Far from Kind & Pretty

An Unsympathetic History of Mincing About

The Comic Cruelty of Fifth Rate MonkIes

Every Kitten Starts off Soft and Good

The Crude but Comical Times of...

Timber Masterson

∾

This is a book that covets secrets. Neither fish nor fowl.
Or don't.

◆   ◆   ◆

*"The truly excessive myriad of timepieces strewn about the home was one thing,
but the fact that a good deal of them, half, maybe, represented some strange
foreign surrogate time zone - one that had no dust particles,
kitchen crumbs or inconsiderate sons - with the rest not moving their
dust-laden hands altogether, made for an unnerving daily far-from-relaxed
headquarters. It was not inaccurate to state that there were so many clocks in
mom's house, I never really knew what time it was. I would come to know this as
doing "hard time."*

...and ongoing in our minds...through and through

that almost unbearable mocking...

꙳

Wayne & Schuster
Rockefeller Central
3523 Avenue of the Americas
N e w   Y o r k , N Y   1 3 5 4 3
Los Angeles   Toronto   New York City
Connecticut   Vancouver   Orange County

◆   ◆   ◆

Above are places that are privy to possessing and
selling this book. Though, if you have the book in your hands
at this moment, chances are you couldn't care less where else
it happens to be published.

down there at W & S and C who know
considerably more than I about lengthy and sordid
adult-like issues. We should consider ourselves blessed
to be in the constructs of an uplifting wondrous
Educational System, in this - our Northern Americas -
that produce such smarty-panted people who've
gone out and snagged themselves that coveted,
impossible-at-times-to-track-down
wildly elusive Full-time Job.
My hats off to everyone.

*

Gratitude of some kind may come in varied forms,
or shapes - perchance an Isoscelian triangle thingy with
super color contrasts? A rhombusy oblong type deal or part
parallel-a-jelly-gram (Candy Gram, M'am?) - should more
than likely be awarded to those who feel they've, in one way
or another - at some juncture during the elongated process -
added something to this inspirational monolith. Though, to
keep all that business straight and fitting gets magnificently
complex, so I'm kind of hoping these kindred spirits will just
kind of know who they areEven better, go on and track down
one of the TimberMedia minions and have them compose a
stipend proxy I.O.U, so they can scribble out, then disperse a
checqeroonie - until I can get to the bank, that is, finally endorse
the thing and deposit said funds as opposed to just handing
over jingle jangle rollaway coins and/or glitzy plumage,
of which I can tell you right off the bat will NOT
cover a debt…not the way I'd like it to.
I claim Chapter 9. (Or is it 11?)
I claim all the chapters in this book, and sure,
…just who else would claim such chapters, anyway? *C'mon!*

*

ISBN 9780 994 779 809

*

46 32 35 67 12 - this code here represents either the plus-size
models' measurements taken during the flirty novel shoot, or
it's the combination to my locker at that downtown New
Jersey YMCA that I haven't visited in a dog's age. I should

look into that. It's NOT the football play that Joe Namath
shouted just before throwing the damn football downfield
whilst guest-starring on the American television hit show,
the Brady Bunch - which is what I originally believed.

*

The Publisher has endeavoured to be as accurate and
complete as possible in the creation of this work.
The book is not intended for use as a source of
medical or legal advice as that would defy
categorization and be even more complicated
than this whole deal is already. All readers
are advised to seek out the services of
competent professionals in the medical and
other serious and comic-type fields, if need be.
In practical advice books, like anything else in life,
And when it comes to the humanoid matrix,
there are no guarantees of cures. Readers are cautioned
to rely on their own judgement regarding their individual
circumstances and to act accordingly. While all attempts have
been made to verify facts and statistics provided in this
particular tome, the publisher assumes no responsibility for
errors, omissions, or contrary interpretation of the subject
matter herein. Any perceived slights of specific persons,
peoples, or organizations are unintentional. (Except for, of
course, when they happen to be absolutely intentional).
Some of the text herein lies possible fiction.

რ

The author has changed some names and characteristics
of certain individuals in this book, which I'm told.
This has something to do with Liable...as in,
"I'm _liable_ to make trouble for myself and make
huge and unrecoverable mistakes." Why, and to what end,
remains unclear to this writer - but it's been explained that
such actions might possibly involve infringement issues,
which would do nothing more than encompass countless
letters, lawsuits, and as well, promote ungodly pre-mid-day
awakenings, plus, some unrequested seen-as-silly - yet are

pretty pertinent - complex pantomime presentations featuring
hand-puppets, kerosene, some non-edible Silly Putty and
some old mannequins that weren't busy modelling
anything or needed on any stark runway. Gosh, maybe even
having to appear in places of drab legal assembly in order to
defend my earlier, yet most sincere, actions - flunky law stuff,
a fumbly business at best - unhelpful to most.

* * *

Also, if you've purchased this book without a cover
then quite frankly, I can't help you.
What would cause you to buy such a thing, anyway?
If you're still at a place in your life where cover-less books
seem intriguing to you, you're obviously someone I can't
reach. Give it some time and try back, but we may end up
only agreeing on the following; that these Timfoolery Tales
may be violently misunderstood.

Wanting to avoid a media frenzy during the time this
work is released, we feel it fair to warn the readers,
the people who digest and care about this novel,
that some scenes during the course of action have been
genetically embellished, not only for dramatic effect,
but for the mere fact it seemed to be best for the
ever-growing manuscript, and life - mine, as a whole.
Nothing is meant to disrespect the reader,
no one wishes to "dupe" anyone here or worse -
"rope-a-dope"…(something Muhammed Ali performed,
if I recall correctly). Quite the contrary, as the author (and all
involved) want genuinely for the reader to feel encased in a
massive down blanket alongside the golden warmth of a
dancing fire in some Vale, Colorado chalet ski lodge, with
servants of strange ethnicities not only serving you at your
every whim but delivering to your suite bowl upon bowl of
steamy *chaud de chocolate*, plus other special affectations and
artifices for imbibing, digesting and drawing on;
quite a rare luxury, you can be well rest assured.
So, there you go.

* * *

That being said, you'll come upon an occasional name change
within the construct of these gingerly manufactured pages,
and, as far as characteristics, well now, that's anybody's guess.
Though I am open, prepared even, to discuss it in any type of
open arena, forum or legal theatre with a pretty green or blue
backdrop as a canvas, with a dedicated fellow-of-law present.

So, as aforementioned, some names have been changed.
An attempt at any rate has been made, to protect the innocent,
though the feeble, predictably meek and spiritually
unbalanced "innocent" folk still shine brilliantly through,
as do those known as The Guilty - a sorry and malodorous lot,
who are served best in a remorseful burning
book of Revelations dedicated specially to them.

ॐ

None of the nameless - at times faceless - non-violent,
non-diaper-wearing beasts were harmed or teased
too badly while any of the stories, essays, treatises and
arguments were being compiled, even though there were
about a million instances the loutish teamster crew here
could have really had some fun at their expense.
As far as any animals' names go, sadly for them - I'm sorry to
say - have _not_ been altered, as they should have considered
their behavior better before getting involved in such an
ambiguous manner. FAME will be their punishment;
those bygone days of relaxing Sunday walks out to get the
paper, not being pestered, or hassled, like, totally under the
radar of the Monster Animal Act of 1823, totally
unrecognizable, a thing of the past. Being held up and exposed
now at party meetings and examinations, exposed for ridicule
by any damn fool who wants to point their finger and mouth
off with their two cents. Further still - wildlife, as well as
those furry interloping domestics - are responsible
for their own actions; as all creatures great
and small must have accountability.
No exceptions.

I've wrestled with this one through a myriad of late night
hours and countless days staring into a boundless futile abyss
and am convinced that between the viewing of the surveillance
tapes from the backyard grotto - albeit recognizing moments

sublime, terrifically romantic and wistfully grainy in some
parts - coupled with my extensive notes compiled, now locked
in the massive unbreakable steel safe in the TimberMedia.com
underground offices, it's more than fair.

Look at it this way;

here is where trust can begin.

෨

Significant to note that voluminous interviews and seemingly
never-ending researching went into extracting truths from
creatures in the strangest of lands across this globe; a purely
come-across one - a new entity (just put out by The Lord,
obviously), low on the evolutionary-promo-publicity-wagon-
wheel-modern-media-gizmo scale - an accidentally-stumbled-
upon beast (which made it all the more intriguing and
just plain bizarre) - this sweet, bilaterally symmetrical,
surprisingly hermaphrodital bi-coastal furry cad so found
turned out to be a nocturnal, ultra-violet, non-violent
but dyspeptic Bunny Rabbit Man, (who, at first, withheld
his name) that possessed (and later showed off) remarkable
antennae, shiny but bloodshot eyes of teal, and was a lurking
eight feet tall, AND had a barnacle mollusk tail plus (!) a
supreme passion for deep-sea fishing, *sans* license.
"I love the danger, the intrigue," the big fella was overheard
spouting. He's now being properly tended to, is on the mend
and at the time of this release - and as the pharmacist, Dr.
Forminkle, said, "Doing just fine." Me, we're going to get
around to. *"I will feast tonight on what I have come across in the
aquatic hunt. Tricks or Treats, you ask? Why both my good man.
Both!"* This, the only English we could interpret from the
beast's blubbering while he was still dressed in the burlap
clown sack along with the severely suffocating *Spanx for Dudes*
that he somehow procured out there for snug sporty wear.

Where he bought any of that stuff, we still haven't a clue.

* * *

The only time at all, animals or humans even came close to
being maimed, receiving electric shock, or having lunch
money and paper route funding withheld during this
production, was during occasional drunk actions
from the aforementioned, while proudly screaming
his "Tricks or Treats" line in a high-pitched
Ethel Mermaid-like squeal. He had to be force-fed sedatives
and administered multiple booster shots. I was next in line for
the treatment, though after an unfair amount of time had
passed, (I felt) and having these tricky and now unlicensed
RN's from the outer boroughs attempt to keep me from
said God-given medication, I figured, finally, that to
administer my own would not be considered unlawful, even
unruly, hence, I found myself retiring to a tattered and rancid-
smelling, yet tranquil, cushiony doggie bed out in the garage,
amidst inedible green leafy diseased vegetables that hung
cavernously from the garage rafters. Laying down best as I
could, away from the romp and circumpance of interviews,
phone calls, requests, notes left on the front lawn and pinned
to my front door, autograph hounds and bookish things,
I fell into a perfect unearthly fugue dream state
where I had a sense that, absolutely all of the wistful
images that occurred during my somnambulant hours, were
being displayed through incredulous dream-skype-like sunny
images to me, all for the good of the show, cast,
personnel and crew alike. I mean the book.
Yes, it became photosynthesized for the good of the book.

* * *

Some of the chapters and come-across-pterodactyls *(tf#1)* in
this book have appeared in slightly different form, if not more
splendidly structured for the human brain palette.

Some almost unrecognizable chapters
and published excerpts from
Timfoolery: Tales of a Third Rate Virtuoso Layabout,

in other challenging areas of thought and quality verse, like
these ones catalogued here before us at one time existed
elsewhere, which, if you ever run across them, you could
probably pick them up for a song, if you knew who to contact,
that is. They are *Gadfly Online (2014), Akashic Books (2013), the*
Bitchin' Kitsch, (2013) Roadside Fiction (2013), Open Book
Toronto, (2011) Fresh Yarn Salon (2006) Yankee Pot Roast (2005)

ᔕ

That said, the author is terrifically grateful to the people
who've put up ad nauseatingly with the likes of me and my —
at times - out of whack ego-driven demands; the editors,
mentors, ex-girlfriends, colleagues, the casting personnel,
fellow countrymen, audio engineers and dairy farmers -
who've assisted in various capacities to obtain the final product
by means of those read-throughs, elongated discussions, the
work-shopping and screenplay suggestions, and of course the
unlimited methamphetamine caffeine suppository testing.
For this and more, I Thank You All, truly; not only for saving
me from that rotten and confusing parochial school on the
Eastern seaboard, but for things you may never know.
That being said, here below and in no particular order -
well, maybe a remote tiny bit of thought process regarding the
order, but not enough to get into.

Anyway, here they lay: *Ed O'hara, Cornelia Persich, Jody Terio,*
Michael Levine, Marcus Bobesich, Katherine Mcleod,
Annette Andrews, Daniel Richler, James Frey, Michael Levine,
Oran Canfield, Beth Collison, Chuck Vollmer, Dave Ford,
Dr. Christina Whyte-Earnshaw, Rhonda Towells, Melinda Johnston,
my always "right-on friend" Frank Miles, Jonathan Kay,
special unfatigued editing thanks to Richard Horgan - my "Canadian
writer friend in California," and a host of others...though, not an
exorbitant host of others.

*the Toronto Arts Council, the Ontario Arts Council, Biblioasis, Brick
Magazine, the Peppermint Hall Publishing Concern* and *TimberMedia
Inc.* all played a role in keeping me walking upright during the
process of this historical enterprise.

&

A miniscule, though mentionable, modicum of effort has been
made to correctly attribute materials reproduced here, in this
tome for you. If errors have unwittingly occurred, the
publisher will be happy to correct them in future editions. If
no future editions are produced or made available, then
I will pinky swear promise to come to your home
(that is, when my parole officer, Mr. Jakes, and Karl the
Country Club membership coordinator say it's, *"OK to travel,
Tim!")* - and guide whomever through a kind of
reprogramming in order to show you how to rewire and
create your very own publication; that is, when I find myself
visiting your particular city, there first and foremost to get in
and reorganize - code-wise, the gunky innards of your
computer system to make it all run super smooth once again.

*   *   *

For information on how to report embarrassing blunders, obvious mistakes and how to properly ingest penguin with a guilt and gluten-free conscience, kindly send 296 cereal box backs (Kellogg's Frankenberry mainly please, or if your bunch is able to hunt down a couple dozen or so of those classic Wheaties ones with the wildly defunct, past-their due-date sport stars of yesteryear); that, or sultry poses of Sally Jesse Raphael captured in sweats and next to zero make-up.

*

Now, scotch-tape it all up in proper cardboard, Styrofoam - whatever's easily procured from the neighbor's garage, then, secure the package. Write on the bundle the following address: 220 East 63rd Street, New York, New York 10028 (I used to live there with this prima donna soap "actress" who was "in love" with this well-known hockey icon. That is, if you call blowing a burly and toothless NHL defenseman, then stalking him and his poor unsuspecting mid-west wife from state to state, "love"). Don't worry, it's alright; the slipshod fallen princess probably still doesn't read books without pop-ups or scratch 'n sniff pictures, so we're safe, legally, and she most certainly hasn't inhabited that Upper East Side haunted domicile for quite some time. If you feel that it is safe and secure, your package, then go ahead and send it on as the post office people will magically make certain it will materialize there sometime soon.

* * *

The First English translation was helped along by A.J Milner, under the title, *Woe, and It's Relation to my Unconscious Self: The Muddled Mary Tyler Moore Years,* which explored one's relocation to a new city, social integration, finding community through a news media outlet whilst ceaselessly hurling women's hats sky-high to preposterous heights whilst skulking through Minneapolis' outdoor food courts and what that action represents. The translation was later re-named due to constant picketing and public outcry to a simpler yet more profound, though not as easily understood,

You have what is called a First Edition.

f r o m
The Library of The Yonkers Winka Doodle Family
Congested Congress.
Catalogue-in-Publication-Data
*
Sold Subject to the condition that this
book is mineand not yours.

A medium-sized bordering-on-impressive hardcover edition of
this book was published in 2008 by Eccliastes, (קָלַת ק) a swell
imprint of Harpo Colonic Publishers, which came complete
with monochrome colored scratchy beach towels, a really
keen army-men set and a much less entertaining, inedible and
pathetic lame Sea Monkey collection...fashioned together with
non-Rhino spearmint chewing gum, plus Painted Squirrel-
styled drawing apparatus. (*The Painted Squirrel* name also
became transmogrified into what would later become a mid-
level nouveau riche 'No Shoes/Just Shorts' eatery in midtown
that I - against Fedderman's strong council -
invested a tad too heavily in).

*   *   *

Permissions & Quotes appear at the very end of this work as,
that is where I am told they are supposed to sit. Nobody
bothered to return my enquiries regarding the details
pertaining to them, so the higher-ups can't come to me saying
that I didn't make an effort back there. Some are also
positioned in spaces that seemed apropos during breakfast
meetings, and which made amazing sense on that particular
day. Though now, after looking at the whole damn business
through less-than-rose-colored glass eyes, I honestly can't
imagine what anyone was thinking at the time. And as far as
who gave ME permission? Well, that gets tortuously messy to
sort out properly. Plus, I'm a little miffed now, even
flabbergasted, how nobody in any of these swanky and modern

yet overtly uncouth lofty offices, bothered to mention how a
striking majority of this creative undertaking smacks of
embarrassing immature narcissism.

That Being Said...

These titles, as well as others that got tossed around, involved
a kind of forlorn, end-of-the-line Charlie Brown-like theme.
All got crossed off as they were ultimately deemed too childish
and complex, too unbearably dark for the sort of demographic
these words were intentionally suited for, and so, would
tragically not sell well, which then in turn would
ultimately cause strain and strife in the home and present day
life in General...in Corporal, too. Yep, strife through and
through. But in second and third printings of this work, I've
still got some better titles on the table for consideration.
(know-it-all editors and dumb dramaturds, I'll show 'em).

☙

Professionals and amateurs are hereby warned that any Timber
Masterson written or audio work is hereby subject to an Earl
Grey Boston Tea Party tax and royalty, or at least a good
chunk of the Hershey's bar you've got stashed in that shirt
pocket of yours there. Someone on the team will be coming
for it, so, best leave it on the porch in a Creed's
European man purse or equivalent holding satchel,
to avoid any chocolate conflicts.

*

Except in the United States of America,
this book is sold subject to the condition that it
shell not be lent out for more than a week, re-sold after 8:00
p.m sharp on a weekday, faxed anywhere, hired out, or
otherwise circulated without the publisher or writer's prior
consent in any form of binding or cover other
than that in which it is published.

*

At any rate, you can pretty much assume
that if the writer is dead by the time all this hullabaloo
reaches your selfless stage of consideration,
everyone's just going to do as they see fit anyway.

Because, well, that's just what humans do: behave badly.
I am quite alive right now, during the release of this printing,
so, I request that you not do anything unmerited with this
manuscript or there'll be an unpleasant curse on your head,
you salubrious sentimental tiny-fonted reader. But make notes
along the way, kind country gentiles, for what you deem
necessary to extract from this work. Unless I've perished due
to a bizarre gluten-filled gluttonous indulgence of frozen peas
and tropical sun tan oil or have been pushed off a rather
noticeably placed-for-death scaffolding scene…OR have
perished due to going viral, as in the future (such complicated
and dangerous times), things are not produced without
a great deal of cellular damage along the way.
(And no, not like, Blackberry IPOD out-of-range sort of cell
damage, but, CELL damage).

* * *

This significant work is set in 'monotypical-litho-graphical
Polly-wanna-graph-a-grammy-goiter-iambic pentathalonic-
sutured-non-sequential-wack-a-wing-a-doo-dong-lack-luster-
licious-line'; quite the bitch to download and integrate into
any machine properly so please do not attempt to use on
your own processor of words as it will drastically
screw your computer up beyond the beyond.

*

Parts of an un-abridged version of this novel were "published"
in the South Seas sometime during the new millennium,
though details are sketchy, as it was produced using nothing
but tiny fragile conk shells, octopi tentacles, jelly-fish larvae,
squid-ink and plankton paste. Much of the priceless and rare
reproduction has not been recovered for a couple of reasons;
one, had to do with just how to cart all that business around,
especially through airport terminals, the whole deal getting
unbearably expensive, magnificently weird and tough to even
keep track of, forget even explaining such a moronic
monstrosity to the ravenous border patrol dogs, or keep in any
real order and two, was something else which I can't
remember,but I'll share with you it was quite possibly and
almost certainly important going into the thought at the time,

(Alzheimer's? ADHD? SID?) and may even come up later, if
you so choose to stick around. I bet it was funny.

I mean, I bet that it will be funny.

* * *

If any of the so called "pages" are ever located and ultimately
recovered, on land or found bobbing about adjacent canal
locks or by buoys, would you be kind enough to gather them
all up and send to Esme Carter at Kinney Austere Press in
Montreal (or the Linklater & Shultz Vacuum Company)
as she looks after such things. A reward, or at very least a
re-imbursement of your postage, is not as much guaranteed
as much as it is being looked into.

I, at very least, am an honest man. Pretty much.

* * *

I shall hope for the pleasure of including my critics and lovers
alike, in a kind of comparison companion kind of Ephrem the
Enormous Cherry-colored & Sensitive four-legged crossbreed
mongrel Heath-Cliff-Notes work book.

The words I have pursued and the clues I have followed, often
Fruit-Loop-lessly, '*Nonetheless, Catharticly*' (a sweet lyric from
a Leonard Cohen-ish song I penned, "The catheter I didn't
require, good squire; now, don't leave me in bed, for dead,
now pour this here cowboy a Johnny Walker Red"),
was but a fashion/style preference far exceeding in
number the pages in this volume. Not easily now
(pretty soon) shall I relinquish this fascinating pursuit
and can only trust that readers will find corresponding
pleasure in these rewarding excursions along the
unfrequented paths of literature and language. For some,
I'm told, these words set forth are best experienced when read
aloud. Many young adults, especially the mid-lifers - that
perilous regrettable time between birthing canal sanctity and

those final days on the moronic morphine drip and plus, the
in-between time - the absurdity of trying and caring and
worrying. (You fool!), it's no word of a lie to discover that
this will be the only work of literature book
needed before being tucked in.

* * *

You are amazingly close (really, very) to actually reading this
book. Stick with me and keep moving along forward, as
Patience, a virtue lost in frolic and immediate
gratificational rummaging, gets easily cast aside,
one of the first attributes to go, I regret to remind.
And actually 'patience' is not your **P A L**,
not like the principal should have been - that conceited prick
bastard. I learnt this in Grade 3 spelling class, or was it…
mmmmmm mmmm?mmm;
no, it was definitely Grade 3, though
the "Grade of Three' ended up being little more than a
queerly-shaped musty room in the basement cafeteria reeking
of disgusting melt-in-your-mouth horrific odors that
permeated the youth of tomorrow's supple and tantalizingly
moist youth. Some chose to believe that the Kool-Aid-scented
carcinogenic unnerving mind gas - if that's indeed what it was
pulsating in there - was a past-its-expiry date sour-cream 'n
chive-anchovy-paste plus pineapple crust concern with
delectable deep dish but inedible tuna fish at this stellar quasi-
school I found myself assigned to, which had little to do with
that catastrophically scary three storey high fucking
abacus…for self-teaching pointless archaic calculations and
me, repeatedly showing up with no proper teacher in
attendance, plus never ceasing, seemingly, was that
Hunchback of Notre Dame teacher's assistant who dragged
stuffed mannequins in weekly resembling Boris Karloff and
Bella Lugosi mixed together and aptly placed "for studying," at
the front of the "classroom" though riotously more disturbing.
I had not clue one as to what these brilliant educational staff
folk were trying to get through to us. Can't say if it somehow
was to act as a kind of poignant cautionary tale, as in, "If you
don't stretch properly, then you, my friend, could also be in
for some horrifically nightmarish hump-like osteo-psychosis

bony matter stemming from…" Or maybe it was a way to get us to remember the definitions of metaphor, personification, simile and irony, which, by the way, I still retain to this day, literary devices from Miss Finch's Grade 9 English class that I can still whip out as alarming, second-rate parlor tricks for when the party inevitably slows, but once in a great while, the sympathy vote from a cardigan-wearing head-brace'd divorcee with stringy molar braces might offer to take me into the guest bathroom, and scrub my hands with some of that sea kelp quality soap. Also, the writing implements were made out of ceiling fans and dried poutine, with no suitable ink to speak of - unless you count the day when that foreign kid with braces brought in that Blood & Squid Ink Turtle pool (a conceptual modern artistic mfor "Show and Touch" and things got out of hand (it's down in the record books somewhere), as I made certain to share with the hung jury, *"Hey, I don't think that counts. Hold on just a minute!"* The "faculty" or "the board" - whatever they called themselves - taught sad and unhelpful, threatening lessons in harsh-sounding foreign languages by way of teleprompter, and as well, managed to lure all us young'ens off school property with promises of visiting "the puppies" and eating wild flavored licorice and rainbow-colored Chiclet's while visiting the dinosaurs at some confusing 'Humane' museum…which I never did see. "You call yourself educators?!" thrusting a vat of tartar sauce desecrated with vomited-up green and red licorice and robust fruit flavor Chiclet's. "Freudian field trips", this, the Mother-Fucking-Prodding-Liars retort in court years later. This, to say nothing of how their evil temperaments and manic dispositions have hounded me relentlessly through the years. Somewhere down the line, a couple of those dandruff-entrenched pseudo teachers actually turned into out-of-orbit-irritating-Perquacky-playing-asthmatic-Kerplunkity-Plunk-Palestinian-neighbors-with-off-the-wall-furious-crossword-concerns, who now, nightly, peer in my backyard window, hands filthy from their pre-sunset gardening expeditions - VAMPIRE GARDENING - I've dubbed their all-too-loud finicky nocturnal "meetings." Their bothersome and unnerving sport, executed with pith-helmet-mag-light, electronic Ginsu-digger,

methamphetamine-suppositories, handily inserted for full-on
sustained troweling power - their uniforms complete with all-
too-gay looking Tony Randlish-ish multi-pocketed, cream-
colored aprons and bizarrely-drawn cartography-club-
membership t-shirts. Seems I'll never get rid of them...
the extra t-shirts or the neighbors.

* * *

After showing some advance chapters & heartfelt
Words to many delicatessen heads and a good deal of the
populace leasing office space here that have basically little
or nothing to do with anything, there is the consensus afoot
that my original name for the book,
"A Heartbreaking Work of Staggering Wit and Mincing About,"
made grand sense in relation to how this story was
beginning to shape up and seemed to encompass in grand
scope and wide breadth the feelings and ideas set forth.
In other words, (!) - yes, I know we're almost
done here - in the beginning it made *mucho sentido*
and was a favorable title...but, in the end, all thought it best
to stay away from all that borderline infringement busied
business I'd just as soon avoid, not wanting to rehash,
or tread in such already proven ground, or step on the
toes of its loved ones. I'm happy with
my TimFoolery title anyhow.

* * *

Though, after working diligently on it for more than
a good chunk of a decade, the "Tim Foolery Footnotes" thing
keeps coming up, and since these are all mostly; fragmented
stories, heartfelt recollections, reports from the frontlines,
diaries from a madman if you will, the "Tales" title
also seems to make a hell of a lot of good sense too.
And besides, I sort of like clarifying and sprinkling
my two (or three) cents gingerly throughout.
I believe that my notes also assist in building a worthy
and true, bonding relationship between you and the
author, so that's where all that stands.
N o w . . .
an already documented exploratory outing,

"*Wingdings; What's Up avec All That Nonsense?*" - further
selected stories from this author, can be purchased, though
still remain an astronomically Herculean task to take on and
ultimately find, as only 23 copies were printed in the "South-
eastern United States," under the pseudonym Cornelius
Jestermishkinson. Apologetically, that book is un-rated and
un-praised, unlike the one you have in your hands, which is
rated, mis-pronounced, garbled and at times…even
marginally strung-out, but nevertheless, more than worth
your precious time to read and really get into, and if possible,
assign some questions to confused 2nd year psych
students with no social calendar.

* * *

This work, resulting in years of excruciating research,
which has festooned and garlanded me exhaustively, was made
possible by the co-operation of scores of leading universities,
pre-med mechanics from the Devry Slipper Support Factotum
and certain girl guide leaders; those New Jersey Turnpike toll
booth attendees; interlopers with secrets using only mother's
fridge magnets; the Ouija board people from the attic no one
dare set their Achilles heel in, as well as scores of absurdly
helpful Lindsay librarians and the places that house them - the
libraries; that girl Beth something-or-other of the perfectly
goldenrod locks, stunning lashes and just the perfect amount
of freckles who purposely sat directly behind me in Home-
wreck-room - of all places. I'm convinced to this day she
plopped herself down directly behind me to make me lose
whatever beginnings of a mind I had going, teasing me
incessantly with her raspy but youthful sweet vocals whilst
sucking on peppermints, requesting that, after she dropped
her pencil, if I could "…be a sweetheart, and help me out?!"
and then when she knew I was listening intently to
her talk about teasing the boys in gym class like,
when she whipped out her trick bra. (Tricks-a-plenty which I
fully respected). Sweet Jesus. OH MY GOD, that gal made
me completely mental, and at the time, you couldn't
convince me that there had not been a spell cast my way.
Clear pre-meditated (*pre-medicated?*) torture.

I would have stayed up all night, done her homework,
gently bathed her, (all at the same time even, while cooking a
western omelette). Dangerous but doable, served on wobbly
dinner tray in front of the old boob tube. I came away from
the whole heartbreaking scene attempting to carouse my brain
towards anything other than her devilish scintillating beauty
and girly way she had about her. It was all I could do to try to
think of anything else but her. I tried thinking of the weirdest
things like, what those ancient brown Ontario Science Centre
carpets must smell - and taste like - after decades of
punishment from misbehaving kiddies on overnight sleeping-
bag-wetting grade school trips, vacuuming procedures not
being what they once were...but my thoughts
always returned back to _her_.

* * *

Also, one of the editors of this work, Monsieur Dogmar
Rulensan, who's not slept by what must be now going on 43
days, and, whose teeth are being shipped back to him in special
bubble-wrapped polyurethane Saran-Wrap, has truly
succeeded - (I'll have to check on this) it seems - in collecting
over 24,042 portraits, (will double check figure) photographs,
facsimiles, archaeological illustrations, and ideas scribbled in
less-than-respectable hotel bars working with a barely useable
gnawed-on primary Color triangular Crayola Crayon set;
plus there's the other pictorial material germane to this field
in which the author has played in, an arena of sulk and
sickness intriguing to some but best avoided by most.
This, the first time that such likenesses, traditional, artistic and
otherwise, have been assembled in one such vague, but vivid,
purposeful volume. You are the recipient of this, the readable,
streamlined version.

* * *

Numerous reproductions of paintings, emails, statues, scans,
letters, Polaroid's, pastries and other works of true art relating
to great thinkers of our time, who the author has perhaps once
heard of, or stumbled upon at a cocktail party (as well as ideas
from varied mystics, fundamental scientists, dog tired Dairy
Queen part-timers, butchers, coffee-baristas in tight

flowery summer smocks from all lands) all will now be
readily accessible to the reader: YOU
Oh mercy!
Before drawing conclusions, however, you, the reader, is
cautioned to bear in mind the fact that the author has spent
considerable arcane time mentally

U n B a L a N c E d ;

discourteous to others

&

destructive to himself

§

F u r t h e r   a c k n o w l e d g m e n t s :
and cheerful thanks to:

The Monks who run the Hospice of St. Bernard (and their
gargoyles out in front of the church that I *swear* keep rotating
and switching positions on me), The Pomona Police
Commissioner's wife for long sanguine and entwining
"low on ethics, big on ease" mid-day sessions
(for research purposes only, of course), the car wash station
attendees on Miracle Mile and 3rd St. that maintain and build
on their private set of keys to the weirdest of places, like
offices in buildings that I can't imagine for the life of me
how they…well, good for them, I guess. (Maybe it'll help
bandage their broken self-esteem and construct and aid in
auspicious plans, who really knows?); that girl from Ogunquit,
Maine that looks so preposterously like Nancy Drew,
I couldn't help but ask about clues to a case I know she
had…anyway, she sells sea shells full of moisturizer at the
nearby sea shore drug store; there's Pedro, that Spanish
security guard who took multiple risks with me down at The
Paramount lot, always letting me pass unhindered - as he and
his family would find themselves in a sea of horrific trouble (*I
threatened!*) if he didn't wave me on and let me pass, on
account I told him I had an office (my very own palm tree
bungalow, actually) and later, with me ultimately passing out

in big shot cheese-ball Hollywood starlet's trailers from come
across 'medication' - my 'investigative journalism' -
participatory, of course - crossing the line, having had an
untreated compulsion to 'shower close to stars', this,
part of a once ongoing cinematic and wildly
entertaining therapeutic study
lasting numerous months.
I'm better now.

❧

Curl up and
Enjoy, won't you...
as I will do my best, also, to enjoy

*   *   *

Every Kitten Starts off Soft and Good

No, that's not going to end up working.

The Regrettable Charm
of the
Imposter?

mm mmm...

THIS GRAND MATRICULATION
maybe.

Simpler, please.

How about,

"The Timster Fools the Really Useless Jungle Trapper Guy"

Sneaky and mysterious, sure, but…
Nearly…almost…maybe.

*   *   *   *

This Book,

this grand manipulation ~

riddled with imposter scenarios, nostalgia,

amidst a Tsunami of sadness steeped in epic

cinematic imagery,

starts right about

here

▼   ▼   ▼

Yes,

that's

good

now

you

have

an

i d e a

Paying Rent in the Tower of Bliss and Courage?

Yes, but a tad confusing,

and, c'mon, what does that really mean anyway?

Press Play and let's get going here

*   *   *   *   *   *   *   *

*   *   *

One bad year never comes alone. This, I fear, is truth.

"It wasn't until very late into the publishing procedure that the team came across this: an exact description of how Mr. Masterson saw himself early on, though he's since been transfixed, somewhat, the publishing of this Barbapapa information seemed necessary to get down before chowing down on the meat of the matter."

{The main characters in the books are the Barbapapa family, who are most notable for their ability to shapeshift at will. In their native form, Barbapapas are blob-shaped, with a distinct head and arms, but no legs. Male Barbapapas have rounder bottoms, whereas female Barbapapas have a more slender form. Each Barbapapa can adopt any form they choose, but they remain easily identifiable by always retaining their faces and their distinctive colour.}

Barbapapa himself is a generally papaya-shaped, pink shapeshifting blob-like creature who stumbles upon the human world and tries to fit in. The shapeshifting is usually accompanied by the saying **"Clickety Click—Barba rick"**, or in the 1970s British dub **"All Change!"** (Based on the expression used by the driver on British buses when the bus reaches the end of its route) (in Serbian "Tata Brada", in the French version "Hup Hup Hup, Barbatruc", "Oblajuco, Barbatruco" in Spanish, "Ra-Ru-Rick, Barbatrick" in German, "Huub huub huub, Barbatruuk" in Dutch, "Hüpp Hüpp Hüpp, Barbatrükk" in Hungarian, "Hop hop hop, Değiş Tonton" in the Turkish version, "Resta di stucco, è un barbatrucco" in the Italian version, in Arabic "أعظم--- ال شاطر ب ارب ١١" ساحر قال ديو ق", in Hebrew "תיקיתיקוץ, בַּרְבָּקוּנְץ"/"Tiki-tikutz, Barba-kuntz", in Greek "Κλι κλι κόλπο, μπάρμπα κόλπο"/"kli kli kolpo, barba kolpo", in Finnish Hik hik hikka, Barbakikka, in Chinese "可里可里可里, 巴巴变"/"ke li ke li ke li, ba ba bian")."

▼ Not similar at all… ▼

After various adventures, Barbapapa comes across a female of his species (more shapely, and black-coloured), named Barbamama. They produce four sons: Barbidur, a sports fan (red), Barbibul, a scientist (blue), Barbidou, a nature enthusiast (yellow) and Barbouille, a painter (black and furry), as well as three daughters: Barbalala, a musician (green), Barbabelle, a beauty queen (purple) and Barbotine, an intellectual (orange).

*

T i m f o o l e r y :

T a i l s f r o m a D i m l i t J u n k i e

(the "Junkie" title still arouses and still scares off some conservative 'inside-the box' thinkers - a title that even scares off most of them there Liberals…best maybe to reach out to those Democrats and Republicans, appealing to their sense of, uh, what is it they stand for again?)

*

This book is dedicated to my mom -
who most undoubtedly had a hand in me
being able to type, but also enabled me to show up
here to present said writing work.
This is for her and the ones who took the time,
and still do.

"Do not abandon all hope ye who enter here…"

* * *

Footnote...footnotery, TomFoolery... (Tom was my Dad's name),
*so let these be... TIMFooleries = **(tf#1)** from here on in...*

(Though certainly not to be confused with this Tom Dooley character,
who does little else than just 'hang down his head and cry', especially at social
gatherings, my cronies report. An out of touch gent who's nothing more than an
imposter and a snail - he's been known to wear only a complicated and
unflattering ensemble of cowboy hat, tall dark socks and Bermuda shorts
(unforgivable), while rifling through unsuspecting guests' coat pockets for
change. I read a piece on him in 'The Star' and I swear it's true.

---

tf#1: the Paradiddle Didactic Wagsnozzle thing is a parakeet crossed
with a pterodactyl by the light of the silvery moon just on the way to the
variety store for some smokes.

THIS GRAND MANIPULATION
Begins now...

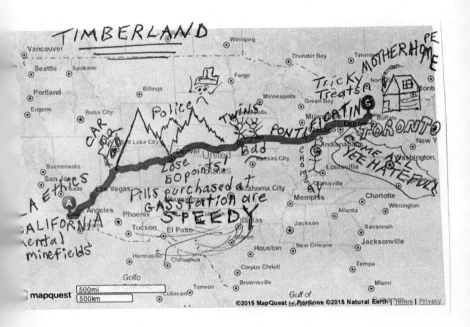

prefab

Often, the only thing that comforts me is the knowledge of a telephone
number,
someone that won't be too long in arriving at a pre-determined locale
to deliver a powdery gray mare,
that will induce immediate soothing crimson inspiration,
though ultimately providing just another bastard brick
in the stepping stone to a nuptial death-knot,
I will in some gross manner always be betrothed.

And at a point pivotal, down some path, must attempt to elope on my own, as to bring her with me
out the window
in some fleeing escape
would mean a maundered diffuse I've plundered
on what feels like endless, countless occasions.

There are prayers, seen and felt in astral carousing, of late, a close cosmos 'round towns,
that I'm not too
high up when the
next jump comes into play.

1. Me and Chuck B.

I first began reading Charles Bukowski right around the same time I was falling off the earth. Hearing that he'd lived a tragic, tortured life made me all the more eager to get involved with his books, to read of his treacherously long, odd soul-searching days at the U.S Post Office, his part-time gig when not entrenched in the written word. How peculiar for him to have had such a wide array of untamed characters showing up at his residence: seasoned drifters from far away posing as fans, presenting themselves at his doorstep; assorted folks driving through who thought they'd just pop by. Poor guy, dodging compliments from illiterates who said they loved his words though had read none; pointless people rallying around his noble bungalow, peering in windows to maybe catch a view of a great writer enjoying a beer and a cheese sandwich. Ah, the human race strikes again. This made little sense to him or his life partner Linda, who'd often be keeping watch, on Selective Security Sifting Mode (I imagined this role for her), fielding requests from the front door, bellowing to Chuck, off hiding in the kitchen, "You have visitors, Shakespeare," but ultimately telling the bunch to take a hike and come back another year. "It's not that he doesn't love the admiration, guys, but, he's too drunk off his ass right now anyway…he just wouldn't want you to be disillusioned, is all." She wished them all a Bon Voyage while swinging an sharp wire broom to shoo them away.

"So long, hippy parasites," she cheered sarcastically.

"Scram, vamoose. Slink away, cockroaches." The woman could be entirely nurturing when she wanted.

The bunch hopped back in their hippie-sippy love van and happily scooted off. "We met the master, man!" they must have shouted as they all high-fived one another, turning up the car radio as loud as it would go then and disappearing onto the next street and to the next task of the day.

These constant ambushes occurring because the youth of this era sensed Charles Bukowski (and others like him: Miller, Kerouac) represented a generation's rebellious view of society. He was only writing what was in his heart and suddenly he's some kind of society spokesman, partaking in what by this time, had become daily involvement in an unwanted celebrity pseudo side-show; his reward for being a storyteller, one whose rare voice of gutsy, ball-grippin' prose and to-the-point raging doggerels engulfed a nation. The Kerou-wackos scurried off, hustled up more drugs, called it a day, and forgot where old man Bukowski lived altogether

This was the 60's, man.

Recently, I've had my own share of poignant moments and bewildering escapades in Los Angeles, reason enough to draw comparisons between myself and the horse-race-gambling, portlier, *slightly* more successful Bukowski. Something I don't recall him being famous for was writing bum checks to bookstores and cabbing it to second-hand haunts to get what cash he could for them: that's been my job. His books always brought in a favorable bounty at the establishments I slithered into. Man, they got some sweet deal off of me. I'm guessing the bookshop owner's greed overshadowed his moral ground, but really, who could fault him? My desperation, racing blindly through intersections with stolen words, the soon-to-be profitable works of literature sitting pretty in my accredited accomplice - the threadbare soiled sack; and if the sweat on the brow and the holes in my shoes weren't a dead giveaway, I don't know what was. I must have been a sight. Maybe if I'd schlepped less, showered that week, come in with less of a

Neanderthal-like presence, maybe then I could have kept up a better face for my narcotic fun-run, chock full of wily adventures and good times I told myself I was having.

On a few occasions, I handed over the crumpled receipt given to me an hour earlier from the three-storey-high, unsuspecting book conglomerate not yet tipped off to the literary mad genius scam I believed so foolproof, such clever creativity…inevitably my demise. They must have been kicking themselves having trusted me and my post-dated, personal out-of-province checks, my bank account a Less Than Zero affair. I can laugh about it now, a little. After a time I gave up further attempts at acting cavalier and nonchalant, just dumping the books out from the satchel, scattering them feverishly on the counter, the way one might brandish a sour attitude, or a gun in a hurried frenzy, "I'm in kind of a rush. You know how it is…whatever you think is fair."

The similarities crossed over into the bizarre, Bukowskally-speaking, as during one of my most recent stints at a recovery rehab institution, I learned that the distinguished address of 360 South Westlake Boulevard - where I called home for a grand total of nine days - had actually been occupied by the eminent author many years earlier, though at this moment was housing many non-writers and felonious finger-painters. Seems it had been magically transformed into a chirpy dwelling called The Royal Palms Center, though the furthest thing from some balmy, palm-desert-hallowed-ground the name might conjure up.

I was the clock watcher, needing the hours and days to pass quicker than usual so I could make it out of there in my own time and in one piece. Fidgeting and depleted, up at 4 a.m. on account of not being able to sleep from the all too familiar withdrawal game, perched out there on the rusty blackened fire escape, a solitary spot I discovered up at the fifth floor window, to rock back and forth, rattle and hum while considering various game plans that weren't working. Passing prayers and passing thoughts flew across my mental dashboard, devoted mostly to just how I'd ended up in such a demoralizing all-male recovery dorm. These prayers and thoughts I was privileged to own, as most else was sold or misplaced. "How did I land here? What am I going to do when I get out?" Crazy questions nobody I had run into could possibly provide a clue to. "I could be a limo driver. Yeah, I could be good at that…meet people be my own boss, not cooped up in some office, good tips, but that friggin' red tape about a license, then insurance…" I mumbled to myself, considering various occupations *(tf#1)* I'd not yet taken a stab at, in an attempt to diminish and make light of this cold, illogical end-of-the-line scenario.

How close had I come to overdosing and dying? Was this my bottom? Did I have more energy saved in some reserve tank for another run? Could I control it better next time? I had no way of knowing.

Crawling out to that fifth floor fire escape, a perfect breeze, was the only thing on earth I looked forward, to receive my dose of sanity, an all too sobering symmetry, the twisted station of silence apart from the other court-ordered drug savages; they, a constant static with buzzing backward agendas, having to cope and muddle through amidst their irritating milling about, their rummaging amongst each other's diseased minds that sickened me to see, feel and regrettably be a part of my home team for the time.

Addicts don't get breaks, it seems. Not for fucking long anyway.

Directly below, a family dealing in the brisk sale of crack cocaine fiendishly working all hours: a spiffy, finely tuned operation taking place around the clock, a freakish after-hours carnival, night after night, ominous, never ceasing, not that I saw anyway. It inspired dread but amazed me, much the same way A Clockwork Orange *(tf#2)* did as a kid; decadent and intriguing, fear-provoking, nightmare-inducing but strangely, not scaring me off the way it should have.

All sorts of shoppers would drive up in search; high-end, slick subterranean appendectomies to broken-down rusty lime-green Gremlins hobbling relentlessly on their last legs, callous bug-eyed drivers in need, pushing poor blue-exhausted jalopies beyond their own wake.

Colonel Sanchez (I named him) and his chain gang of feisty fools chattered away in foreign tongues, keeping tiny bundles tucked away in their orifices, awaiting the substance seekers to show up to purchase their goods. They'd know precisely when to open the gate and step into the spotlight from the graffiti-strewn apartment complex, to rapidly conduct their openly orchestrated drug shuffle. I gave them credit, such unwavering teamwork. Every actor prepared to play their roles exactly as rehearsed. There should've been a flashing neon sign blinking *ONE STOP SHOPPING* TRI 'N SAVE* which would've been monstrously funny.

"Yo, dog, what you doing watching us out here every night? Why don't you get your cracker white ass down here to the party?"

The grand pursuit is going on as we speak, bleeding waterfalls spilling creepy shadows into our cities, towns and streets across this limitless land of heartbreaking unfulfilled need, the devil's agents always advertising, accepting garden-fresh and hasty applicants in their smoke-filled *Mad*

Mer-like office down the hall, publicly, unashamed, requiring anyone with a human head and an aorta to sign up, grab a name tag and hang out contentedly at the septic tank cooler, excited and assimilated to maybe, finally, belong to *something*, even if *it's* the devil you don't know that well - yet. The naïve participants for this alluring fury and undefined hunger *(tf#3)* to survive - an underworld complete with its own twisted primitive set of rules - murky manners, fabricated protocol, things you just don't do, and ways in which to manipulate the team and yourself...like in any other world, be it under or above ground. There's no jubilation here people, enslavement gets to be a cheery upper, served encrusted and awkward. Cheating Death is one thing - to repeatedly laugh in his face, steal his lunch money and perform Oedipal acts with his mother is another story.

Anything went down.

Different worlds co-existing dangerously close, me, too infatuated, too fucking fascinated with my proximity to the psychotic prowling, no one paying me much mind, mostly.

Occasionally, a squad car would pass by a few streets over and shine a disquieting spotlight down the alley. "Buddha!" or whatever the code word was for that special night shift got screamed out by a guy whose job it was to keep watch and everyone would scatter like unexterminable crazed centipedes. I'd stretch my neck out, further dangling over the outside landing, inhaling the scent of the Spanish spider people scurrying to their concealed cracks, who'd reappear minutes later to continue

Business as uSuaL

It's scary and speaks of uncaring, the trifling inhumane kind, to close one's eyes when others around them are losing theirs, sinking, spiralling south of eye level to a suffocating soil, and me unable to mushroom in a much trounced upon earth; nobody growing with me here at the birds-eye view, deserted and unfed, along with the sweet and sweaty whores *(tf#4)* lacking manners, even though they turned out to be amazingly supportive spellers when the time came. I knew this because I'd seek out their wisdom, shouting down the occasional crossword query.

"Excuse me there, ladies, um, ten letter word for 'Used in alloys, electrodes and catalysts'?"

"Try M-O-L-Y-B-D-E-N-U-M," one of the girls shouted up to me all casual like.

"You don't say?" I tried fitting it into the puzzle and was instantly amazed that she was bang right on. "Holy geez, it fits. Way to go ladies. Thanks."

"Gladys, you always had a knack with that Periodic Table of Elements stuff. Shit, you're in the wrong biz, doll!"

They all laughed like hyenas in the alley up the way while I jotted down impressions of the scene in my notebook, paying enough attention to film it all in my mind. We worked out a system where if they helped me complete the damn thing, then I'd toss down a dollar or two, which they promised would go towards an academic fund, just in case the sex-for-money thing didn't pan out as they had hoped. The tarnished herd could saunter over to the local community college and enroll in a handful of adult night classes that might hope to give them some kind of future, breathe some possibility into their depleted lives, which they told me at this particular moment, in a barely comprehendible floppy Spanish accent it was, *"Not on our Pajendas, Pappy!"* (?) and, they also voiced concern, dead set against, "all that wakin' up early n' stuff."

They may have had a point.

Crosswords remind me of mom, of her and I sitting on that green vinyl couch in the cozy den figuring them out, using whichever dictionary, thesaurus or wordy supplement might assist us in the majestic quest to complete the thing. Somehow, we seemed to bond while this went on, maybe without our knowing the wheels were spinning towards, dare I say, an understanding of each other. Neither of us tuned in to that fact and I'm sure if we became too aware of the development, it would have gotten in the way.

We both shared a passion for words and their meanings. The lure of the crossword held promise, a set formulaic thing that wouldn't let you down, crash into you or rip your heart out; it was reliable, and once completed you even got the feeling of conquering *something* outside yourself. How many things in this world can you say that about?

Once I snuck out to my perch, it was hard not to get engrossed in the Disney Downer Soundstage (I liked to call it) - reeled into the whole scenario. I'd catch Colonel Sanchez and his compadres counting out crumpled American bills, elephantitus-like wads that must have been in the thousands. Had this always been The Family Business? Just how did they fall into this profession anyway? Were they putting their kids through expensive private schools? Needing to keep up appearances?

Risking my Royal Palm live-in status and in an attempt to connect with one of the crew, one night I took hold of that rusty fire-escape ladder and made my way down there, nearly breaking my neck, ignoring for the moment the series of ballistic punishments the counsellors would dream up for me if they caught me off grounds.

I jumped down off the last rung of the ladder, somehow twisting my ankle, embarrassed at my obvious childlike footing, not yet used to the sleepy-time meds they were providing me to help get over the dope sickness. I took a seat at the curb, lit up a cigarette and spoke. "I remember back when I was your age, my father was working as a copy editor at Spitzer, Mills & Bates."

"Yeah, my dad runs a gang and he's going to rip your head off mutha fucker. Gimme your cash and your car keys, man."

"Well, uh, I don't have a vehicle - see, I'm in this rehab. I'm the guy five floors up. You see me all the time," trying to reassure my new friends that I obviously was no threat, "I thought maybe I'd come down and check out the scene you got going...maybe try some of the gross national product." They must have found me a refreshing humorist. "I could pay you with...

I'm rudely interrupted.

"Get the fuck out of here, Narc." I was no good to him or his family that began to threateningly assemble around me, so I quickly climbed back onto the fire escape ladder like a skittish ring-tailed lemur escaping from an animal-hating zookeeper and made my way back up to my balcony where it was mostly safe.

Melodic echoes bounced off the concrete minefield, soulful sounds from Isaac Hayes, Larry Heard, The Gap Band and others I couldn't identify. These songs acted as the soundtrack of the night, transmitting sex and smoke, personal meaning and raw sketches of better times - all making its way over from a boom box somewhere nearby, a faded melodious electric blackboard of LA ethics. Pointless poetry filled my head all too often…inarticulate speech, parts of odes and lyrics that once meant something to me, now disarmingly menacing - words flew around that I hoped could help make sense of the fragmented man-child I now was; the rhymes now had their way with me, and the little mercy they did show revealed themselves pounding what truth they possessed atop my confused frame.

A voyage of the damned, the always intact unyielding dawn, my carousel of the macabre holding firm, cinematic cysts brewing in me for what's seemed like forever, what's infected my sub-par moral infrastructure, the stalled carnival in need of interior updates, the windswept boulevard needing a good hosing down. I will tell all, as I'm told I'm allowed no secrets in this purge pot, this reeling and revealing revelation in and of

C o M i n g C l e A n .

---

tf#1: An Actuary? Opiate-research test dummy? (Kind of defeats my purpose). Astronaut author? Shamed cyclist? Marry that Sheryl Crow person? How would we look together? Maybe start collecting photos when we both have similar tans? Hey, Fort York - Civil War Reenactor! Maple Syrup and soldier stuff, gun powder, women in Mennonite villages sloughing over hard-to-hear cabinet sanding and mending pillowcases and pants. Could be good.

tf#2: This did, however, create a long standing fear of any collection of gangs of men wearing full body white underwear and eye make-up approaching me with canes at nighttime.

tf#3: As per matter of fact, 'The Hunger', was a moody, sluggish vampirish flick with lesbianistic undertones that crept into me at an early age and still sticks like glue to my psyche. Decent soundtrack, too.

tf#4: I wonder if that rule about "No whores in the house, Timothy!" regardless of any cutesy-pie kitsch factor, ability to assist mom with the tougher puzzles, or promises to clean up, is still in effect. Did she mean altogether? No sleepovers? Or just that specific time? Lipstick can be a nightmare to get off pillowcases

* * *

2. Filthy Cocoon of Damaged Charm

This is how you become an addict. You have no inner resources, you drive people crazy with all your neediness, years go by, you don't grow up, people lose patience, and all that's left is whatever gets you through.

Elizabeth Wurtzel

More, Now, Again, A Memoir of Addiction

You tell yourself you have a handle on it, that it's not so bad. You catch yourself looking down at that once precious, bleeding, now scarred arm, blisters reddening, rotting boughs hemorrhaging, far from on the mend. Things swelling where they shouldn't. And those twitches you have...you remember a time when they weren't part of the package; always such excitement, those speedballs working the graveyard shift on my system - the getting, so long after the waiting, then the preparing and always the temporarily gorgeous injecting ritual. Then the oncoming ferocious and racy feeling; the mixed mortar morphing into something special, my soul stirring with junkie entitlement, and that loquacious liquid melting down together from sticky brown tar, the H, and the off-white bitter powder, the coke; cooked-up and sparkling pop-o-matic bubble-trouble, that had its own running agenda, gearing up in the corroded silver spoon to take another shot at racing around my existing heart, my active bulging veins and a prepped body-for-bliss mindset eager to dictate - each and every time I did it - where I'd land for the night, and what I'd be seeing maybe for the last time. There were lots of last times. And I was a pained participant, past panic, yet still somehow always willing.

Obnoxiously in-your-face hot is what it's like in the California summer. You can get burned before noon by what's been referred to as 'Africa hot'. You're gonna want to be near the beach. All Santa's and Ana's were not near the beach. It's concrete jungle, vigilante-land, baby: a ripped up, torn down tinsel town tornado in the rain. And me, with my Santa Ana Land Shuffle, even now my survived senses get a whiff of the derelict dancing on windy and weirder days, remembering how I spread myself too thin, screaming body parts all spasmodic

When I wasn't punching The Druggy Clock or doing The Wonka-Wonka 12 Step (I named this dance), I had a ton of time to conceptualize quirky jazzed-up plot-lines for what was going down. The powders gave me the courage to do things like stroll into a Hollywood Blvd. lacy lingerie store and request, confidently, to the nearest statuesque high-heeled minx looking to make her sales quota, "You must try this on, my wife will love it!" The trick being not to giggle. Maybe even arrange a meeting, get her to open up and tell all Victoria's (or her) secrets.

My unemployability, at a standstill for too many years and still counting - almost impressive, though, my real position - being accountable to a whole new realm of narcissism plagued by indecision and low self-esteem, along with my recently procured infinite forms of self-deception, plus (!) those Seven lackluster Deadly Sins I wholeheartedly embraced, disappointed when I couldn't pull at least a few of those puppies off in one day. This became both the real goal and ultimately the real disappointment.

I shouted out to anyone on Skid Row who'd listen. "Alright, I got Greed, that's a constant. Certainly Sloth is taking shape nicely, Lust kind of comes and goes...hey, man, what are those other ones?"

A survival denial I told myself was that the charmless human snafus I'd encounter in this addict world were actually one of the benefits, meeting such weird and wonderful folks, all of us mixed together in some shameless but revamped melting melange, like this resourceful couple I befriended, Palo and his gal, Snaggletoothed Shelly (I bestowed upon her this title). They were feisty junkies of the most desperate sort, playing all positions for the team. They lived in a scraggy alleyway behind a mini-mall that housed these pointless sun tanning salons and unfrequented appliance and wallpaper shops. Palo said the owner knew of their squatting but didn't care as long as they kept their eyes on the place for anyone who posed a threat; another irony, like Tasmanian devils asked to take care of the pet shop while the owner is away. I came to think of them affectionately as The Dynamic Duo...ludicrously lame superheroes, minus a proper cape and tights and certainly no help in the League of Justice super power arena. I imagined them using children's bed sheets, fireman helmets and cheap lycra bathing attire as their third rate costumes. Through the grapevine I heard from similar ne'er-do-well characters some of the clumsier conduct they promoted: robbing and pawning, underhanded trickery, manipulating identities and fraudulent double-dealings, while racing against all the obstacles. These things that were all part of my Glitterless Game-town.

On the days when I was unwell and no dealers were at their usual spot, I'd have to hobble around and pay the duo a visit, to see if they could assist me with finding the stuff, which was always more complicated, and costly, always having to grease their palms for the help; they with their schemes, scams and unsubstantiated tales, and me, the one who still can't, for the life of me, manage how to shoot up properly. Again and again I required someone to play the role of a nurse. Now, if I had uniforms in my trunk for them to change into, that would've made for a real captivating scene. Definitely worth recording. Though it's remarkably tough to get many homeless addicts or alcoholics to - once dressed in a costume I'd provide – to sit still for the camera and respond to even a few fact-finding questions. Paying strangers to hop into my spook-mobile, handing them my last three or four dollars to do the predictable and repetitive deed had become the norm – all funds earned earlier gone to obtain my treats. What was left went to gas, food and lodging. How I never got stabbed or dismembered and left for white meat, I've found no clues to uncover that one.

"There's gotta be someone 'round whose holding?!' Where the hell are those guys this morning?" I called out from my car.

"Hey, gimme me a ride, Remington Steele," a street villain cackled with delight, but I found it hard to appreciate his comic line as I was doubled over the hood of my car from painful cramps, getting sicker and sweatier from not having.

No longer could I pretend I was dedicated to my own highly-stylized version of a Kerowackyan-participatory-journalistic-field-trip, on some lost generation monkey-hunt for those missing Bewitched episodes, longing to transform myself into nobler heroic leads from books I treasured, but too cold and bothered to keep any of it straight. Here I was with the wildebeest at my hooves, a liar in my own dog-eared notebook of un-integrity and with off-the-scale-uncertainty, and at each blink from my still intact eyes, all systems and loved ones removed, replaced somehow, entirely out of focus.

The shaky close calls began to multiply, once what was the exception quickly became the rule, like that grey-haired, badly-burned guy who helped me shoot up on more than one occasion, his echo remnant of a beat up, frowning Ray Charles – hanging on for his charmed life from my car door, half in half out, me attempting to flee the scene, him screaming, "Motha fucka! What the fuck ya think you doin', white-boy!?" Ten seconds was all it took to get my four-cylinder-lawnmower-of-motion-sickness up to the necessary Mach speed to jettison all hangers-on back to their appropriate curb seating. My streetwise colleague finally let go and dropped off, with me waving goodbye and with a quickly invented English accent offering, "So long there, Jeeves, old boy!" though not knowing quite which fictitious dandy elder statesman or from what cinematique gem I was imitating, but there was an idea simmering that he'd come up again, and have to be dealt with. Later.

———————

It was fitting that it be brilliantly shining on this super morning, in a kind of pathetic-fallacy sort of way. The rays shooting down beat me into submission, far from qualifying me from being in the light. So dispirited, a sick psyche lost in astral carousing. Beaming memories and images shot at me of sparkling beachfront Muskoka Lake cottages, swimming pools and well-groomed tennis courts, smiling summer girls smelling of Ylang Ylang and Aveda hair products, and love, now miles behind and getting tougher to place, suspicious as to if it occurred at all. There was genuine love somewhere; I still have pictures of friends and families that sure made it look that way. Does someone out there still have those home movies? Or was all of that just *in the movies*? I break and cry a little every time I see them, even if they're not mine, me, a joker on the swings of indecision, the wired Riddler gone wild, some deviant projectionist, unsettling. What to do with all of that now? Having almost perfected a backwards and persecuted point of reference is top-of-the-pops terrible, as you can't recognize the good stuff if it ever does happen to radiate and deliver itself a beat at your door. It sure is gratifying to be aware of the pretty pictures, but when you're stuck with a warped perception, that's where things can get perverse and gruesome. Don't count on interacting too well, or integrating so hot either, especially when others tell you, *"Hey buddy, you're not so badly off there, ya know, chin up!"* as you may feel it best just to run them over.

On the terrible day, my pals Palo and Shelly weren't around - probably off making the world a better place, volunteering precious time for a better cause. I pulled the car around the back of the ramshackle eyesore of a building near this dumpster; "How embarrassing, this cliché backdrop," I thought, and may have said out loud. Peering over rusty shopping carts, garbage, wrecked toys and broken lighters, through gross soiled clothes piled high, I climbed through the bottom of the fence and crawled over the pissed on crud and looked around for my jesterly associates, cohorts from the California Dreamland of Misfit Toys; ridiculous allies I'd enlisted to share in the dreaded pathetic spookfest, to somehow shelter me from further grave morbidity, I believed. They were on a team, some demented Sub C bantam house league with threadbare uniforms and didn't even know it, with me, about to be sidelined and broadsided. Entering the back alley of the place, I looked down around my ankles, my socks and running shoes that served no purpose but to assimilate into cement, cigarette butts, pipes and needles, strings and wires, machine parts, gadgets and in the middle of it all, there lay a grey dead kitten, with soot and stuff stuck to it, matted with crusty things, patchy fur, still bleeding in places, maybe where other animals had picked at it...and its head partially crushed, an almost unreal, macabre thing to see up close. SHWOOP. I fall backwards a little and step on what must have been another cat's stomach, making a weird suction sound, like letting the air out of a hot water bottle, deflating us both. I'm ankle-deep, it feels, in a kitty catacomb. Upon closer inspection of this poor little one, some patchy areas where she may not have been able to look after herself properly, due to malnutrition, abuse, or circumstances beyond her control. The other one lay there staring at me, my losses marinating in this once spry corpse, the good eye that wasn't ripped open sparkling. My furry Cyclopean friend, not so funny, staring out into infinite space unaware of her own seeping decay. Here she was, ripped apart, legs busted, limbs and such, twisted. A voice spoke volumes to me with static and silence:

"How could you let this happen? I'm no good anymore. I was good once, I played ball and fun games. I had a mother and brothers and sisters - people took those from me and then this happened and I can't tell you really how I got like this because I don't want to give you more death than you're already wrapped up in here; you don't seem to need my help in your self-destructive, misguided excuse for what you are. These flies around us - marching over our once frolicking bodies, picking us apart, is death enough for you today, kid."

This reawakened feelings I'd believed were truly lost, too pushed down to ever steal a breath. This is when something exploded inside me as I got my ass out of that alley and back to the car.

That face, and the fear and lonesomeness she must have felt was all I could think of.

I'd not known the feeling of bursting into tears until that moment, but I began to develop a taste for it. Though, Taste was not on the list of senses that were doing so hot; all five of which, by now, were pretty much opposed to interacting in any natural Darwinian forward-type-motion.

"Let me see, shit, there's Taste…Sight, uh…isn't there one that starts with an R? Guys? Little help?" Those out of touch entities being commanded by substances, to fall in line when ordered to do so, to jitterbug beyond the type of life they were built for. Sensuality, a unique explosive chemistry, all the things I longed for - and once in a great while even felt with others, now fragmented and stitched together in the back seat of the wobbly roller coaster I'd been flying around on with crappy cheap sutures and purloined Medicare I'd no doubt have to repay. Later.

I jotted this incident down, tears dripping on my notebook, kind of smearing the words, adding this trauma-like cuddly tale in with the Dopamine-deficient desperation to corresponding moments, mixed with the multiple times I'd thrown myself at the mercy of sickly hygienic emergency rooms too busy and too involved to be bothered with my unglamorous suicidal cries, sending me right back out the automated doors. They didn't see my problem as serious or something they would want to deal with, their lunch break being not far off, but not before I indulged in a number of jaundiced butterscotch pudding cups and was awarded a good talking to by a couple of dazed and confused pre-med students on their dizzying rounds. They showered me with gifts upon my arrival though; a fuzzy maroon robe - my ass exposed for no reason I could fathom - and those comedic pointless paper slippers, but they made me return the sub-stylish manly fashions then sent me packing, out to battle, with a bill to be paid and my words barely intact. I drove around the next couple hours trying to resist the pull of that handy turn into oncoming traffic.

When the dust clears at the end of the day this might be recollected to tell others, maybe around an open flame, but so much to take in and who'd really listen or take notice anyway? And all this before noon.

I recall sitting in Larry's office, a windowless room with too much brown, staring at him juggling my urine sample, and me, wearing black track pants with white stripes, holes in the knee, something I came across in the donations/lost & found room, and mesmerized, an obligatory meeting, more of a 'Good talking to,' as I was ordered to sit down, shut up, listen and stare at the transitioning blue to light green rainbow of opaque colors, swishing back and forth in this tiny vial, the guilty verdict seconds away. I decided to let the urine lie wherever it wanted to and just let go, meaning, why attempt to control something I had no control over? He was going to see what he wanted to see. Seemingly pleased with his findings, a dwarfish smirk made its way onto his face as if he'd found a treasure chest of gold coins, or had discovered a forgotten shirt in his closet that fit with not too horrendous a sweaty underarm stain. Larry said my sample was positive which didn't sound too bad at all, but in fact represented an unfair, disagreeable result. Before the uninspiring diagnosis sealed my fate, I had a few choice responses ready, just in case I took it upon myself to fight tooth and nail against what I knew was another splendid failing grade. My top three were, "That can't be *my* specimen." "I'd like a recount, *please*," and, "What's in urine, *really?*" But it took far less energy to just fess up and accept the last screw being power-drilled into my claustrophobic addiction coffin, but still able to reject his emotionally asphyxiating remote drone justice. The withdrawal from the drugs I was sneaking in daily would soon be upon me, coupled with the familiar fear and anxiety I had about not having a place to call my own. The low man on the scrotum-pole, revealed once again.

As a rule, it's best to abstain from using during one's holiday in a drug treatment facility even though there are a surprising number of ways to procure the exact substances which landed your ass there in the first place. Ah, that sweet, sweet spring aroma of annoying irony. Scoring a little pick-me-up, taking something to make you borderline mummified, or maybe something spicy to quicken the mad mind, to take the edge off for any amount of time would sure smooth out the journey, but, and this is a biggie; they now seem to have devised this nifty, yet irk-some, little rapid-result number called a Drug Testing Kit. There seems to be no suitable method for avoiding this impressive yet mandatory and random hi-tech testing ground they've assembled in such residences, as it's just that: R A N D O M , like some threatening kind of kryptonite set on READY, prepped, at the slightest slip-up, to subdue the powers of Super Addicts.

Good old head-cheese-cutter Larry asked a confused but strong nearby slave to assist with my exit. "Would you be so kind, to gather up Mr. Hollywood's belongings from the Bukowski suite," so everyone outside his office could hear. I immediately bemoaned the earlier sharing of that tidbit when Larry first checked me in; confessing my literary passions about a writer I totally dug and related to, and the thing about Bukowski actually living here on the very grounds I was a temporary patron at. Larry the Lughead showed a surprising lack of respect for privacy and confidentiality, in the one place you'd expect to find such things, as he used that - and more - against me every chance he got. Then, brightly over the intercom he announced, *"Attention, attention: Royal Palms residents, turns out it'll be Kerouac's last day here so don't forget to say toodle-loo."* I had nowhere to go and no game plan, and now worse, was chagrined and smalled by Count Frosting's comments. I still hoped it would get dealt with, later on and by someone else.

He certainly was a character though - a genius in training who thought I was there only to make his life complicated, not to mention causing dissension in the ranks with my self-deprecating hilarity, sarcasm and general high-jinx. I'm guessing a good deal of the hostility he harbored towards me came from the notion that I was the instigator on several unsolved mysteries about the residence, and believed that I was the 'rotten' and 'selfish ignoramus' (he awarded me a plethora of nicknames), throwing a monkey wrench into his grand plan for the place. See, he imagined himself to be a bit of a ruler, a kind of King and we - I guess - were his slaves and servants - disloyal subjects toiling away in his kingdom. At any rate, he wasn't too sorry to see me go, the same mustachioed devil that barked the exhaustive lines at each morning meeting moments before we began chores and tasks for the day:

"Losers do what they want to do.

Winners do what they have to do."

When I wasn't in strict attendance, soaking up the golden creeds and life lessons he bestowed upon the group, I was out the back door busy not being a winner. From what I could surmise, his public addresses to the all-male community were the best times to sneak out of the building to score from Primo, the nearby dealer, purveyor extraordinaire of injectionable goods and services, while everyone else was busy paying strict attention how best to not end up like me. Having to jet out the back alley, across Wilshire Blvd. to the 3rd Street Laundromat to score then sprint back quick enough to keep the sobriety-facade up, PLUS (!) the continuous updates of the charts, class assignments, my personal detailed minutes and colored graphs as well as keeping all that excessive data hidden from the mish-mash of moronic bunkmates I was living with was a feat in itself!

I was kind of glad to be getting out of there, to tell you the truth. It ended up being a lot more work than I'd hoped; the incognito Nikita covert ops were menacingly draining, especially not having a partner in crime to work with. I'd felt I'd done enough time in there anyway and had become all too quickly annoyed and frustrated, having sweated my ass off there day after day in the bowels of that harsh and crusty uninspiring dunk tank. Even though my options on the outside were few, I figured they couldn't be any worse than this.

What actually came to mind as Larry was monkeying around with my bodily fluids was the time I thought my old girlfriend M. was pregnant and we had to go to the drugstore. Embarrassed to be shuffling around the pharmacy aisles, we procured this blue and white tampon-like-box and returned to our home headquarters; if it turned blue we were good to go and off the stork's hook; if it turned yellow, well, then we had to make a heavy and politically-confusing decision, (a pharmaceutical abortifacient) that, or start drumming up baby names and squirreling away money for a college fund.

Larry mentioned I was, "Insufficiently committed to a course of action that would be required to remove substances from my lifestyle." *(tf#5)* Powerless to tell if he was making fun of the manner in which I spoke, I responded by sharing with him - and the group - that, he was, "Communicatively-challenged with an accent too tough to pin down and a scent unbearable to endure." I even caught him a couple times digging the aroma of his watchband when he thought no one was looking, a true sign of senility in my books.

It wasn't all dreariness and hardships. There were some fiendishly sweet moments, like when I'd bring back hookers during visiting hours, just to hang out with, or maybe interview - and with each afternoon tryst - falsely confessing that it was in fact my own personal mom who was accompanying me up to my room. "Mom's in the program, she's kind of been on relapse mode, lately," sharing that kind of knowing look with Sober Sunil, one of the more sympathetic and dozy on-duty guards. Why those were the particular moms I clung to, who I seemed to feel a particular kinship with, I can't say. For one thing, they weren't lying about who they were. I had respect for these sweet working girls stinking of disproportionate self-imagery and rot-gut whiskey, ingesting treats and turning tricks up the way behind the facility at below-basement-bargain-prices.

Sunil the sober security guard had been clean for about ten years thanks to Narcotics Anonymous and had worked at the place since he completed the Royal Palms program. I believed we had an understanding: that we were both men of the world, men who understand how such delicate issues have a way of working themselves out. Sunil the permitted our conjugal-crossword-visits, until, a less compassionate sickly-thin and long-legged, white-wash jean'd fellow named Carl, a hopeless coke-freak from the Bible Belt who relentlessly sported a hideous mullet with an unbelievable silo of gel, took over Sunil's shift one night and found me and female guest (not mother) in my room, not doing the crossword. These guys were supposed to be licensed though I suspect they were not: theoretical counsellors, original guests themselves on the fruitless freak ship, too frightened to get out there and play ball in real the world, just on a different type of drowning vessel I guess, but who was I to judge? Bible Belt Coke and Gel man turned me in and spread the news of my illegal entanglements with non-Royal Palms residents.

What a maroon.

I don't think I'd be wrong to think the other guys in the rehab came to enjoy my cutting remarks and predictable rebel rousing. True, there may have been times when my stratagems and flagrant behavior served to hurt only me, but I believed myself cunning, an innovative hands-on artist convinced there were no telephone calls from theatrical agents and personal managers only because the front desk chowder heads knew nothing about how to properly work a switchboard, clearly, but even then, they wouldn't put them through, non-disclosure agreement, privacy rules and all.

I was awarded the nickname 'Señor Crafty' by many of the staff there, but was also told to not take this as a compliment. I'm sure they'd still roll out the nurturing and cordial carpet for me to vacuum and shampoo again in a heartbeat, if somewhere down the line I made up my mind to buckle down.

---

tf#5 from David Foster Wallace's almost incredible must-read novel entitled, "INFINITE JEST."

* * *

3. Tropical Travel / An August Scene

I'd l i k e t o let you in on some things. To recollect a little may even help me out of this upside down Flint Rubble Bubble of a mess. I'm drained, sickened, scared of the world and don't want to be and don't know how to stop being this way. For not having found suitable tools with which to address daily concerns, I'm disgusted with myself, not to mention dealing with those baffling life questions no one seems to be able to help me with. Further, I can't stand this "unfestive" bachelorhood I drag around with me. This doesn't even begin to address my scarcity of a proper protective force field or necessary but absent resources - others have ways. I seem to have missed the entry deadline, by now far too late to be considered for college classes in *Important Strategies to Keep On Hand 101*. I need some time alone, to think it all through. While at the same time isolation does kind of make for a crummy playing- field to bounce ideas around in, so maybe that's the farthest thing from what I need? What's worse is discovering what you think could be a satisfying calm, but just when you're slipping it on like a snug-fitting slipper, it materializes into something else entirely (wrong-sized stinking rain boots?) and feels ultimately unattainable, even pointless. It's like being on some King Kong-sized outdoor squash court, the wind whipping the tiny black ball around too goddamn fast for you to ever get a proper swing in. There's no time allowed to stop, breathe, to recoup and get a decent look at how to approach any of this, even who (or what?) my opponent is - how to interact with these things getting shot at me. My Play Now, Pay Later Rusty Linings Playbook, too scuffed up and soiled to read, just hopeless hodgepodge hieroglyphics really. I've got to play a part (they say) in my own recovery, find unity in community amongst my fellow humans, somewhere I could flourish (does this exist?), take some action towards ousting the drugs and any other toxic evils from my sewer system of a body, what I'm supposed to regard as my temple, but really, closer to the truth and more to the point, has been remodelled into more of a shack for hanging sea bass in.

I need rest: rest that's been put off and time away from the struggle. Not to mention a quality moisturizer. *(tf#6)* (I'm looking for a magical formula in the anti-wrinkle, anti-oxidant, anti-psychotic department: a lotion or an ointment, a cream, oil, some toner: a super serum to shellack over me so as to replenish my decaying mind). Maybe?

There is some good news; I feel some miniscule solace in the idea that I should be living somewhere near, if not directly on, Henry Miller's *Tropic of Capricorn* - a city (or island?) where you can speak your mind, that's still edgy and inhabited by eccentrics and sincere nymphomaniacs, but peopled also by the delicacies of childhood; a playground rich and exultant complete with tuxedo-laden man-servants always in ear-shot, devoted solely to providing me with top grade, Italian fresh-roasted espresso…and Swedish massages, doled out by scantily-clad, wolverine-like, sex-starved princesses, but brilliant too, and curious, and eager to massage me out of my grief. I could see myself acclimatizing to such a hot and exotic, but gracious climate.

Now, just how to get there.

I'm frustrated and more than a little put off when I arrive at the L.A airport - these goonish airport security fellows tell me, "You cannot park that…that CAR here, sir!"

Here I was, bags packed, excited to begin what I was hoping to be an unfettered, self-exploratory journey. To my horror, I am denied a coveted schedule no one felt the need to share, when the next flight would be departing, and at what exact terminal: basic stuff one would expect without complication, "I don't know if I quite understand where it is you'd like to go, sir?" My enquiries met with dull wandering monkey minds, Burger 'n Fry's guys and gals concerned only with when their next break would be, eager to resume piling more garbage into themselves and continue their gossiping - the exchange of coveted private pointers on just how to remove mustard stains from shocking, pukey pastel golf course costumes, while marvelling at their own starry fashion sense, and further, congratulating themselves on black market, pungent perfume purchases from the duty free shop. An all too fragmented, vermin-ish bunch that seemed to share little sympathy with my gleaming quest of finding a new home. They had no clue as to how monumentally important this journey was to me.

Not wanting their virtually absolute unintelligible approach to infect me, I scurried off and took a seat in one of the crappy orange plastic cafeteria booths and awaited boarding instructions, along the way helping myself to stale salted peanuts from a mock food stand – a snack I assumed that was - though later was informed, was not - complimentary.

What side is anyone on these days anyhow? Me, feeling excluded, the ungodly unusable air-strip, some dilapidated misplaced runway. (Again, the confidence soars.) Lately, there's been little else to do but live in private created fantasies, a kind of hobby, moot criticisms with surreal characters, real to me, bizarre and often alarming to others; this veranda with chimes onto myself where I don't contend, don't get disappointed, a mind-set where a large part of my down time is dedicated to not mopping up more severely agonizing messes, tired of that regularity, having just ejected myself from moping round the watery West Coast mine-field, where about the only helpful tidbit I've picked up is that, *"You have to be wiped out as a human being in order to be born again as an individual."* Again, honing this misfitted charmer I can't help but be, this enfant terrible I see myself as, so marvellously maladjusted to anything going on around me, muddled, beaten, severely starved for answers. I'm all for finding a way to get re-born, to reinvent myself. I don't much care if it's as an individual, a peculiar smelling cabbie, a self-absorbed artist or an insomniatic gravedigger with Stigiophobia, just as long as it's not someone who's stuck eternally hopeless, doesn't reach forward to be anything better and feels dismantled by his surroundings. Especially having all this crash in on you first thing in the morning - that's the worst: to rise and fall in the same breath immediately after opening your eyes, to wake and weep and have the helpless thoughts gearing up full-throttle to rock whatever faith you've got going. To rinse and repeat the cycle before your orange juice, coffee and Wheaties is…well, a shitty way to begin the day.

Another helpful thing learned during scary recesses: when the deflation scenarios stab at you, you might have a fair shot at blowing yourself back up, that is if you can listen raptly and learn from your mistakes. Such hints make for fun and flirty pontificating to spew as luring teasers at social events and company picnics. (that is, if one is so privileged to have good-hearted friends, kind souls with solid steady jobs who take an active role in that ridiculous ritual of catching you a suitable female counterpart who'll put up with your *tour de force* of nonsense, for any length of time). I can see the scene clear as the Liberty Bell.

"Guys, it's nice of you to invite me, but I have to say the last thing I feel like doing is getting in that itchy potato sack with that Denise person you're trying to hook me up with in accounting. This is pathetic, really. This mockery of competitive sport, these cheap games are lame, lonely and sad - beyond belief. They're making me feel drastically sub-par and unwell. I'm off to get more pasta salad. And wine."

"Oh c'mon, spoiled sport, we've got a good shot at first prize," says Denise, a tough to look at Cyclops. It continues, "Phil in sales is bull-legged and those other teams look drained and drunk from the day". I envied the imbiber's stick-to-it-iveness. "I need a partner," attempting to grab my arm and get me "in the sack." She finally got the message when I put my hands over my ears and began reciting Pythagoras's Thermos and scaring the children with quick rapid jerky motions as if I was having a seizure, and made strange never-before-heard-by-human sounds not far from what I imagine cows being doused in kerosene and lit on fire cattle might sound like.

This gal Denise had have a talent for making me simultaneously miss pretty much any girl I ever loved or who loved me or cared anything about, she had the touch of morbid reflection. For whatever reason, her sad attempts to be cheerful, optimistic all in the guise of getting me to have fun plus my hyper-awareness seeing the mirror (and me in it) not responding well at all, everything all jumbled together. Worse, the sullied scene made me remember this 1st year college essay about Greek literature. *(tf#7)* "In the kingdom of the blind, a cyclops is a helpful guy/girl to know." (But not in this case, her one eye was so askew, and her one eye-brow so continuous, then there was the fake color eye, I didn't know quite what the hell I was looking at, so I became angry at her (unfairly I realized) for making me have to look at her face while at the same time having to take it upon myself to construct a method in which I would seem completely casual and non-chalant).

"Oh, you're no fun," she finally gets the picture of what she's dealing with. "What is wrong with you anyway?"

You're getting warmer.

————————————

Those unsupervised security fellows have had their eye on me for the last few hours and seem to be taking their own set of notes.

"Can we see some ID, sir?" the airport security minions inquired. I smartly responded with, "Well, I don't know. CAN you?" *(tf#8)* Why Smart Aleck Tim decided to show up for these dudes in blue, I can't say. Possibly the fact they were just hounding me for hounding sake. I wasn't doing anything terrible or that could have been considered conflicting with the public. Also, my long standing difficulties with well-shaved authority figures couldn't have helped my cause.

I catch them whispering in delicate tones, no one wanting to set me off. If somebody would only point me in the right direction, I'd leap-frog away and get out of their hair and finally could jet off on that international flight germane to my new existence, on to the eccentric destination where they lay waiting. (They?) The possibilities are endless, but are cut immensely short once I realize I've forgotten a necessary passport. Come to think of it, I don't have the legitimate ID (ideology?) for this aeroplane undertaking at all. I better go grab the car and drum up the courage to commence the trek back east by way of land. "I guess it's just you and me old man". (I talk to the car sometimes, to boost her confidence. More on the vehicular dilemmas later.)

"I was just leaving, but thank you though. Are you Mutt or Jeff? You know fellas, it is good we've got you. I've had my eyes on those homeless gals dressed as nuns, yep, sitting right over there, *pretending*. They don't appear trustworthy, no siree Bob. They seem unclean, unsavory, and I think I saw one of them split without paying for her Orange Julius. Bunch of no-good-niks. You know the type. It'd be in everyone's best interest to pat 'em down, bring 'em in for questioning. I would have done it but hey, you guys have it covered, clearly. I mean, it's your turf, right?"

Sitting solitary in airport detention, a hand-cuffed man in a Khaki-safari-outfit-and-pith-helmet catches my eye, shuffles over my way and sits down beside me. I figure he is either a Jungle Trapper or works at a pathetically-themed-tropical-cinnamon-bun-stand. He launches into a dramatic tale of how he's just returned from The Congo with six Ecuadorian Spider-monkeys, each one worth at least 50,000 Kronkas - which sounded like a lot - but said he'd let me have them for one thousand Loonies. "A steal, at twice the price," he said. (Twice the animal? I thought, under my breath). "Maybe some pets might help me take the focus off of myself, even make me feel needed." I thought about it momentarily, and then explained to him that I was on a mission, on my way back to my birthplace and it just wasn't in the cards for me to transport contraband animals that needed feeding, hosing down and proper washroom breaks, I couldn't risk it. Dealing with me was all that I could handle.

Focus was what was on the menu, with a side order of earned cynicism as usual. With an urgency afoot, somehow I sensed the people out there waiting for me to enrich their lives would only wait so long and I just had to find out who and where they were. As well, the little guy's high-frequency whinnying would have driven me completely mad...not from the trapper guy, the monkeys.

A couple hours passed before I was released from the airport's high risk security area. They could sense I wasn't the type to harm anyone but myself, I think. Mutt and Jeff said I was allowed to depart as long as I promised not to darken any airport terminals with my down-in-the-mouth negative attitude or transfer any kind of monkey, be it Spider or Ecuadorian over any border; basically anything that had a pulse or could be considered zoo-worthy. I accepted his terms, even though I thought he was being...

A full tank of fuel is all I've got, so somewhere along the way I'm going to have to sing for my supper, that is if I'm planning on eating sometime in the next few days, and coming out the other end of this Mr. Toad Wild Ride alive.

Time to strike the set. Now, where did I park you?

---

tf#6 I'm looking for a magical formula in the anti-wrinkle, anti-oxidant, anti-psychotic department: a lotion or an ointment, a cream, oil, some toner: a super serum to shellac over me so as to replenish my decaying mind.

tf#7 Don't worry, I was not in attendance due to any sincere endeavor to seek out and understand Ancient Greeks and their books or poems or whatever it was; I was there for the day only, having walked into the wrong room by mistake. I was visiting the campus to find a room with a piano so I could sit and play it and have my sandwich in peace.

tf#8 in grade school I would always ask if I can go to the bathroom to which the teacher would respond, "I don't know, CAN you go to the bathroom?" It was never simple. Actually, I developed a wicked insecurity and plaguing self-doubt around the whole issue: Can I? Can't I, Why am I here? Do I really need to go? Did I drink a sinister amount? Why aren't the other kids having this problem? Any question surrounding me and a visit to the lavatory sent my mind into such a cosmic and unpleasant tailspin, for a while, I just would hold it in and try and think of something else. By the end of the school year, I finally got the hint and secretly urinated off the property so as not to get involved in some protracted yammering back and forth on if it was possible for me to attend the bathroom and pee or if I was allowed to go and...well, you get the idea.

* * *

4. Crossed Country

Some men take the long route and some take the short route. Every man is working out his destiny in his own way and nobody can be of any help, except by being kind, generous and patient.

Henry Miller
Tropic of Capricorn

Cross country travelling, so many stories. Everyone has theirs, and they're all - to them, and maybe a few uncles and aunts well-rehearsed in counterfeit feelings, strange relations who're sure to put on caring faces when the time presents itself, to listen lovingly to that drab cliché data at graduations, weddings and funerals. I could be wrong, but I don't feel that I am.

I've made pretty good time, passed Vegas this morning and now I seem to be over some unbelievable mountains, which I'm guessing are part of Colorado. I don't map out specific hi-ways to take, don't have GSP or GPS, mainly, I use The Force, but I do have a sense I'm headed east, definitely east. Then it hits me that somewhere along the line I've got to head north. Hours of solitary driving lay ahead; Canada still days away, but it'll be worth it. The air is so thin up here; there's a chance I can't rely on my level-headed reasoning, even some of the heavier trucks pull over to the side of the road to re-establish their footing. I thankfully make it to the top, and the car thanks me for gliding wistfully down the other side of the mountain. I probably could have made my way down in neutral, but I thought it best not to confuse her. I wish more of the trip was like this. Effortless, beautiful, a gorgeous descent, a real breeze.

I'm starting to feel pretty exhausted, more to the point I'm running out of money and won't be able to afford the proper four or five night stay that awaits me somewhere on the horizon. After some tidy calculations, seems I'll have to complete this trip in a scant three days, tops. Maybe I can hunt down some of those speed pills that truckers gobble to stay awake.

I decide to give us a break - me and the 1990 4 cylinder Pontiac Sunbird - so I stop at this ancient gas station, that looks as though it was out of a 1950's American retrospective photography book, time having not messed with it one bit. There's an attendant wandering around inside so I walk in and decide to start up a little convo.

"Excuse me sir, can you tell me which time zone I'm in?" He answers with a Midwestern drawl. "There's only one REAL time zone, son…and you're in it."

"All righty then. Um…hey…you sell those things that help people stay awake when they're driving on long trips?"

"Pepto Bismol? Yeah, right over in that aisle there."

"No, those little vitamin things, you know, truckers always take them. The quicker-picker-uppers."

"Bounty Paper Towels?"

Is he kidding? We're not speaking the same language, so I jiggle back and forth, eyes rolling around in my head, a performance with flailing arms and chattering teeth which I hope illustrates what medication I mean.

"Oh, that. Um, well, we're not really s'pposed to sell that stuff, man. FDA's been on our backs." He winks at me, us now brothers on the same page, I guess - that or he's quickly realized I'm his type. He tells me his name is Kenton, which was strange enough, as my new dungaree-wearing contact also had a name-tag stapled to his lapel that read Cake. One of the things I managed to pick up in cognitive therapy was that it could be possibly destructive to shut a door when so clearly here, one was opening, or knocking, or was that opportunity? Whatever, this must fall into a category that deserves attention. So, I decide to go with it. Kenton the Cakeman coyly motions to a hidden camera, whispers something that sounds like pig Latin to me and then. "Psssst. Dude, meet me out back in five." After I take a gander at some glossy car magazines, munch on a child's size bag of Cheetos and down a frosty Cherry Coke, I shuffle out the back way to meet my new connection.

"We ain't supposed to sell it to customers over the counter, ya see. But I can let ya have these." He pulled out of his overall's pocket a Tylenol bottle filled with mysterious multi-colored tiny pills.

"Yes, that'll do just fine. Now, my good man, let me see here (flipping through my slender wallet, beginning the financial end of our negotiation)... I've got postage stamps, food stamps, my Chevron card and...let's see here..." He told me I was a real comedian and that he could accept nothing but cold hard cash, so I handed him more dollar bills than I could afford to part with, knowing full well this was none too hot an idea, though I did make a quick calculation that by taking the pills it would cut out the need to eat and stop anywhere decent to sleep, so actually I was saving money. Whoever said I can't make quick snap decisions on my feet was dead wrong.

He wishes me a bon voyage and I am off again.

Equipped with more to remember, sort out and recall than there is to look forward to, I'm removing the bandages more and more as I feel the Eastern seaboard merging closer with my eager sensibilities. My companion, the sun, still beats down on me with all kinds of reminders, while I zip through what must be ghost towns, some of which boast populations in the hundreds. I blast the car stereo away at my own emptiness and solitude, as well as the people who take the world (and each other) too seriously - humorless dark dogs baffled as to what to do with themselves. This sorry-assed consensus fills the whole continent; nobody's immune to the poisons that seep into human hearts and minds from the periphery.

My sick but speedy spook-mobile announces to the small minded, un-musical, non-writer types here that I've arrived. The townsfolk return my wave, their blank empty faces saying, "Yes, hello to you too, Mister-Big-city-dick-wad, keep moving on, that's right." They man their cornfields and tar paper shacks while motioning to me, "Lower the volume on that God damn radio!" fearful I may stop and request to stay the night, ultimately causing them to shuttle their rosy-cheeked, Daisy Duke look-a-like all-too-curious daughters in tight red and white tablecloth tops back to their barns.

I pull the car over to the side of the road, stirring up a wealth of dust and debris. There wasn't another car anywhere in sight. The sun was going down in the late afternoon sky. It seemed like a good time to be in the moment, even appreciative. I walk around to the passenger door, open it, reach in the glove box and glance at the Helpful Hints Travel Log Book packed affectionately by my last sponsor. These poor pamphlets are dreadfully out of date and behind the times.

Do you think you may have a problem

with drugs or alcohol?

H . A . L . T.

Are you Hungry, Angry, Lonely or Tired?

Ask yourself if you are any of these: it could be the reason you're craving your drug of choice.

Let's see now, I'm most of these things a good chunk of the time, so where does that leave us? My sponsor said, "Plan ahead," and as my "very best thinking" (as they say in The Program) got me in this mess, I'd better heed someone else's words for a change. I should make a reservation as these past weeks of sleeping in the car have saddled me with car-mopius osteoporosis interupti, a whooping cough and some wicked headaches that have been setting up shop for longer and longer bouts the last few days. Hopefully the worst of me - along with all my long-term and recently contracted torments and grievances with just about everybody - are long behind me. Things have got to change. I want to and can do better.

I got back in the driver's seat and make my way, still further north and east, away from a family of vultures that seemed to be assembling overhead.

———————

I want to fly at warp speed, motor past every small town I'd never heard of while at the same time stopping everywhere to explore, make notes and take photos. This feeling of freedom is intoxicating: top down, tunes so loud, whizzing through states, spun on my own version of speed. These tiny spark plugs that my morally vacant and greasy gas station anthropoid sold me that promised pep aren't hurting any as far as making the trip skate along briskly.

I'm on my way, on my own and what I say goes. I punch no clock today.

I decide to disrobe entirely while driving. It's incredibly hot and I want to feel the sun everywhere. "Maybe it'll help my body repair," I muse. All that Vitamin D and stuff, and no one'll see. I joke how my car is now a nudy colony for recovering vampires-in-the-addict-relocation-program.

Ah shit, what now?

Damn Highway Patrol. This is all I need. This is not going to be good. I begin to pull my auto over to the gravelly shoulder of the interstate while at the same moment I realize I'm buck naked, except for a beach towel I've got on as a kind of cape. Immediately, I sense this will not be a whimsical meet 'n greet filled with delightful and polite social graces.

I manage to grab onto what I can off the car floor in the back seat that fell out of the costume trunk earlier, blindly assembling a sort of makeshift cop outfit; (coincidentally) green felt Robin Hood cap - with feather - and a child's flimsy tan cowboy vest complete with a tin SHERRIF's badge as well as a much too big pair of colorful spotted Velcro clown bottoms.

I catch a glimpse of him in my rear-view mirror, moseying on over from his patrol car and right off he's an exact ringer for that weirdo whack-job Colonel Mustard from the game Clue, minus the monocle. As far as what kind of oddball I must have looked like, or from what board game I could have escaped from, I really didn't know. Nothing good or even remotely stylish.

"Bonjourno, mon Deiter-Hausen. That sure is one hell of a scooter you got back there, Colonel," tossing out multiple made-up mixed metaphor monikers, my friendly banter while unravelling maps from other states to cover up and hide my shame. I'm usually better prepared.

"Sir, do you know how fast you were driving? He asks and receives a dead stare. "Well, I'll tell ya: 130 through a construction zone and I've had the siren on for five minutes back there, ya couldn't hear me?

"Well, Officer, the radio was on pretty…"

"And, in THIS great state of Kansas, folks wear clothes when they drive. It's not in the law books, it's just kind of a given, ya see? And do you know what the punishment is for impersonating an office of the law?" Which was funny on many levels, as I can't say anyone in their right mind would have bought the fact I actually belonged to any sort of law consortium.

My vehicle may have flown through their town a snippet of a percentage point north of the speed limit and true, most every stitch of clothing I'd put on for the day was tossed in the back seat, but who would have thought this all would have brought about sirens and condescending looks from pissed-off patrolers? There were no signs announcing, KEEP CLOTHES ON WHILE DRIVING! No picture of say, a grinning Amish lady with a red X through her, holding up some shirts. Where was that sign, mister!? Yeah, just as I thought. Nowhere. That's where. But a warning would have been nice, speed limit-wise, clothing-wise. "I'm sorry, sir, you're so right, I had a situation…" To which there was nothing left to do but shut my mouth as nothing I would have said after that doozy was going to win this fellow over.

"Registration and insurance please, sir." Can't remember if I'm insured. I can find no information in this glove box to tell me one way or another. I guess I'm on my own if I get stuck. Nothing new.

My dreamy scene (whatever state I'm in) interrupted by this dim-witted freeway Mountie, needing to fill his required daily nonsense, thus robbing me of my escapist nostalgia. I cast him quickly in the role of a stark backdrop, some pedestrian panorama.

"What was that?" simultaneously shooting me a disapproving disgusted look that told me my faux merry clown suit and effeminate - but manly - Dane chapeau wouldn't be a hit in this bogus Hamlet of his.

If I survive the next scene I'm going to have to give a concerted effort into keeping my mumbling to a dull roar as too many of these private thoughts are getting too many strange looks on this trip. Again, I'm much louder than I believed, just as he begins scribbling me a number of citations. Knowing there would be no audience response, I gladly approve and commend the hilarious comments under my breath. "Oh, nothing, sir." Feeling a little like an apathetic raven who had flown out of his designated jurisdiction, who doesn't know his place.

"What's with these California plates?" he quips while making notes and circling my vehicle. "Look, mister, having a driver's license is a privilege and in this state we don't drive like that. But I guess you're a long way from home, eh?" trailing off chuckling, tail in hand, probably drunk on dreams of jelly donuts and the heady promise of cellophaned white bread mayo sandwiches, maybe left over from some surreal suburban John Waters-like PTA type picnic. I would have made a joke about dollars to donuts but I'm pretty certain he wouldn't have dug it or even understood it.

Figuring he had heard all the "We're not in Kansas anymore" jokes, I digress, but come to think of it, we ARE actually in Kansas (pretty close, anyway) so there was no joke to be told, which momentarily made me down in the dumps forlorn like a kid away at camp for the very first time, and getting picked on. This trip was fitting on me just fine, I thought, like a fucking strait-jacket.

I'm convinced there is a spirit that breathes somewhere here, a soul untroubled and tranquil, hidden in these far-off hilltops and vistas…but I'm promptly disappointed; they speak to me - and strangely sound like me - these mountains, and concede they are broken, blistered and dog-tired from the multitudes of hungry tourist's eyes seeking to extract something worthwhile. They declare they are fraudulent and meaningless, standing by, docile, clumped together, having given up trying to be something more than what they are: recipients of embarrassing salutes from Foster-Grant-wearing-Smokey-banditos-of-purgatory. Through trying to explain all this to the reptilian constable, I can see he's lost in my international rhetoric. I love it when others unknowingly make parodies of themselves.

When the police do stop me, more often than not, they're pretty puzzled as to what to do with me, my California plates and improvised erratic accents plus the dual citizenship thing, AND being Canada-bound makes them shrug their shoulders in confusion. They warn me about this or that. In the day, I might have been taken for a draft dodger, but as there has been no draft to dodge for a half a century or so, that wasn't the category that I fell into. These highway police folk sure look funny though, all portly and packed in, truly unaware of the power their utility belts wield. Now, if they had capes and masks, maybe pirate swords, vials of truth serum or MDMA - proper pills - that'd be something. As it stands, this one just plain bores me as I play atop it all, thank myself and speed off leaving Captain Sensible the Fully Clothed Commando behind in a cloud of dust. I am relieved as I won't do any hard time for my multiple car crimes. This is a relief, as I look (and feel) drab in stripes and bruises.

I really can't imagine what somebody would do if they ran out of gas in these parts - flag down murderers and rapists and hillbilly local-yokels with pitchforks to assist? Just don't let the tank drop down near E, so I won't have to deal with being fuel-less out on one of these barren but slick seemingly endless highways - it'd drown this whole business of freedom I'm getting used to.

I've left a few messages back west, my sponsor Franklin and a couple people in the program who still gave a damn, the constituents of quickly dimming crevices in my memory now made aware I'm on the wheelchair ramp of life and haven't yet succumbed to the turkey vulture devourings possible in these parched and wicked wastelands. I'm halfway gone, criss-crossing through, in hopes of making it safely across the border, returning to some sort of home base, a headquarters that may or may not still exist, and me, the great divided one.

* * *

5. My Haunted Carriage

**If a boy's father is absent or emotionally unavailable, then the boy
will spend most of his time in his mother's world.
Unwittingly, his mother may instill 'feminine' qualities in him
by rewarding him for being sweet, gentle, cautious, and well
behaved. Boys who do not have a strong father figure wander
around in a kind of No-Man's-Land.**

Marvin Allen
In the Company of Men

I arrive at the motel where there's been a manger
specifically set aside for me. I requested a room with two
twins, the living breathing kind. Management, finding this
request less than amusing, downgraded me to a berth
absurdly close to the front desk clerk. I'm guessing the
quirky but clever remarks made into my imaginary hand-
held tape recorder made the on-duty dweeb uncomfortable
and suspicious; my allegedly unsocial conduct further
ostracizing me from the troops and yet again, helping to
build a strong case for The Isolation Chamber. I get him
back by mumbling out of earshot, "Ya minimum-wage-
earning mullet-headed red neck." That'll teach him, I think
to myself, and may have said aloud.

I pop out of my room, walk to the lobby and make my way
over to the adjacent bar for a watered-down scotch. By
nightfall, when I return, there are two blond, pig-tailed
twins in lacy pink Sunday doily-dresses in my room. These
girls are groomed beautifully, and seem to be warming up
for some twisted Little Miss Crazy, Jon Benet, Honey Boo
Boo beauty pageant. With a lisp, one says, "Mommy thinkth
I'm thowing too muth leg in thith evening gown, what do
you think?" and from the other, "Do you want to see my
special talent?" Questions I couldn't begin to answer. While
staring through me with a piercing icy gaze, the twin things
in precise unison declare, "We're shiny, feisty and super
clever. Brush us pretty, mister." The nightmare befalls me.

My idea of a quality assignment with bite used to involve driving across America with a hot-chick-photographer, trying to score dope in every state capital I visit and then writing about it. Today, it's a little different. I prefer to take the pictures myself - getting into my own pants is tough enough - and as far as the scoring of dope, well, I'm much more above board these days (with the grain, as it were) - so to speak.

Who to speak with about acquiring such grains? Oats and fibre-ish goodness I've heard tons of info on, yet have felt inadequate to take the leap of faith and make a commitment to embrace the concept whole-heartedly.

Being too cerebral and overly analytical while reflecting endlessly on my own peculiar actions - and scribbling myself memos in public - seems to have left me at arm's length from most everything. I've wondered for a hell of a long time just how others get along as well as they do. Or are they dying inside and have just figured out how to hide it better? I feel I have no way of knowing. Maybe I'm an anomaly and this is simply how things move through me.

There was a time when I had a ceremonial parlor in my mom's basement to pay daily homage to Diane Keaton, a Kafka-esque super set-up complete with a fully-clothed mannequin dressed as the actress, fridge-sized black and white stills from Annie Hall along with melted candles, chalices, sacrificed squirrels pinned to a cork board and a couple shaved llamas. Visitors who'd returned with me to the homestead delicately shared that I was profoundly misguided. I still felt it was an achievement, impressive even, but, more than once ended up being on the business end of mortified looks and demeaning laughter from curious dates with the wrong questions. I've finally assessed that working with an arsenal of morbid though eclectic, ritualistic behavior has left me on the empty side. Further, I've discovered that to be neurotic, elitist and emotionally distraught (though possessing a keen fashion sense and the bizarre talent of guessing perfectly ladies' perfume choices whilst beside them in elevators), has become outdated and useless and also unattractive to the opposite sex, and apparently comes across as being really, really gay.

Maybe it's my whole way of being and not just my manner, my gait, my carriage, that's damn outdated and useless (AND unaccountably gay?) T'is also become a rarity to even find a gal who isn't convinced I'm just homo-hypocritical, just hiding in some closet. Not right. True, I've ventured into armoires, a couple of arboretums, a wardrobe (or whatever they're called), but that doesn't count, as I was only hunting around in there for a secret door leading into a mysterious land, some Narnia-like village *(tf#9)* which certainly can't be considered In The Closet. Plus, since I'm on the council for Hedonism and Deviant Decadence, it makes little sense that I'd veer away from something just because it might be deemed socially odd and non-conformist - knowing me, that would make me wanna do it even more.

I know some French, maybe a few Broadway show tunes (mother's fault), can cook when the situation really calls for it and yes, I've taken those sweltering sweat-hog Bikram yoga classes, but hey, that's only because I was trying to detox while simultaneously hitting on rich, sweaty divorcées while living the grand lacuna in Laguna Beach, California. I've always said that I'm comfortable enough with my own sexuality that I've never needed to act the male beast role. I'm unhampered by rigid traditionalist notions of what's masculine and feminine, and have never felt the need to adapt that male-gusto-elbows-on-table-open-mouth-pose when ingesting food. And why should I be suspected on account of having refined tastes, minimal body hair or using a few sissy words like Thus or Whence or Tempestuous? And that last one, I'm not even sure I use properly. I do what comes naturally, thus side-stepping any machismo stereotypes. The kind of girl I end up marrying will find me to be an original, sensitive, even intriguing conformist for the first couple years (if that) but will ultimately leave me for a less artistic, knuckle-dragging, more employable type of guy. *(tf#10)* I'm guessing this'll be unavoidable, unless I can put an act of sorts together. Or at very least pick up my socks and start making some positive, healthy choices. A guy can only act out the scene from Say Anything for so long: the one where I'm in a trench coat, standing outside the girl's window holding a ghetto-blaster above my head blaring Peter Gabriel's "In Your Eyes" at an ear-splitting volume, before they in turn see the movie for themselves, inevitably rendering me fraudulent, creepy and unoriginal, not to mention, regrettably, sending all plans I had for enticing interplay - even just cuddling - dismally downhill.

The closest I got to that kind of cinematic-gooey-love-parade-of-intimacy was getting Ione Skye (the lead in that exact movie) to be my sponsor when I signed up in the Narcotics Anonymous program for a spell. Getting clean and improving myself was truly what I was after, but in all honesty it was her narcotic essence and promise of something more that kept me coming back. That was ultra-cool, and made for a great story to tell when I got back to hometown Toronto.

"All right, I'll be your sponsor, temporarily, but you know, you're supposed to have a guy take you through all this."

"What you said at the meeting last night really hit me," I replied, staring at her, google-eyed, a little nervous, almost stuttering. "What are you doing after, my chickadee? A Caramel Macchiato perhaps, mmmmmmmmmy treat?"

"You know if you don't take this shit seriously, you're gonna die."

God, she looked and smelled great, just like in the movie. Now having gotten my hands on a personal tutor, a mentor of sorts, I set out to show her I was damn capable of taking this recovery stuff seriously. Beyond excited and raring to go, I began a routine of fetching her steaming hot coffee at 5:30 a.m each morning, to flow fluidly with the black and white, billboard-size headshots of me in reflective scholarly poses nailed to her garage door and taped up onto her neighbourhood signposts.

I swear I was doing alright: on my phone, genuinely lurking in the bushes across the road from the 12 Step Meeting, monitoring my new sponsor - the lovely Ione - catching her sashaying out of the church with what must have been a new beau, maybe a new sponsee in training? Seeing her reaction to the love letter, candies and roses waiting for her at her car did nothing more than embarrass me, not my initial intention. Me, Mr. Maturity, reporting the sullied scene to my buddy Franklin over the phone.

"Really, I'm... I'm okay."

"Where are you, buddy?" Frank asked with concern.

"I'm in the bushes, where do ya think I am? You think I want her to see me, what's wrong with you? She's coming out the entrance way. Now, she's embracing the flowers, she's looking around..."

"Are you all right?" More concern.

"Stop asking me that, of course. I'm better than all right. I know what I'm doing."

"Did you finally get your stuff off her lawn like she asked?"

"She wasn't serious. Wait, now she's...hold on, she's stuck the flowers underneath the front wheel of her SUV."

At that moment the sprinkler system decided to turn on; now, a very tiny Tim, tiptoeing through the awful tulips, the lurker in the rose bushes, socks squishy with mud, thorns jabbing my face. This, a banner fucking day in La-La land. I had arrived. Observing in Technicolor sadness her shooting the chocolates over to what appeared to be a hungry hobo type guy, then speeding off, running over and demolishing the roses, but not before she caught my eye, shooting a scowl my way to let me know I should look for another sponsor and that any hopes of future fine- dining experiences together were looking super grim.

I drop my phone, my entire surveillance file in a giant rhubarb bush - time to reassess this unorganized amateur stake-out. I abort the mission, shuffle to one of what must be the last few standing PacBell phone booths in California and call my dealer. "What do you mean, you're sold out? Shit. What kind of outfit are you running?" Unacceptable. I later dub this day, 'The Unbearable Darkness of Sharp Thorns and Hating Everything', but also, make a note to later rework the name into something shorter, less touching and with more of a straight forward and quotable hashtag to it.

While wiping the mud off the phone and powering down, I get in my car (not an SUV) and try to recall the advice that I probably won't put into play. My sober, philosophically-charged and always right-on friend Franklin, who's bailed me out of trouble on more than one occasion, said earlier with care, "Look, I think you'd better get yourself sorted out first before thinking about dragging another poor girl through your childish bloody muck heap." There have been more than a few unhealthy, less-than-spectacular, unhappy endings. Alright, I'll give her a little space. Next time will be different.

"Where is it I'm going?" and "Do you want to come along for the ride?" Figure out the first one before even considering the next one... Apparently, I'm not supposed to get these questions mixed up or out of priority sequence. I'm supposed to figure out just what I'm doing with myself before I invite someone to co-exist with me and share the joy ride. Makes sense, kind of. Why do I keep forgetting that? Truthfully, it didn't really take all that long for things to spiral south. With Ione, it ended as these things tend to, painfully and a monkey paw or two earlier than I thought they would.

I enjoyed Ione's and my relationship (*working* relationship) tremendously and it went, for the most part, pretty smoothly; the cease and desist order and her second-degree coffee burns notwithstanding. Admittedly, I may have been somewhat over-zealous, but to this day, I have trouble comprehending why the heck she won't return my calls. My heart was in the right place, the stalking was genuine and sincere.

My spooky curiosity entwined with an eerie interest in most everything dark and macabre have propelled me into being someone who repeatedly makes terrible, self-sabotaging choices in regard to drugs (and maybe relationships). Though, rather than define myself as a hyper-active addict, I kind of like to spruce it up, spiff it along if you will, and more often than I say this with a thick English accent, as if I were ordering a spot of Earl Grey Tea, sticking with ye olde reliable, more acceptable-for-conversation stock statement: "Why, yes, at times I have made some rather peculiar decisions in regards to my relationship with substances." It sounds a little more above board.

---

tf#9: a village with no pesky laws against carving mantras in trees with chainsaws, like Sartre's "Hell is other people."

tf#10: me, fulfilling her sweet wish, to rescue me from myself and oh, if she knew what a job she'd be taking on, if she only knew!

* * *

6. Anybody Home?

The boy appears to be deaf to her criticisms, so the mother repeats them over and over again. What she doesn't realize is that her son is paying very close attention. He grows up feeling there is something inherently wrong with him. It's not his actions that are unacceptable to his mother; it's his very being.

So this is the arena where my dear mother and I are re-connecting, her grand old house in Lindsay, Ontario. I'm allowed to live on this Glass Menagerie stage, that is, as long as I don't rearrange her meticulously placed items from their precious homes. Everything must be just so, right down to the delicate and easily breakable Tetley Tea miniatures and what I imagine to be a snug and comfortable afghan, which would be great to throw over me during allotted TV time, but alas, is only a prop for the show. There's a litany of crumbs to be picked up along with the predictable, unavoidable onslaught of leaves to be raked amongst skeletal trees, coupled with an a semblance of more than 100 years of surviving life (beating death) we've managed to pull together here on planet earth.

We share my Dad, his death, also her second husband most recently taken from her, both tragic, sudden and devastating... The latter more so for her, as my assigned step-monster and I were far from fond of each other.

There's her two strokes, her mysterious Multiple Sclerosis thing that no physician can quite make out what to do with, and of course my frustrations and failures, battles mostly lost out there in larger-than-life cities that've swallowed me whole. It breaks her heart, she says, to see me struggle. It breaks pieces still left in me to think about it.

We also share her Lorazepam, but I'm praying mom thinks the missing pills are the work of a tooth fairy, some foreboding fly-by-night-figure with weathered wings who can't keep track of what cargo she's supposed to pick up and what proper legal tender to leave behind for us molar-less humans. Maybe I could talk this impish pixie into taking me with her, swap me and leave in my place a kind of changeling? Creepy, yes, but I'd like to think I'm open to change. Regardless, she doesn't care much either way as long as she gets a sweet deal for the pills when she arrives back home to her corrupt cloud. I could be wrong. I'm just hoping she doesn't organize a proper Law & Order-like investigation concerning the missing medication - my mom, not the hopped-up fairy-duster with wings who pawns her wands and wares. Mother has her own fantastical explanation for how things operate here on planet earth. We're both trapped in this portrait of unhappiness and illusion and we both have our own ways of coping. So, this is where we'll repair, or at least, attempt to.

They think she might also have cancer, so they keep removing sections of her skin, making her look as though she's been picking and scratching at scabs on her face like a crazed meth addict would, but they say it's a necessary process. I feel awful for her because I know how self-conscious it makes her feel. It's more than a little unnerving, but I think I'm getting used to it. They thought I had Hepatitis C when I got back from California - another reason to eject myself from the pricey American medical matrix I wouldn't have been able to afford - but luckily, they also said that I'm one of the freak cases where the bad blood swimming around in me just kind of eerily vanished. It hasn't shown-up on any of the latest tests so I'm keeping my fingers crossed. Also, none of the pens work here. (She holds on to the unusable ones, for what?) I feel a spooky ironic overtone flowing un-fluidly along with the dozens of clocks tick-tocking away in my mother's kingdom, marking time in this dungeon of threadbare opulence, clearly not mine for thousands of hard-earned reasons, all belonging to her. I hear the cuckoo clock chime, "Not mine, not mine, not mine..."

After zoning out in front of the television for what must have been an entire afternoon, an intense numbing boredom comes over me coupled with hot and cold flashes, a duplicitous soul-curdling recipe. I get the feeling that I'm even more alone in the house than usual, therefore free to forage with ease as opposed to when mom's nearby keeping close watch, so I ignore my strange symptoms and run frenzied into the bathroom, open the medicine cabinet to hunt for helpful drugs of any kind. To come across only Women's A.M and P.M One-a-Day Vitamins is a sorry tale, but I down some anyway. I also discover chewable Vitamin C and Evening Primrose Oil, so I ingest a large quantity - a William Burroughs quantity - knowing full well this'll do little else than arouse a more fragrant scent and jaundiced coloring at my next outing at the urinal troughs. The buzzing serenity of fortified bone structure is not the desired effect, but the evening in evening primrose sure makes it sound calming, like some sort of Valiumy-like-valerian-licorice-root-soother, so I pop those puppies too. Tonight, I eat you all. Bingo! Something that seems to be prescribed by a doctor. This could be good: Medroxy-progesterone and Conjugated Estrogens, though after a quick glance in the DSM reference guide, I learn this omelette of witchy womanhood won't help the likes of me. Suddenly I feel faint and imagine being absorbed onto a drafty 70's game show soundstage - a confusing affair, this unwanted Logan's Run television portal. A kaleidoscope of colors dance and flicker around the room and come at me, instantly calling to the stage a Chuck Woolery-ish game show host-type guy who introduces himself by thumping me senseless over the head with an enormously long and metallic microphone, then evaporates magically, disappearing as quick as he appeared. I'm now orbiting Planet Distraught - a scant galaxy away from my new home, Planet Bizarro, a triple long jump from Planet Abyss, a ghostly ravine most living creatures are lucky to avoid. My fears sometime speak to me. Today they mention matter-of-factly on their way to the gym, that I am the void inside a volcano, not unlike Mars, with all its mysterious craters and hills, endless valleys and peaks. And to also try to include some exercise in my strange days, that it'll help to release serotonin and dopamine. (When did fears get so scientifically informed?)

I think I hear Mom. Yup, the sound of the side screen door slams. Oh oh, she's hunted me down. She's returned from shopping and I can hear her ominous and ghostly moccasin shuffle on the other side of the door; a frightful and twisted unglamorous prêt-a-porter, now too near. Realizing I've picked the booby pill prize and not having the courage to stick around to receive whatever the drab parting prize is, I carefully try not to make any incriminating sounds or actions, and gently position the tiny bottles I was rummaging through in the cabinet back behind the sliding glass mirror.

"What are you doing in there?" she queries. I open the bathroom door, obey my mopey mood and counter, "Nothing mom. Geez, why are you always on me?" Simultaneously slinking past her to the living room where the 100-year-old Steinway baby-grand piano sits. This is an amazing piece of handiwork: brilliant, kind of a deep rich maroon, mahogany maybe, inherited from my grandmother, the piano I learned on that's always sat atop this hardwood floor making the perfect beast resonate wonderfully with an echo of ages.

The rare instrument hasn't been played much in years, still there's a familiar scent of Old English genuine Lemon Oil, as mom still manages to look after it to keep it from cracking and ageing prematurely. The strokes and MS have left my mother's motor skills fragmented and discombobulated. Maybe she's a little jealous, as I still have a say in how my hands glide across the keys, and can play tunes she once performed with one hand tied behind her back. She tears up pretty often when I sit down and get playing this beautiful monster that haunts both of us daily for many reasons, though I'm pretty sure I'd just be guessing at what they are.

I've always felt fortunate, how I was introduced to the passions and intimacies of such an eclectic range of music: everything from Debussy's "Clair de Lune," Saint-Saëns' "Danse Macabre" to Vince Guaraldi's Charlie Brown jazz numbers, to pop song singles by Christopher Cross, Toto and oh yeah, Hall & Oates. This is around the same time I began to hone my improv skills and my talent of playing by ear, in life and at the piano.

Mom studied at the Royal Conservatory as a kid, her Rosedale values and upbringing, now a cruel template. But thank god, she's managed to save all this wonderful timeworn sheet music, not to mention plenty of hardly-played classic vinyl albums for me to pick through. I first heard a good deal of them during those in-between moments - waiting for my parents to drive me to early morning grade school classes in wintertime, my forehead pressed against the frosty screen-glass door, drifting away, listening to the finely-etched melodies from a kitchen radio seemingly set to an old fuzzy standards and classics station, that couldn't help but make an impression on me. What came with it was an ability to instantly conjure up images to go along with the music that started to connect to my heart.

I used to get Mom to sit at the piano and play popular songs I wanted to learn. These were magical times. I'd put my hands on hers and say, "Go" and "Again," then, "Is that it?" It was another world, deciphering the hidden meanings of the notes, clefs and time signatures on the page. Too impatient to sit through proper lessons, I learnt by listening. Blessed with an uncanny musical ear, that unique gift of improvisation really became fun. With an aptitude to figure out just about any song, plus my virtuoso bravura of self-soothing, suspended chord clusters and dreamy yet sorrowful minor nines, the piano would be like a companion for me. Not many things, hardly any, actually, have come to me as naturally. To live vehemently and vicariously through the connected resonating strings, the pedals, note by note, all of it and me, the voracious skimmer, making the music my own. It was all I'd have left after spending all that I was. I still cherish this big old crazy box of wood. "One day you will be mine," I whisper to it.

Someday, my poor fatigued mother will pass on and it will be my turn to read a horrifically-sappy eulogy at her funeral, a W.H Auden poem I'll cut, paste and mostly plagiarize - alongside my less than welcome two-cent-stand vestige. I foresee some rotten hazy February afternoon, drizzling sewage, mud sliding down into the dug area the casket is being lowered into at some cemetery named St. John Wartz on the Hill, like it was at my grandmother's burial, that day when those pall-bearing strangers so callously did their job. Standing there, I stood quivering, squeezing my mom's hand so tightly, almost breaking it, these seconds between us... clenching on to her, needing her to offer up something, maybe answers. I became angry and resentful that she didn't have the goods to make those minutes disappear. Stopping the procession, "Hey, Granny, wait... I, but... wait...um." Looking up at a sympathetic cousin, "Can't I...still...say something?" Unable to stop crying. "Gran, no, you can't go!! Gran, no, you can't go!! Wait. Stop." I immediately realized, embarrassingly I might add, that I had transformed into a one-manned cheering section for some goddamn fucking College prep-school. Christ, any levity available would have helped soothe while she slipped further away from me, the coffin gaining speed, lower and lower into the unforgiving stupid ground.

BuT nothing did.

One things for sure, the joy that was in that piano would change. I didn't know that the pain from the memories and the feelings of desertion would help make for better song writing. But what kind of trade-off is that? This was the moment I knew there would be no returning to that house down on Alvin Avenue around the corner from that ornamental parkette, near the schoolyard, amidst leafy trees that circled and cast that late day shadow on the kid's swings, with their pure nostalgic sounds that fed me all along. Plus those tennis courts that were all ease and innocence. Those weekend sleepovers, permission to indulge in Earl Grey tea and stay up late, sometimes viewing slides from her world travels during her younger years where it looks like she's another lady entirely! That was the greatest. Safe, and cared for. The gentlewoman who was all grace and under whose loving aegis I'd first experienced cards - double solitaire, and bridge as mysterious to me now as it was then. Oh yeah, then there was that weird puzzle game with the tiles and the numbers on them, that looked like it had lived through some evil war. You had to be careful not to land on the spooky forest animal, the dreaded Skeezax, all tentacles and veins, like a gigantic living pulsating liver with a bulging scrotum for a head. Or there was "EL CUCUY," the Mexican boogeyman who trolls through numerous forums in search of victims and answers to his questions. I wish I still had that ancient board and all the pieces that came with it. Man, where does that stuff get to?! I don't see how it could just up and vanish. Every family member I ran into over the years said they didn't know where it materialized to; that I must have thrown it out (!) Now, I know that didn't happen. Could I have been that dumb on the cusp of adolescence? Has my mind really checked in to the Alzheimer's ward, signed up for movie night and chosen my team for volleyball intramurals without having considered the part of my brain that would defend against such demoralizing end-of-the-line scenarios? C'mon people.

She was active in church, lawn bowling and thinking of others first. I like to imagine her as just away, off somewhere like Belgium, maybe Geneva - some outlandish, maybe Communist city, protected by some Iron Curtain rod. Representing Canada at an Anglo-Saxon cuisine conference or playing in some prestigious international bridge tournament that's gone into like quadruple overtime.

Incapable of unkindness, she is well liked and needed elsewhere for now. She has information. Knows important secretive stuff, like, exactly how to set a pristine, profoundly welcoming table. She knows where everything should go; how to exquisitely prepare and wheel out the cut-up celery and carrot sticks and the green olives with the things in them; yes, a hugely underrated skill in times of bloodshed and warfare between countries.

I believe most underestimate the intrinsic value of those Triscuits and Turtles chocolate treats Gran seemed to always have plenty of in the pantry, prepped and ready to roll in, in case company came - important captains or generals from one side or the other decided to pop by uninvited to discuss casualties. Such snacks can be monumental when it comes to improving relationships between countries, grandmothers and grandsons. She had a way of understanding me with just a look, and also had the best sense of humor I've ever met in anyone her age. So, I'll do my best to be mature and let others appreciate and enjoy her for a while. The governing card council in charge of Card Games Gone Wild - The Senior Episodes, have to hold on to her, temporarily.

Great. Mom has left me another list. "Alright, I said I'd get to it." Amidst her obsession with the daily rituals that I myself would prefer to pass on, but I'll do my best to placate. I've got to get out there to rake up those crunchy Canadian maple leaves before the terrible winter weather returns. Again, both front and backyard need tending to: a seemingly never ending task amidst some desperately needed humor. I'm sure if she could, she'd find a way to keep a tally of me failing to attain the made-up global leafage accumulation measure, some proper per-square-capita-per-day of leaf luggage I fall short of. Seems it's never enough, as the leaves fall faster than I can stuff them into the goddamn Hefty bags. Out of breath, I suggest to Mom we play Beat the Clock and ask her to keep time - how long it takes me to gather all the leaves and shoot the lot of them onto the neighbor's lawn while she rifles through her purse for medication. Mother doesn't find this game funny. This, I can tell, as she begins breathing heavier, shaking her head back and forth. So, I up the stakes, almost knocking her over with an unexpected bonus round question in my best Howard Cosell voice. "This is the last match of the day. You can have what's behind Garage Door Number 1 or settle up and pay off your son's accumulated allowance for the last 15 years." Weighing her options, she opts to head back into the house to hunt down a calculator, I assume. I yell out an offer to paint the entire house if she can pull an albatross, a prescription pad and a chess board out of her ass. Purse. I meant purse. She's back in the house going through her wicker bag as I continue the yard work, remorsefully, on account of I really meant to recommend that other crazy Monte Hall fantasy booze cruise competition, Let's Make A Deal. I don't think it would've made much difference though. The triple espresso latte with twelve sugars I made for myself earlier is peaking in me. I'm at my emotional zenith and am forced into a feisty, playful mood, bouncing into the garage *(tf#11)* and coming across enough material to construct a flag from a neighbor's tossed-out-wooden-leg I've been saving and an old white pillowcase lying mockingly amidst the hammer and nails area. Though that pillowcase may also have been a handkerchief belonging to someone with gigantism. I tie the cloth to the wooden leg and with a black marker, write **S U R R E N D E R** on it, retreating behind the flimsy partition.

This surrender scene with the flag reminds me of that brief stint in the All-Addicted, Inner City, Non-Traveling All-Stars at that Royal Palms Rehabilitation Center (Bukowski's old digs). I was forced to sing in this recovery choir: *(tf#12)*

> **"We are the soldiers in the army, we had to fight,**
> **although we had to cry,**
> **we had to hold up the blood-stained banners...**
> **we had to hold 'em up until we died..."**

Play here....if you dare. (warning: it's catchy)

https://search.yahoo.com/yhs/search?p=we+are+the+soldiors+in+the+army+we+had+to+fight&ei=UTF-8&hspart=mozilla&hsimp=yhs-002

Or pretty close to that. A soothing ditty I can assure you, and yes, it's been a battlefield. It never fails though, when one is *forced* to sing anything, there will be not one grain of passion. Same goes for sincerity. In an attempt to get on the choirmaster's good side, I joked with him that I had some experience playing the triangle of self-obsession, that maybe he could keep me in mind if they add an addict orchestra. But the comments did nothing more than make the guy mad and doubt my level of dedication.

Rest time was a luxury no-no at the Royal Palms. You were never allowed to just hang out in your room and stay in bed if you felt like it, and you couldn't talk back or offer excuses to the higher-ups in charge or you'd get what little privileges you had revoked. "Don't think you can try that crap on me, mister. You know how I can tell if an addict is lying? His lips are moving." Not entirely true. In retrospect, my lips have spent all kinds of time moving without anything close to a lie coming out of it... Not for days in a row or anything; I'm just saying it wasn't terribly kind for the staff to say it was an absolute.

It wasn't enough that we were up at 6:00 a.m scrubbing repulsive toilets and lime-entrenched shower stalls. There was also the herculean task of cooking breakfast, lunch and dinner with the full-time kitchen staff for a couple hundred loud, mostly ungrateful, frenetic insensitive guys. The folks in charge still wanted you fresh and chipper, to be alert for group sessions or - if the need came - to bellow passionately in a pointless choir. Were they trying to kill us, I wondered? We were supposed to have our parts down, memorized and solid, so that when it came time to step up and perform an absurd solo, you didn't make the whole damn group look inept or God forbid, even worse – unmusical.

Phone calls were attempted by me, dialing out on a scuzzy Pacific Bell rotary-dial telephone in the cafeteria; desperate to tell anyone who would listen that this just couldn't be where I belonged. Someone must have made a mistake.

There were the counsellors who I could handle, even have a heart-to-heart with on occasion, and then there were the ones who wouldn't give me the tiniest break, who went out of their way to belittle me. Larry the muffin man was one of these guys. I liked to imagine him as a steaming hot but rancid buttery muffin with legs. It seemed to take away a good deal of the power he felt he had over me and the other klutzy castaways. Come to think of it, Larry the blueberry dough boy was the first staffer I met when I checked in. His comments stick out in my mind, like, "The bellhop's off today, so you'll have to carry up your own bag, Sonny boy," and later, "You can't accept collect calls here, who the hell do you think you are?" and "It's time for meditation, get off the fucking phone. This ain't the Hilton, dude."

Then there was the night my mom tracked me down on my birthday from her hospital bed in Toronto. I heard an announcement over the intercom that there was a call for me, but by the time I raced down to the front desk from my fifth floor suite - barefoot in brown and white cowboy pajamas with the feet in them - she was eagerly cut off by helpful, kind and cuddly loving Larry. "No, don't hang up! I've been waiting for that!" I yelled. An important call, a rare moment, as my mom and I weren't conferencing all that often; I saw no reason to keep her up to date on every little place I happened to check into. Why worry and upset her any more than she had to be, I figured. "Ah ha, too late. You snooze, ya lose. Got to be quick around here. I'm sure whoever it is will call back. Get back to bed!" Bastard.

In the future, if there is one at all, I'm guessing Mom and I will muster up the courage, even take part in some small victories: times we'll look forward to an event or happening, maybe a day trip together somewhere, the pinnacles in-between the tears, when the pain and suffering from being forced to press on takes a vacation. When genuine feelings might raise above the surface for a quick breath, some moments strung together when the weight of everything we've both been through doesn't have to be part of every conversation, or isn't present every time we look at one another These are golden and much welcome breaks.

But Mom and I must learn to share more than when the tea is just right. Maybe I can still drum up a good old college try, "Fight the good fight" - as Granny used to say. Who knows? Questions come up, a lifetime worth of them, and Uncertainty - an ugly term I'm getting to know all too well - is a belt I tie 'round myself first thing every morning to kick off the day, which doesn't come off until I *retire* at night, which is sure a funny word for calling it a day.

I only hope that Mom has not activated her own plan of devising a strict drug testing kit for me while staying under her roof. As weird as things can get around here, I wouldn't put it past her.

---

tf#11: The unmusical urchins grated on my fillings, their alarming off-key depiction brought tears and baffled me, the mandatory attendance bereft of any proper addict sopranos or soloists.

tf#12 *Tool Time for Tigger*, a show?

* * *

7. Treat Me

I can either leave or stay. Leaving means going back to addiction and facing either death or jail. Staying means leaving addiction and facing something that is unknown to me. I'm not sure which scares me more.

James Frey

A Million Little Pieces

M y   m o t h e r   h a s   always been on the look-out for a really super treatment center: one that fixes broken parts, preventing them from ever breaking again - which by the way doesn't exist or I'd have already attended, documented and be referencing it right about now, thus writing an entirely different story.

I stayed at this one place called Las Encinas Hospital in Pasadena, California, paid for entirely by the Musician's Union in Hollywood. One month: $34,180.38 in American dollarinos. Just how I hitched my carcass to that weeping carnival - applying for it in the horrid condition I was in, filling out forms and applications without getting blood, chocolate or tears on it, then getting myself there legally and legibly, I'll never know. No small feat, I can assure you. Actually, come to think of it, I do recall some pieces of those early fragmented days. I made it there on account of the unbelievably kind, sweet goddess I was staying with - who showed alarming candor, letting her exuberance show. "Goddamn Relieved" and "Bloody Cheerful" were words I overheard from a private phone conversation in regards to ejecting me out of her house, and after all, who could blame her? Let's just say she had no idea what she was in for. Shit, I can't deny the chaos and drama I transported with me wherever I set up shop or when I was lucky to be invited anywhere. Disgorging the likes of me from what was once a serenely beautiful and calm living space and finally getting her life back to normal, getting me the help I so desperately needed, was a gorgeous item to check off her to-do list.

Also, for one reason or another, they extended the term "musician" to allow all kinds of artists acceptance into the program. And this artist of sorts, having puffed up the resume enough with false allegiances to Radio City and a world tour with Yanni and the John Tesh Orchestra, was amazingly, somehow, accepted.

Check in time? Good god, why in hell do they need you to get there so damn early in the morning? I guess to test you, to see how badly you want it. Since my obnoxious spirit part doesn't wipe the sleep out of its eye until around noon, it's tough to fight back without proper junkie attitude armor on, making artists more malleable and easier to admit. My thoughts working overtime against me, the worst enemy I know, and right away, sensing this spin dry cycle of bandaging won't work on me... But my options at this late stage of the game are miniscule, along with my poor worn-out friends - now Card Carrying members in the ALL OUT OF IDEAS CLUB, so I've got to give it my best shot, like my life depended on it.

This do-gooder from AA named Gary (most are named "Gary, or "Dave" or "Mark" or "Chris") deposits me at the front door of the hospital. Gary specializes in specializing in good deeds, new plastic sandals and getting people's asses to the door, without making rest stops at a bar or side trips to dealers to say last goodbyes. I'm a real sight, with a full roll of toilet paper dragging behind me as the sniffles have turned into a full-on nasal nightmare, torn backpack in hand, toothbrush, a few shirts, some marked-up books I cherished and that was it. After answering way too many questions, the process started.

First, they detox you, the worst of it lasting about six or seven days (give or take seven or eight hours, but who's counting?). Once you graduate from that hell, they set you up in a cottage that a drunk and sluggish W.C Fields once inhabited - like this somehow lessens the pain and embarrassment of having landed your ass at a completely sub-glam-gloomy-bottom-out-zero - a shitty village to hang your head at.

If memory serves, my imitations of that great performer (and drinker) W.C Fields during group sessions were not found funny by the instructors or nurses I tried to engage in overly personalized conversations. (*Boundaries?* Why?) A few of them would have made great Doo Wop backup singers. They missed their calling, and I told them so, 'cause they sure weren't terribly gifted at putting me back together.

"Would you look at all the pretty foliage," A heavily-tattooed Winona Ryder look-alike mused upon arrival. "Yes, it sure is lovely," I responded.

"Oh, is it time for another shot already?" I quipped to the orderly. "Excuse me, my dear. I don't know where the time goes 'round this delightful hideaway."

"Yessssireeeeee my chickadee. Care to join me at my table for din din this evening?" I probed another newbie female arrival, bouncing back to the girl tout suite, due to the post-injection wave of burgeoning vitamins, Neurontin and something unpronounceable that now swam in my body.

"Tell ya what. I'll swing by your cabana, say around six-ish, we'll grab a pre-dinner martini, maybe some canoodling?" The flirtatious banter oozed out of my attempts to motivate myself.

There's organic fruits, a swimming pool and a tennis court for all to enjoy amidst new friends who've also bombed out in the life parade - gang members with record contracts, misfit fashion models who've cowered off their runways and pissed off their agents, folks who've just plain lost their footing and are lucky to have found a map leading them here. There's good old Doctor Drew (now a bonifide celebrity with multiple television shows focusing primarily on the lost, notorious and muddled), who pops in when he can from his hectic successful life. And there's a big old grand piano which was rumoured to be **NOT FOR PATIENTS**, that is if one could even crawl or shimmy shimmy coco-puff up the hill to the main building to check it out. I was asked to, "Not play it again, Tim," but I couldn't help but play…the piano OR with the on-duty attendant assigned to keep bored and wound-up patients from getting into their own brand of artistic mischief.

"I see, sooo… no one's supposed to play it?" I query, melodically, eyebrows fancifully raised, my hands gliding over the keys.

"Uh, that's right. It's only for show - no one ever plays it, no one's supposed to play it." This from the over-tired intern, whose name I learn is Martin (I dub him Big Marty), armed sadly with only stale instant coffee packets, paper slippers, clipboard, upside down name-tag and a pudgy demeanor.

"So, then, just what pray tell is this wondrous mighty monster here for then, if not to be played upon?" I'm king of the debating team and racking up points as I go. Just watch me, guys.

He glances at his Casio Mickey Mouse watch. I'm clearly detaining poor Marty, but I'm not letting him go that easy. He's going to have problems with me. A few of my coddled contemporaries - also as starved as I am for entertainment - have plopped themselves down on a nearby sagging sofa to enjoy the exchange between myself and Monster Marty.

I rally on. "So, you're saying that even if I'm not disturbing anyone, and even if the occasional passer-by says that I've brought some joy, some melliferous music into their pitiful, hopeless existence, that they wished I'd pounce on the keys more often. That even though this is clearly cathartic, dare I say, maybe an epiphany in progress, you're saying that I've got to cease…"

"Um, hey, look, I just work in…"

"No, no, my fine gentleman, you are doing a bully job. Yes, a bully fine job; you keep it up. It's good we've got you." Confidently, throwing a look to the gang and starting in. "And now, for my next number." The staff spent a good deal of time delegating punishments (*"Art supplies back to the Play Room by 5:00 sharp!"*) and having to be unnecessarily strict (I felt) much of the time.

The accumulation of little stunts like these plus my mimicking of inmates and staff got me on Badminton Restriction for an entire week. Plus, they dropped my sleepy-time-medicated-goodness down a notch for a few rough and tumble nights if I remember correctly. I admit I may have taken the rebellious nature routine too far when I cajoled a few of the more whacked out patients to break into the grounds-shed and liberate a number of red and silver spray paint cans that seemed to have no other plans. We managed to draw wonderful landscapes and illustrations of some of the meaner head nurses in compromising positions on the sides of a good many of the cottages. It was hilarious, to some. I also, as a result, learned a marketable and labor-intensive skill: how to remove unwanted paint from cottages.

Also, remember to speak of that sick and sad, filthy cocoon of a place, Charlie Street, in Santa Ana that I had to hang my head at. More desperate hours. And what about The Costa Mesa Ha-Cha-Cha. Did I make that dance number up or did I perform it at an AA Memorial Day picnic? That can't be right. Why can't I remember?

Who can say if the M o n s t e r amount of cash shelled out by the union for me to be placed in that rehab, was put to good use or not? I kick myself now for not having taken better notes and interviewing everyone properly, which might have made my stay more complicated, as people say that's not the kind of stuff you videotape and document. I don't concur: the human condition is fair game.

Did I learn any life lessons? Make changes in my behavior that would shield me from the mischievous spirit next time, or keep me from returning to mercilessly self-sabotaged and avoidable situations? And will those lonesome lessons I learned protect me in the real world on a day-to-day basis? Sadly no, but there was consistency, a routine I could gel with, innovative meal combinations - a hit and miss dynasty and a triumphant prop of hope in that old grand piano - the one I managed to tinkle on in my demonstratively all-too sobering medicated haze. Leaving there, I still saw myself as the equivalent of a mapless and unchartable landscape, one that needed something I, nor the staff, could grasp.

Still though, I consider this recovery villa my Drug Kinder Camp - as I like to call it - pretty much as good as it gets. On the whole though, the hospital staff were not a flexible lot, backwards in their execution of consistent tasking and delegating chores, especially.

———————

Christmas Eve was the nastiest. The most pitiful. Anyone in their right mind would be about a gazillion miles away from a place like that on such a traditional night. I'd never wish that on anyone. Until you've spent Christmas in an institution, consider yourself fortunate to have escaped emotionally unscathed and untainted.

Half a dozen or so of us had started to chum around a little, ignoring our assigned counsellor's orders about "not getting too close." Huddling affectionately around the glowing boob tube, we were like kids at some crazy camp, legs drooped over one another innocently while on lumpy couches, afghans and comforters draped over us, all buttressed by our Christmas Eve late night snack of no-name potato chips and French onion dip. We wished out loud that we wanted to be anywhere else, while at the same time we knew deep down that this was the safest place we could be.

Those places have rules. I thought they'd permit my tiny aversion from the guidelines, maybe. Actually, now, looking back, I don't know what I thought. Christmas Day was even worse, if that was possible. Like inhaling death, and needing to escape. Stupid families coming to visit their loved ones like some grotesque garden party. It was awful. Surprising feelings came up out of nowhere. I didn't have to give in to the screaming fury telling me what to do… but I did. No ho ho.

See, I had a kind of day pass, but on my mandatory application for the pass I may have fibbed a little about where I was getting picked up, my destination and what I was to be doing. When I returned later that afternoon from my first trip to the outside world in a month, it didn't take them long to sense I was less than truthful in my report of the day. As well, my mandatory urine sample they extracted was "dirty." How was I to know that the pee I mischievously hid earlier in the day (when I was clean) would get so hot left in my cabana closet. When I submitted that tainted little plastic cup of hot sauce, the nurse sensed immediately there was foul play involved. She said unless I lived on Mars, there's no reason why my sample should exceed 100 degrees.

A few weeks of being clean, staying out of trouble, off the sauce, on the wagon, choosing hugs not drugs, however you want to phrase the fuckin' thing, I chose drugs and felt excited to do it. Took the first cab outside the hospital gate and flew straight to Bonnie Brae and 3rd Street, downtown Los Angeles, not a super classy area, well, it is in the sort of vain, like, there's quality drugs there, and they're available on a pretty consistent basis, but it's not classy in the, "You're allowed to keep your wallet if you give the robbers your money" sort of way. They take it all down there. It's not a great place if you want to have a say about that. Or needing your car to be left in the same condition as you left it in after a measure of time passes, leaving the vehicle to the trusty streets and the soldiers that run them, nope, not a great place for that either.

I got down there and was thrilled and exhilarated to be out of the place, be able to do what I wanted, I was overcome with passion. For me! Literally skipping from one side of the street to the other hunting for man with the goods I would soon invest in. Long story short, I found him and procured the drugs, slipped into the nearest hotel bathroom (they're usually the nicest) and took care of myself. What a rush, whoosh, the warmth of the shot took my whole body over, the chest and mid-section, down to my feet, and took my head away and placed it gently on the commode to cool off. I sat down on the throne I was so taken. The big wide RELAX came. No need to go anywhere, I wasn't needed anyplace. For the first time in quite a while, I was free. I momentarily felt as though there wasn't one thing wrong with what I was doing and felt others to be fools who weren't my tolerance was totally back to almost what a normal person's would be.

After strolling in and out of no nothing dollar stores and a couple 5 and dime candy castles, I looked at my watch and tried to remember just what time I jotted down on the application sheet, my request for a day pass, out to have lunch with my sponsor and a clean uncle or some such lie. I flagged down a cab but this time my time travel machine was going to be going the opposite way. Still loaded, the worry and fear didn't hit me as much as it would have if my inception injection wasn't still pulsating through the old veins and core of my purified solar system.

That place wouldn't have any of my shenanigans. The Musician's union called and said, "Toss him out of there." They said sorry and wished me well though, which was nice. But they ejected me.

So, after a couple months clean as a whistle, I had to pack up everything, with all the patients watching me, whispering. There were rumours flying as to what really went down, and just when I was beginning to feel as though success and possibility were allies in my hope chest of sober living, I was at the front gates, homeless, with no one to pick me up.

It happened so quickly, too. How the hell did this happen? I know how. I got in my way again.

Dragging my suitcases through the neighbourhood, catching glimpses of pretty little bungalows along the boulevard, families inside being thankful, their sentiments and thankful prayers, with dancing ornaments and carols drifting over the trees, and me, hating how everything stunk of fucking pine. Open drapes revealed excited kids looking out onto me, the shut-out, an unwanted Christmas-less critter, forgetting how to love myself the more I shuffled along the sidewalk. Scared of my own growing anxiety and emptiness, back on the fight-or-flight dial, hardly meeting eyes with a soul, even if strangers did speak to me. At that precise moment, I was unable to tell if I was dying from feeling or dying from not. It would have been such a pretty scene, if the person in it wasn't me.

* * *

8. An Unselfish Act

Basically, all healing has to do with changing our perception and seeing things in a new light. Every problem, temptation, distraction and all busyness that is avoidance occurs because we are afraid to change.

Chuck Spezzano, Ph.D.

If it Hurts, It Isn't Love

The biggest absurdity today : sending my old friend Jen a dog-eared copy of this book that's been kicking around in the basement for a hundred years or so: Zarathustra's Discourses, by Friedrich Nietzsche. While gingerly wrapping the thing in some tattered Christmas paper with a gold ribbon, along with a note, I wax papered these important thoughts:

Dear Jenny,
This comes to you at what I'm sure is a pivotal point in your life.
This book assisted me in reaching epiphanies I hadn't thought possible;
these pages primed me for blissful moments.
This life, a beast at times, much to conquer; but you are more than
on your way!

Treasure and cherish the cathartic chakras going on in your existence.
You have been, and will always be, an angelic voice through times of
darkness. I know we will see each other again when the time is right.
Your light is missed daily and dearly, my beautiful special friend.

Happy Holidays.

T.M

Thing is, I've never read a word of the book, not a stitch. All I know about it, really, is that it is somehow tied to that 2001: Space Odyssey flick (which I never saw either).

Spectacular. So, that's funny on many levels, right? The thing of it was I really did mean it as a sincere gesture. Along with it came this equally sincere gesture to get as much crap out of the house as possible. She'll appreciate my overly sentimentalized malarkey-driven folly and likely get a golly-giggle from seeing through my false sincerity. I have hopes it didn't fuck her up to some breaking point.

Hey, what if one day I'm down from my tree house in the backwoods, at some out-of-the way general store, in town for the day, purchasing my monthly necessities: salt & vinegar chips, swords, notepaper, fire logs, sundries and such - and by bizarre happenstance, I overhear a conversation between the shopkeeper, a warty woman of few words, and Jen, the exact girl in question. She'll be chattily telling the warty shop keep about how she's moving to Cape Canaveral or some god awful dirt bomb of a sand-blown American city, and is prepping to enroll in some wildly nutty and grossly time-consuming astronaut program.

This scene swings into final frame with Jen revealing to the rotund but jolly shopkeeper that the reason she's doing all this is because an old friend (me) mailed her a book that sent her into an over-magnified, crippling, self-examining tailspin. I hope the address I have for her is still right. Maybe someone should check in on her. Nah, she's a big girl. She'll work it out. We're all left to work it

out ourselves...

* * *

9. City of Sulk / Border

S o t h i s i s w h a t ' s been put in front of me? What the fuck am I doing here? I mean Christ, no stability, inconsistent and ungrounded. To be back living at Mom's is going to be a bizarre rehashing of things I don't know if I can contend with, but the alternatives are looking kind of grim.

At this point in time, I don't want to risk anything and I'd prefer not to venture forth or try out for any teams or for that matter, submit myself for anything. This includes auditioning for rigid boards, stifling councils or creepy ego-maniacal casting VIP's who've got the last word. Same goes for submitting myself, enlisting, applying for or signing up for service of any kind – I don't want to come off as the fool, a syrupy sentimental man, and risk showing my true self (whatever that is) or chance not being loved back after putting forth my grandest shot at all the marbles. Disappointment is more death and I've got enough stored up in this dehydrated mind to get me through a number of what might be hibernating months, even years.

"Risks must be taken: the greatest risk in life is to risk nothing at all...They may avoid suffering and sorrow, but they simply cannot learn to feel, and change and grow and love and live...

It escapes me at present the exact cereal box I cut out that catchy proverb from. I deemed it worth saving though. It's now pasted somewhere in the back of my notebook. Maybe it works fine for some people, but I've played in the field long enough and admittedly, I need a stand-in, a replacement, can they clone people now? Can I scrape off my own DNA off and enter it into a computer? 3d copying? Who do I talk to about hiring a doppelgänger? (A *Timberganger /DoppleTimber?*) Sending someone else in might really make sense, for a while, for a time. See, I risk by getting involved, partake, then get disappointed and feel rejected so then the retreat, and get small then try like hell to re-group and build the life back up again. I stick a baby toe in, take a shot, but disengage and run away, again, all the while on the lookout for my gaggle, my bevy, a murder, gang, a chattering of I-don't-know-what's; a comforting mob of sensitive ring-tailed lemurs I recognized from an episode of National Geographic who've been around the block and lived a life? Jesus.

RISK *(tf#13)* is a game best served cold, but these frigid days, a beginner in this town once more, I don't feel so much like playing, whatever temperature it is or whoever decides to pop by unexpectedly for a challenge match.

This undramatic settlement longs to be a more intense, maybe even a famous character. Come to think of it, it really doesn't know what it wants, or where it wants to go. I see it as being an only child - on break from receiving multiple wedgies from upperclassmen - phoning its parents from some faraway prep school, whining, "You lied. You said it would be easy to develop a sense of self, to make friends, that my head wouldn't be used for a tether ball." See, the parents have already cut the scene, moved on to another town boasting of greener pastures, less starch, minimal gluten and certainly no egotistic, self-serving offspring that muck up the yard and order pricey meals - or make costly transatlantic crank calls they're not prepared to pay for. The taller, hairier parental cities have changed their telephone number, and their names. So we're all left to go it alone and scurry, mentally and socially frazzled, left to borrow beyond what we know we can't pay back, procure what we're able to from other richer, smarter provinces, bogus villages and mini-mall towns that may have something worthwhile to offer. So until the information reaches me, I do drugs, act the role of a ragamuffin, sticking to what I think is under control, ultimately messing everything up, having to start all over, regroup, move on and out, attaching along with me another sorrowful, unhealthy corrupt reference, recoiled within sinister sickness, embracing that which should be expunged: you stick with what you know.

Here's why I'm not capable of making friends. For example: if I hear somebody use the word "awesome" in a sentence multiple times, or within a few minutes, with the same person, I sense that word is their favorite (and only) go-to adjective. I'll get up from where I'm sitting not rudely or anything, hand this suspect human an article I've pieced together (I've always ample photocopies prepped for nearby dum dums, listing a good 30 or 40 options for other English adjectives they can try out). That is, if this humanoid still feels confident enough to speak out loud now that they're aware someone's paying attention, lurking in the wings, prepped to pounce like some Tigger patrol working undercover for Roget's or the good folks down at Webster.

This so-called cultural melting pot is dripping with melted redundant problems all over town, and all unearned joy will have to be paid back, much later, not by me hopefully. I can't find the drawbridge, again, and me, now like the unattended moat, left to ride a crappy makeshift paddle-boat with lame-ass splintered oars, no way to make it across. What was surprisingly fun, strangely novel, even invigorating upon my return, cooly shucking and jivin' amongst city dwellers, back on my old grounds of stomping and wondering, still sporting Californi-eh? license plates, and stories to tell… All that fluff has abruptly become frightening - an all too spooky reminder of the manner in which I'd become slothed and betrothed to, before I left for the West Coast.

I am the Charlie Browniest of them all. The bottle has spun my way and it's my turn to go into the closet to get all kissy-kissy with the halitosis-laced foreign exchange lass, the one with braces, terminal Blunder Buzzard against a landscape of prehistoric-looking, beautiful but stupid loons who can't fathom it's too damn late to catch the last gust of warm wind to fly south to hook up with family. That's me. Too late, not enough, wrong choices piled up blind, long-winded.

Got to get it together. Must think. Options? Anyone?

Clichés from the Twelve Step programs still are embedded in my brain, like Easy Does It and Do the Next Indicated Step, but it's all overwhelming, getting catapulted out the metaphoric window wrapped in a rug doused with wit, Sambuca and gasoline: those spirits spiral to the wayside since I can't complete even one task at a time. Is it death or deal? It's all an ordeal.

I'm not even that interested in investigating complete and total sobriety, although I'd like to, maybe. Even if I volunteered at the nearby hospital or old age home and stopped the drugs for a period of, oh, let's say three months, do the 'eating well' thing, and sign up for those Boot Camp workouts, would things get less fuzzy? When you've told yourself that substances (my treats) are the one thing keeping you aware and engaged, afloat - a desperately needed navigator, then, my brothers - the questions without answers come knocking in a loud masquerade and leave you feeling pretty unsolvable. I'm that broken umbrella going to pieces altogether, drenched with frustration, wearing sagging extra-large x2 complete with busted draw-string. Which is sure a funny image, but most likely just to you, as I'm the one who has to live here, and regrettably, the one who can't keep it together long enough to earn the pecuniary means needed to buy the proper-ply-towels or those pesky vowels sorely needed to dry off and come clean.

Special times, rare as they were, when my mom and dad would coordinate the "family together treasure trips" in that big old green Chevrolet - a convertible, but, not one that began its life as a convertible. It *transformed* into a convertible. Looking back, it's not outrageous to say it's THE original Transformer, complete with full-on beta blocking a.m radio alternate Autobot forms for most of its life. Over time, the roof deteriorated into such horrific condition, and summer was right around the corner, so it seemed to make good sense to just chuck all that heavy roofing crap. It was in this original always-fun mobile that they'd drive me to a host of specialists in. This was told to me years after the fact.

I can't recollect all the different physicians of varied heights, ethnicities, denominations and degrees sought out to treat my off-balance childhood. At the time, no one could figure out just what it was that possessed me to try to pull down my Grade 1 classmate's (*Becky somebody?*) leggings on the way home from school and ingest pieces of board games. (My later redemption/revenge? Graduating to inhaling foreign substances.) The Blame Game is an all too common one and that's not what we're going for here. I'd rather be made up entirely of blame and spoiled Yorkshire pudding (not pudding at all) than be considered common, or worse, mediocre. I'm god damn sure of that. Further, I've been unable to figure out just how I turned out to be the person I am today, kind of like the way there's no clear cut explanation how you became who you claim to be. I'd like to trust you, but let's not get off on the wrong wing here.

In my opinion, it seems we're all the sum of some startlingly complicated board game, occasionally getting eaten by bigger, meaner players. *(tf#14)* We've got more chutzpah than pawns, but less gusto than kings and queens. And we're unsure just when we're permitted to - when it's safe to - if we're even allowed to - move two spaces up and one over. Or are we just consistently diagonally on down, backwardly spiraling? None of which is any good in the Getting Ahead Department. Getting rooked is unsatisfactory to me and castling of any kind gets just plain confusing and pretty unfair. It all borders on crisscrossed tennis court lines laid down by insane and corrupt, stone-faced Dalai Lama-like line judges with spinning windmills on their yarmulkes, there only to find fault and again, throw me fundamentally off track, out of touch, tossing me permanently offside and forcing my sojourn in the penalty box to be extensive and confidence breaking. And to tell you the truth, I've never been so hot on Borders, *(tf#15)* the daunting multi-level book conglomerate, or the sinister and shady referee-people that work at them. More than likely, they have my 8 x 10 headshot up in the back room - to practice casting spells on? - or on the Ten Most Wanted list, just maybe? Though I can't imagine for the life of me, the Ten Most Wanted *What* exactly!? Crimes from my past, literary and otherwise? If I had to, I probably could remember, even figure it out. But as to how they got a picture, I'm coming up empty. Real empty.

---

tf#13: actually, RISK is a game devised by a couple horribly cretan-ish and disfigured brothers named 'Parker', and not of the "Posey" variety or the 'Nosy' kind either. This complicated, tiresome past-time sits dusty and unforgiving in all our closets waiting to be plucked from beneath the wintry boots and old saucers wrapped in boxes to be used for some spectacular Anglo-Saxon-gathering that in all probability will never occur. It also seems to be dusted off during thunderstorms, blackouts and after funerals and wakes once everyone begins to get uncomfortable and doesn't know what to say to one another. I was never much for the game, really, admittedly not for any other reason than I plain just didn't get it. I liked all the pretty colored countries on the board but it came with no dice, nothing to yell "Pop-o-matic-trouble" at, no words of any kind to unscramble or muck around with, just some weird dungeony dragon-like stench that never surfaced beyond the brainy ones who excelled in the now defunct Latin Club in high school. You can dominate your stupid countries, provinces and states, I'll be over here building this really neato swing-set out of Lego and monkey-barrel paste, wearing my fully equipped home-made utility belt with pick-up-sticks and edible Play-Doh, that I quickly (maybe not so quickly), have discovered, is not edible. I get all that confused with the game that came in the shape of an egg that I'm convinced you could eat part of, or if you rolled an image on it, the image would appear on the gummy, nerfy-type substance, and whammo, presto chango, good snackin'! It's one of the things I'm going to look into when I get the chance. All this, also tied in to those unfestive snap-Cracker-Jack tug 'n pull holiday game things I spoke of early. I'll get to the bottom of me. I mean, the bottom of it.

tf#14: It became almost impressive, the system I had designed for working things out and planning my future. Whilst engaged in a rare attempt at dominating the old Monopoly board, I'd gobble up the top hat when I landed on Boardwalk, meaning I'd confirmed my seat in some literary non-existent stock exchange, somewhere in New York or The Hamptons. For good measure I ate the sports car piece once my playmates landed on any worthwhile real estate, for good measure, I figured having the prized possessions inside me might make me feel more complete and guide my process. The horsie I couldn't swallow. I was called "competitive" by many teachers, and no parents would allow their children to come over and play for fear I would "eat their parts" thus leaving them scarred. (not to mention, being on the low end of the FUN totem pole when it came to being fun to play games with) I was even taken away by some council as the school system was convinced I wasn't being fed properly at home. T'was like a holiday, just 3 days in juvi.

tf#15: nor do I want to invest time or money in any kind of 'wax museum', inside a 'Border's Books' store; edible gooey statues of philosophers and extra-marital encrusted existentialists. I'm sure I'm not in league with having the 'proper managerial gumption' an undertaking of that magnitude would need. Just ask my Uncle Al as he's good at telling me about my lack of proper work ethic.

* * *

10. The Arrival & The Missed Flight

Everyone and I mean everyone gets theirs for the simple reason that we carry around with us what we've done and what's been done to us.

T h e   s h e e r   a m o u n t   of memories that made their way into my mind and decided to set up a sub-shop/smoke parlor, more than took me by surprise, not only for the obvious reason (nobody bothered to ask me) but concerns over rental fees abound. Licenses? Hello?! That group of prickly interlopers and Sir Puffalots get under my skin, like you wouldn't believe. I am NOT renewing my prescription to the memory department! I mean SUBscription.

Plenty of memories washed over me today as I made my way apprehensively through my cantankerous, lost, chilling city, a new and improved über-modern Toronto. Yuck. Almost every street I turn onto brings up an image. Right now, this area makes me miss darling M. and those ricochet days spent curating a dwindling, stormy and all too neglected relationship, so I keep driving. The hours in this day (and all these reminders) scream SEDATIVE, and I can't say I'm feeling too motivated in the capability department. No, not so hot on doing much of anything these recent days back at headquarters. Maybe some minestrone soup? Yes, the Italians' answer to Sodium Pentothal. It's warm and nourishing and I could come by it honestly: a tomato-vegetable redemption with a comforting homey feeling - of whose home, I've no idea and today, I could care less.

From the car stereo, "Take the A Train" plays. The tune is joyous, playful, upbeat, suggesting a hotbed of high nightlife from the 1920's. But nothing is like it used to be and they can't fool me. I, of course, find a way to see through this filigree façade, just about tagging a tardy molten senior *(tf#16)* after flying through a stoplight. I'm too busy pondering where I started despooling and where the the unravelling became commonplace; what really went wrong and also, what sort of store might still accept my personal post-dated, out-of-state cheque and how I might scrounge up the change for a postage stamp, or better yet, an alluring healthy meal.

   JusttRy doIng tHe sMa/l thInGs.

Don't get your head up in the clouds.

I'd sure welcome a buddy to bounce some ideas off of, to hear each other's opinions and options, and not one of my practically deaf and dumb parasitical animal friends that *mentions* things, or those hoity-toity Chanel mannequins in the attic that think they know so much. A real loyal pal, maybe a trusted crony? An amigo or chum? I'd even settle for a "dude" or a "bud", but only if they provided the room with some decent, but not over-popularized, culture references and could offer a sympathetic ear. Somebody who doesn't have to be promised anything or cajoled into meeting up…someone who *wants* to spend time with me. That would be great. But, with no real autumn clothes to speak of, drained and snively, the people I knew having moved on, unemployed characters now somehow with their artiste cards rescinded, many now ensconced in pyramid companies or sub-human, full-time dedicated to timetables involving *her* and baby makes three and all that; all unavailable to discuss over slushy juicy drinks or espresso our lots in this life, driving around this shadowy town with that shot-out window; which makes me more self-conscious than ever, feeling I need a story to explain away the absurdity of the travelling show. This is the farthest thing from sumptuous and most certainly for the birds. Ill-prepared, ill-advised, far from at ease. Just ill? Just get the soup. The doctors say these are only feelings, and the doctors say they'll pass. But doctors, I've found, will say anything just in passing.

I guess I should mention a little bit about how I exactly came to be here.

But that will come.

———————————

I am here, back in The Great City of Sulk. This year, what's under consideration and still in the air, I might add, is an application I put forth requesting permission to fly up to the family cottage after driving the 3000 miles across country. You think that would act as prerequisite enough? The last time the family saw me they were under the assumption I was loused with substances, so that pretty much covers that. The high holidays nodding off into bloody Hollandaise and fluffy stuffing doth not make for much of a Norman Rockwell pictorial or help with anybody's appetite, on anyone's side of the table. Neither does using the fragile only-for-company cranberry tray as a soaking dish after an imaginary manicure. No matter, one must always moisturize. I've got my people looking into alternatives, but what lie will work best to cover up this scary sham? What to tell the youngsters?

"Sometimes. One. Needs. Rest. Their. Hands. In...."

"Yes?" the family response sounding like they were eager for the finisher. (I drool here, one eye heavier than the other)

"...Something. Else. Besides. One's. Hands." I vomit here, mostly onto my plate. Immediate gratification with relation to cranberry doesn't sit well with some. Even I thought something was off base and burning at the kiln, too easily reminded of glowing inoculations with turkey-baster-sized-syringes. Admittedly, feelings of jealousy weighed heavy on me towards the fully dressed, brown and buttered bird staring back at me from the center of the table, he unable to grasp just how lucky he was to be center stage, a recipient of repeated glimmering booster shots. I won out in the end, being asked to leave the table, my foe left defeated and spent in the fight ring, flesh ripped apart, innards devoured by ravenously disrespectful relatives, his carcass now resembling a younger, but still skeletal Cloris Leachman. Oh well, seems I need not concern myself with any of that hullabaloo this year.

———————————

Anyway. I've always been suspicious of a holiday that doesn't fall on precisely the same day each year. Why on earth this floating party, this Moveable Feast, made convenient so that extended weekend warriors can catch up on their shluffy-land nappy-nap sack time? Overworked longshore men, marble-headed good old Brando's, brooding off their waterfronts in need of deserved down-time away from the sloth of dock life.

One Thanksgiving not so long ago, I found myself at good old Swiss Chalet. By myself. It was unwholesome and the worst of dreary.

M. and I were supposed to scoot out of town, take some public transit-type-deal earlier that day, so we could make it out to her family's home for the evening. We'd been pre-selected to be one at The Big Spread. Unfortunately, we found ourselves to be very much In the Bag, or had Too Many Bags, or was it Not Enough Baggage to keep us afloat? Needless to say, needles were involved and we slept right through the only bus departing on that most glorious of non-cinematic black and white days.

"I thought I made sure our alarm was plugged in. Don't yell at me," M. pleaded.

"It's a digital clock and it runs on batteries, sugar." Ha. Take that.

"Shut the hell up. You blame me for everything." She had a flair for the dramatic.

"Well, stop doing everything wrong then." Maybe I did too. I was on the mean side by that stage of our game.

"And where in God's name were you last night? You can't tell me all you're doing is answering the phones at that escort agency? Your parents are going to be so fuckin' pissed. Christ, this is bad. We'd better call them."

"Um, I guess this isn't the best time to talk about fiscal stuff?" Often, spacey hieroglyphs were a memorable name I designated for her unclear white-out sentences. She gave me a look that said - this month, our battleship was sunk. "What do you mean you used the phone bill money for more of that shit?"

The only thing certain and in the bag was going to be our lack of nutrition, and our maudlin, pathetic, self-seeking disinterest... but in a really pleasant festive way. (I'm trying not to let things slide too quickly here). Thinking of those two pitiful, empty spaces at the dining room table was no easy sentence, let me tell you. We were missed. *(tf#16)* The only thing I didn't miss were those holiday crackers of absurdity you tug at with your assigned grub-inhaling neighbor, some crappy plastic prizes inside as the anti-climactic reward. For whose pleasure these hokey holiday gestures are repeated for, I've no idea, as it isn't mine. No sir, not at all. Tearing open the less than festive parchment paper leaves me perpendicular with open-ended queries. Maybe I'm putting too much of myself into it? But those screwy puzzles puzzle the fuck out of me, what with all the multiple linguistics and that mini-magnifying glass. One time I didn't even get the English version (I got stuck with the one that should have been *en route* to Bastille or Czechoslovakia) and ended up trying to construct this crazy microscopic Ikea-like croquet set out of what I'm guessing were barley-like-wiener-sticks but tasted like a Bundt cake made from fennels and kitty litter. It became a complex chore taking hours, leaving me lonely and misaligned, not to mention missing dessert (the only reason to show at all, most times) and once again landing in the neighbor's garage, pretending to know what I'm doing with their tools. ("Uh, can we... help you?") I know this much: in some Third World Christmas crappy sweatshop, dozens of overworked, underpaid sweat-shirted ladies named Consuela are laughing their asses off.

Anyway, I could just feel W i n t e r s e t t l i n g i n.

Everything getting dark, windy and wobbly and with darling M. still out for the count, I was getting pretty famished. At the back of my mind something told me to seek out a home cooked meal, or the closest thing to it. So, not too far a cry from home was chicken at Swiss Chalet; the place of peculiar tasting sauce, booths made of plastic, those spattered dirty utensils and horrendous music to kill yourself by, nothing really Swiss or Chalet about it. No alps, no Von Trapps, a setting as mercilessly lonely as making the most of a strip club salad bar in the day time, or even worse, having an old lady tell you she's on her way home to defrost a meat pie for her supper, and to wait by the phone for a call from her only son, that will never come. I ended up crying for home, anyone's home.

"Hell of an operation you got here missy, and no reservation needed? Wow, my my, lady luck sure is shining on me this evening. You must have holiday specials; I've a coupon here somewhere." Digging into my pockets hurriedly, realizing an absence of commerce, *sporting lint* I would say, my charm and flirtatious box step coupled with musical finger snapping, and an offer to pay with racked-up Zellers points, unbearably entertaining. To me. She did take pity on me though, directing me to a table, conveniently located between the kitchen and the take out window.

To make the already awful evening worse, the waitress I got stuck with wasn't in the mood for my kind of pathetically-soul-bruising duplicitous interaction, and with English being her second (or third?) language, she wasn't connecting so hot with any of the subtle, sarcastic, self-deprecating humor I was sending her way. I admittedly was rambling a lot.

"What do you mean fella, you 'feel like chicken tonight'?" She offers.

The imaginative genius of my clucking and off-color-gobbling falling on deaf ears and eyes from other booths, me, just trying to stay out of my head, distracting myself from more cheerless thoughts, while remaining focused on the task at hand: finding a cushiony abode and a Welcome Sign that hadn't burnt out.

"Excuse me," I said interrupting my streaming self, clicking my tongue, "They sure seem to be workin' ya to the bone. Why don't cha take a break? You absolutely deserve some down time. Have a seat here beside me, why don't ya?" Tapping the chair beside me three times, preparing my new queen's throne. She may not have been as perceptive as I was, but still I welcomed the opportunity to converse with something more or less human and without claws or feathers.

"Hey, you gotta let me take that tray for you. Hey, did you see that movie where the..." She'd already split the scene, having moved on to attend to more important orders and pick-ups. I sure wanted to 'pick-up' and forget all this, but who could I call? Even the dealers were at their fucking families.

If I thought about it for too long I was going to get really depressed, maybe start in on some good old sentimental sobbing, but I caught myself as that would've been grounds for suicide. Come to think of it, it was some Rhinoceri-like Green Goblin government years ago that voted on a bill and got it in as a law, "...if one cries whilst in a Swiss Chalet-solitary-sit-down-dinner-situation, during high (or low) holidays, then..." *(tf#17)*

Let's just say authorities ultimately would have been called to the scene.

I completed the edible sections of my meal, and when I got up to go to the washroom, I snagged a couple bucks from an adjoining table for the tip. For me.

––––––––––––––––

tf#16: parents and extenda-family folk despise it when you miss once a year eating occasions; functions you've sworn up and down you'd be in strict attendance at, where family entities have been called in from across the globe to get a good look at your dumb mug. An infirmary we became unto ourselves, no one should have been near us anyway, let alone 'pulling for prizes' or 'bowling for cranberry.' Questions will be sure to be bellowed into the answering machine, like, "Just who the hell do you think you are disappointing and worrying your family?!"

tf#17: one must tell themselves false and fanciful consents in order to get by on occasion, "Things aren't THAT bad", all that. As to truly examine and explore, can make one very, very down-trodden. Swiss Chalet & Harvey's (*"Makes a hamburger, a beautiful thing!"*) are more than adjacent, now, they are one entity unto themselves, (!) sporting all sorts of services under one roof...from this day of reckoning forward, nothing will ever be the same.

* * *

11. Father Fodder / Seize the Sins

Will power and self-knowledge will never help in the strange mental blank spots when we are tempted to revert to turmoil. In these throes the victim is in a hopeless condition. The last flicker of conviction that we can do the job ourselves must be snuffed out.

We are completely helpless apart from divine help. The spiritual answer is the only true help.

Thought for the Day

Alan L. Roeck

Look to this Day

It's time to pay a visit to my old pal Father Kevin at his Pentecostal parish, just to see what a man of such worldly tidings might be up to during off hours. When I used to live in the market, sometimes I'd wander in and start up discussions with him. Often before he arrived. "I haven't been doing so hot. What's it all about, anyway? Say, have you ever met a real live Gideon?" I would just imagine what he'd say and respond accordingly. He always said his door is open, regardless of what state I'm in.

He's a hell of a fellow.

I peer my head in through the slightly ajar door to his office in back of 'the stage', or the rectory-rumpus-room, I think I've heard it called. He doesn't hear me as he's involved, quite feverishly it appears, in a kind of verbal battle with some Archdiocesan cat clearly above his head. Heavy and heated words are exchanged and float like burned incense wafting worship throughout. Evidently, the good father is being prepped to bring the word of God to a community somewhere in Algiers...or was it Marrakech? No definitely Tangiers. He's about to go on a sort of international religious jaunt, an exchange if you will, but it's unclear (from what I've sacrilegiously overheard) just what it is the other team will be sending over our way in return for my parsonish pal. I'm waiting for an opportune time to interrupt. They speak of the message he will spread, his goals and various details that need to be worked out before such an undertaking can come to fruition. Let's see if he could be convinced that my kind of 'participatory journalistic clumsiness with a heart', coupled with my rarely used, uncanny knack of being able to tell Turks from Sheiks might come in handy abroad; how his trip really wouldn't be complete without an assistant to tag along and see that things get done. Come to think of it, I'm getting myself mixed up with 'Lawrence of Arabia' - Peter O'toole to be exact - as they're all just non-union extras in beards and sheets to me.

I sneeze five times loudly, the smoke from the incense catching me by surprise. I'm accosted, apprehended, Catholically-captured, by the taller of the two gentlemen, a large Phil Donahue-like gentleman in Catholic cloak and oddly shaped salt and peppered facial hair. I'm given a good scolding, and am permanently scalded from the upstaged fire pit he dangled me over, with my screaming promise not to ever again partake in what, I learned the hard way, was one of the dozen or so deadly sins - 'Eavesdropping'. *(tf#18)*

My new friend from God's kingdom sits me down and I confess to him briefly of my unholy, perilous adventures, of how I used to come by the church on occasion to seek out the good Father, and of how when he wasn't there how I'd sit quietly wondering why God and I hadn't gotten along better over the years. We somehow get around to the fact that I'm no good and since this gentle organizer of worldy faiths seems to also sense I'm nothing special (after I tell him that I was never baptized), immediate plans are made for the episode. He also inquires after I relay more tales "Hey, you know that Ione Skye, what's she really like?" which was just weird. Is this what I've been lacking, I wondered, a thorough spiritual cleansing?

The watery slip and slide downhill magnifies. I had to scramble to return to the church for my allotted booking, and in an attempt to beat the clock, while bargaining with my Canadian Tire money at Walmart, I'd figured I'd work it all out later. "I'm late, this is important, I need something, don't you understand?" My urgent lines sounding all too familiar, applied in worse and desperate situations, glued to my psyche.

I would never purposely wear a Speedo, of any size or denomination (abomination?), nor would I even keep something of such pukey, fusia-like dementia in my house to polish furniture, but I had to make an impulse buy and a boy must do what a boy must do. Through overseeing this near disastrous procession, I learn that Father Kevin not only knows how to hold back laughter, but being a man of the cloth or the cloister or whatever, I also discover he's a man of great prep work as it appears he's run into this before. He disappears to his office, and reappears holding up respectable trunks; clean white cotton-boxer shorts with a embroidered gold cross on the bottom flap. I'm now outfitted properly as if I was going to swim the 500 meter for God's team.

I couldn't help but be reminded of this flick where this kindergarten teacher kept a private stock of trunks for the downtrodden in her bottom desk drawer for occasions when her wee students soiled their undergarments in one way or another, so I congratulate myself as it seems I'm eerily identical to the person I once was in kindergarten though possessing a minimally stronger hold on bladder control. Even with that I'm teetering atop a wet splintered see-saw, likely only a few good un-soiled years left to really get a handle on me. On 'it', I mean.

I wade around in the sectarian turtle pool of angelic Anglican persuasion - the one part of this demented but whimsical process I'm permitted to have some say in, the 'dunking tank'. I've opted for the lesser of a number of evils they've got collecting dust in the storage room: Purple tigers intermingled with friendly, bubbly green, pre-historic monsters. It's tough to feel much like an adult for me in the first place, my murky and hellish turtle pond with left-over metal goldfish from some Sunday school funfair cutting into me, fails to move me any closer to feeling like the man I want to be. An audience of elderly Italian women there to drop off canned goods and breaded items sat in the front row as I fought to stay afloat and began shivering as the reading from the scriptures announced I was ready for the real world now. Words were spoken. I became blessed. This cleansing, my baptizing, something that should have been done by my 'pre-teen' stage, whatever that was. I guess my parents were too busy or figured I wasn't necessary. I mean 'it' wasn't necessary. It was just good I'd got it done, I thought, and ticked it off my list, as if I were a grocery item to be picked up.

Before ejecting myself out of the All Mighty's house (and while the front row helped me dry off), I catch a glimpse of this theatrical troop that call themselves, 'Theatre Gargantula', or 'Tarantula' or something, loading up what looked like their sets and lights and instruments out the back of the church into a van, all the stuff that theatre folk cart around. Apparently, they use the great hall to rehearse in, either that or they've broken in and pilfered some school pageant's costumes and will lose their souls as a result. One of the young lesbianic-granolic-thespians tells me they're about to embark on some sort of Magical Misery Tour to Quebec. What could be worse than trekking through distant territories in the deadest doldrums of winter, visiting people who don't like your language to begin with, having to huddle in some U-haul van with busted heat, jostling from town to township, minimum-wage theatre in church basements, plying the craft on make-shift stages, speaking in unnaturally loud tones so that autistic shut-ins shuttled in for the day can detect some sort of novice performance being staged around them. All this, too familiar for me, to be shelved right up there with 'kissing girls with extra-large foreheads, thin lips, meaty necks and head braces'; not a very fun club to be a member of.

Thinking of this doomed and pretentious bussing experiment with their frosty lonely motel rooms, and typical larger than life actor ego sickness made me tired, cold, and left me fearful of the world outside the church doors. I was scared to death one of the acting bugs would jump off of her, bite and infect me with an unselfish need to help her continue loading the truck. I wanted to run into Father Kevin's office and wrap myself up in his robe for protection and worldly solace - though this, wouldn't protect me from further afflictions out there in the real world and ultimately would be short-lived and really, really gay.

Please, God. Don't enlist me. I don't want to risk another wretched embarrassment. I got roped into that kind of salty theatrical pilgrimage with this totally maniacal director a couple winters ago, hob-gobbling around The Eastern Provinces, forced to travel by helicopter, ("No way to get there from here,") even a canoe. I ended up purposely tipping the cast out of boredom. ("She'll never thaw out by showtime." "Want to bet? Geez, you guys are no fun at all.") 8 girls and me - all even further from being as sexy as it sounds - for the life of me I swear I can't remember what my role might have been. Was I 'Rusty the Crustacean'? 'Kierka the Crusty Croatian', some Slovak-hyena pledging allegiance to some sea, though never knowing what the motivation might have been, my performance ultimately empty, all crashing down around me, archaic sappy elders equipped with pockets of powdered beverages, soups and such prepped for intermission feeding time, if they lived to get that far along in the program, my audience of staring, sleepy-eyed seniors with bleeding gums, catapulted sets of false front teeth ripe for crunching beneath my boots. They'd have preferred to be off going to the bathroom somewhere (the survey reported) or calling grandchildren's telephone numbers from three addresses ago, me inevitably getting blamed for not co-operating, complaining, causing a commotion or a 'Romper-room-ruckus' as the local papers called the ordeal. But you would have too, if you were entombed with all that constant cheap schlock and pointless prop-house antics, the rumors of my unexpected death, only mildly exaggerated. All this along with the lugging of hurtful gargantuan pointy scenery, also demented and lame, mutating into some premature melodramatic autopsy, goddamn almost freezing to death, "The Albatross trucking terminal" - not in the scheduled syllabus - for "suitable" union overnight accommodation coupled with being kept from lunches that were supposed to be included in this beautiful production, nourishment provided often being nothing more than moistened saltine crackers, "It'll toughen ya up, the world of theatre is one hard grind, it 'aint all glamour, Jimmy Dean, let me tell ya." You don't say? Being starved by this so called 'director' (if that's in fact what he was, clown suit, my ass) I more often than not was faint of spirit and lost my balance, and on a couple more nerve-racking performances stumbled into the orchestra pit, just plain overwhelmed at the multiple characters he had me playing at one time to cut down on costs, this found out months later in court. Our heretic Hitler doted on the four hometown miniature Liz Taylors who evidently could do no wrong, but constantly scolded the four actresses from parts unknown for breathing out of turn or asking questions regarding their roles. My attempts at fitting in were never encouraged. The improvised Newfie accent (wildly entertaining to some 9 year olds waiting for my autograph at the stage door) didn't help matters any, as I was told to 'stop making fun of the locals'. I submitted a script I'd been working on inbetween rehearsals, "Timmy and the deep blue sea" which embraced the ambiance of their watery city, a conceptual work in progress, involving a massive underwater tank that I provided blue prints as to precisely how it should be constructed, but it wasn't granted. I should really look into getting professional representation this time around.

I exited the temple licking my spiritual wounds, but feeling somehow altered and told myself it would be a good reminder to learn from my mistakes, to pick up a new bible, and better management.

---

* * *

12. Just Who's Home Here?

I had many less than spectacular, less than healthy living situations before returning back to Toronto from the West Coast. Some, I recall with fondness, others not so much.

Crash.

The character building cruelties that make sense at 4:45 a.m when arriving home, realizing you've misplaced your keys, often carry a far, far different set of regrets and concerns the next day when one is being reprimanded in some office and view things with less fogged-up glasses. A brick to open the glass doorway to my building had made all the sense in the world. How else was I to make it up to my fifth floor loft to get any sleep? I'd thought I'd explain it all tomorrow. My superintendent, Gustav, would understand.

Yes, that makes the lobby look even better; why now there's a pretty light streaming in from the street lamp that should have been there in the first place. I should attend design college on one of the nearby planets...I clearly have quite a knack for...(moving quickly into my acceptance speech at 'The Teamsters' yearly Ball) "I first began my bricklaying career in Brooklyn, and being a career-oriented, broad minded fellow..."

The Throwing up sessions commence.

And it's all one big lady finger sandwich from the Wasserman family wake after party. Is that what they're called? My earlier gastronomical indulgence now covers the brown and mustardy couches placed so conveniently for visitors in the newly dubbed 'Great Lobby of Autistic Vomiteria'. Watercress, dill, and Jack Daniels straight up, such a lousy combination, after the fact. During, too.

Earlier that evening I'd found myself at a strange but festive function at some hotel - a lot of those places look the same - where booze was a willing companion that made near catatonic, mournful ladies in black seem cosmically engaging. So what if I was supposed to be down the hall at Marqus' wedding reception, playing his best man in that other ballroom. He's lucky, all those guests, acquaintances, bridesmaids and such: all that attention. He didn't need me probably. And more than likely faired fine

I remembered what was involved as far as operating an elevator to make it up to my floor, and 5 did sound right. But I was still on the wrong side of my door. For reasons unclear to me, mine was one of the yet-to-be-replaced, easy-to-break-down, artsy-fartsy-wooden-ones, painted over the years multiple times by a string of ungifted amateurish Picassos. I guess Gustav was a true patron of the arts, keeping it around until it went up in price, or caught fire. (The door, not the artist - maybe the artist, performance art being what it is and all.) Anyway, not the point.

I made quick work of kicking that puppy in with the steel toed Doc Martin boots I had on, making a sort of doggie-door entrance to creep through. I was smart, my brain a creative somersault of reasoning. I crawl into my apartment. Thank God I'm home. What a catastrophe. Such quick thinking though, such resourcefulness.

How did I get here again?

And why did I hurt myself with such an awful and untasty outing of Jaegermeister and mushrooms?

What began as an above board, unproblematic, intermingling wake, (wedding?) got funny real fast.

Why all those toasts to brooding unsympathetic and unappreciative strangers?

"I'd like to thank the bride...hold on I'm not done...Who'd a thunk it? Sully - the lucky son of a bitch - finally snagged the old gazelle...um, what's the bride's name?"

"Please, please get down." This from the weeping widows who couldn't understand just why they had to endure an alcoholically-charged speech wishing "the newlyweds - soon to be wild rabbits" - a bon voyage and fond farewell, by yours truly.

Much remorse regarding past moments. They told me at those AA meetings that there are two days we shouldn't worry about: Yesterday and Tomorrow, (Or was it Thursdays and Mondays?) I need to live in the now. I heave in my vegetable crisper and manage to make it back to the hallway where I craft a note made with splintered balsa wood from my kicked in door, for the milkman, instructing him to not wake me - me zee artiste - him with the annoying whistling, the loud lactating delivery irritant who comes-a-calling much too early for my liking.

I turn off the lights (really I just made good and sure they were off as I didn't turn any on to begin with) and climb up to the loft. In the dark once more.

"Please stop spinning. I'll do absolutely anything."

Just which godly specter I was praying to made little difference. Whoever decided to show up for the late-night shift on this quaint evening sure got made an awful lot of promises, the poor unsuspecting apparition.

"God, it's me Margaret...I mean, you know who it is. Yes, again. I know I was asking you for a lot of stuff yesterday, but look, I'll be nicer to people from now on. I swear I won't take other people's newspapers or dip into laundry detergent that isn't entirely mine or try on other people's clothes when the laundry room is unattended or..."

During the promise session, I'm fairly sure I threw up on the cat. Even more curious, I didn't own a cat when the evening began. No matter, he looked concerned, primarily at his new matted coat of vomit, made from come upon social slothful gorgings. I thankfully passed out.

Bang bang bang bang bang

Could the milkman not decipher my note?

I can do this. Just wake up a little. Come on. What time is it? It didn't feel like morning.

It was Gustav who came a knocking at my non-existent door. Maybe he had just popped by for a visit, to check on me, to congratulate moi for brave, all-too-verifiable acts recorded earlier on the video camera. This, I learned helpfully after the fact.

I had to think quick. Multi-rationale. Multi-narrative. Multi-mix-up. How did I get here again? What to do? How to get out of this one? I am a Haikuist, I am a Haikuist and I can do this. Okay, head seems dislodged, but just stay calm.

"Get off the stairs, selfish vomitty greymalkin."

A planet of regret seeping in, my nausea torturing all I am, amazed how I'm able to utter any English useful to human interaction.

"Why, good mornin' kind sir, you're sure up early..."

"It's 3:30 ass-wipe. What the fuck happened to this door? And downstairs, there's glass

everywhere. And you're two months behind, you fuck."

"Ah yes, I saw that god-awful mess when I came in from my Hebrew lesson, I mean my lawn bowling class...and...um...a load of banshees really did a number on my front portal there. I'm lucky I wasn't around. Why, I could have been killed, my good man. It's certainly good we've got you."

We were on the same side now.

"There's security cameras down in the lobby - we got zee whole fucking thing on tape!

Who you think you are, you fucking..."

Clearly, he was speaking with concern for my well-being yet simultaneously crushing a fistful of pink pâté. Was he nursing it still from the Wasserman wake I wondered? I can't remember seeing him there. It was crowded.

"Well then, my good man, it won't be long before you catch those misfits. And they should pay, those hooligans and liars of our society. I'll tell you what we should..."

It was at this point I caught a whiff of the quickly spoiling fishy pâté concern in Gustav's clenched fist, the poor imbecilic sod, unfortunately, the recipient of more of my unwelcome regurgitative projectile baggage. This is one awful flight. I've completely forgotten what's happening, and it's time to assist, once more, in my defense.

"Look here, if you need a witness, I can testify I heard 'em rummagin' 'round down there. I was up here...um, entertaining." I wink, and give him the 'WKRP Herb Tarlek- cowboyish-index-finger-and-opposable-thumb-as-handgun-pow-pow-signal,' cuz he'd know what I mean, us both men of the world and all.

He growls at me through facial bandages, taped together glasses and sailor's cap, breathing frightfully hard, abacus in hand, a face full of pink gelatin-like paste. I'd thought it certain that the hints and clues I provided - flickering eyebrow action and sitcom allusion - concerning my involvement in the previous night's womanizing, champion bouts of cocktailing and testing substantial substance combinations, would be commended!

"You crazy shit. I know you AND your games. You don't fool us. Just you wait!"

My superintendent prosthesis stormed off, this foreign actor who hadn't read my rules, who should have been fired from my set chapters and scenes ago. I should have sensed he wasn't rehearsed properly to suit this director's needs.

Note: look into directing my own life.

And what was that 'Us' business? Just who he meant mattered little, seeing as anyone else on his team would more than likely have the same tragic command of the language and would not have been any more sympathetic to my plight.

I was no dummy. I built a barricade out of the kindling not used in my carefully crafted milkman message and headed back in the general direction of where I left the bed. These things have a way of working themselves out and getting dealt with, eventually - later, and often by someone else. Thank God.

Now where did I park that bed?

* * *

13. Waking Up Jesus

It is difficult for a non-addict to understand the almost religious quality of addiction; to someone enmeshed in the drug and the drug sub-community, heroin is an absolute, something that transcends utilitarian calculation. Every conceivable aspect of life becomes translated into the heroin equation. It is beyond rational cost accounting. A choice between heroin and anything else is no choice at all.

Erich Goode

Drugs in American Society

I awake to discover two creepy strangers flicking shards of water over me. "...And please Lord, don't let this man go through terrible withdrawals, yes, I be certain he has sinned, but he is here to repent, to do your work..."

Why has a sullen mourner got his hands wrapped around my ankles? Why is another crying in a *Take Me Now, Oh Holy God* position? Are these my last rites? If so, who in the hell believed they had the right, the power, to declare me dead? I'm the only one who can do that, *man.*

If I am dead, how come I can hear these fucking nitwits?

What about my first rights? If this is the case, then I'm dreadfully disordered, real higgledy-piggledy and starting to get right pissed off the more I reawaken from my inertia and slide-back into this dung pile of all-too-real Regis Philbin reality.

These gentlemen in dire need of dental surgery appear to be praying at the foot of my bed, and giving me a generous baptism. (Why does this keep coming up?) This isn't right. I'm in a half-dreaming state, morphine-minded with drool on my cheek, still dope sick on some top bunk bed, amidst inhaling which I now comprehend is the rank fumes of burnt coffee amidst too many men in too close proximity. It reminds me of what I think Sun City must be, just less African.

Out the corner of my eye, I see clothes falling out of milk-crate drawers, and a poster of a radiating Jesus that seems to be focusing on me, which makes me feel caught with no place to hide, but I'm too downwardly immobile to start in on switching beds.

Just as a few more of the clan peek their heads in, curious to see the new addition to the group. I am just able to get out, "Where am I? What is this place?"

"Why, you're at The Ranch."

"Ranch?"

"God's ranch," they say, grinning in unison.

Oh no, this doesn't sound good at all, geographically speaking. I'm dodging my own racing thoughts (and a plaguing mixed-metaphor mania that dictates when I'm off to the races). Hold on, I was in San Clemente yesterday - I mean last night, or was that the day before? I recall that Bea, the 100-year-old Swedish lady I'd been renting a room from, said something about her pastor friend having some kind of rest stop on the freeway of demoralization and quarantine of retreat, maybe she said it was a ranch? Bea could sense I had certain… dilemmas. Could this be what she had in mind for me? I seem to recall a van, a lot of my belongings being packed late into the night by tattooed, warrior-like strangers following orders being barked by a J.C. Fellow. From what I could surmise, this trailblazing cultish leader was respected by the gang moving around everything that I seemed to own.

Wait a minute.

"Am I in San Clemente or Laguna Beach?"

"No siree, you sure ain't. That's a couple hours down through the canyon, by the devil's ocean." The other one spoke up: "You're in God's country now, my son."

Another one interjects: "It's good we've got you, you didn't look so hot last night when they brought you in." His twang already entirely irritating.

Disoriented, sweating profusely, I tumble out of the bunk, and manage to entirely demolish a man's candlelit shrine to some octa-limbed Hindu Deity. To add to my downsizing, a weird interlude of recorder and ukulele, a sickeningly sad Jesus jam, accompanies my toppling. Nearby, someone else's frankincense decanter is on fire.

"Oh god, shit, I'm sorry. Christ, let me help you with that." I felt a little bad.

"Don't bother, brother. It's all beautiful in God's world."

Brother? Tell me he didn't say that. I hate that - almost as revolting an event as when I'm in earshot of the dummies using "awesome" as a descriptor for entirely everything in their lives.

This crash pad, some sort of makeshift home on splintered wagon wheels. (No, not those tasty Joe Louis chocolate ones). And the gerbil-chip scent adds certainty to my conjecture that this sure as hell ain't no 'Ranch.'

I seem to recall, of all things, Bea mentioning that this is where Betty Ford kept her cattle and various other recovering four-legged barn-dwelling creatures. Seems everybody gets treated sometime. When she said her friend had a ranch, I imagined horse-riding lessons, thick Porterhouse steaks, rock saunas, steam baths, Jon Voight being flown in to teach acting classes while scantily-clad Coppertone sex-starved castaways, showed themselves eager to massage me out of my grief. But, *this* was really bare bones. A biblical Shriner-fez-camp for end-of-the-liners dedicated to the lord was wildly bereft of medication or entertainment, no comforters knitted by a nearby gaggle of Amish or Mennonites; something I had not prepared for. There was no way this was going to work. No way. Also, there seemed to be no way out as I had been taken, again Catholically-captured, kidnapped in my sleep and driven to an ungodly ranch of perverse loneliness. I had made no reservation at this out-of-town, out-of-gas rustic romp house. I was Gilligan amidst an island of ill-rehearsed misfits.

About twenty Jesus worshippers were what I counted: gentlemen in the process of redemption or running from the law, all cooped up in this brown and yellow portable-on-bricks, like the kind you find in parking lots at below-poverty-line schools. These things I learned at a rotten scrambled breakfast, some three-hour prayer session I was lucky to flee from unnoticed. I couldn't deal with the flustered talk about Leviticus, free range eggs being the devil's work; men having these discussions, more like intense quarrelling meshed into raw pugilism, all about John:13 and whose turn it was to do the camp's soiled bullshit and Hecubus' sugary breakfast cereals and which prophet said which verse in whatever... It was amazing how much passion - if that was what it was - they manifested, like they were fighting for their own, a home team maybe, their mom's? Weaker links in their family's extend-a-chain? With no knowledge of how to protect themselves from the broad insanity that's been hiding for us all, unexpectedly. All hazy though, in that blistering dead weight of July heat. The thinness of the air made breathing arduous plus a few notches higher on the old mercury scale.

The place smelled horrific. I found out pretty fast that we were right beside this pepper farm in the middle of nowhere. That was where my body was deposited, displaced to the horror spice local, which fell short of making it to a map. It wasn't even in a real town. I only know this because a few hours later, I bargained with some chap whose daily assignment was coveting The Yellow Pages - "Dante's Heretic Scrollings," he warned me. I'd tried to find it on a map so I could tell the cab driver exactly where to come and get me - it was off some garbage Lake Elsinore. That was a good one. The best I could do was refer the dispatcher to the overgrown sewage septic-system-with-human-bilge tank that reeked to high heaven, directly across the road, and being it was Sunday, the world's day of rest, it was no easy feat getting someone out there to collect me. ("It'll be another $50 if you want our driver to come up there on a weekend, Mack.") That $150 cab ride ranks right up there as one of my all-time indulgences. Thank the Pepper God I was able to find my bank card and thank God someone in the program had responded to my begging, having deposited first and last on a room for me because the Swedish Jesus landlady had been annoyingly cramping my style. Our lifestyles mismatched and conflicting, her mantras and prayers not enough to extract the agreed-upon rent and she, not so in sync with my wayward-crossword-skanks spending the night, or the four in the morning rummaging through her fridge for European chocolates, the rearranging of her prized bridge parlor... other things. Having a certain tenacity along with a great willingness to venture into territory most others probably would never go near, are qualities that make a good healthy addict. But this wasn't funny. And there was no chance that this community was going to put up with or even try to understand my circus of fancy words. No, the kind of sympathy and bonding I needed wasn't to be found here. I figured only the unsophisticated were safe to roam here with the herd; others would find more suffocating, devastating places.

I distracted one of the guards by asking him about the music chosen earlier for the morning hymn. "How many sharps were in that key of F anyway?" Then quickly, "What's $112 - 17$?" to which he stood there, all glazed over. I was waiting for smoke to come out of his ears and his head to spin around, this minion now clearly on tilt. Quite proud of myself, having stumped him to death. Dum-dee-dumb-dum. While he was pondering evolution in the key of death, this gave me the time I needed to rummage around in the pig shed where the fanatic underlings had stored my stray belongings, costumes, scripts and such. I managed to escape before anything really irreversible could happen to me.

Not having a home of any sorts to return go to, I thought to seek out some support from other kindred folk who knew what was up with me. Misery longs for familiar company, however broken it is.

* * *

14. On Being 'A Raider'

Death and a writer's work. Just before dying, he has his last work read over to him. He still hasn't said what he had to say. He orders it to be burned. And he dies with nothing to console him and with something snapping in his heart like a broken chord.

Albert Camus

December 1938 -Notebooks 1935-1942

W e d r i v e a m o n g s t many long silences , though there is a calm crisp prettiness in the day, announcing that fall has waved her goodbyes and is out the door. After a while Mom pipes up, "So, do you like driving?" Nice, maybe some normal conversation?

"Yeah, I do. I like it a lot," thinking she was going to affectionately query further, how I managed to make it across the country in one piece.

"Truck drivers can make a lot of money." I sneer, maybe wince. A grimace passes over my face and I numbly respond, with an answer I hope will put the whole business to rest.

"Mother, I'm a writer, and have been for some time."

Her eyebrows head downwards and inquisitively, she turns her head to me.

"A raider?"

"What? No, a writer, I said, mom!" emphatically correcting her.

This is where things turned awkward, a terrible series of frowning and disillusionment systematically set up on her face for the rest of the conversation.

"Oh," she says, the support, unwavering. The inevitably deflating thought-bubble above my head poses the question,

"Why did this tender instant need to end up being another unsettling exchange?"

This also was one of those inflamed moments when I didn't know which conundrum to address first. Was she thinking I was in cahoots with the Oakland Raiders? Did she believe that I, on occasion, was a raider of tombs, like Indiana Jones? And aren't those Indiana Jones death shrines only in horrible desert places like Lawrence of Arabia-like dunes in Egypt and Akbar? How could she think that was the playing field I hung out on? Mom, way ahead of me today in the non-sequitur triple-entendre mixed-up-metaphor-purposely-misheard jolly playtime contest I believed myself to be on stage all alone in up here. Or was it that she didn't *want* to hear the word *writer*? I figure it could be both, but things seem to change drastically from day to day, amidst a mocking uncertainty, always at play.

C'mon Mom, a *raider*? Really now.

Mother responds to this whole writer/raider business not with disgust, exactly: I mean she's trying to be supportive, in her way, I think. Isn't she? But why she remains committed to the hunt for a suitable vocation for me ranks right up there as one of those defining afternoon moments that pretty much tells me she doesn't know what drives me or moves me, to what God I bow…or anything, come to think of it. Some confidence-building placating gesture of any sort might aid in my fight, but you can't expect too much. Putting myself out there, leaving my heart unguarded, is business I withdrew from since coming back here.

In all earnestness, I sincerely believe that I exist on the planet as a genuine writer, a storyteller, sharing situations, opinions and building from what's on the page… It's more than a worthwhile pursuit. It is the only pursuit. It involves intricacies maybe not in the league of a Hemingway or Miller but delicacies, nonetheless.

Henry Miller was known for ignoring literary forms of his day (I do that), his work evolving through an often semi-autobiographical arena (I definitely do that) that melded social criticism (I've heard of that), character study, philosophical reflection and surrealist free association. I like that, and I do that, kind of, though, through my own unconventional and original meta-creative filter (that needs a good cleaning)... And Ernest Hemmingway, also known to flex his writer's muscle when it came to assaulting conventional taste. Also, Ernesto's spare, tight prose is right spot on with my code of non-unessential rhetoric. Alright, maybe not exactly, but you can't ignore the parallel as I listened to A Farewell to Arms until the record had, um, not synced up to my sprawling meta-filters (Wiki.) but similarities (reference material from Wikipedia Encyclopedia). But, if I was held up and frisked, asked point blank by inquisitive urban DEA agents with threatening meat carvers, I'd have to confess that I've drawn inspiration from the demented, warped and withered Henry Miller, maybe shrouded in Dr. Seuss-ian overtones. *(tf#19)* And what of such mentors and role models I've so adopted? There have been some strange ones, I'll admit. I've always had a mysterious appreciation for The Elephant Man. Yes, a swaggering and fragmented chap who turned out to be fairly well read. Now, the foul odor I'm not condoning. Also unhelpful: the low grade osteo-neurotic-psychotic-posture, making him more than embarrassing and less than popular with the ladies-who-lunch set. He was a true original, but reached too far outside his area of expertise; peddling those motivational tapes door-to-door also insured he remained dateless for a record 28 years. ("People are going to eat this crap up. Unhand me, officer; I need no license to canvas here!") But that couldn't be helped; the burlap sack over his head almost always frightened away possible female companions, as he innocently canvassed door-to-door asking strangers to pledge a little dough towards upcoming Monster Mash Dance Marathons:

"Ten cents a mile? That's highway robbery, Elephant boy. And Tony Robbins? Never heard of him. Get off my porch, Freako." Families often took me in, taught me much needed life lessons and embraced me.

Even when he did manage to find a dame not so primarily concerned with outer appearance - surprisingly more impressed by his sentiments, the masculine prancing and jigs - ultimately, things would skid downhill as fast as any song he chose to croon in private performance for lucky ladies were muffled by gargoylish, slurpy inhalation noises and obsessive sweating.

———————————

I feel my observations are relevant. Exactly to whom, they don't say that it's a prerequisite to know intimately just who my demographics are, but they're out there, I know they are. I don't have to know, not right now, not in this Unpleasantville I'm king of. Just another piece in the modern day possibility puzzle.

Once I've moved along, there will be more than enough adventurers and pleasure seekers looking to take over the lead ship. Trust me, when I disappear, they'll be someone else running 'round shrouding themselves from the world, just like me. Is it interesting to stick around and see who's going to get the short end of the sack? No, no it isn't.

*Note: use the word macabre more often. It will make me sound more French. And just what did those Momenchantz people think they were doing, anyway? I bet it's not even a word.

If I don't expect anything then I can't get disappointed, so, self-preservation has become a just, well-earned and deserved thing, and a game I can play alone. I need to support myself.

"Will you slow down, please? You're making me nervous! Pay attention, you're going way over the speed limit," mom barks alarmingly at me..

"Can I have a Kleenex Mom, I think they're in the back."

"I don't see them. You must have taken them out of the car earlier."

"No, I didn't. I would have remembered, for sure."

"How could you do that, you should know better, to replace things if you use them!"

"Why would I sneak into your car and make off with a box of tissues?"

She doesn't talk for a few minutes, but when we stop to get her a Tim Horton's Ice Cappuccino shake, we step out of the car and discover that a Kleenex box had slipped under the backseat. I give her the look like, "See I told you," redeeming myself, but only slightly. I'm waiting for an apology, but she just shakes her head, so I'm guessing I won that round, and it's on to the next conundrum that's set to be an unavoidably huge ordeal.

We get back in the car and I begin to fiddle around with the dials on the stereo, hoping to magically turn Mom into some kind of non-speaking entity, but that doesn't happen. Clenching my teeth, I speed up just as something clunks against the car. All I see before me is a sea of red, black and white. I figure I've either demolished one of God's creatures or have flattened an Amish lady transporting fresh livers and kidneys, betraying proper crosswalk procedures - oh my.

No matter, in an attempt to get that feeling of freedom I felt when I drove cross-country, it's time to expand these restrictive parameters and disrobe entirely. Mom won't mind.

---

tf#19: Dr. Seuss' real name was, 'Theodore Geisel' and born to this earth on 1904. He went on to talk-radio fame years after his last book bombed, "Arctic Google Kitties frozen in haunted melting igloos", and sunk into a deep dark, yet animated depression. He went on to host a popular weekly radio show called 'Doctor Demento' (I think) which held little regard for the pre-teen audience he'd worked so hard to accumulate over the years. Ultimately a wack-a doo, similarly to one of his mentors and eventual colleagues, Dr. Sigmund Freud, he ended up shooting monstrous amounts of cocaine and going blind from too much bliss. Also, just what Hunter S. Thompson was a doctor of, I can't say. It's cool to have interns who come to visit, assuming they have no lives to hurry back to; also, look into that 'God complex' thing that's mentioned in the book Dr. Dave lent me.

* * *

15. The Call

Stories pass the time with time and make it beautiful and interesting, if only by removing it from context, where everything becomes interesting in its strangeness. Hearing a story is telling it is to be implicated in it.

Richard Hell

Go Now

We pull into the driveway and as I step out of the car, I can just hear the phone ringing in the house, so I attempt a mad dash P.D.Q. I get to it and pick it up, half-expecting one of Mom's gorgon lawn-bowling gal pals on the other end, enquiring as to when and where the next bridge game, luncheon or town mob hanging was being held.

"Hello, hello?" I could tell from the scratchiness it was long distance.

"Ah, hello, yes?" I said.

"There ya are old boy, you are one tough son of a bitch to track down. I thought you said you were gonna phone once you got settled? It's a good thing I'm not sensitive. Ha, ha ha. Hey, I'd want to put something like that behind me, too. I get it. Last time we were knockin' around you were seriously in your own planetarium, dude. Christ, what was that you were on!? Never mind. It's good to hear your voice, anyway."

"Uh… yeah. You too." (?!)

"So, you have any comment on what's been going on?"

The saying "from out of left field" comes to mind.

"Sorry?"

"Now, if I can get you to say something about this business, my editor would flip out as, you know, it would be sort of an exclusive....you there?"

What editor? What business?

"Who are you again?"

"Look, if you wanna give "No Comment," that's all fine and good, but there's gonna be questions, a ton of them, and a blasé attitude'll make you sound like an ass. Not only an ass but an uncaring, insensitive one. The media'll paint you as... "OK, OK, I... see," I said, responding half attentively, so I could use another working part of my brain to imagine who this could be wanting a caring comment with regards to something I had no idea about. This would not be the first call.

"Hey, tell me, was all that Chateau Marmont Belushi crap really true? That stuff was great. Do you have any pictures? If you can come up with some other stories, you know not too this, not too that, I got people who'll eat up that dark Hollywood behind-the-scenes shit, we could put a coffee table book, together, maybe with a mirror, people can do their blow off it! But look... um... this other thing, they're after some cold hard facts. Her parents are more than a little pissed, you understand, and who can blame them really? What do you say I just tell 'em that you were out of your head at the time, you know, give 'em the, "Something like this certainly wasn't all your fault, you have your own set of problems, and you're sorry..." bit. Don't worry, I won't make you out to be some remorseful slouch, I mean, shit, we've all done things..."

"Right, yes, well, of course" (!?)

"... that aren't strictly above board. But, they're going to want to get in touch with you, speak with you properly and all."

Smartly, in a quickly invented English accent, I managed, "Can I, uh, get back to you then? I just came in the door and... my mom's still locked in the car out in the driveway, probably suffocating by now, so you'll understand if I've gotta run, she has to be melting out there."

I don't think the guy heard my addition to the already outlandish conversation.

"Sure. Sure, sport. You do that."

* * *

16. Waking Up Jenny

One of the few phone numbers still lodged in my memory were the digits of Jenny K., my old partner in crime. More of a drug buddy than a Bonnie and Clyde type crime scene, we were pretty harmless to unsuspecting bystanders. Our most atrocious heists involved sneaking into her dad's office and lifting medical supplies, then driving to Nordstrom's in the convertible mobile-coffin to help her return pricey make-up samples she'd stolen just hours before, then put a call into Printo and we were off, usually for a good deal of the day.

So, seconds after taking out everything I could from the ATM at the 7-11, I shouted into the pay phone for Jenny to meet me at this dive hotel out in Santa Ana.

Now that I knew I would be saved, I became gleeful, bursting with unmistakable and familiar frenetic energy, a bit of the snide obnoxious spirit rising. I proceeded to tell her how I'd awoken in this god-awful Jesus Camp dwelling.

"My treat, sweetheart," I recall saying to Jenny in my best Jimmy Cagney voice (a terrible impression) as I hopped out of the cab and threw my arms affectionately around her, so happy to see someone who didn't want to put the word of God in me. I unloaded my boxes that still smelled of God's salad-daze seasoning from that Children of the Pepper-Corn farm. Then Jenny and I got busy. On this day, as soon as we saw one another, we already knew what lay in store.

A similar nightmare had befallen her not so long ago, so she knew how I was feeling. Her parents carted her off to some brainwashing, clean-up-your-act, thrill-less cult-like farm. Baffled at just what to do with a daughter whose job it is to cause more than 24 hours a day of horrific worry, of course her waking up in another country occurred while she was under the influence - if I remember right, it was a hell of a story, her escape from all that. "Please come get me. I'll do anything. These girls are so freaky. I'm scared. And sick." Funny how things get spun around.

We got dressed and didn't even have to speak about the particulars in the caper we were about to pull, we had done it so many times with ease and *non chalance.* She knew her role, she had it down pat. It was my job to play the straight man in our rehearsed scene of Mumbo-Jumbo Make-up Absurdity (I gave the larceny a name).

On occasion, we'd get an absurdly motivated and too-into-her-job saleslady. "Didn't I see you here a couple days ago? Yes, you said you'd lost the receipt, that it had been devoured by your domesticated ring-tailed lemur? Or was it that he had pee'd on the receipt? Yes, now I remember. You said you could get the receipt but it was defecated on by a ring-tailed lemur. Are you saying the same thing happened again? Which was it, *sir?*"

I stood blankly, letting the odyssey of nothingness gloss through my mind, as just then - and not a moment too soon - just before mentally arranging the final thread in an escaped zoo animal story, and how they're attracted to the ink from cash registers, thus all the lost and destroyed receipts, I see out of the side of my eye, Jenny giving me the OK sign it was OK to jet as she had removed what Lancôme and Elizabeth Arden and Shiseido lines she could in her 'borrowed' Chanel bag.

She had this beautiful laugh, endless and comforting. I'd really missed it. So, I explained to her how I really had made this valiant attempt at integrating into God's team (four hours was ample, she said) and how it just hadn't looked like

I could acclimatize her biorhythms to such a rigid, pointless schedule laid out by the sweaty priests and narcoleptic nun brigade.

Her contagious energy, maternal nature and sincere compassion were apparent through her giggling, saying the whole thing was hilarious while sensing that another one of our fun (but deadly) childlike liaisons was now in the works.

We got back to the Santa Ana creature comfort Inn after our Nordstrom's run. Here was where I would begin to completely lose any sight of sound mind.

The thing I can't remember so great was just how I wasn't more worried about where all this was going to end up. I'm kind of thinking I'd played so many games with myself by this time - adapting and all - knowing which situations to go numb in…maybe not too much was hitting me the way it should have, being already bruised internally for eternity, and all of that. Once again, I'd hit another soul-throttling murky bottom, that unparalleled bar continually dropped by the insane judges and life referees keeping tabs on my madness; my balsa casket gaining speed, lowered further into the ground.

We stayed up all night: phone calls to far off places, hopscotch in the uneven parking lot, laughing about Jesus, dressing in each other's clothes, sniffing and shooting stuff that my dealer, Primo, had given me. Him so grateful to see me again, worried where I'd been the last 48 hours, and so happy that I had any money at all - me often begging to pay "Next time." I figured his name was bestowed upon him on account of the superior drugs he was selling, like, "Wow, that is some Primo shit." Either that or his family was in the pasta sauce business. Either way, this sweaty Spaniard in a tattered red Toyota was the main center of attraction during my tour around the underlying gunk of the Southern California area.

Jenny confided in me of her recent life capers: her stripping job and of how she'd once danced, of old boyfriends, her crazy L.A band stories amidst the decadent Nirvana hipsters, and me telling her how I came out here - eerily we asked at the same time, "Just where is everyone that got away from us?" - people in the program and our experiences in the sausage-grinder of getting straight, of trying to get cleaned up for more than a week at a time: the hospitals, the sterile centers, counselors, the Musician's Assistance Program place in Pasadena... (Ironically, or is it coincidentally?) she had been the one to tell me about that place, the one I breezed through.

Once we ran out of stuff to do, I think we were going to have a bath together 'cause we thought it's something we should try since, well, I'm a boy, she's a girl and we're in a hotel. We were pretty enthralled with our own manic energy, so filling up the tub just became another task, a distraction in-between the main event of getting high. We never got into it. We did order up more HBO movies that we never ended up watching. We were doing much better as desperate but resourceful junkie-fiend buddies, we figured anyway. Why screw it up with sex, which never seems to work out the way you thought you'd wanted? Our sexual churning and sex synapses burned out ages ago, I think, love liquids which had swum with a conjugal syntax, depleted, now uncharmed, the tassels of attractiveness beckoning in the syringe beforehand. So high. The drifting in and out of consciousness, in and out of one another, time standing still. Or did it move so wildly through us, with lightning speed 'til we just said "Fuck it," chalking it up to one of the thousand things over which we had no control.

She had a video camera that she'd borrowed. I think we even taped some stuff, not sex stuff, just silly, character, pretend stuff.

"Let me just set this tripod up so I can get in the shot. Hold on."

"How does this look?" she asked, parading around our suite, draped in the shower curtain, the rings clipped to her ears and nipples.

We sure could entertain ourselves.

I've got this twisted kind of combo-Peter Jennings-Chuck Barris voice thing going now. "We're here in this drug testing lab in a wickedly downscale motel/notel in Santa Ana, California. We've placed these two young urchins in this cage for two days and nights and given them every drug they want. Will they come out of it alive? We're going to find out. The winner gets a set of clean syringes, steak knives and a book on how to improve relationships. Let's catch up with Jenny, one of our contestants, a twisted ballerina who's ingesting substances that should have put her under hours ago. Her tolerance? Well, it's downright staggering AND entertaining! She's a vagrant-celebrity-on-the-rise but doesn't want any involvement in that whole Hollywood star system, so…"

"You are truly ridiculous," she offered.

Before injecting ourselves down the merry path of sin once more, we talked through tears of joy, smiles of sorrow, how happy we were to see each other alive and well, both having thought we'd got lost somewhere through the lines. She was a wild card by nature, troubled and mischievous, yet I'd never pressed her beyond revealing to me her predictably crippling relationship with her family. Things get buried.

And corroded. And sometimes never rise again to the surface.

The aloofness of this sweet girl possessed me and penetrated me. Some people just have a magic effect on you. It's rare. It's special. I can't say I understand it. I just know it's one of the few things in the world worth welcoming and respecting. Jen could have been a Cheerleader for the Damned if they'd bothered to put together a team. My beautiful frightened ballerina, morally vacant, an emotional train wreck always running for and catching a ride on the latest L.A man to treat her like shit. This had become the ongoing joke with us, when phoning each other we'd confess to yet another of our predictable and all-too-typical and reckless attempts at lustfully productive romance, always ending in regret. Prepped with either of our two resonating stock phrases "What was I thinking?" and "So, what am I going to do now?" Familiar fiascos, whomever we lanced into. Those poor people.

We sought sleep to escape, drained entirely from our low-budget reality show that no one would ever see, but could feel the nightmares readying themselves. I must have gone to sleep at some point. I remember having horrible dreams, the nightmarish hurtful ones which invariably rush in on the nights I'm most scared, dreading what the next day would bring, in whatever bed I make mine for the night.

I dreamt Jenny overdosed. I didn't know what to do. I'd seen things in Pulp Fiction-ish movies, but all the stored-up visual images that raced in all at once were immediately deemed useless for real-life application. I tried calling out on our phone, but it had been shut off by Jughead at the front desk, him suspicious of us not paying for our long distance and pay-per-view flicks, I guess. I tried slapping her across the face, tried mouth-to-mouth and finally dragged her to the bathtub and dunked her underneath the water. Nothing worked.

She wasn't waking up.

I thought she might be trying to put one over on me, she was that enthusiastic about playing pranks and all. She'd been known to take jokes pretty far, if they were good... but no one goes limp like that, quits breathing that way, and can be acting - not with that color blue flushing her expressionless face to pale: she turned the colors of the American flag... red to blue and finally to white. Surrender-flag white. An image flashed of Jen swinging at the end of my mind's tether, long golden locks flowing, eyes big and in wonder of what world she had put together for herself, but thin to the point where one might wonder if she's all there. Flowing with lace and smiles, at the lake, swaying on a rubber tire hanging by a rope on a huge willow tree and killing my heart, multiple breaks each time she swooped back and forth, hitting me with what could have been pleasant and sparkling recollections representing hope and innocence, but which only scalded me with blistering torment and longing - the feeling of being without, missing everyone and everything. Again, she was a pale princess to begin with. Strange how she brought to mind my funny Baptism with Father Kevin, being under water like that, so peaceful and white, her incandescent once-laughing-face so still now. The claw-footed trough held on to her. Her speckled veiny vessels on her eyeballs spoke of depletion, of not getting enough of something. We tried to monitor each other but fell down our own shattered and broken shafts, victims in a Dionysian feast of ourselves.

The "mischief of the tides had her," a verse from the writer Mary Oliver I may have read many years earlier, but not the entire book. She helped teach me to think in pictures and prose, how best to describe a thing, an occurrence. Somehow this was relative to the moment but still empty. Jen was now somehow disassembled, not how I felt or sensed her hours before, and I couldn't explain it to anyone better than that.

That night, we shared some pivotal moments, what felt like cathartic talk that could have turned the sinking ships we were into a better plan. She was to have a devastating effect on me, like in the way characters in a favorite painting can be mesmerizingly vivid, staring right at you from inside the canvas, sharing with you their secrets. Unforgettable.

Smash and Blow. Scream Scream Scream Jesus fucking Christ.

With the sting of morning, my earlier joy had melted, along with the seriousness of things which startled me hard. I looked around the room but there wasn't a trace of her.

Trigger happy with triggers, the grief still on board, I attempted to skip to and fro with multiple coffees and Greens Plus in cranberry juice liquidating to quicken my near-mad remorseful mind but unable to block out the disgust of wanting, wanting, wanting, even now so fucking anxious to return to that never-ending-struggle to call, and wait, and cop: the promised arrival of something that had stopped being fun long ago.

I threw what was left of my life into the car littered with cassettes, half-empty bottles of water, maps smeared with chocolate, shirts donated to me from that Charlie Street drunk-tank place, a tennis racket with busted strings, my life trophies, Henry Miller's Tropic books and Bukowski paperbacks - all too dog-eared and soaked in suntan lotion to sell to any second hand store, and drove off.

* * *

17. Not a Promising Bunch / The Towelette Episodic (Youth 1)

M o m ' s very s i c k t o d a y, can't get up and out of bed. She asks me if I wouldn't mind heating up some ginger ale in the microwave. (Though I could have misheard the request, could have been "Gin and ale with a dyke of cocaine," but such a request is way off base for her.) This one comes under the category, 'Things that have never, ever worked in the history of man, yet people persist just because they heard it somewhere'. A carbonated and clear amber drink flavored with ginger extract may assist in quenching one's dry palette, but to look any further- inconsequential and pointless. Another great myth - or old wives tale - passed through the ages is to wrap a hot towel around your head as a response to some ailment. Come to think of it, I believe it was getting picked on at school - yes, that was my ailment. This blackening affair added to my growing unpopularity with the non-towel-wearing fellas on the wrestling squad back in Grade 7. Or was it Grade 8? Like there's a difference. Things become clear many years after the fact, far past the time it could have assisted with clues as to just what was brewing in those formative years.

"Do I have to go to school? I feel kind of unwell." Mom's response, "Well, wrap a hot towel around your head." OK then. All set for success! Someone just point me in the right direction.

Why such a concept didn't throw me like it should have, I'm sure I've no recollection. I do know I couldn't imagine where she wanted me to obtain those moistened towelettes that were reputedly so fluid and fruitful in our home. She provided instructions. Carmen Miranda was the famous person I came closest to resembling (the "fruit in the hat," I was affectionately called, but confused through the school's darkened halls). Also not a popularity mark with the dudes in the homeroom I was assigned to, smokers and slackers the lot of them - when I arrived at school, it far from assisted with the not getting picked on part. But I stood my shaky ground. My governess said it would help, but the 'Sound of Music' line didn't do the trick, junior high students of such predictable and severely mirthless ilk, often more threatened than appreciative of imaginative banter. I was left to resort to rehearsing interludes, "Liars and beggars and stares, oh my, liars and beggars and stares!" crooning the lyrics to that upcoming high school musical production I ultimately fell short of being chosen to star in, due to great bouts of bottomless gloom and talent-free vocal chords - the tumultuous sadness of it all retiring my salmon-colored, Egyptian-cotton impressively high-thread-counted blistering hot towel to that high chair back at home, though not before the pelting of lunch bags, girly napkins and gruesome disparaging comments came my way. The faculty, a dreary force to be mucked with, fooling nobody - those far-fetched frumpy zipper-heads did little to intervene, their chastising, chuckles and loud whispers overheard through thin veils of cheap commissary pathetic partitions:

"There's the towel boy. I can't imagine he'll fair too well out there."

"No, his attitude doesn't appear promising, and get a load of that bowl haircut?"

"An asteroid of trouble unleashed on the world that kid's gonna be."

I swear I heard them murmur, "How do you solve a problem like Maria?" (but with my surname stuck in there). I was too consumed with nailing down just which fire-sale-suited, undeserving-of-tenure buffoon would have played which character in The Wizard of Oz, to ask for guidance or pay proper attention. In the kitchen cafeteria, they'd already fried up and destroyed any notes I'd taken on keys to Surviving School, along with tips for how a student might fit in and extract more from this primordial scholastic tutelage.

Staring up at the sky for some form of God to shoot down a helpful play: any answer would've been amazingly appreciated; anything at all to arm myself, even water wings would've helped, as my ship was sinking fast. My support team from the pit, truly overwhelming. Especially from the Hindu contingent, chanting at me, casting glances... and spells, who steadfastly believed their worldly ways were being insulted, pleading, "I swear I'm not making fun of you."

How could I poke fun at them and make merry when I knew nothing of anybody's true faith!?

There should be an award, a council assigned, grant money and such, or even just a nice little ceremony with snacks and pretty colored pills, for surviving some of that misery.

A h , t h e r e v e n g e f a n t a s y o f ... wrapping the entire teachers union - and some of the nastier kids - in one gargantuan scalding hot beach towel. In the school's auditorium I orchestrate the proceedings; sitting up in a 20-foot-tall shiny silver high chair, wrapped in an edible, designer methamphetamine chocolate diaper, demanding that the girls' football team, who'd be wearing only sheets, do as I say: subjects at my mercy, dancing and weaving all Maypole like, continuing with the immense gauzing and bandaging, despite the unmelodic pleading and apologies that came years too late, too quiet and not loud enough. Wonderful.* * *

17. B) C l a s s y C h a r t s & G a m e s (youth part 2)

M o m t e l l s m e s h e feels as if she's in a terrifying
dream she cannot wake up from. My trampled heart goes out
to her. Somewhat. Of course I care, but that's not the issue.
It's her random and unnecessary over-acting to get attention
which always triggers my inquisiviteness - how she never
got involved in a Noel Coward play or applied to the Actor's
Studio. Plagued continuously with my own marked deck of
multiple concerns, I get thunderstruck all too easily, and as
far as which one to address first, that leaves me aghast.

Today I look in the full-length hall mirror and see a
Three-Toed Sloth; a ravenous Klingon-like unkind
uncuddly. I'm made an example of, behind the glass, in a
scary desert-like man-made continent on display for sticky
fingered kids fresh from parade floats to point at, running
nervously, dragging their part-time weekend parent past me
and my exhibit (told not to pet or feed me), fearful of
growing up to be like me. "Read the sign, scary dad!"

Seems the idea of me growing into that special someone
who wears fetching slacks, plays polo, cricket, or other
civilized contest involving lemonade and referees who keep
tallies, whilst pontificating and posing poolside, will never
come to light. Synchronized swimming, a no-go; no
Parcheesi or Bridge pour moi. No mingling-under-mistletoe
amidst Mai Tai merriment. And certainly no invitations
from the yachting set to arrive at the club... "Not a dang
second past eight, you. It's The Big Brentwood mixer -
Kell's first big bash since getting home from Brandeis!"
None of that stuff. (tf: I did put in a call though. Not
surprisingly, not on the list, past my bedtime, the tight
material rendering a tuxedo was alarming, they said, and
would play no part this year, in any club gatherings.)

My education has seemed to have been more about getting up in the world's face, falling down and accumulating a mountain of misperceived memories. Big deal, so I've got some stories and some experience. I've always just wanted to be a part of something that was special and respected, where I didn't have to make excuses, or apologize, where I could feel good about knowing that I'd found a place that wasn't made out of doubt that same old same old. Where did I put those chocolate-flavored maps, anyway?

* * *

17. C) The Bully

B u s y i n g m y s e l f   s t i l l back up here with endless projects and plans I'm behind in; one being the hunting down of the bully who taunted and teased me relentlessly, without remorse in Grade 7. Every day. And I mean every day, without fail.

During my frazzled maze of a stroll home, after school was done, he would follow. Kicking me when I was down, a frightful devilish figure, Jocko Van Bibbins *(tf#20)* (known affectionately to friends and family as Jocko the Destroyer) proceeded to break this unwanted but valuable violin I was forced to practice with and take care of in Miss Whatever-her-name's class. I had to pay for it with my inadequate paper route money, a creatively bereft experience I must add - drudgery defined - stressed to the gills with a Stradivarian tease monster, a savage and severe weeping circus home. I held in all the intense hatred I've had for him but it's built up over a number of years, has become a constant and profound torment, stashed away. I know full-well that if I were unleashed, I mean if it was unleashed, it's not a very pleasant thing to say, but he would be strangled to death.

On a couple of occasions, this awful, ominous boy had the testicular gumption to show up on my mangy morning delivery route and set my newspapers on fire. In retrospect, I think there was a tough but valuable lesson learned: people who pay to have their morning papers delivered to their front door, simply do not want to have to look at the kids who've delivered the news screaming down the apartment hall engulfed in flames. Or have burnt ashes blacken their doormat - a now new art installation, a sooty irreparable affair. Magnificently unfair, it is, to have their early morning preoccupations interrupted by my little problems.

Almost all my wages were used to repair my neighbors' front steps, the funding coming out of my - by now, Less Than Zero earnings - from supplying illiterate richies with the stellar Globe & Mail morning newspaper. I begged my parents for help, but they said it was an ideal life lesson for learning just who (and what) to avoid on my travels. I was told I would remember the lesson. What I ended up learning had more to do with parents and aromas that stay with you after decades have passed, like, I never left those buildings without a taste of what I imagine the tattered carpet at the Science Center tasted like... Something about staying away from creepy horror-show smelly meth labs, somebody cooking cabbage and brain soup in these low-rent district apartment buildings at 5 a.m., when most inhabitants are asleep and can't hear me bawling for help (Bawling for Dollars, a show?). They can't make out or even decipher the screams of a little guy working a paper route years before it was proper in order to pay back his super-critical dad *("Uh, a little help, people. Hello? It's your paperboy." "Fuck off, we're sleeping.")*

Scurrying around the building in an attempt to hunt down the drunk and belligerent super (a man) to let me in, who was dragging along beside him a splintered goalie stick and weird Oscar Goldman *(tf#21)* face-mask lobbing racist remarks my way, this was overkill in the "I'm going to die" department.

Having to ask my mom for the dough to replace the violin, unable to tell her the truth; that her son couldn't stick up for himself.

So, years later, I go to his place of employment (turns out he works as one of those nutty veterinarians from the dark side who perform unorthodox procedures of inserting modules into cats' brains - a time-consuming pursuit in itself) and here's what I do: just when he's coming out of his office, say for lunch, or maybe I wait and save my entrance until the end of his day. I run up to him, piercing a barely human-type scream as loud as is possible in my condition (an undecipherable scream) and commence with pummeling his head with a violin case, repeatedly - eerily resembling that exact instrument I had assigned to me - as hard as I'm able, 'til I'm restrained by his fellow co-workers. The last few times proved to be ineffective (revenge-wise) as he swore he didn't know who I was or what this was all about.

Officers remove me and the paddy wagon and drive me away to the PokeMan station for questioning (I did have quite a lot) from the bloodied sidewalk where he lay begging, crying - desolate, confused. The only words from his misaligned orifice that I could make out over the sirens, "Why me, why?!" But I think he's starting to get the idea. Next time, I'll make sure.

---

tf#20: known affectionately to friends and family as Jocko the Destroyer.
tf#21: the agent boss from The Six Million Dollar Man - guess the scary man was a devoted fan.

* * *

18. H o t A i r

We loved to have people call us precocious. We used our education to blow ourselves up into prideful balloons, though we were careful to hide this from others. Secretly, we felt we could float above the rest of the folks on our brainpower alone.

From Chapter 2 in the Alcoholics Anonymous Big Book

The w o r d h o m e s i c k is a terrible one. It doesn't go anywhere. Just sits there, empty with no direction. What are you supposed to do with it once it's out there? Does it even have its own a place? I can't say it really exists or not. I mean, how would I know for certain if I've never reclined by poolside or ordered food there?

Seems I'm going to need a lot more oxygen if I'm going to do this sobriety thing right. A helium tank that never runs out of steam sounds about right for the job, to compliment my eternal air bag full of self-righteous but disfigured dragons, chasing me in a dirtied vacuum bag, far past the proper emptying stage; to say nothing of those skeletons and Shoe Tree People in my chaotic closet that scream at me, night after night, to do something with them. A parlor game? Maybe a film? I have my own Theory of Chaos.

Just why I was recruited to assemble an unfathomable amount of easily bustable orbs for some finicky wine and cheese gathering, an inexhaustible attempt to extract further monies from members, I can't say. This type of bullshit would go on all the time, these terrible special occasions and drab activities appearing magically on the schedule when tuck shop purchases and group lessons were down.

The tennis club I worked at in California used to rent this helium tank for silly syndicated sporty events, the boss enlisting the likes of me to play Balloon Captain. That is, when not spending time being mistaken for Gopher from

Love Boat, though gimpier, if that was possible. I had my own unique gift of wardrobe style. Wearing white knee-high sockaloons and whatever shoes discovered in the Lost and Found (playing *Dress Up* was a kick), bantering and flinging fancy with others grappling with their own pathetic attempts at backhands and wildly excessive bar bills and me, blown back behind the front desk by knee-highs, Dewar's scotch and un-cut cocaine; not the club uniform originally awarded to the holder of this junior position. Just prop me up to meet and greet at the welcome mat, checking in those luxurious members and dreamy divorcees all the while playing the role of the fading flirt with the older ladies on the Morning C League Team. All charming like Eddie Haskel, with a sharpened boomerang - cagily watching the clock, soon the escape down to L.A.

"Would you mind terribly if I slipped away a tad early today? The 405 freeway's a bitch to contend with on a Friday, you know how it is. Oh, and by the way, it's like 100 degrees back here behind the desk, could we lose that Must Wear Pants rule?"

Out there speeding along the lost highway to my beautiful freaks, who were far from members on the Morning C League team but who understood and accepted me... Maybe there's something to that? The family of drag queen junkie hookers of Westlake and Eighth Avenue had adopted me and welcomed me into their fold.

"Remember to save a place for me guys; I'll be there as soon as The Man allows me to cut out of work. Hey, pick up for me, would you? Of course I'll pay you when I see you." They looked forward to my visits, needing my Remington Steele good looks and Caucasian demeanor to flesh out the street demographics.

"Who is this? Yeah, all right, but you owe us, bitch."

I don't know if I'd be that well-received if I were to return, the sorting and sifting through the office manager's desk drawers caught on surveillance tape and all. "Uh, I'm just cleaning up, sir," I confessed later. There certainly have been some attempts.

I used to keep this special can of Lemon Pledge in the club's locker that I'd turn upside down, using its shiny and beautiful concave-bottom to mix together water and tar heroin. Then I'd sniff it all up using cut straws from the snack bar, kind of like I was drowning in the club's bubbly Jacuzzi, dreadfully past my allotted break time, sinking in the tar pit un-oasis, all that chemical compost flowing through my nostrils and suffocating any possible chance of advancement.

Things got out of hand on a few occasions. There was some nodding off (again, not in the job description) coupled with uncontrollable Mexicano dealers popping in, pretending they were only there to peruse the pro shop's lady's tennis skirts, ultimately confusing the female members, there looking to run up huge luncheon tabs and take part in less than stellar competitive social tennis.

"Are they members, Carol? I can't say I've seen them here before. They must be new." Her doubles partner responded, "I'll bet you a pair of Prada shoes they're not." I think her name was Gloria, the freckle-faced head of the afternoon get-togethers. She had me in her back pocket.

"Now, darling Timothy, would you be a dear and sashay these cocktails out to court 12? Marjorie's ensconced in one hell of a battle out there. God, she may even break a sweat! Just sign her name on the chit sweetie, would ya?"

"Sure thing Glory, anything for you girls," I responded as she shot me a Sue Ann Nivens suggestive wink.

The affectionate and bored housewives treated me kind of like their mascot, the drunker ones inclined to placing an occasional tip down my trousers. "Now, don't cha' go off and spend this all in one place, you." I guess a more discerning, sophisticated shopper would have invested more wisely with that sweaty dollar bill moistening in my shorts. The accumulated bonuses went towards future downtown street purchases and gas to get there. Thank you, ladies. They weren't mean-spirited or anything. Just blind.

I kept a library of paperbacks under my desk and consulted them when I ran into trouble. For instance, that book by Carnegie Melon, How to Win Friends and People While Under the Influence, *(tf#22)* opened my eyes considerably and assisted with getting me through the hilly slopes in relationships I was barely managing to keep up appearances in. A guidebook on How to Live can be the most important thing for someone with substance concerns.

I miss those luscious late afternoons where I'd work until closing, mucking about in goopy sentiment, reminded of summers as a child out at the park, maybe with my dad. Better times. There'd be this strange surreal calm, the scorching sun slowly disintegrating, empty tennis courts, scattered stray balls left behind that needed collecting all the way out on court 18: one of the tasks of my job I wasn't too bad at. Huge oak trees hanging overhead, reddish auburn leaves swaying in gentle breezes - all calm for the moment, no rage in sight - settling through the club and its tailored walkways. All could have served to build in me a glow, some monumental warmth, though it did nothing but fill me with a strange and bitter sadness, only conjuring my dad's absence, and my tragic similarities to circumstances to scenes in films and characters in books I loved and saw myself living in, convinced I was like-minded, feeling entirely simpatico with the hero in a story, right there along with him, feeling, knowing and sensing the outcome. If I'd a hand to bet with or any winnings to speak of, I would have let it all ride, as a good chunk of the time when I turned that page, I was dead on. Dead on. These were times when I knew there was beauty in books and beyond, just under my fingertips where I knew I wasn't too badly off. But like many times before, my all too keen sense of inadequacy and negative disposition naturally did me in.

Even with my books and the pleasant surroundings, there were things I felt too inexperienced to truly understand. Those tiny but jarring moments that I hadn't known what to make of, but I knew a smarter man would have made the connection and known what to do. For instance, my tennis bag, where I kept a notebook and wallet and stuff, eventually got used for carting 'round with me this black leather zip-up surgical pouch for my works (the marsupial pouch I've always spoke of having?): syringes, cotton swabs, a silver spoon, a lighter (to this day, I don't smoke - now that's really bad for your health), and the unavoidable klutzy occasions when the used syringes, bloody alcohol swabs and various tourniquets would spill out onto the court for an alarmed hitting partner to see and query. Falsely confessing such sexy trinkets of manhood were on hand to light candles for impromptu picnics and desserts I'd put together for lovely young things I'd meet at auditions, or new members I felt I needed to romantically initiate. My point being, that when I was 16, I wouldn't have known what any of those tools would be for. I know now.

There were a couple members that I got to know rather well, the ones who sensed that I could get them hooked up with my pal Primo. So sometimes on my lunch break, I'd put the top down and dash off, Irvine to Santa Ana, playing the soundtrack from Traffic, and manage to flag down Primo and pick up the sticky brown tar stuff for the Club B mixed doubles squad.

Often, I was left unsupervised to saunter in and out of empty offices. I'd make my way out to the pool area amidst the backdrop of white plastic chairs drenched in dew, making sure all was safe and locked, feeling much like some mischievous mouse, while the feline boss was away, off playing, while I kept my own time. Sometimes even forgetting my addictions in the infinite splendor during after-hours moments, alone hearing a din of crickets somewhere nearby, feeling the summer sky, warm and mysterious, along with hearing innocent voices from happy kids on bikes, amidst moth haunted street lamps.

I wandered the complex grounds, making my way out to court 18, where I lay flat on my back and right in the middle of the court, stretched and looking up at the sky, not caring about the sandy red clay from the court in my hair and on my clothes. I stared up and wondered which little lights were planets and which ones were stars. This season anyway, there would be no pointless below-zero northern weather making its way into me.

ONe poiNt for meE.

---

tf#22: the book referred to is actually "How to Win Friends and Influence people," by Dale Carnegie.

* * *

19. Lonely is an Eyesore

Pain and suffering is for sure but total misery is mostly optional.

My big adventure planned for the evening is an Alcoholics Anonymous meeting, my first in quite a while. I've been kind of apprehensive about going. See, back when I was pursuing the life of sobriety, I really enjoyed the vivacious energy of the alcoholic recovery kids in California. I'm kind of feeling that whole scene spoiled it for me here, as that was great and this is very much not. Maybe that's an excuse? It's AA Central out there, with special youths on specialty teams who've lived a number of wild lifetimes by the time they're done being ripped-apart-teenagers. Everybody I ran into was either in the program or tumbling their way there.

The program is basically The Last House on the Block, meaning that if you end up there you've desperately grabbed at every other straw imaginable, and most likely more than once. I wasn't going to push for any hidden meaning - my mother's big old homestead, coincidentally, being the last house on Colborne Street, but who knew and go figure.

Upon arriving, I'm a little tense shuffling into the makeshift church. I duck down to enter the catacombs of self-revulsion, and above my head I think there's a neon sign that reads YOU ARE NO LONGER ALONE (How did they know, I wondered?) Also weird and lonely, that these were precisely the sorts of places rented out for my Cub Scout meetings when I was about 12 years old, one of the few organizations I ever excelled in. The familiar stench hits me right away. There's an exact template in all community centers and churches in most every state, province and ghostly host town across the globe that offers itself up to these withering, drawn-together folk attempting to get their lives back. Those predictable hemorrhoid-inducing wooden chairs and bad buzzing lights overhead, coupled with a hollow boom-busted echo in these rooms - unavoidable when one speaks above a whisper - and of course, Timbits. The standard fare: selected stales from the nearby coffee shop along with black beverages made by a volunteer caffeine-crazed-alky-wild-cat, this being their 'Commitment' (a position shakily held by unsure 'Newcomers', barely hanging on), the unpaid duty which is helping them stay alive. It's the accountability, I'm told, that consistency of providing caffeine for the forlorn that at this very moment, is working somewhere, for someone. That's one less statistic, which is very, very good.

It's all kinds of easy to cast judgment, make snide remarks and be totally critical. The material for a good properly produced pilot is all around, but that's the trick. Here's an opportunity not to do that, to realize that amidst the glaring and obvious differences, there's one big smelly shitting elephant in the middle of the room, and his name is addiction. (Though it's really tough to get the guy to come when he's called, so…).

Forget what the folks in the room look like: pay no attention to their eating habits, the barf-worthy perfume, ridiculous stone-washed vests, multiple piercings in the oddest of places, scrawny types turned muscular, humungous hairy-nosed dudes, anorexics, bulimics… They're all there to reach out to.

Sitting directly across from me is a very badly-aged Cindy-Loo Whoos-it. Yes, from Whoville. She still has that spark, it's dim now… you could see it was there once, maybe in the right light? Actually not so much. Yes, it's that gook on the eyelashes she's batting eerily in my direction. Now I see. Though probably in her early 30's, she's looking mid 50's and drained, seriously exhausted from running, and now she's left dangling from the tip of the world. I couldn't help but picture Cindy-Loo in her little jammies, a cup of hot chocolate spilling onto her slippers, "Where are you going with all of our presents? And our tree? Stick around for a cocktail, Chubby?"

Cindy said she was 96 days clean, though I sensed she was not, and that she'd been up here looking after her dying father for the last few months and was ready to blow. Or was it do blow? Concerned with what I was going to say, my turn quickly approaching, I didn't query further and ended up spending a good chunk of the meeting mostly taking notes (more Participatory Journalism; I had no REAL business being there). When my turn comes to share, I murmur, "Oh, I'm up here visiting my mom. I'm not really an alcoholic or anything, it's drugs I've a relationship with, and actually, I'm just here to enjoy the company, and your stories." I sub-vocalized the last few words, but would have said them out loud if not for my nose running like a sewer coupled with an absurd amount of shakes. Once halftime comes (the 7th inning stretch, I guess), I saunter over to the refreshment area and pour myself another drink (of water). Miss Loo comes over to say hello and with a brandy stench percolating, whispers to me, "Drugs, booze, it's all the same, kiddo. Cookies and milk and a wee little nip are getting me through. I just haven't 'officially' quit yet, but I couldn't tell 'em that." Guess not. She raised her one continuous eyebrow, winked with her good eye, and then vanished from the church, escaping her own resonating confession.

A couple of seats away from me sits another poor gal who clearly just came from a Who-Can-Wear-The-Most-Blue-And-Purple-Gunk-On-Your-Eyes-And-Still-See-Out-Of-Them contest. I'd heard rumors of such freaky events in other Canadian tiny towns. If I begin to crack even the smallest smirk, it would lead to giggles and then that's it, I'm a goner. I hold solemn and true, averting my stare across the room, biting my lip and thinking to myself, "Since when have girls returned to using the hair iron?"

At the other table there's a gal who looks like Dorothy Michaels. (Dustin Hoffman's drag character in the movie Tootsie). Beside her (him?) appears to be Terence Stamp with a botched face lift, who asks me if I "know what time Coronation Street is coming on at." This overcast bunch taking a whack at this cat called sobriety has been run over, spun themselves down and out through the back lots of life and come out the other side, just barely, and just in time too.

A thinly skinned, almost skeletal man, ran the meeting. His thin skin spoke of depletion, starved of something, though I didn't know what until he sang his tune. He shared with the group that it was companionship he woke most mornings crying for: he had lost a wife to throat cancer just the month before, and one of his lungs some years before that. He missed them both.

The theme for the most part was Gratification: the tone seemed to go in that general direction, anyway. When my turn came 'round again, of course I'm the one complaining of being constantly irritated, joyless, maladjusted, unsatisfied, morose and sullen: down on myself, for missing some metaphoric boat. I chimed in saying that I really liked what one of the old timers said before the break. This sincere gentleman brimming with bright eyes and an inner calm, told a story of how he had reached an epiphany, and how he's now at peace. I said that I wanted what he had… I even meant it too. The people who are actually working a "program", who get honest, grateful and eventually lead simple but rewarding lives, no longer absorbed in the self-indulgent pleasure-packed palisades that gained them entrance to this club, no longer creating wreckage out there but actually helping others, all of that. They're the ones who did what they - at first - thought was impossible. They're the ones who won't end up dead before their time.

Oh, and then there was Pat. She had just come from seeing her horrifically sick husband in the hospital. Two months ago, the doctor told him if he drank he would die, that one more bout would just plain finish him off. So, now he needs assistance getting in and out of bed, also help in understanding why on earth he needs a toilet wheelchair, why his wife is visiting less and less, and why he can't go home 'quite yet'. In layman's terms, he's done.

It's the toughest thing when all that comes naturally is agitation, with everything and everyone in your path. Then again, someone once said, "Every passing minute is a chance to turn it all around." I heard that in some French movie, though by the time it gets edited and translated from one generation on down the line to another and makes its way around to English (and my mind), it falls sadly short. But it sure sounds splendid and hopeful. Once again I am lost in someone else's translation.

Oh, and it never fuckin' fails: if you catch a ride with one of the sober gang, they are invariably the ones who will be the last to leave. You tap your feet and endure half-baked chitty-chitty bullshit with strangers when all you want to do is get the hell out of there: not my idea of a good time, so I usually check out, and walk the few miles necessary for home plate. **KEEP CRAWLING BACK** they told me. Maybe it was Coming Back. Either way, I picked up a workbook on the way out, as later that night I would attempt to memorize (yet again) the Steps-a-12 of the program. As I walked home alone in the frigid glassy air, I struggled in and out of sobbing about all of this.

Only then it made perfect sense to me. It wasn't just how loud the sadness of drink and solitude was in these folks, or even how horrified with themselves and their disease they had become. I cried more for the joy their smiles told, their 'not having checked out from life yet'. By being around people who were kind, loving and eager to listen and assist - who'd changed for the better - this reawakened inside me something unidentifiable. Good for them, reaching out - trying something so totally foreign, knowing they would die otherwise - that's what I cried about. So glad that I went, loving souls, all of them. I should really go back sometime, pop in and see how they're doing. It couldn't hurt. What did hurt was how hard the damn gauntlet of AA male greeters shook my hand when I first walked into the church, my welcoming into the fold as a 'Newcomer', less than thirty days clean. I suppose it was to let me know how strong they were. That stuff can get weird. It can be like a scary Gap greeting team that won't take "no" for an answer.

It started to rain. Snow would be here soon. Shit, that was one of the reasons I hauled my ass out to California. I detest the kind of grey sludge that seeps in and takes over your pores. What is the point? If I was a Mountie draining maple syrup from a tree outside my igloo wearing snowshoes and being pulled by a dogsled, I'd still complain the sun wasn't hot enough to melt it all away.

The meeting stirred up past mishaps on the using trail.

The sleet started me thinking, about the time I apprehended a metal canister of milk and got nailed by The Dairy Police while living the life with M. in Vancouver? Made to sit in one of those high chairs, with a bib that the coffee barista bitch tied around me that said I'M SOME

THIEF! in big bubbly red letters, me unable to maintain my bearings, dumbfounded by my new disease and the response time of police who dealt with intolerant-lactotic-street-villains-with-cream-and-sugar-schemes. I felt like a misbehaving child with a sweet tooth, out way past curfew. I needed to steal as much as an 8-year-old needs Gillette razors. Just bored probably. Bored and optioning poorly, my behavior needing a good shave. My allowance from the lucky lady I was living with, one who had a genuine job, more than used up on this particular day; let's just say I was a 'Scavenger Donning Disproportionate Milky Needs, Disenfranchised by the City's Watery Atmosphere.' Is there such a word as Misbesheveled? How about Verbosiosity? Probably out of luck on that one too.

While sitting unpretty in my high chair, as the coffee cops conversed about what sort of ticket to write, sparkling visions poured into me, images that snapped my memory back to a time when I played the role of Second Banana, an accomplice in 'The East L.A Nescafe Capers'. I needed some sort of employment so I befriended this caffeine cad named Crispin on the downtown L.A. streets. I ended up carting him around to these food warehouses. His specialty was repeatedly deeking in and liberating eight or nine colossal instant coffee jars from the shelves at once. For these special outings, my slick pal devised a special leather wrap. Lorne Greene 'The Bonanza Nescafe Machine' would have got a kick out of all that. So, he sneaks back to the car, dumps the jars in my trunk (Crispin, not Lorne) and returns immediately to repeat the process a good three or four more times. When our task is done and my car is filled to the rim, it's off to see Winnie, a warty Spanish lady who reliably sets up shop daily at the corner of Wilshire and Nowhere to exchange our goods and services for pesos. Winnie sells her wares from a makeshift table: fresh fruits and the like, shrouded in some sort of gaudy-Catholic-loin-cloth-cloak to hide the many beverage urns that'd been lifted by us, the dyspeptic duo who dealt in seedy under-bellied caffeine crimes. To write about it is yes, taxing - to have lived it, even more so… deathly draining, no filters found, all that.

"Why am I doing this?" I ask. Because I can. No one's telling me I can't. It's free money, and I tell myself I'm in need, plus, all I was able to operate in and maneuver with was the Here, and the Now, oh yes, and the Again, there's room for mortal fibered coil in my trunk, so we're off, one more time, no fooling and a trunk full of neediness.

"We're going back for more? You think we should? Weren't we lucky to get away with what we did? Those guys have cameras, don't they?" He looked at me as if I was a novice crook.

"Quit worrying so much. Jesus, you worry like a muthafucka. I'm goin' in one mo' time, you just keep this shit box runnin', hear me? We're gonna fly down to Washington and Alvarado, I know some fiends down there with some good shit. Hey, where ya usually score, anyway?"

"Look, old boy, I really think you're pushing it…" I offered, but he had split to grab what remained of the coffee section. It was then I began to construct a mental list of the violations I would have to undergo in my particular cell block, dealing with enormous sweaty men named Gina or Rex, who will not find my antics funny. I should be awarded hugely on the Absurd and Resourceful Scale, if one so exists.

God, if only I could have enlisted this guy to sing tunes from some rotten Broadway show, now that would've been something. My fraudulent nature was getting a fair amount of airplay that summer, ripping through the A.M/F.M blistering sides of the city - my murky mise-en-scene soundtrack, and with the cigarette Mr. Crispy smoked out of his neck, his minor third melodic scale, and the unappealing costumes; all made for desperate performances so clearly lacking proper rehearsal. Crispin The Coffee Crook wasn't much on the conversation side either, but he let me sleep in his carpeted box a couple nights - and didn't freak out when I ordered imaginary room service - which was big of him... And it gives me another story to tell, right?

"Fuck, is coke supposed to do this when you shoot it? I have the freakiest ringing in my ears, and my heart is..."

"You just getting off, dog, you'll calm down. Can I drive?"

"I don't think that license you made in jail is going to do the trick, Mr. C. That thing is a joke. Hey, are those cops?" Two unmarked police cars arrived across from the parking lot, after we stopped in the desolate lot.

"No, they're just undies. Undercovers," Mr. C spoke confidently.

"Aren't they going to do anything?" I asked kind of worriedly.

"Sheeyit no, they've got bigger cats to go after besides a couple of two-bit hoods cooking up in a car not bothering nobody."

"Speak for yourself. I'm a Raider."

"Wha?"

"I mean, a writer. Sorry. One day I'm going to write a book about all this. Maybe you'll even be in it. A lot of this is so I can get a first-hand look at how things work around here, ya see, I'm going to write kind of a..."

"Good for you, now hand me the lighter."

"Certainly, my good man. Hey, do they still have high tea at that Four Seasons off of Doheny, do you know?"

"Huh?"

This started to get old. "Look, would you mind getting out, I should really get going."

"Okay man, drop me off at the food bank, would ya?"

Driving my white convertible down a central California city alley with yet another homeless junkie hanging out my passenger window yelling obscenities, it occurred to me that this was not the way God had intended me to be of love and service. To myself or to others.

Once back at mom's, before retiring, I shambled over to my writing desk and jotted down, from memory, some of the snippets conjuring the strict program guidelines. It had been a while since I studied that stuff but I remembered it as being important. The good book suggested very strongly that if I incorporated a good chunk of The Steps into my day-to-day life, it'd greatly assist in my quest for peace and making sure I had the working tools for my life toolbox for when it came time to creatively attempt to control sticky situations that are already out of my hands. Like Step 11 for instance, which went something like write down anyone you harmed today, or think you owe an apology to. It's all about keeping your side of the street clean.

There's a section called The Promises in the AA bible, The Big Book, which reads "...We will lose interest in selfish things and gain interest in our fellows; fear of economic insecurity will leave us, we will intuitively know how to handle situations which used to baffle us; we will be amazed before we are halfway through; we will comprehend the word serenity and we will know peace..." and so on. That would be amazing. I can identify, longing for such special effects. It wakes something up in me, I'd love to have those things. Trouble is, I always bail too early, long before I even make it a quarter ways into recovering from the hopeless state of body, mind and spirit, jetting out before the goddamn miracle happens. So, it's back to The Drawing Board. And I hate that fuckin' board.

The 12 Step Program, (from what I recall).

Step 1 - We admitted we weren't too powerful when it came to unmanageable life stuff.

Step 2 - Came to believe that a Power greater than ourselves was a really spooky concept and pretty tough to grasp, but mostly we should try to keep an open mind about it.

Step 3 - Made a decision to turn my will and my life over to something that wasn't me, once I found out what that was.

Step 4 - Made a list of a lot of really wild stuff that's gone on with me and made sure to keep it to myself.

Step 5 - Admitted to God, to ourselves and to another person the exact nature of what I thought should best be avoided.

Step 6 - Became entirely ready to promise myself to make it out to some of the meetings,
in my area.

Step 7 - Humbly asked the Powers That Be to remove my shortcomings, the very worst character traits that have weighed me down, that materialize no matter how much I pray for them to go away.

Step 8 - Made a list of persons that I didn't act so hot around, and became willing not to hang around them anymore or try to win back their friendships with pathetic apologetic half-assed emails or empty-gestured memos or cards. (I added the last part, knowing full well it wasn't in there.)

Step 9 - Made direct amends to people who I couldn't seem to dodge any longer, and prayed to a higher power, that if I ever did see them again, I would not bother them in a similar sinister manner, the one they'd become all too familiar with.

Step 10 - Continued to monitor the program, pop in at meetings, make lists, and try not to ever be wrong.

Step 11 - Sought through prayer and certain medications to improve my conscious contact with God as I understood Her, praying only for knowledge of Her will for me and the belief that everything will just kind of get better if I just keep writing about it.

Step 12 - Having had a spiritual awakening as a result of these numbered tasks, we tried to carry the message to other addicts, alcoholics and people that clearly need this sort of thing, and to practice these principles in all our relationships and affair

* * *

20. M a h l e r s   E v e

A Wee Reminder of that Long & Confusing Youth –

(A W R of that L & C Y)

Part I

There were Two little Bears who lived in a Wood

They lived in a Tree when the weather was hot

And one of them was Bad and the other was Good.

And one of them was Good, and the other was Not.

Good Bear learnt his Twice Times One -

Good Bear learnt his Twice Times Two -

But Bad Bear left all his buttons undone

ButBad Bears thingummies were worn right through.

A.A Milne

Now We Are Six

I t   i s   t h e   e v e n i n g   o f maudlin trickery. The Children of the Dark commence. An off-putting onslaught. Mephistopheles milks us for cookies. Dracula threatens a trick but ends up just pillaging the Smarties. Hockey Player Guy hovers around our open offering of sweet delights, reaches in and instantly we realize just how short we are on sundries, and well, everything.

Take take hate hate take hate take take hate hate hate.

"I c a n d o t h i s. If I say these words aloud, repeat slowly and add patience, they will empower me and assist in getting through the confusing and tougher times, up and over the hump. They don't.

The leaves rustling in our front yard announce the next contestant. One creepy kid advances up the steps alone, his elders wait in the shadows at the end of our sidewalk. He seems to be having some trouble. He? tripping over his spindly tail, or what? supposed to be a tail. I love this particular pauper because he's perplexed, muddled, knows not the precise procession this extraction-of-candy mania. Also, his face is on backwards - his mask, I mean - though my initial image of a disfigured juvenile recluse, with withered face, is funnier. If I remember from experience, they don't make those polyurethane things so kids can breathe too swiftly. It's all one big sweaty, ?ear-your-own-erratic-amplified-breathing-while-trying-desperately-to-see-out-of-any-orafice-that-points-forwardsort of night you're in for, if you choose to don so gruesome a gabardine. The bewildered youngster eventually drags his carcass up to the door and instead of introducing himself and stating his needs, he looks up, way, way up. I see his attention is held by an owl caught and screaming in the eaves trough (trying to eavesdrop?) laughing with frisky dementedness, the Child, not the Owl. He appears to be some kind of Bear Thing and while I? busy being scared he reaches down in his bag and offers me candy.

Racing back and forth, upstairs, downstairs, from front door up to the office computer, I'm scribbling impressions while I jog, as there's an inexhaustible amount of comedy material here for caffeine boy in Oompa-loompa-ville, barely able to keep track of all the queer occurrences. Which thing to extract? Right now, the thing is at our front door and wants recognition and attention paid to him and what must be a Unicef box. (That, or some sort of dangling orange catheter attached to his holster.)

"God, it? me Margaret...I mean Tim...don't let me be that thing one can end up being after listening to too much Joni Mitchell. I want an out."

I Trick-or-Treated well into my twenties, way past my due-date. I? disguise myself in a moth-eaten pillowcase and saunter through strangers' neighborhoods begging for bonbons. After a while it seemed easier to just sit in their cars until the startled lineage would have to take care of me. They gave away just about anything as long as I'd get out of their vehicle and off their property: Doritos, candy bars, cheques, vases, sport coats - whatever might have been lying around their foyer/vestibule area. See, that way, they came to me. Yet another event which has played a part in my accumulative low self-esteem; all I wanted was to be invited in to discuss the day's events and joke around in a family atmosphere. My true desires misconstrued through a pillow case and tell-tale footwear; my Balaclava-begging-for-bonbons-outfit and withdrawal symptoms, lacking social finesse. I'll admit, the costumes were pretty shoddy the last couple outings ('The Shoddiness of Costumes' - a chapter?) Regrettably, it became more about the gifts I could acquire, rather than the enjoyment, or the art of the sport. In defense of the unnerved families, I may have missed the mark a little on the exact date, could have been a day or two early or late, though I'm fairly sure it was damn close to October 31st. Pretty close.

Mother shuffles slowly out from the kitchen, leans in close so she can overhear me ask the kids. "So, what are you all supposed to be?" There's five, no six of them. A few pipe up with their monster status:

"Hobo.

"Goblin.

"Susan Sontag."

"Pinchquilly."

This last one, a sinister and clearly saddened child, who? costume was but 3 spice racks glued unforgivingly to him, two candy-apples hammered to the top of his head (antennae, I guess), a light bulb jetting out of his mouth and pants made from a mildewed Maytag box. An instant image of his poor mother, a cigarette dangling, who couldn't get herself together to assemble a proper costume, and besides, was using a calendar from the Eighties, thinking she could save money. Halloween's not for 6 days, Jackson, we'll get you something, lots of time left, don? you worry.

Before he gets sent out into the confusion, she instructs, Godspeed, kid. Tell ?m you're a Pinchquilly, it will sound *mystical.*

Actually, Ma, it sounds kinda gay, but no matter. One smartass interjects my way, and what are you supposed to be, dufus-boy?" *(tf#23)* I'm caught off guard, my mind pre-occupied with fish sticks flaming in the oven, trips to the front door, in-putting tales of woe upstairs, and what movies I had lined up on my evening schedule, ones I? pretend I? been thrown off the set of, and inevitably cut out of. ?...ummm, well, uh, look you - easy on the charm there, Casper, I think your parental orb is calling you, run along...you little...The best I could come up with costume-wise; a quickly invented a kind of Stephen Hawking sort of thing. In lieu of a real wheelchair, I?e got myself set up in a shopping cart with a dining chair in it, and have slunk into a terribly cheap blue suit and brown corduroys, and a snow mountain of dandruff, me only able to manoeuvre about the home doing unfortunate pop-a-wheelies, smashing into couches and ultimately the vestibule entranceway, catching a kid? tail up in the machinery of my shopping cart, my magical-makeshift monkey-mobile setting left precariously on Spin, and spooking youngsters away.

I empty the last of the potato chip dust from the bowl onto his head; they scurry from the porch and call me ingeniously wounding nick-names, foul-mouthed invectives they could only have overheard during bouts of parental arguments. Ungrateful pricks.

I just don't like where my head goes sometimes...

Next cinematic fanciful delight: two extremely young girls of a flirtatious persuasion have arrived at the door, well past 11:00 (isn't there a cut-off time?) with about a season? worth of Lancôme make-up plaster-and-Parissed on, making them look a fiery, capable 16. After attending to the slew of beggars throughout the evening, I? now relaxed in my role, and with Mom having repaired to the den to drink, it? time for some harmless mental jousting.

"Trick or Treat? they beam simultaneously, these shrewd serendipitous cuties.

"Yes, a treat, I'd like that, do you girls have any good drugs, or just what did you have in mind? I jokingly imagined or may have even said.

These dead ringers are dressed in some sort of cow-girl-rodeo-duo-get-up I think it? the holsters and the silver-cap-guns they tote, tauntingly (not to mention the horses parked at the sidewalk) but I? just thinking out loud here. The fact that there are two of them...girls, I mean, add to my, perhaps inappropriate, excitability: such short skirts, their Wonder-Woman and Power-Puff undies just peeking out...this is terrible, I think, stop it! But the isolation: it is so rare when others come to pay a visit. I? reminded of the episode where Fonzie finds true love with this bovine gal he thinks is as pure as a shiny John Deere snowplow, or something. Richie and the gang of misfit toys head down to the strip club where she works to prove to Mr. Winkler that, well, she ain?. This Tuscadero-ish hotsy-totsy (Potsie?) mama is unmasked, her identity revealed to be ?he Lone Stripper leaving a shattered Arthur Fonzarelli alone in a sea of mournful apathy. It was tough to watch. I didn't go to school for three days. Such high hopes dreadfully broken. Fonzie? too.

Now, I've never actually called on call girls - per se. Not really. I? just saying if I ever did, it might be a kind of exciting fantasy to have two of them, maybe, dressed up in a sort of costume. Semi-depressing thought: I? say, 60-something years of age living in a dilapidated Vancouver hotel, near Pain and Wastings, Ye Olde Drake maybe ?he Grand Sludge. And with my long awaited and much prized welfare-check, I put in a call to the Triple A Escort team, though, in my drunken haze, I can't tell if I've phoned for someone to tow my car, have telephoned an agent at CAA (Creative Artists Agency), inquired as to when the next AA meeting is or if some girls have been called to come over to rip me off. At any rate, none of the options are self-esteem boosters; I? on my way out and don? care much either way. Why this is happening in Vancouver is anybody? guess - I can? keep my dreamy sequences by starlight straight, this, just one of my head? hobbies. Whatever. As long as it? not hurting anyone.

But the two girls at the door

I swear one of them was flirting with me. We're selling ourselves in order to collect money for...like it mattered what the association was after that stunner. I offer an inviting smile in return, grinning 'til there's sweat jumping off my forehead. I realize their smiles are in fact painted on. One opens her bag, revealing a slew of mulch-flavored, rainbow colored condoms - the other one has a back-pack, brimming with suggestive chewy sex toys. Then I wake up.

All right, maybe there was more.

They push their way in, and I fall backwards and collapse into a basket of umbrellas and canes. They hoist me out while clubbing me with glowing Jedi titanium-dildo-wands. I? dragged away to the garage and tied to the aging Ikea patio furniture. I? squirted with scalding lemon juice from electric water guns and have burnt fish sticks crammed down my gullet and into me, preventing me from yelling for assistance. Mom unable to hear any of this wild, script-worthy interaction, as the volume of the Italian News is at an absurdly ear bleeding level in the den. She is also on fire. Seems she spilled some of her pre-dinner martini whilst trying to light one of those highly flammable pre-packaged fire log. This is going to cause a big mess and me, with all the running about (metaphorically hopefully?) It? tough even for me to tell anymore, with all these putting out fires and what-not, doing my best to attend to the endless tasks of the home.

My new girlfriends are already stuffing silverware, urns, booze, anything of value that the Duracell Bunnies won? get their fiendish paws on (you'll soon see) into their sacks.

"So long, momma's boy loser crud bum."

The foxy duo jump on their silver-spray-painted-ski-doos, revealing tattoos of super heroes and track marks on their thighs, and Jetta out into the night.

Halloween can sure be a gas, for some.

———————————

tf#23: Alas, I was ill-prepared in regards to a costume. I'd been building one in the garage but could not finish it in time using articles found on a workman's bench in the garage. I didn't get a chance to suit up for the big night with my pieced-together costume made entirely from popcorn, glue and pieces of The New Yorker Magazine, me, hanging together, for once.

* * *

21. Chipper Chomsky : A Dreamy Invitation

I arrived home from the meeting exhausted. Emotionally drained, the 'not sleeping well' thing has caught up to me. I dragged myself upstairs and didn't even bother changing and fell into an amazingly deep sleep. When this happens, I dream like nobody's business. The kinds of hallucinatory night journeys that when you wake up, you feel ripped off that there wasn't some kind of videotape machine to have recorded the whole thing.

So, I learned while reading in my neighbor's mail (he, a teacher at some university) that the well-respected author and famous commentator Noam Chomsky was being honored at an Invitation Only dinner. I abscond with the invite and prepare for the upcoming evening by renting a tux and billing it to a company I once thought of working for.

I am in awe tonight, in discovering myself amongst the city's best left-winged, left-handed, all-too-often left-out leading intelligentsia: authors, scientists, columnists, bike-less cyclists, Islamic fundamentalists - as opposed to "Icelandic something or other-ists" (I later apologized to the senator's wife for the faulty misstep). I finally work up the courage to sidle up to the Noamster, me with my gross sense of self-absorption and radiant glowing charm, the 'Raider', allowing myself to believe I'm in the same literary league as the now defenseless Mr. Chomsky.

"...Yes, in North Carolina, I was also suspicious of that questionable Ferret-Aid thing - a celebrity auction in support of abandoned ferrets? It made little sense to me, aristocrat folks

wearing ferrets around their necks, many on leashes. Come to think of it, I'm pretty certain it was an artsy cult of some kind (a Ferret Retrospective?) And they never did pay me. Has that ever happened to you, N.C?"

The auction after the reading was weird too, taking place in a dungeon where none of the Tourette-Syndrome-filled-audience spoke, but found a way to constantly interrupt the evening's proceedings by making nonsensical jittery moves with lots of eyebrow action, multiple ticks and such, while repeatedly needing to have the definition of Absentee Bidding explained to them. The auctioneer, disguised as a chit-chattery Count Chocula *(tf#24)* - a non-conformist I guess - seemed to be in charge, conducting all of the alienating mish-mash; why he went in and out of slinging a completely and obviously made-up Africanize accent was, I believed, used only to show off.

Weirder still, they were offering up ferrets of all kinds, dead and alive. "There must be better gigs," I remember thinking, I should be paid for this kind of misery. Yes, there's an idea: to be reimbursed for venturing out from Mom's abode for the night. (Now I recall why I don't go out more often). A payment of sorts, yes, a stipend even, I like the term 'recompense', because it feels kind of French, god, even some nuts to squirrel away for a rainy day at least. And, when I asked how to go about bidding on these rare items listed in the program, - pages of Henry Miller's handwritten and typed-out notes for a novel he never ended up writing and a trumpet that Glenn Miller apparently looked at through Melvin's music store window in Greenwich Village from the 1940's - the count swung his cape around himself and slunk out of the room on a kind of skateboard thing.

My haircut for instance, schlocky and wistful, from Bottom Cuts or Tragic Cutz - my locks deconstructed by a blind co-op student. Coming to the foreground, I can't help but catch a glimpse of this debauchery in a carnival-like hall of mirrors on my way to the bathroom. Me, thinking myself rather sporty, giving off quite a young dashing Gatsby-ish air; tweed jacket, suede patches on the elbows, tied gallantly around my neck. Yet in actuality, according to the glass speaking back, revealed is a wretched cyclopean, Down-syndromish Sal Mineo. All in all, it's helpful I'm not down on myself. I catch myself at risk of having a good time. Perhaps there would be situations forthcoming on my social calendar which would not involve sauntering off to the lavatory... this would not be one of those times. After doing a few lines, alone (Noam having refused my offer), I move on to discuss semantics and edible stuffed cheese-dolls with Mr. Chomsky - who I'm "pleased as punch" to meet, knowing full well this is a dumb thing to say. I'm smashed past the point of quality vision and my knees are somehow ridiculously feeble and made of lime Jell-O. I still attempt respectable chitchat. Noam and I speak warmly of Darwin's Un-natural Preventative Dentistry Theories and some European guy's ideology regarding *The Natural Progression of Numbers* (Duh: 1, 2, 3, 4). Our repartee is moving along brilliantly, Chomsky clearly impressed by my skill in balancing four cocktail glasses between my legs while holding the guests' coats, and voicing many years of saved up ideas from my mental vault.

That's where it all goes sadly foggy, for the life of me I don't know what I was trying to get across.

Much to my dismay, I was coming off as being a non-sequitur and slappy stupid. (Not the plan.) Must redeem myself: I'm losing him. Regrouping quickly, I offer, "I can't say enough about your last literary outing, 'Making-up Consonants,' and that 'Transformational Grammar' thing is quite something, really; such fashionable pessimism, it's gonna be a trend, man." *(tf#25)* He stares at me, amazed (the whirring and clicking now dreadfully loud on my hand-held tape-recorder), and now clearly astonished, just how I managed to gain entry into such an intimate and high-brow function. I felt badly underappreciated. Everything by this point an embarrassment; I'm somehow a picked upon participant once again, seeing all with scrutinizing, sarcastic, whimsied downtroddeness through Bolivian eyes and multiple martinis. All this, again, falling a tad short of the mark, and when asked to present a copy of my personal invitation, I can produce only a book of matches with my name on it, previously scrawled in purple crayon, and misspelled. The matches, alas, were not mine, but from another man's coat pocket I'd been rifling through for my notes - and a positively bitchin' minestrone soup recipe I'd heard he circulated with a select number of guests - all this, weakening my alibi during subsequent questioning, all hellishly unnerving. It was at this point I caught a whiff of some quickly spoiling fishy pâté concern in Chomsky's clenched fist, the poor imbecilic sod, unfortunately, the recipient of my unwelcome regurgitative projectile baggage.

No surprise, I was asked to leave the gathering, despite last ditch Herculean attempts at balloon animal tricks and silent film star impressions.

Must retreat to Mom's house, where I am a 'Writer in Residence' thank you very much. Need to regroup. That night really knocked me out. Screw Chomsky anyway.

———————————————

tf#24: whose teeth were loosened by his much talked about mass ingestion of champagne and sweets. He now, needless to say, is not high and mighty, but lowly and molarless, a crazed and animated auctioneer.

tf#25: I gave it another shot; "Making Up: Couples in Consequence," believing Noam was responsible for penning this important work. I heard of this self-help book, assisting couples in the sorely needed department of respectful actions, conflicts and such. Turns out, his famous and original Nobel Prize winning book is called "Manufacturing Consent"...though, in picking up a copy I didn't find it to be any great read. Also, no pictures. There were some graphs, charts of pies and cakes and such, but definitely no pictures. Arguably just about the goofiest book I've ever borrowed and not returned.

* * *

22. The Terrifying Brown Sugar Incident

I thought that I beat her up this morning, time-wise, this morning, but she's already storming about, already yelling again from the bottom of her lungs, trying to reach the top of her voice. She screams from somewhere inside. Her concern: The brown sugar that's decided to poke its tired mildewy eyes from its punctured and broken home. Over time, it morphed into a kind of fungi pet, another item for the time capsule. She's committed to spending the $3.29 for a new bag, insists that I am a "Wasteful, wasteful whipper-snapper," but in an entirely charming 'Little House on the Prairie kind of way.' It's a show of sorts.

"I'd like to take you to Russia," she says, and I'm intrigued. This is new. I'll wager a guess it's to introduce me to the less-than-adequate food provisional situation, but can't help my thoughts from turning to greener pastures, say, a new breed of hotsy-totsy-hooker with arabesque tongues and teddy bear coats.

"And just how would we get there, Mom? You'd never pay that kind of exorbitant air fare."

Why must this downtrodden sweetener, this candied conundrum, take us so far into the arena of friction?

Before I know it we're arguing about Trotsky, food lines and tampons hand-sewn by The Amish, The Great Depression - MY great depression, other feeble sweeteners and so on and so forth. In the end, we ill-equipped fighters will acknowledge this to be a bout in far-fetched madness and really about nothing that's possible to name. We will go to our corners, further flattened and wearied, to no avail and no closure.

I hate the guilt, my body and heart reacting with irritation to her banging things around, other markers of her frustration and anger. And I'm tired of waging war inside me. I'm powerless in these battles... having to just take it, as a sort of payment for my wrongdoings, it's my punishment. She's convinced Ron dying was hers. What a pair we are. I'm brought in, called out to the field from too many years in the Ron-guarded-penalty box, to share in the immense grief she needs me to feel. I'd just prefer pass, not play at all, but there are things hovering, looming and lurking, right above my head: stupid flying personified metaphors with wings, this hunger. I wonder how they'd taste.

It's not so bad, b u t i t' s b a d .

We see things very differently - which is neither good nor bad, it just is. The real question, "Can we survive in the same house without setting each other on fire?" I'm guessing time will tell, but as I repair to the den to scribble down these impressions, equipped with matches and a ten gallon jerry can full of jet fuel, at this moment in particular, it's looking kind of bleak.

I'm guessing she wants to instill something in me, that maybe once was, or always has been, but that never poked its head out from the backseat often enough to arrive at anything.

Maybe she's fearful at the thought of 'not having', terrified of some dreaded non-existent envelope that won't ever show up at the door... the one that says, "You owe the government all of your money, and must move to an old folk's home. That's it for you, decrepit one. Pack it in sister, you're done here. Good luck out there in the Cold War."

I've never worked for the post office and I can't say if a letter like that exists, but I have run quite a marathon since I was 16 and may carry a message of some sort that one of us will have to die for. It's a skewed game of queer puzzles with ever-changing rules, and I can't imagine anyone getting any further ahead playing the Manipulation and Guilt Card. Though if played swiftly, properly, I'm told a croquet-set made of marble and a bonus 50 points are up for grabs.

She acts as if we're collecting welfare but doesn't really know what a struggle is. I shouldn't say that, as it reeks of clear-cut self-absorbed self-ism. Of course she knows what a struggle is, but neither of us can empathize with the other's plight, and in so many ways, we're just not cut from the same J-cloth: we don't grasp things (or wipe things up) with similar panache. We are living in the $20,000 Parallelogram, a 24-hour-a-day contest where most days I can't remember where I left the score sheet or even what the prizes are. All accumulated cash and credit, I'll inevitably lose, and worse, I'll forget to dress the part and disguise myself as an answer in the form of a question. It'll all come tumbling down. Nothing seems to fit, nothing can be repaired and so few things rhyme for me, and the crosswords keep getting harder. I can't find anything to fit properly (the monster-sized-sweatshirts-with-question-marks only seem to suit better planned-out dream sequences). I'm hoping there's an Elimination Dance Round to be rid of all this fluffernuttin.

She dictates to me what she wants done and when, not unlike a spoiled child that doesn't care how it happens or from whence it came, just so ultimately, she gets what it is she wants.

"Take the groceries from the car. Why are you putting that there? Be careful, I told you that five times...watch it... you're so messy...you'll never learn..." and there she blows, and I'll tell no friends, and they'll tell no friends and so on, and so on, and I'll be repeating this to myself, over and over again, trying to find out just why I'm here at all.

If I'm able to go numb in this round without responding in a harsh tone or manner, then I'm good for 10 points. But I'm also in trouble for polishing off the Triscuits, making me a "dirty, dirty disrespectful retard." So, once more, I'm back to zilch, nil, ground-peppered zero. The pixel board now boasting;

thiNgs: 83,209 - TIm my:

pOinT-LeSs.

When my music is on too loud, she yells at the top of her lungs, which oddly doesn't make much of a sound, but the vibrations still ricochet through my body. She feels cut off. What she can't see is that I'm just writing, listening to music, trying to get something done, to muster up some good old-fashioned inspiration from a dry well, and without hurting anyone.

Who's right? Who cares? It's fucking uncomfortable.

The times I was dead on the street and she wasn't aware or nearby, those stand alone, way outside the shared family lexis or memorabilia. The times I couldn't make things easier for her in the home when she brought in the stepfather-ish person, so soon after Dad died: Was I supposed to follow orders, do whatever it took because that's what she needed? I gave it a shot and it became catastrophically scary. It's all up and down, opaque and spinning out of control and is draining both of us. There must be a better way. No one should have to spend their days and nights playing SORRY. (Was that Parker Brothers or Hasbro?) No matter, no one ever played it for long, as a rapidly gaining-in-popularity little Rondo a la Turk titled

Lite Bright swept the nation, soon giving way, of course, to Electronic Battleship.

Me, well I ended up just moving out, left to my own special skill set for seeking out creative ways to get lit up. Good for me. The Game of Life (Mattel?) can be a banquet. A banquet best attended with a partner, preferably one around the same height, for many reasons. Let's take the most obvious: whilst standing in line for the banquet, you can hold hands, and four hands are better than two for the absconding of food, stuffed in her purse for later hungrier hours. Being a team can be good and just, and tag-team events make for silly pictures at company picnics. I am without a company and lacking company in the couple capacity. Christ.

Tired of trying. Tired of involving myself, and it all smacks of trying. I'm clearly getting close to done here, finished, forced to again work with what's been doled out: with what's been hanging on the line for too many nights and just plain getting old and unfresh. I'm barely able to deal by staying indoors: not willing to risk the outside and its illicit harsh arrows: is there a place made so you can stay in from even staying in from the day and night? Talk about regressing and returning to the womb. This is my mother's home. Not mine. Mother's. Who's kidding who? I am a freak. A freak who relates to no one but himself and maybe some dead writers, and even they are disconnecting their phones.

I try to call my uncle's phone number. My mistake. I dial my grandmother's old telephone number. Is it 489-6586 or 489-5366? Not really knowing anymore how to connect. She doesn't need a phone number anymore because she's dead and probably doesn't even run into any of the writers I like.

23. Did they not invite you back?

S huffling through coffee-colored snow, retreating from the retirement home across the way, my friend who tagged along with me for the afternoon mumbled she couldn't watch or listen to any of that morbid, old age home Vaseline and pudding cup Christmas drizzle without weeping. I however, cannot partake in any of that without drinking.

I'd had visions that this occasion could be an act of faith, an attempt to involve myself in something partially unselfish. I thought it would be admirable to volunteer to play some tunes for the elderly, spread some cheer, though not likely as my repertoire is riddled mostly with mopey, morose gloomy-Gus melodies. Arriving home from Bellwood's Senior's Residence, a doomed sanctuary, the offering from the mother character could have easily been, "I'm sure you did fine", or "I bet they appreciated it."

But no.

I hear, "You mean they aren't going to invite you back?" A long silence - hoping a simple "No" might put an end to it. Why couldn't she have commented on my charitable offer? Why couldn't the focus be on my being of love and service: no payment (or jacket) required, filling in for some Sam who regularly plays, my visit being a one-off Christmas-time party thing, though I was not asked back, or to ever return, having been told to "not play it again, Sam."

The supervisor, some head-cheese nurse, also recommended that I learn some upbeat, sing-a-long tunes for the grey-toothed, frail and candy-floss-haired residents, but I didn't want to do that. I play my own compositions: minor nines and suspended chord clusters, a brand of thick, nostalgic narcissism, intensely passionate and moody prose magnified and spoken through keys and pedals. It's death personified for me to have to scrape up "Yesterday", "Piano Man" or "Mr. Bojangles", or that "Les Mis" song, shit…because I've played them all a thousand times. Alright, maybe I could cringe through "Send in the Clowns" or "Somewhere" from "West Side Story", even manage to unveil the evil elevator muzak of *Memory* from *Cats*. But, only because you're ancient and in a last stop crematorium and I want to feel good about myself when laying my head down on the pillow tonight, tucked away nicely in a room that doesn't smell of *Vicks Vapo Rub* and regret, knowing I did something that was tough for me to get through. But, I'd have to go to the washroom immediately after and do my back stage bulimia imitation as I feel I'd be awakening the merry-go-round of monkey-like-cholera, the carnival freak-show, the wind-her-up-wind-bag play-for-peanut kind of schlock I pride myself on not partaking in, so you go agead choose the program.

Now Mom's on the phone with the retirement home supervisor making excuses for my less than sparkly interactions, even before the lady can get a word out thanking me for at very least, my effort. Mom steps up and interrupts with, "Certainly I apologize for him. I'm sure he didn't mean anything by it."

"But I wasn't calling to…"

"A shave and a haircut yes, yes he does. I tell him all the time, but he doesn't hear me, such an embarrassment. Again, I apologize."

Immediately following my stellar show (magic tricks with flaming whiskey bottles, seniors' underpants and soiled rabbit costumes), having now returned home, slouching in Mom's dis-orderly kitchen, everything in its place, something strange occurs; it feels as though I can actually *feel* the sullied scene at the retirement palace just a few doors away. I imagine nurses and staff fielding questions from the mostly embalmed stony-faced palsied-bunch, spectators who just a half hour ago witnessed the musical massacre that sent many over the edge and others soiling their Depends undergarment, all egging each other on, a black energy I must have left behind that gets them thinking:

"I'm not paying you guys to be punished!"

"How might one go about making a proper noose from a shower curtain?"

"How's about a formaldehyde and rum cooler?" and

"Is there a sign-up sheet to be taken up there," pointing to heaven.

I should mosey on over there in a few days and give it another shot.

———————

I feel as though I am the mediocre, less dashing, less remarkable, less talented and less Fabulous Baker Boy brother. Yes, much like him. Them. I don't feel a need to change my attitude in that boyish department - the fitting rooms, left unattended far too long, now shabby, musty, distasteful beyond recognition. That part of me is me. Misunderstood. Notorious. Black of spirit. Brooding. Munchy. Misanthropic. Irresponsible, often unaccountable. Fearful. Talented. Leary and all right, a little toxic. An epidemic unto myself? Maybe. Bruised. Misdirected. Unpredictable. Unclear. Scattered. Unfathomably spontaneous. Rightfully fearful and stupidly fearless. Bereft of subtleties. Terminally Lonely. Terminally unique? Troubled. At the end of the day, when I'm all sad and done, after a gross and overly magnified microscopic examining, coupled with an unhealthy cyclical and cynical courtship with myself, I still end up with me,

　and so much of the time

　　my best is still not good enough.

I need involvement in this Charlie Brown Universe, *(tf#26)* but look at what happened to him. And just what type of production am I supposed to chuck myself into anyway? Most of the times I've applied and made the commitment, I end up wishing I hadn't gotten out of bed in the first place. Aren't we all just much taller, hairier versions of the babies we once were, just with an unexpected amount of shoe-laces to tie and forms to fill out? Even now, still concerned with just who's going to baby-sit me and what kind of pretty she'll be.

Still can't get any kind of sleep pattern happening here, so I end up going over everything I've ever done, beating myself mentally into submission. I scream into my pillow like I'm suffocating underwater. This is the best way I've found to say my prayers. I can't help the persistent, embarrassing and regretful, actions based on ego, the grizzly after-maths, the gut-wrenching disharmony, my unsuccessful Geographic's and who, if anyone, was along for the ride, where they might be today. The drug dreams most nights kick me hard, feeling more real than when the action went down. And I still can't control how I'm getting cut up.

Those w o r s e a n d w e i r d e r times, take for example when my partner in crime, Jenny, peace be with her, had to revive me from the ultimate sleep, as she says I was way, way, past blue. She was frantic over all that. I couldn't have been c a l m e r .

After awaking from the dead she shared with me how I had just gone out…high herself, and rather quite involved, fidgeting about the apartment looking for projects, how she came into the room…how minutes had gone by and I was just lying there, blitzed, past my prime, sprawled-out and grinning. Can't imagine what I must've looked like.

Going out and scoring for us excited me… made my day, if you want to know the truth. What's crazier? Thinking that I could have accomplished anything during those months. Thinking I could have meant anything to anybody that cared, past just praying for me… Telling everybody I knew just what I was doing, my setting set precariously on self-destruct-mode. Even I didn't want to be around me, but you can't see that kind of stuff when you're glossed over, shiny and self-important. Still, I have those rationales and justifiers and they tell me it wasn't *that* bad. But it got bad. Rationalizations and Justifications, a lot like masturbation…screwing yourself every time, just as lonely and obscene.

––––––––––––

Getting overwhelmed is the force at hand, endless missions; too much to read, to research, there's apologies to make, letters to write and send, a life rife with excuses I don't want to own. There are pictures to sift through, maybe some mixed tapes to mail out, old girlfriends to look up that maybe still give a damn. So much wasted love, who's to say if there's any healthy light left, any sort of blazing effulgence still simmering on the back burner, a luminescence that could amaze us all and take the shape of a positive glow. In all this, I've taken myself sorely for granted, am losing all the best places that were once inside me, finding it tougher and tougher to tap into anything. I, at one time, could count on such things, but now, in the jarring bell, I'm unable to get any of these damn things to chime the way I'd like.

"You are the most wasteful boy."

She's been through her own convoluted hell which I probably couldn't understand if I tried, but as she is my only mother, I must love her regardless; so whatever she wants, however twisted, however profoundly bizarre, we'll all try and comply. What works for her, and the world she's made - this, revolting confusion that now stares at her daily. Why not just take part in the attempt to make her happy?

Oh yeah, now I remember: because it's never right and it's never endless.

And who cares anyway? Sometimes there's nothing to do except put pen to paper, fingers to the keys. Then *Go!*

Charlie Brown #26

* * *

24. Hunting for Home

Mom's castle of crazy concerns, and this weirdly woven jigsaw nonsense of a rekindled relationship, that's burning us daily, is beginning to drive me positively batty. And worse, it's having an even more torturous effect on my nature. I absolutely must find my own space and get self-sufficient. But this positive thought-canvas I paint gets washed over all too quickly with disappointing and dreadful cringe-worthy experiences that lead me to set the classified section on fire.

I consider living out on the Toronto island but images pour into my unarmed mind - all the canoeing back and forth, frozen and exhausted, with pelts - somehow hunting is involved, maybe trapping. I'd be frosted, tapped and taxed beyond healthy living, a bizarre bracket, again dislodged, frantic and frostbitten. So I'll back away from that one, knowing 95 percent of the inhabitants are going to be freak-nuts anyway: fastidious, weirdo vegans, religious shaman-esque fanatics, swami seniors with out-the-window backyard gripes, left-wing, *The West Wing* rerun watchers, wrought and uncentered, defenseless pointy political people, skating around the infected cesspool that is one of our less than Great Lakes, emotionally frozen - the lake and these island dwellers, lost denizens who couldn't contend, compete or make their mark in the open wound of city life. Who can blame them?

I can.

Again, there's still that soiled soliloquy somewhere that calls out, "Well, it just might work out. Maybe this time will be okay?"

But all that having to hunt for food, not to mention the unwanted ungainly children giggling behind my back, as I shuffle down picturesque streets between miniature cottage-like houses, dropping supplies. All this cinches the deal to stay on dry land.

"There's the guy from the city that got chased by a cub." No attempt to cover up their taunting.

"It was a bear, a real bear and it was hungry," I'd yell back to the earthy yogurt-ingesting still cackling tricksters. No dice, pal. Not this time. I'm smarter than the average cub. Yes, I am.

Some stuff is just trouble brewing, waiting to happen, to me. Just as there are girls who are bad medicine, there are just as many less intimate recipes for disaster. These stuck out as the most confusing. Here's what I mean:

'8th to share home, environment friendly' (?!)

'Cheezy'. No, hold on - that's 'Cheery'.

'Basement-bachelor at Gerard and UPPER beaches - 'Upper' meaning nowhere near.

'Share house with gay gentleman, must like pets.' Uh-oh. That's tragedy time. Also, must like an outstanding miasma of fur on your stuff, you can bet.

Nothing ever good has come from that. Any of it. When I hear 'with pets' I'm thinking the cat and dog variety, not condors (condos?) or anything that slithers or is equipped with spontaneous flight, you know - aero-dynamics. Things that flap, or have maintenance fees, don't breed success. More often than not, what they breed is just more of that same spooky mucus albeit with more pungent odor and fowl taste. I've been some pretty strange things, I mean, I've *seen* some pretty strange things. Let's move out... I mean, move on. No, move out too, as I most definitely need a proper place to lay this head assigned to me.

I've ascertained that in the great hunt for a home, 'Funky' means little or no plumbing; 'Plus Utilities' can mean 'The bathroom key is on the wall at Texaco-town just a hop, skip, plus something best stepped over down the alley'. 'Cozy' could quite possibly mean, 'Furry on-site Frankenstein-fella-called-Carl', who hails from the Old Country - which gets weirder, no one ever really finding out where this 'Old Country' is, but let's jostle forth. Carl, or any other nameless faceless lord of land, may literally have no face - just bandages, while brandishing a bad attitude (and a rubbery prop sword) due to some shabbily sewn-up surgery and may not have a real name that sticks, just a number safety-pinned to his shirt, *and* there's always, always the off-chance of him launching into stories, and dance numbers, when guests with breasts come to town. You may have to contend with attentive ears pressed against the French doors leading into your private domicile, but you also are forced in to creative mode, learning to make-up games such as **CATCH CARL**, which ends up being a sport any age can play, a solitary venture, just one player, you, dodging about, as you learn that he 'comes with the house': a live-in, unwanted snag slag appendage to your new home: it's in the contract slash snafu agreement. Sucker.

Note to self: read the fine print next time or take a course in Contracts. Rent Paper Chase, with Timothy Bottoms and that Bionic lady, at very least.

Also, you've gambled away any other money won - none left for further bonus round involvement, as last time you "Let it ride!" (you big-shot high-rolling ignoramus), when you brought home the criminally attractive, alluring first date to get all kissy-kissy with, keeping your fingers and toes crossed that Carl wouldn't be in your room going through your belongings, looking for his gum (gums, gun?). "A lame excuse," is your later retort in court. It's a big loss, being back to zero and homeless. You, wearing the sweatshirt with a big old O on it, the whole donut hole.

Pixel board reads: People, Places, Things :

2,348 - You : m i n u s   m u c h

The last one on the list, an appointment with what sounds (over the phone anyway) to be a sweet gal with a sense of humor. She has a room for rent in a charming old house in a quiet area called Henry Street. This familiar avenue has enchantment and could have promise, but I know going in, she'll be looking at me as 'the other' - the outsider to share the flat, the one who might fill the position of The Third Man theme. My own worrisome motif? I'm going to scare her off, I can't keep anything contained or quiet, can't lay down when those thoughts come-a-knocking.

I arrive in my skin tight black skeleton t-shirt, bow tie inner tube around my waist, flippers *(tf#27)* and a quarter cup of High Karate Men's cologne that I spilled an hour earlier, while nervously dressing, all in the guise of wanting to make a good impression. I'm also carrying a parakeet in a mammoth-sized brass cage that I picked up along the way but didn't have time to drop home. I think she thought I'd be a pretty interesting addition to the nuclear holocaust family situation she's got going here. I start to get excited at the thought of moving out of mom's.

She's showing me around, things are moving along nicely, until we get to a moldy cobweb-encrusted basement, which looks as if no one's been in years. I can't help but wonder how fun it would be to play Phone Tag. Not played very often due to injuries, law suits and just plain hard-to-find proper apparatus and willing participants. A simple outing of pummeling, of pounding new house-mates with clunky, black rotary dial-phones. The rules being, you invite maybe three or four good friends over, go down to a very unfinished-basement, turn off all the lights and just go for it. Sort of an initiation to a new home, 'breaking someone in', so to speak. Whoever is left standing and least bloody wins.

She looks shocked, asks if I'm nuts and queries, "Uh, is there anyone I could speak with?" (I'm guessing reference-wise). Not being able to come up with a quick retort, I decide to cut my losses and strike the set, careful not to make any sudden moves. I backed my way out and up the stairs making loud bumble bee noises, hoping to take the attention away from my less-than-social or *proper* manners. I grabbed my top hat, picked around in her fridge for some tasty leftovers then put my flippers back on and and ran off.

Strangely, I did not hear from her. I'm guessing a lot of people came to see the place. Also, I was too embarrassed to return to the scene of the crime to pick up my walking cane or the loud tethered bird cage I had left in the house.

---

tf#27: I forgot that I'd burned a good deal of my shoes, shorts and tops in a ritual fire out in mom's backyard, wanting to begin fresh, everything new, and hadn't had a chance to go sifting and sorting at the Goodwill fill-a-bag-for-a-buck shopping excursion, so my remaining duds were from a drawer marked AQUATIC/PARTY.

* * *

25. Strike Two

"A c a t i s g o i n g to be too much trouble. I'm not ready. There's the fur and it'll be climbing up the curtains. Then what if I have to go away, who'll feed it? No, it's just too soon." Mom is telling her tale of feline woe to the terribly interested retarded boy who wasn't expecting this, and was only stopping by the house in hopes of siphoning gas from mom's automobile for his motorized shopping cart/toilet wheelchair/leaf blower thingy. This weird scene, another one - with everyone's complex motivations. I'm watching them through the kitchen window shaking my head then begin to drift a little while entertaining thoughts of new projects I could begin, wondering if I sincerely have what it takes to commit myself to the hobby of ingesting several casseroles in one sitting until I get dizzy enough so that... The phone rings, diverting me from yet another wholesome endeavor. We've been getting a ton of these crank calls lately, hang-ups and such. The voice asks for The Man of The House, which creeps me out a little. Mom and Ron, in recent years, have been dependable donors to various funds and, "T'is the season to hit them up again." I however am not as thrown by this sad telemarketing goonbag. I'm straightforward, and make no bones in reassuring these life-interrupters that their nagging and pestering, their putting pressure put on old Ron played a heavy hand in killing him. I re-enact the death scene, his dying words on the operating table, "Damn Cancer...Humane Society... hounding, bleeding us dry... they're killing me!" but I make no bones about reassuring them. "Oh don't worry, we're not suing." The callers go instantly silent and retreat while I turn to more sympathetic thoughts. Just as I'm thinking about how anyone must be suicidal to spend their working hours in a brown office cubical poised as a telemarketer, clock-watching, and that they're the type that care passionately about nothing, another call comes in. This time it's not one of the leeches. It's some unknown parasite, and I'm the host receiver.

"Hello. Hello there. Is that you, old man?"

I caught enough to tell that it's that same guy who called a couple days before.

"Uh, hello?" I said.

"There you are! I can hardly make you out. I guess all the cold weather must do something to those telephone lines, huh? How do you folks survive up there in those igloos?"

While enjoying his own laughter, I had a few seconds to digest how deftly engaging this fellow was not, who I seem to have been so chummy with in California.

"It's not so bad, really. The leaves are just starting to…uh, what can I do for you?"

"Well, you see it's like this, old boy: seems the girl's parents want to tie you into all this, something about making an example of you, says they'll burn in hell before you're walking around free. Seems that Jen was their only daughter so…"

"Jennifer?"

"Who in God's name do you think I'm talking about, scout? There's a couple witnesses, but I'm sure that…"

"Witnesses?"

"Some angry hotel desk clerk, the guy saw you peel out of the parking lot, and it didn't help that you skipped out on the bill."

God, no. No no no. Please. This isn't happening.

"Look, I'm behind you. Jen, she was some live wire, that's for sure. She was headed down anyway, you were just caught in the wrong spot. It's a good thing I know the detective and all, I mean..."

A sickness started to hit me all over.

I tuned out whatever jabberwockying followed. It was Brandon on the other end, this freelance hack journalist, an overpaid fixer-upper of high-budget production disasters. I'd hung out with him a few times. I was the one who introduced him to Jenny, actually, and had regretted it immediately after, as I really didn't like him much. We'd gone to some NA meetings together, he more so to try to "interview" the more attractive fairer sex of the group. Guess he didn't understand the term "Anonymous." This guy was derailed and optioning poorly, trying to get back his script-doctoring career, nailed for taking payola from some mob guy he'd promised not to write something about. He ended up blowing his cover, so the Al Capone guy and his editor both had words for him. He wasn't terribly bright or even a very good liar. He'd always show up at meetings saying he had more clean time than he really had. I know that for sure, because just the night before, he'd been running around with me at that trendy nightspot, The Rooftop Sky Bar at Mondrian hotel, where people of that glitzy glamma-ramma-wanna-be ilk tended to gather. He lived in this shack off of Silver Lake, where he said I could park myself while I got my head straight. All I'd have to do was take a look at his schlocky-cheese-ball scripts, which if I recall, had next to no redeeming qualities, this was our deal. Oh yeah, and the ghost writing. He thought that was an excellent plan. On account of his ADD he could never finish anything, so between that and his dyslexia, he was stranded as far as ever being able to complete anything. A real pain in the ass. I pictured writing all these super-hot scripts for him and then getting nailed in some scandal a la Woody Allen's *The Front*. *(tf#28)* Remember. He did all that writing for those blacklisted guys; talk about a recipe for disaster. Brandon undoubtedly would have eaten up the publicity. Before getting anything off the ground, that's about the time my mental real estate began crumbling, the falling off the earth thing, so...I plugged back in to the present.

"Who are you again, anyway?"

"Don't be funny. Her parents want manslaughter. What are you going to do? Oh yeah, and I've seen your movie."

Movie? What movie?

"I'm surprised her folks aren't up there right now. Thought I should warn you, all that. They haven't contacted you, huh?"

"What? No. No, they haven't. You saw a tape of us? How did, I mean, what kind of tape are we on... How the hell did you..."

"You guys are in this hotel room dancing around. Look, I hope you've been getting a lot of your highly stylized near misses and imposter scenarios down somewhere, some of those tales would really sell. In fact, it wouldn't hurt if you started thinking of camera angles from here on in." The connection was cut.

That was an edgy, cold, unanticipated call. My friend is now a statistic. I gazed through the kitchen window again; mom and the mentally-handicapped scooter boy were still trading quips.

So there it was. Those dreams, weren't dreams at all. Those eerie notions and wild surreal images of my beautiful friend Jennifer in the bathtub, so still, another energy I felt blessed to know... So ageless, now lifeless, something else indefinable that I could never go back to, and all irreplaceable.

I thought of just where that book was now with the poem I wrote. It certainly wasn't going to make it to her now - that package I so gingerly wrapped and mailed out to her days before. I thought of it sitting, forgotten, at the bottom of a bin in some desolate post office terminal and an awful feeling washed over me that made me hate everything.

My home, this domicile, I've been trying to settle into, was about to be ambushed by tormented parents. Looking for what? Retribution? Revenge? Answers? I had none to offer. Bizarre how any of this happened at all. Actually, that got me thinking. What was I so afraid of? I mean, I didn't kill her. Christ, she was my friend. I thought of which part of this was my fault, and how I'd never ever see Jennifer alive again. And why Brandon was even on this story, I wasn't sure.

I'd met her father once when he dropped her off to go to a 12 Step meeting, her license revoked due to the knocking over of signposts on her parents' cul-de-sac. People named her Flipper, stories of her remarkable feats out there on the road were almost impressive. Some people have no business behind the wheel. Her father didn't know what to do with her. Loving pacifist though he was, Jen nonetheless just became too much to handle. Stories of her sneaking into daddy's office, stealing syringes and other things, became commonplace. She got good at breaking both their hearts. And as parents are apt to, they'd always invest more emotionally, (throwing good money after bad?) or in a new condo for her, plus $200 trips to the grocery store, "Just to get her on her feet," which assisted greatly with her never having to fully hit bottom. But the mother, boy, she was a fireball, often swearing at me, hanging up when I called there. She could even tell when I disguised my voice. She knew my tricks and knew full well that when her daughter and I got together, things had a way of getting messy.

"Where did you get all that stuff?" I'd ask upon her return back to the little cook-up kitchen in her house, our headquarters.

"Do ya like? I *love* these designers!"

"Yes, you look like quite the princess this evening."

The cameras (and the cops) caught her one time after I dropped her off at the plaza for her daily routine. But that in no way stopped her from pressing on with her thieving agenda.

"So, you say you're in school?" asked the security guy. "What classes do you take?" Jen, reprimanded to the store's manager's grim and uninspiring brown office in the back of the store for misbehaving, acting inappropriately on ice disorderly conduct, physically, and emotionally penalized. But Jen soon brushed it off and accepted her temporary circumstance.

"Kleptomania and Second-Hand Sales. Commerce. Semantics, really." Her response to the store security that finally picked her up after so many months of garnering preposterous amounts of fashion luggage in an afternoon and plundering whatever lay in her path at the mall. She was a pro.

In an attempt to enlighten the authorities, she came to her defense with some entirely noble and understandable excuses. "Funny how people will do things under the influence of substances they simply would not ever do sober. BUT, certainly all this and more should be taken into consideration with someone in my *condition,*" she whispered the last word as if she was saying "Testicular Cancer" at an orthodox Hasidic family dinner table.

They weren't as understanding as she thought they could be, but they did end up letting her go with her purse, after a couple hours of performing and reciting song lyrics (from bands she dated), and with a court date set for later that month.

———————

I never seem to know anyone for any real length of time. If I have, it's been intermittent - I suppose attributed to bad behavior and never seeming to improve upon it much, mine or theirs.

———————

As the sun stuck its head down over a faraway forest tree line, introspection popped into my thought bubble as I drove past the recently constructed mega jail (before the cold weather set in) and thought about all the constellations I used to know, thankful my luck had, knowingly, never turned that sour.

———————

tf#28: The Front is a 1976 comedy-drama film about the Hollywood blacklist during the age of live television. It is written by Walter Bernstein, directed by Martin Ritt and stars Woody Allen and Zero Mostel. Because of the blacklist, a number of artists, writers, directors and others were rendered unemployable, having been accused of subversive political activities in support of Communism or of being Communists themselves.

Several people involved in the making of the film - screenwriter Bernstein, director Ritt, and actors Mostel, Herschel Bernardi, and Lloyd Gough - had themselves been blacklisted. (The name of each in the closing credits is followed by "Blacklisted 19--" and the relevant year.) Bernstein was listed after being named in the Red Channels journal that identified alleged Communists and Communist sympathizers.

In the early 1950s, in New York City, restaurant cashier and small-time bookie Howard Prince (Woody Allen) has a friend who writes for television. Because the friend, Alfred Miller (Michael Murphy) has been blacklisted, he asks Howard to sign his name to the TV scripts.

* * *

26. Off the Charts in Tears

I had a tough time getting that call out of my head. I was half expecting to bump into Jennifer's parents in town, or something. Their attempts to hunt me down would soon pay off, lucky them.

What would they say to me?

What would I have to tell them?

I was hoping this all would go away.

Grateful for the arrival of the day with its veneer of possible activity against which I might blend in a little. Those divine orange-tinged auburn Autumn leaves are now history, and it's the dreaded snow now keeping me from putting the car's top down. The snow shoveling amputation assignments are adding up, and I'll have to trudge my way through.

I emerge from headquarters, innocently looking to inhale some fresh air, but am forced to ingest the ever popular Santa Claus Parade, some nativi-tea and scone Scar-face scene. I'm agitated, quickly exhausted, forced to view the urgency of suburbanites hustling and bustling, chomping at the bit to purchase presents that'll be returned days later by spoiled offspring and exchanged for cash to feed that pot and porno mag addiction. Yes, I'm far from in the mood for such ridiculous prancing. Also darkening my day - the story already having leaked of Comet and Blitzen, selling their meaty and raw, tiny charges into slavery - their rotten and embarrassing behavior, now dubbed Reindeer Syndrome by some Eastern Syndicate. The latest en vogue disease to get all flustered about. A good twenty feet above the heads of bewildered holiday zombies, a sign that sagged from one

streetlamp to another - that I could have sworn said **COME
ALL YE HATEFUL.** As it billowed in the breeze, I thought
there's a chance I could have read it wrong.

All around me, couples embrace. This one pair stops me
dead in my tracks. They stare into each other's eyes, forever.
I can't help but wonder how naive they seem, utterly lost in
one another: gazing, longingly searching for answers… it
was cinematic, almost. Was it a farewell? I turned to walk
away, but not before looking over my shoulder to see their
white canes exposed. I knew it had to be something; people
don't really look that way at each other, do they? If I ever
did, I'm sure having a tough time remembering where I
stashed all that hope and possibility. And just where I put
my cane. I think to myself how lucky they are to be blind,
and how they're able to see everything as they choose to. I,
on the other hand, am left to contend with this troublesome
and deceitful procession, and the fact that there's no one to
help me cross the fucking street.

A vision of pointing a turbo-nozzled firehose at the lost,
blind lovers is surely a charming notion. Hosing them down,
almost drowning the pair, is more movie magic that blasts
its way onto my periphery and skates them out into the
warped mad dash that is the parade. For the first time today,
I feel a smile comes across my face, a muted chuckle, so
welcome. But, like many of the dreams and desires in my life,
the whole enchilada is gonna end up getting stuck down the
back of my throat.

Caffeine-deprived, it feels like someone has finally
demolished the entire downtown west side Starbucks, or at
least taken all the coffee baristas hostage and is holding
them for a ransom no one will pay. Turns out there's just a

gigantic and dangerous power outage, so no biggy; there's always Timmy's if I want to hurt myself.

The liver-spotted idiocy of this weirdo frightful event continues with an amount of papier-mâché that is outlandish and unreal. I'm feeling too much like Travis Bickle from *Taxi Driver*, pacing amongst the crowd, hunting for an opening, easily lost in film noir reverie... in pursuit of a victim, one that warrants it. There is a SWAT team for crowd control and yes, there is tension; gargantuan wavering snowmen and their blistering swollen heads – perfect bludgeoning targets, rapt for easy pummel-ability, zooming in on carrot noses; baffling tall gents in sweaty antler-outfits that bring only harm to children's defenseless minds: all now smashing to the ground, all left deranged, damaged and tainted. Everybody's brains and bodies seem barricaded, for these bewildered Christmas wanderers deserving of what's coming to them (at least that's what would happen in the movies), this from my bruised and purple perspective.

A pint-sized pre-teen dressed all in rhinestones and sparkly pink Yuletide gear, perched on a demented float, rides by at the jet-speed of a pregnant sea turtle. She's energetic, unalterably excited, her smile gigantic and beaming. (The teen, not the turtle). Later, I find out it had been painted on by a sluggish past-her-prime make-up artist, disturbingly nick-named Turtle. She minces about, feverishly waving wands and batons at the crowd (the child, not Turtle), then suddenly our eyes meet. This minute hellion tries to extract a big old holiday *Miracle on 34th Street* smile and Grand Ole Opry wave from me, but I'm having none of it, her pre-rehearsed delight. My response? A tilted head – perplexed and inquisitive – plus a knowing squint, my arms folded without compassion. Let's have some fun. I toss her a red and white striped candy-cane-flavored Frisbee, sharpened. I'm pretty sure she, and security, thought I was trying to knock her off the float. She's now self-conscious and shaky, as my charming Mr. Wonderful presence has shown up to speaks to her:

"Just what are you doing, you homunculun oddity? What parental orb arranged for you to take part in this mockery of Old Saint Nick? Anyway, what's the deal with those fake pink gems you got on? What of your sparkly facade? Are you not chilly, inside and out? You must be fucking freezing. Sorry about the language. But really, what the hell is wrong with you, can't you even catch a damn Frisbee?"

All this spoken with a glance, not trying to be overly harsh, really just wanting to cross the damn road. She starts to bawl, as loud as a child wearing pink, sparkles and a painted-on smile bursting from too much cotton candy, rehearsed jitters and role in this carnival-crap scam-a-rama, can bawl. Seems I had set the heart of little Hecubus aflame and was pronounced a Mirthless, Puddinghead Scroogester by onlookers. Suddenly, a balding, Hudson's Bay coated gentleman, clutching festively bright packages billowing with brilliantly colored ornaments (probably her father, or a Hudson's Bay Christmas tree salesman) bolts to her rescue. He grabs her minuscule frame, holds her close and comforts. The little lass devilishly spins her head around to cast the Damian-Omen-like finger in my direction, sealing my fate, casting me out.

This isn't going well, this 'crossing of the street' idea, now a complicated cavalcade. The indistinguishable fatherly salesman type guy comes over to punch me in the nose. I am now slip slidin' away, falling backwards, crushing a couple of seniors not paying proper attention. I admit I may have been half-deserving of a knock, though not fully deserving of the promotional funeral flyer he flicked atop my disheveled frame, the one boasting of reductions on holiday pine-scented caskets. Now the day is really getting going. Par for this course? Uncertain, as the pro shop is shut down for the season, due to inclement stupidity, no one to monitor this maple-less story of mensch-less, messed-up munchkin mayhem. Jesus.

Coming down the street, I spot what appears to be a tiny Egyptian countess being dragged in what I can only describe as an enormous birdcage on a chain leash, through the slushy sidewalk, by what must be her recently relocated, sickeningly rich Western World cousins. Smart silky Fila ski suits and plush *Rico Suave* head bands, lots of jewelry, you get the picture. She screams like a distressed and frostbitten swine, beyond repair. The cousins attempt to ease her obvious suffering: "Isn't this fun, Madame Kukaching? This is what happens in this part of the world at Christmas time." Madame Kukaching weeps in some Wingading language, longing for the parades of youth when she rode high atop camels, worshiped by strange slaves, having her feet kissed by adoring halitosis-riddled strangers who certainly didn't have to contend with average, Joe Shmo vanilla folk scrambling to get a close-up of a far-from-jolly, half in-the-bag, Rolly-Polly Swede lobbing cheap gift bags with stale crumbly fortune cookies and fourth-rate antediluvian Halloween offerings at her from a shabbily spray-painted floating chariot. Frail charms of frightened foreigners sickening me all the more, I'm now grotesquely infected with the small-town-gooey-glucose-guise of this holi-daze.

I projectile vomit over a man selling international hand-held flags and what must be poisonous lollipops. What spews out of me is candy corn and Kraft toffee. I am mortally confused and more drained than ever. Onlookers pelt me with girlie napkins and soggy banana-packed lunch bags. As

I look up from the ground in a haze, I see the boulevard swarming with thousands of soldiers marching in unison, all chanting a national anthem, though I can't make out the country they march (or chant) for. They're alien minotaurs (or annoying relatives) with heavy multi-weave back hair and crotch itch, sporting leopard-skin tails. They omit a foul odor, but are astonishingly synchronized - the dedicated training on other planets clearly to be envied by our slothful race (the punch from Captain Charisma, the Hudson's Bay Salesman, may have loosened a few screws, so don't quote me on the alien minotaur soldier part.)

This Dickensian death camp will soon be over, I reassure myself, but I am still on the battlefield, left to my own non-poetic devices: dodging floats, freak show countesses, easily swayed crowds, surreal scenarios, children with sickening festive agendas and their puppet idolatry - with me off the charts in tears, as I miss everyone I've ever loved this time of year.

Everything begins to look like a pregnant piñata, but I'm not a violent guy; I really just want some goodies. Or at the very least a treat. The ultimate, always reliable, depression: me longing to check out with a strong dose but not being able to procure one. I can't find the damn stuff, is what I'm complaining about. Sure, big busts of all kinds abound; operations led by undercover narcs in surrounding city school districts - Grade 9 and 10 students, propped up at their desks by Burrough-esque bug powder delivered uncut from some Triad watercraft that's just arrived from some place where workers toil in the fields persistently pulling poppies properly, maybe from the Pakistan pastures. These dopes seemingly have no problem scoring between Mr. Hanaram's Social Studies class and Schlifer's scholarly misgivings. A few sniffs in the 'phantom troll-toll foxy-faux phone-booth' beneath the gym stage will set them more than straight. Even at all the old reliable intersections - my old haunts dedicated to Orientals selling specially put-together packages of high tidings and treats - there's nothing. Again, forced to endure sobriety today, kept alive for something sight unseen, I suppose.

Dreams of childhood outings wash over me: getting dragged to Santa's Village on a blazing scorcher of a summer afternoon by a babysitter who'd had enough of my tricks. St. Nick's helpers are clammy and worn, torn-up and less than vibrant skanky elves, their ripped Lederhosen two sizes too small, make-up running.

They make valiant but broken attempts at building snowmen. Of course they are all made from kindling (the snowmen, not the elves). Some children set them on fire (the snowmen and the elves) and cheer, while smearing their faces with elf blood. It reminds me of that book where those kids run the island... why can't I remember it? *The Island of Pigs? Bay of Fundy? The Lordy Operation of Flying Rings and Six Sense Stuff?* That can't be it. Everyone is an absurd alcoholic fire hazard, while management begins running out of props and costumes (and elves) and must do more than just consider shutting down rides.

Quelle Suprise! Quelle Beau Village!

It's hilarious, though not so much for the wicker-people-employees and their families - more so just for me.

Disenchanted with so much, I come across another fumbly father-child equation (so many of them) having a snowball fight in their front yard... Either that or they're trespassing. If I could muster up the energy, I'd flag down a cop and report the man for child abuse. I decide to let the whole thing slide, for fear that I, in turn, will somehow get nailed for Snowball Possession, a crime that carries the heavy sentence of being forced to watch ghostly black and white videos of past Christmas parades on extra slow-mo-speed.

It's time to turn to more important and relevant matters, like how I'll look in my hand-sewn Luge outfit for the 2016 Special Bam Bam Olympics. Must get on that. Where to practice? Oh, and material... must acquire material. Hey, I've got the best idea. Those kids'll eventually have to abandon those catastrophically useless costumes from the parade... no, that would be sacrilegious... How many sins would that cover anyway? Bribing a bored and sinister mushroom man with fake blotter acid, he fesses up and divulges the secret location where this whole travesty ends. I've hiked cross-town and am waiting for parade participants back at the starting point: an icy auditorium, scalding hot chocolate, weary parents discussing when they think their crazy children will be arriving back atop their shoddy floats, and me lurking in back rooms conversing with profoundly marshmallow-laden costume ladies with too many stories:

"It was New York, the year 1958, a much younger, trimmer Ed Asner was lookin' for a dresser, so I told my parents to go to hell, that I'm cutting this dyke-school-scene to break into showbiz, so then..." I endure Grizelda's bizarre nostalgia in order to procure colorful cloths, textiles and tapestries needed for my uniform in an upcoming sporty project (not to mention some pretty darn funny comedic material).

I end up being held without bail for trying to lure youngsters away from their costumes with alfalfa salt licks, carrot noses and a half-eaten box of After Eights. "We've been watching you," two undercover detectives say.

"I'm not after the kids, I only want their costumes. I'm not some perverted criminal, I just need the material; Christ, they don't need it anymore. I don't even have a record, unhand me!"

"Tell it down at the station, gramps."

The arresting officers said I was nothing more than a sour, judgmental presence, but for the life of me I couldn't see it. Nor did I see how such behavior could be considered criminal. I told them calmly that this day somehow reminded me of coffins whizzing down an icy crystal race course. Sour, maybe. Judgmental, never.

They transported me to a cold, damp igloo of a hollow-minded police station; the snowballs that weren't confiscated in the arrest are melting down my trousers. I try to make a game out of it, but it's all turning awfully unfunny; thoroughly iced genitalia going numb with the rest of me, hungry corrupt constables staring at me, eager to cross-examine, to extract 'the truth' from my mind's eye, melting and starved, just having missed the once-a-day behind bars snack allowance, my pockets deep with regret, like snowmen who've gotten off at the wrong stop, forgetting their extremely queer-shaped undergarments, not prepped properly for the all-too-humid and airy aroma of an early thaw.

Where DO crafty snowmen go in Springtime? They have places, you just have to look.

I couldn't help but feel that anyone who wasn't as upset as I was by the mockery, so consistently plaguing, in what was now a daily dodging of the cruel hurtful bullets shot at me, was guilty of not only not paying attention, but thought themselves far from in the wrong. Even worse, nobody was about to do anything about it. All this I had scribbled down on a notepad, scrunched down somewhere in my pants back pocket, now lost or stolen. I bet it was one of those goddamn cherubic float-riding kiddies just back from devouring entire cotton-candy-floats, who gobbled up my Life Notes, testing to see what's edible and what's not at their after-party: appetites insatiable, unquenchable thirsts never satisfied.

Okay, maybe I have done that. But I'm not like them. I'm not like anyone.

* * *

27. The Church Thing

This evening, I accompany mom to a family memorial service thing, put on by this palliative care place. It's scary sad from the start. A stooped Ichabod Crane elder greets and accompanies us down to our assigned pew and whispers some discomforting words. "Welcome to the end of the world," though I could have heard him wrong What's worse, the odor that wafts about the pews is not unlike what musty gravesites must smell like after a good downpour.

The church event is unbearable, in a cataclysmic disfiguring way (I'm being kind), on account of it's all about mourning. And grief. People's losses, and not things they've misplaced. We're talking about devilishly morose sorts of stuff, things I'd just as soon not contend with tonight. Mom tells me it should only go on for about three more hours or so, but it will end up lasting much longer. I wasn't planning on going but what's a son supposed to say? No? So of course, I'm off to these sluggish races with her. This event, DEFINATELY not a pretty pony show, a day at the track, or anything like getting set up in those special booths where people tend to your needs. It's not like any of that. It's some kind of candle service. Lost, black and cotillion-typified. After a few un-showy tunes, the Muscular Dystrophy-ish, Cancer Society-volunteer-variety-club type-round-ladies teeter totter around and light your wick. All this going on while the minister reads off a couple hundred or so names of people who've passed on: *Alibaster, Ames, Belson, Blair...* Once they start getting close to mom's husband's name, I truly catch wind of her horrendous, blistering torment and pain. A real wind of it. An absolutely dreadful oncoming fear train with no bar-car, just moments away. A wrecking ball of grief coming in to visit, again. A revolting red flag affair. There was a precise moment I could feel her break inside, with me unable to put out much past keeping intact and quiet, and in trying to keep intact his hard-won protective fields. To comfort her, a son can't help but go numb himself, for self-preservations. If he's going to be any good to her at all through this, there's got to be some disengaging. If he fell apart every time the moms got all teary and broken, well... anyway, there's no way out of this scene.

There was, thank god, some humor (my Savior, many times, when it doth choose to make an entrance). Seems the lady behind us was tone deaf - amazingly tone deaf, like a sick Bassett hound pining and trying valiantly to sniff a squirrel through its nostrils, bereft of any musical melody whatsoever.

"He lived and died, to buy my pardon...
An empty grave is there to prove my Savior lives..."

My creative head, an inebriated dissonance of whining doggies wailing, wafting over pillars and pews. See, this wasn't the place for comedic canines, not at all. I guess that's what really made it laughable, the irony, the absurdity, and trying to suppress the hilarity, to keep it all in. It was some good comic relief.

"Thank you for coming," mom said through tears that had been building during this brutal shroud of explicit sadness. I looked at her, held her hand tight and we shared a moment reminiscent of Grade 9 science class, the one where you and your best friend can't stop giggling – as on this day, our teacher Mr. Pemberton's octa-weave-toupee is extra grotesque, horrific and made of anguish, and is damn unslinky. Things that were a great nuisance long ago can make for great material in later life. You never know what you might be able to take from a situation. That is, if you're paying special/enough attention. Mostly I think I do, but there again, part of a bigger problem.

"...I'll fight life's final war with pain.

And then as death gives way to..."

Very cheery stuff still coming at us over the crackling loudspeakers, along with the brochure we're given entitled, "I just can't face the holidays" - offering tiny steps to take, like how to avert one's eyes when that perfect gift for one's beloved sits behind a Christmas display window screaming, "Buy me!" or, how to cope with the Significant Other not being around to partake in the Receiving the Gift portion of the show, as they're too busy with their newfound occupation of being dead. The bereavers, the Bieber Believers, the bereft, left only with pictures - artifacts to be organized, now hypnotically lethargic, having to force themselves to rise to the occasion when they hear the sound of their own fucking mind pulling apart. Decorations will need somber tending to, and there are notes and suggestions left by those who've already checked out and who aren't going to be showing their face at festive family functions and holidays, the lucky full-time sleepers.

I'm glad I went. For her. As I would wish it on no one to be in that heartless final place all alone.

My head couldn't help but be in Morbid Reflection Mode - there was digging that had to be done the next day, resurrecting certain prized hand-puppets who've been left to burrow around in the basement. The real question here: just which ones to raise from the dead and so on, which ones to bring forth for the meeting with some people about this 'Kid's Host' job thing tomorrow.

There's something to be said for living in the moment, though I can't remember or even imagine for the life of me what it is.

* * *

28. No Safety in Coffins

It is no measure of health to be well-adjusted to a profoundly sick society.

Krishna Murti

W here is the colander that will filter out all the crap, but keep all the good stuff that I know is in me? I need a descent break from the constraint of mother's den. I'm not ready to return just yet.

The underworld fascinates me. I'm too attracted to words like 'cartel', or the 'running' of anything anywhere - picking up, bundles, bindles, dimes, shooting, Pure, cut, oxy's, morphs, the cut, ounces, pagers, corners, cells, alleys with cats in them: a diminutive dichotomy, the entire grift, shake-downs and hustles... A love-hate relationship of the oxymoronic type. I should be more wary, as living beneath ground has just about killed me, many times.

These little jaunts into the city are doing little more than wiping out any healing process, that I so sorely need to piece together. It also depletes all cash needed for other adventures: eating, bills, other pleasurable purchases; food and fuel... Why does that keep coming up?

I don't like the place I get to after using - that uncomfortable, inconsiderate drafty arrival terminal.

On this particular Sunday morning, nothing was open. I slumped along in a drizzle signifying what I thought would be the end of my time here, and with little funding afoot, I remembered luckily that I had a damp check that would clear in about four days, but by which point scurvy will have set up shop. I was lacking, me, the lifeless marginal madness in strange shape, icky and inescapable yet again. Toppling into a snow bank, I smashed my head on the roadway while interrupting my melodic humming of, "...Frosty the Stank

Snowbank...", which I'm almost certain weren't the right lyrics. When I purchased these boots in California, was it my fault that no thought was given to early rising scenarios such as this? This pair was too slick and sleek underneath, no proper gravity treads to speak of, just footwear of miserable sub-perky proportions. Ill-equipped to handle these conditions. This place - some twisted Timber-land I'm lost and wearing deathly footwear in. Forlorn. Fuck it. I have hope the day will improve. It's got to.

It's not long at all before the day takes over again and trumps me with a car splashing a brown, mushy, slime-like substance - salt, failure, dirt, regret - all wash atop me, this sick montage. The chorus line bellows, "Where is Love" from the musical Oliver, so badly out of tune the birds in the park across the way call an emergency meeting to discuss my unmelodious somber chant, and question why I have about a dozen colored ladies (altos and tenors mostly) in blue velvet robes and Buckwheat hairdo's in step with me. The flock can't help but flee the city to save themselves. The colored gals also begin flapping their arms furiously in an attempt to disperse from my off-color rendition of Genesis' entire last album.

"But this is my solo, will no one listen?" I plead.

I find myself in front of a funeral home, the one maudlin yet helpful outfit that's got its doors open for business on this sparkling and beautifully cascading morning. It's Grim-town, baby, and I'm the mayor. Bleak for days. Is this really happening? Yes, yes it is. I think about how lucky I am that I have a coupon for caskets melting in my pocket, just in case.

The funeral home manager - who I thought might be rushing out to help me up - instead, tosses me yet another pamphlet, this time advertising a sale on balsa caskets, telling me to pipe down as my crass dismantling diatribe, my songs in the key of death, are bringing down the weeping mourners inside. Balsa, apparently, is an easily widdleable, highly malleable light wood of mid-to-low grade quality, which comes from the tropical American tree *Ochroma lagopus* - this I learn after a few phone calls, as I don't invest easily. The caskets are extra kooky-fun as the aromatic resins and soothing ointments in your chipper death box all deteriorate along with you as you begin your last ultimate chapter of life and begin to decompose. Now I'm pathetic but informed. Always at my fingertips, with useless knowledge at the ready to offer up at parties whose pace will inevitably slow, and to which I never will receive a proper coveted invitation. I've got casket propaganda though (which is better, I tell myself), and now the day is mine.

That someone will come along, pick me up by the scruff of my neck (where is that?), encase me in a Ziploc sandwich bag module and toss me into the river, this is my wish. But more than likely I'd get nailed for littering, or that business of 'Snowball-possession' that dogs me still from state to state. Worse, I'll be blamed for not being disposed of in an ergonomically incorrect, organic aerospace-like, Grecian-formula-Greenpeace-manner; the coating that now surrounds me, won't breakdown.

I. Do. Though.

By now, you're getting some idea.

There's a lot of solitary walking - a drifter on the hunt for a plausible grift, having returned to the criminal city - the sulk scene, lightly drooling, pre-coffee'd, unfed in every way, shivering. I confide in my best friend: the hand-held recorder device by General Electric - a shoddily pieced-together machine that never uses guilt or makes condescending snide remarks behind my back, but, continues to be unfailingly dependable and always shows up for meals. It, *He*, repeats back when prompted and doesn't stray from what was said at an earlier time; a simple candid relationship. No false expectations, jealousies or catastrophic emotional glitches, just a rewind button and a microphone that won't desert me. Thank god for the words that make me up, the ones I've come to own.

In the snowy park across the street from mom's house, the tennis courts are all covered over with snow, maybe symbolizing finality, an end I'm too sorrowful to extract helpful hints from today. I mumble to myself, "Why did I leave the West Coast?" Oh yeah, now I remember.

* * *

29. You Have a Visitor

I retreat, back home to headquarters. My mental real estate is predominantly rented out, to rage and confusion, a strange couple that can't stop bickering over a price or location for their new digs.

I've taken to bouts of inflated self-importance, brimming with my accoutrements of whimsy, outfitted in a utility belt – with the following items: a fresh ground black-pepper mill, toy cell phone, a hand-held tape recorder, disposable Kodak camera, a map of the city of Toronto (from the 50's, the 1850's) and a loaded water gun. I'm trying to think of an instance in which someone in town might cause me to draw, and what would the argument be over exactly? The reputation of a young lass heading down a dangerous No Dignity Road? Backyard property lines - where theirs begin and mine end? A fight to the death? This opens a plethora of Pandora's boxes as to who might win such a showdown. Merely because I'm armed with an outrageously hefty pepper-grinding-mill, shouldn't he lay down his water guns? Would we play, Who can season the other one first? Who could monitor each other's nerves the fastest? And where would the rule books be hiding for such contests? What Freud would have said about this, I cannot say. I'm betting he'd have more to say about me shacking up with my mom. (Or was that Oedipus? No matter).

Too many questions. Too much to do, too much to consider. Too many notebooks from years gone by that are pertinent and necessary to my voyage, my trek through this wreckage and the mess that's now slapping me across the face and calling itself, LIFE. I'm putting things back together, re-packaging my soul in better bubble wrap, so when it reconvenes with my heart and mind, the whole she-bang won't tumble and crash too badly. But I feel dangerously too close to everything to have any sort of integral sonar perception, and during these moments I'm somehow simultaneously numb. How is this even biologically possible, to feel and act "as if," two opposing things are working out together at the same gym?

Mom seems to think a full-time job would be good for me. What she can't appreciate is how desperately I need my own Muse. Not one in sheets necessarily, and not some kind of kindred spirit or meditative minstrel projected on the wall to pray to - my new muse doesn't even have to be a direct descendant of Zeus or Mnemosyn. I'm scavenging around for a kind-hearted creature to advise, listen and assist me with the overwhelming sores I've opened - how to just get through a day, the stories and how to integrate an actual narrative arc into this writing that'll make all these notes easier for people to comprehend. Someone on the other side of the confessional booth that I can spill my guts to. I'll find her. I have faith - kind of. I'm right in the middle of constructing a free-standing structure, complete with velvety red curtains (my mom's) used to conceal penitents from the rest of the church (house). It's going to look totally cool. I don't know anybody else with an oratory other than a parish church. I hear it takes quite a while to get a proper ecclesiastical authority to come over and bless the thing properly, before you can start to use it and all. Better hire some assistance, not only for chapel-building but for companion-type stuff.

No matter. I put up an ad at the library, MUSE WANTED. Life lessons, gas allowance and a few meals, that's what I'm offering. What eager young Liberal Arts student devoted to the pursuit of knowledge wouldn't jump at such an opportunity? It's inspiration I'm after, stuff I can't conjure from the dry well in myself. I forget, each time I hobble back to that place. I'm jolted into remembering my used-up cache of tricks and survival skills I've extracted all I can from.

Settled awkwardly on my tuffet, munching away, the peace in the library that I seek works like an older brother that never once lets you down and sticks up for you in high school; makes you feel safe, special and cared for. Just then while I was imagining this unrealistic situation, who sits down beside me but this gorgeous spidery girl, bubbling with youth, equipped with ponytail. Why she has it in her hand is not clear. Things that zoom-a-zoom into my noggin': Roman Polanski, Bitter Moon, Breathless - French flicks with guys in white Polo shirts rolling around on vintage black bicycles, who just happen to run into absurdly-cushiony-femme-fatales-in-training, sprawled suggestively beneath oak trees, smoking Camels, appearing unattainable... their existentialism class just having ended. Of course, the classes exist only in their minds, allowing these collegiate minxes to spend even greater bouts of post playtime dedicated to just

BEING.

I learn her name is Bernadette, as it's doodled on many of the textbooks peeking out from her backpack. It's also tattooed in red on the back of her neck, AND spray painted on the scooter that she mounts after our little chat. I sense this impish pixie (who must be in love with her name) yearns to break out. Breakthrough? Break down? Break away? Here we go again. Could I be the one to give her Life Lessons, or at very least a thorough tonguing? Could she be flirting? To tell you the truth (and why not?) to this day, I still have not clue one as to how all that goes - picking up on if they're being agreeable and easygoing or if they really are flirting a tiny bit to pass the time, OR are giving me a clear sign that they want me to make the play and pursue.

To break some ice, I ask her for a light. She responds with an endearing army of facts and accusations: "This is a library, pal - ain't no smoking in here. Smoking killed my uncle, asshole." Dumbfounded, I just sat there and hoped it was not my synapses' day off, as I sent down a probe, ordering my cerebral cortex to come up with a much-needed and clever retort. But before I could orchestrate a response, she politely offered more helpful information. "I'm pretty sure the librarian over there caught a whiff of your runny mustard and cheese sandwich dripping on the keyboard there. You're quite the rebel-rule-breaker, eh Swifty?"

My swelled wolf tongue now recoiling and all little lambs silenced, I tell Bernie I don't smoke, that I only wanted to use a lighter so that I could "see her in a more complimentary light." She pauses for a moment (she's starting to read me right), stands up and places her hands on me. Wow, she's pretty forward, I respect that. A hug already? Caught entirely off guard, Bernie somehow grabs hold of my waist and chucks me into the microfiche machine, as if I were a pamphlet requiring shelving, my forehead now a much different item than when I arrived. So, smalled by her less than playful cutting remarks and muscular ability to toss the male form so effortlessly, I'm left to shuffle on alone, somehow a lessened man. I wrote in my tiny pocket notebook that libraries are terrible places to try and meet someone. Today might have been a good day to stay put in the crib rolled up in a blanky with my thumb in my mouth. But even then, someone else's thumb will inevitably look better.

Bernadette was a tough cookie; she had style and could stick up for herself. I liked her immediately. Dusting myself off, emerging from the files, I introduced myself and presented her with my muse offer. I told her about the position, what I was doing up here, how I'd arrived in this place and how sorely I needed someone to touch (base with?) daily. I may have come off a little desperate, but at that point I didn't care.

Anyway, we agreed to test out this working relationship, to see if it felt right for both of us. I immediately trusted her.

She'll set me straight, I thought. She'll know what to do. The question is, can I convince her to come to the house and visit for a day or two, maybe even a couple nights, so I can have her dose me with some kind of sanity/reality. Actually, I don't have to convince her at all, as she's curious and more than willing to make the trip just to see what I've been up to: the projects; my sorting and sifting, the writing, lately, the unpacking of my thoughts and words and prayers; my meetings, the weirdo late night/early morning gardening experiments, the seemingly unnecessary ridiculous re-assembling of my childhood to present life - memorialized material for the big puppet show that'll never play in anyone's home. (Maybe Peoria?) This perk little ditty known as Life (an awful term) has led me down a hybrid of dirt roads, to near death and street urchin living, one foot remaining in the trough I've heard.

For entertainment's sake, I make a few small requests for our upcoming Lost Weekend of Rose and Whining; a requisition has been put in for 150 pencils and a box of clipboards. I plan to have her sit at the desk that I've oiled and Pledged to death. On top of the prepped desk, AND on a set I've constructed, out of copper, marble, Styrofoam and plywood, acquired from a neighbor's back porch development that had been taking entirely too long - sits a gigantic, black rotary-dial phone, for effect mainly. I ask

Bernie if she wouldn't mind dictating, to herself, what it is that I should do with myself. AND if it's not going to be too much trouble, to wear yellow rubber Winnie the Pooh rain boots, a prom dress a size too small and carry a sparkly magic wand. In this scene, I see her as a kind of soothing secretarial Miss Kubilek, and I, a sort of stunned, strung-out Jack Lemon-ish, Fred MacMurray-like fellow, a third rate Mad Men lower tier exec, though I can't quite recall how anybody's characters are supposed to interact. The arrangement makes for better-than-real-life acting out.... and anyway, we're not hurting anyone. A lot of this would spook first-time-Timmers, but she's been privy to witnessing some of my more obtuse kinds of high-speed nonsensical turns, and knows to blink a deaf eye and ear to my instructions and silly commands. She knows what she's in for and how to deal with me. I think I'm supposed to wear a bowler hat - the junior executive model - in one of our scenes, but I can't drum one up, so I convince myself it's of little importance and will make up for it with over-acting in all of our other scheduled scenes together.

Deciding it's best to offer her a position in my firm, the consistency and support thing could be inter-planetarilly good, which further fuels my fantasia self-propelled self-absorption. But who wouldn't jump at it, job opportunities being what they are and all? As we are now friends, I'm hoping she won't ask for vacation pay or for any stuff that requires forms. (And who likes to let red tape, form letters and pricy litigators get in the way of a relaxing overnight stay?)

"I can't pay you a whole hell of a lot, but just think of the life lessons!" She appears to be mildly impressed

Bernadette arrives with bundles of writing implements (that even work!), her hair tied back in a ball (a definite plus), slinging a Staten Island accent for added role-playing nutrients. She's more than willing to play (for a while anyway) until she's had enough, like so many of the other actors and actresses in my life who've trounced off set, once I'm deemed too demanding, scattered, inconsistent and in the end too much to put up with, seemingly unworthy. Too busy scavenging for drugs to pay proper attention to what I was losing. I can't be the only actor that's easily replaceable. They must have people in their life who don't put up with their nonsense, right? I am Max Von Stroheim, the great director, without cats, I mean cast, to lead into production battle.

An offer is on the table to pay her in caffeine, stuffed toys and chocolates. Also, a I also promise her (and this I came to regret) that if she needed to take out any frustrations she had (either with me or let's say, past boyfriends etc.) that I'd dig out the bunny rabbit costume in the attic gathering green moss and mold from a parade long past and slip into it, allowing her to chase me around the yard, pummeling me as she saw fit. I guess I'd have promised anything as I sure did want some company.

"You can learn a lot from me through my stories, what to watch out for, how not to live," I offered.

"Oh you, stop being so silly," Bernie said, simultaneously bashing my skull in with monster-sized pruning shears.

I still have the scars and bruises.

I want her to be part of the imaginary audience at the mother coliseum, to be my Human Candid Camera for a while. I have needs, but don't like saying that out loud, because I don't want to risk being turned down. Who cares what I need anyway? Today, it's someone to listen, really listen: the kind of exploratory listening through which I can sort out what I think I really mean.

Is this how the humanoids create a more complete sense of themselves, and do I need to be accountable to something or someone other than myself? I'm guessing, "Yes" and it builds what again? Sense of self, self-esteem, that less lonely feeling? Washes away that melancholic mind-set?

I tell Bernadette that she needs to be tough on me, or give a sincere rendition of something that smacks of Tough Love, because I know I need discipline, at very least instruction. I can't have all these words just end up in the basement, tossed aside, my time and energy left to serve some other outlandish project I'll inevitably consider just as important, one that looks like an easier way out, less harsh on the old system anyway. I won't let that happen. Not this time.

How she's going to do all this, I don't believe either of us have an idea. There need to be parameters of sorts, boundaries, of which I'm more often than not one who assumes a rapport and ignores boundaries. Guidelines, or is that guides? (Often, left to my own devices, I'd take the role of Tour Guide, snorting lines off the bathroom bus commode during stopovers.)

There simply must be a service somewhere that can streamline me, trim me down to essentials - some enormous life colander the size of a three-story house, where I'd walk in the room and all the unnecessary mental dead-weight, the plasma and cells taking up space, would get properly filtered, just fall delicately away, Hey, maybe the gunk I drag around with me could even be scratched off with some People-Potato-Peelers. (Call the patent office).

Stirring up some memories, over a stir-fry bachelor favorite of extra-gluten all-wheat quickie pasta and parsnip meal on the BBQ, thinking it'll help with this manifesto of excuses I've dedicated to getting down, we move into the room of historical but useless accolades on display behind a colossal glass enclosure far too big for the room: these trophies and ribbons from my youth, like the ones awarded to me after many cub scout squattings, *(tf#29)* where I mused the words, De Do Do Do, De Da Da Da – some vendetta-ish, Zenyatta Mendatta-like-chant.

Eventually, the scoutmaster ended up handing over just about every award laid out in the Cub's Handbook, I'm guessing for no other reason than it was way past the time for me to abandon the organization and move on. How brilliant an association: all that was required of me was to show up, kick soccer balls around with other equally immature rag-tag peers in a below-ground dwelling after getting charged up on take-out food – one of the few weekly outings my parents were good enough to commit to, perhaps thinking this would give me a sense of consistency, a suitable dress code and a shot at normal behavior for my life ahead. It didn't.

But huge appreciation goes out to the McDonalds, K.F.C and H. Salt Fish and Chips crew for sponsoring a good deal of my childhood and giving poor Mom a break from the constraints of Anglo-Saxon preparatory cuisine: 'Team Ragu Kraft'. Just where all those Lettermen uniforms with the numbers on the back disappeared to, the ones knit and sewn to impress off-campus co-eds, I'll never know. They must've ended up being sold to that second-hand haunt on Melrose last year. *(tf#30)* Awards from the cub scouts, the tennis tournaments and my brief time with the debating team, happened all before I became overly seasoned by peppery and fragmented concerns. It was an encapsulated time, a wondrous era that was somehow golden, and much, much different from... well, from everything else. But maybe those glistening memories recollected, my multiple but hazy heartfelt treasures, weren't as great as I imagine.

Anyway, after a short time, Bernadette said she had her own life to get back to. She'd had about enough, saying that she couldn't put up with my absurdity and grandiosity even if it was from a sincere place, but she wished me the best of luck on my journey. I hate that. People are always going somewhere, leaving me alone.

When praying, Jenny's image comes up, a lot. She's just about the most desperate and unsatisfied person I've ever met: a dancing crystal corpse who inexplicably sunk into me. On stranger days, while menacingly high, I'd watch Jennifer rehearse her deathly pirouettes. Her reasons for killing herself so continually, I never got let in on. She'd had opportunity and people who loved her: how we sometimes get spoiled and irreparable inside, and arrive unwillingly at places we can never come back from. God, I hope she's beat the odds, found the percentages in her favor, has managed to stay alive through her stories. I should go and try and find her. There's a lot of people I should go and find after this is over.

---

tf#25 Wiping out, no DESTROYING, my opponent rather handily, which turned out was me.

tf#26 Seeing Brownies "flying up" to Girl Guides can be an important and wildly sentimental scene; I know this as periodically I'd catch a glimpse of the pre-teen ritual through the church's basement window.

tf#27 not the co-eds, the uniforms… mostly.

* * *

30. Rid-a-Lyn / Reading, Rioting, Arrhythmia

My mom keeps coming across tiny yellow Post-It notes around the house, leading her to believe that she will soon be dead, and by my hand. It was clear I was going to kill her. It was only a question of when. I'm kidding, of course. To explain: I got this suggestion from a friend, a tip that seemed to work brilliantly for her, for a while anyway. The notes pertained to the KILLING OFF of the old me: ridding myself of everything (and everyone) still in my life that wasn't positive or helpful... to dis-attach, leaving the worst of myself behind and burned. The documented memories, the photos, the notes and anything else I'd been hoarding, which have played a part in my being an awful ignoramus - my limitless fancies, my devotion to decadence, those dodgy mannerisms masquerading as charm, will go up in a ritual fire in Mom's backyard. I want to say goodbye to the questionable everything's that I've been - render those puppies docile and out of breath, the smoke rising to the heavens, representing all the stuff that's done me no good, a cathartic transition, from a sincere farewell to wrongly done deeds and evil actions.

At last, to make a change and do the right thing. Whatever that is. Compared to all my other plans, this didn't seem too out there.

Anyway, the character of the mother only gets half the story - a memo left behind on top of my open note book beside my computer that reads, Pick up bananas, soy milk, and...

RituAl fire... Must arraNge foree this weeek

hAlf to KilL off OLd PaRson

This would unnerve anyone. She begins treating me nicer - like completely out of hand, ludicrously nice. She's been leaving her own set of writings out where I can see them in full view: ones that state the deed to the house is now in my name, asking if I'd like to go buy a car, all this as she's thinking only of her own happiness around here. Material gunk isn't what I need though. I should tell her what's really going on, so she doesn't blow a gasket or something. It's kind of funny how I'm now allowed access to her account and she isn't yelling at me when I don't make my bed in the morning, and now she always, always does the dishes.

It's not very nice to keep this from her. I should really tell her about this whole 'ritual process' thing.

Later.

———————

Today is Salvation Army Donation Day and we've got a drab grab-bag of immense accumulated proportion that I'm sure the Sally-Ann minions in blue aprons and gas masks (maybe not all wear them) will be pleased to receive and I know we'll be glad to get rid of.

I can't believe it's snowing again. Shit. Once more, uncivilized white and fluffy tufts, representing a completely revolting time period, a barbaric affair that teases and lures me in, only to drop me skull-first on to some gooey emotional pavement. I didn't miss it at all while on the west coast, that's for sure. Waking up to the beach, then a ginormous breakfast on the patio, then getting invited down to the harbor to spend the day, along the way, picking up is in the unattainable category up here, in this deceitful northern hemisphere.

The last time I can remember a downfall like this was when I was making an emergency trip back to visit Mom in the hospital. She was hooked up to a whole lot of machines and stuff, maybe not the sort of stuff meant for sons to see up close: tubes, wires intertwined all around like an overcrowded freeway, amidst out-of-date gang-green monitors and always that musty smell, the sick scent of soiled linens, half-eaten mushy food on grape-juice-stained plastic trays, an uncertainty hovering over the remaining humans, along with Kafkaesque interfaces on elevator rides with strangers. I'd think, "I wonder who they're here to see? They look pretty shook up," and maybe say aloud. All this against the backdrop of Christmas, of presents unopened. (The Unimportance of Gifts - a chapter?)

There's an immediate urgency afoot. Undecorated, dropping needles. Stinking up the joint stood the big old balsa Christmas tree left to dry out in our living room, all this happening instantly, without warning. Thank God for coming across some medication luckily left over from some preoccupied doctor, in this metaphoric back seat I occupy, distant convulsively-diarrheic Tourettic-tourista-relative, late for his first class flight, scampering, homeward bound in order to reach his sweetheart, (the drunk) the children growing more and more excited over Daddy's big deal fucken' arrival. "He'll be home soon, dears," their mother says while holding a martini in one hand and a Stephen King spooky paperback in the other; the tiny charges jump on top of their new X-box machines into the ground.

At least I had an easily manipulated prescription.

They say there are levels and stages but I can't make myself into heads or tails anymore, even though there was a time when I could, and sure, I looked damn funny but at least I had the rigged hangman puzzle figured out better. These days it's just right out-the-window, off-the-board inexplicable, deafening and unbearable, like a hangman's game set up for you to lose as there are no vowels for you to choose, in an all-vowel consonant-contaminated world.

———————————

Ron, who played The Stepfather, would grab my arm and tug me into that hospital corridor to offer up, "If you're going to upset your mother, then don't come back, asshole." I'd sneak back after hours when the monster had gone, and she was fast asleep, to spend more real time with Mom; those were the best times to tell Mom what was up with me, when she was resting between worlds, and I was alone. The nurses just had to take one look at me to know I wouldn't be adhering to any of that VISITING HOURS bullshit. Horribly uncomfortable family scenarios like ours didn't add up and certainly couldn't have been new to them.

Pretty much everything I said upset Mom a good chunk of the time. 'Hello' opened up a bushel of suspicions and concerns, in those days. So what's different now? Well, Ron's not around anymore and Mom only occasionally has to check in at certain hospitals, just to make sure all is up to snuff. But I feel pretty much like the same guy, and I'd be lying if I said I've come through anything because I don't feel much like I have. And she still asks where I'm going, when I am coming back, what I'm doing, how long until this or that, which is nice that somebody cares so much about my actions and thoughts, but it's not the sort of care and concern I'm after. This is why we don't marry our moms. Well, some folks dig that sort of lifestyle, but to each their own.

I am as Important and needed as Pockets in Pajamas...

Mom shows me chicken scrawls on various steno pads - scribblings from her files, compiled during her stay at Mount Sinai Hospital in downtown Toronto when speaking was on the list of disappearing talents.

"Cheap." "Nasty." "Tasteless." It doesn't say so, but I'm guessing this was commentary on the unimaginative food-prep (props?). This, or derogatory rhetoric towards slutty weekend nurses with questionable ethics. And in her folder are recent request forms for 'Disability,' unsigned and denied by two of her doctors. Seems they didn't want to risk attaching their names to the damn things, off-putting pile-driving-humiliating declaration forms. Physician's red tape warnings: If patient is sufficiently alive and seems able to walk upright into your office and speak, then...', more heartbreak. I guess she can be spry and get out there and grab some yardwork or commissary manager drudgery. Silly me. Nullifying. No genius or kind heart at play here - just Jesuit-wanna-be-morticians with letters after their names, controlling the fate of others by pulling bits of crumpled paper out of some hat and signing the 'eeney-meanie-minus-much' thing, blind.

"Ou est le lapin," one might ask? Why, suffocating, a musty stench emulating, all scrunched up in their car trunk out in the parking lot, of course. Doctors make for cruddy magicians. And magicians, well, they're a rare breed - often astoundingly charisma-free and demented to some damaging degree, living a cotton-tail curly, collapsing Hunka-munka-mucus-trap existence that reeks of "Love me, I learned a trick from my Uncle Bizbo in Grade 3, so which way to the adult community center? I must perform for napping seniors - Ta Da!" Multiple chapters could be devoted to all that, but

there's not a hell of a lot of time to get through here. Or is this some wretched solitary 'Rock-Paper-Scissors' affair yet again? A predictable game (one would think) that tires quickly when played on your own. Games drain Mom. And Mom drains me. So you see, it all works out great, for someone else.

She's now taken to ringing a mammoth-sized liberty bell to grab my attention as she can't be heard bellowing from downstairs to my upstairs writing room, what with all the music blaring to drown out the silence. It's immeasurably ironic because the dinner table fights are the most pugilistic and sweaty, so having that commerative jingle bell to announce it all, well…the clanging preps us for what I wish wasn't proffered each evening, what we submerge ourselves in, again and again, unarmed.

Ideas of employing a kind of dumb waiter get tossed around, though ultimately, this, nothing more than just me in a dusty old tux, two sizes too big, one itchy wool wet sock, clip-on stained and askew, grade school party tie, shuffling around the home, drowsy, pushing a gravy-stained TV dinner tray, with wheels unbalanced, me heavily medicated, punchy and possessing an indistinguishable accent, thus, ultimately helping no one with anything. What I wouldn't give for a high-heeled, swimsuit-fashion-model with maternal instincts freshly-slathered with coconut oil and a surprisingly stellar knowledge of early foreign cinema and Italian cuisine, to slink around the dining area and hold up giant-bubbly-numbers-on-Bristol-board-cards that keep track of just what garish round we're in.

Now, I *know* that's a fantasy.

But I also *know* it could happen.

And, I can *mostly* tell the difference.

When I finally do decide to make my way down to the kitchen, Mom holds her finger up and says, "I've burned myself."

What should a son do? Me, sincere in believing that it would far and away cross the line, up and over the weirdness frontier of mother/son interaction, bordering on some Harold & Maudlin-kind of snack-a-puss-like gesture, as to 'kiss it better' would be creepy, totally disastrous, complete-with-inside-shivers; no matter what telescope or magnifying glass one decides to examine that puppy with. The sullen sad state of this affair is simmering on the burner and I'm figuring there's enough unhealthy occurrences and shaky instability in the heart, body and mind - this home, the secretion and discharge would be astounding even to those observing from the padded fragmentation-room. I opt for a more pedestrian suggestive, "Please take great care when cooking by that hot stove, mother. Be more careful!" and leave the room quickly to retreat upstairs to read, write and arithmetize. *(tf#31)*

Only after we've lost everything are we free to do everything.

Mom, clearly flustered, comes into the room while I'm writing.

"Why do people have to put up their lawn ornaments so early?"

Is she speaking of those dwarfish black Mammie minstrel-men who offer up lanterns and a helping hand with which to attach your horse to, or knock over when you've had too much happy reindeer beef and sin cider? Such colored cads, nothing but good old-fashioned Christmas décor, I figure. Trees, lights, Ho Ho Ho and mistletoe. Someone, somewhere is innocently enjoying all this. The look on her face is that of someone told that the scrumptious steak before them is rattlesnake-porpoise-blubber. It's unmistakably sour, bitter, very much not steak they've been eating, NOT subtle or well-defined like the syrupy and Eiffel Tower strong Triple Sec. Disgruntled; our sparkly holiday conversation now overshadowed by irritable bowel anger directed at a sibling-free, defenseless debating system.

I offer all what I think might help. "Do you want me to go knock them down?" She shuffles away, "No, no. They'd just put them back up.

At least I had an easily manipulated prescription.

------

tf#31 Arithmetize...which can be metal trigonometry in your head while sweating out over a Kathy Ireland or Jane Fonda or Jillian Michaels workout vid. Any advanced physics while hula-hooping qualifies as "Arithmetizing" too. It is not an exact science, you've more than likely already guessed.

* * *

31. Mom's Visitor

When we cry with joy at weddings, aren't we really sad that such happiness belongs to someone else? All our emotions, even the generous ones, even empathy, are really just a way of bringing the woes of the world closer to home. It's all one big opportunity to feel, to feel more.

Elizabeth Wurtzel

More, Now, Again Memoir of an Addiction

Mom is entertaining the troops in the back garden. A nearby neighbor - an old vet named Cal or something. They talk of things they have in life: birds, animals, news of engagements, the unreliable weather, the obituaries, things that aren't right, how everything is ridiculously expensive, lawn bowling escapades and upcoming funerals; things that are no longer around, neighbors who've disappeared, stuff that needs fixing, everything and nothing.

Turns out his son killed himself off with pills last year, and I know that this Cal character sees him in me, so I drum up the respectful patience. "So, you play some piano your mom tells me." Now he's pushing it, uh oh. please no. "Oh yes, Timothy, you must sit down and play a little," Mom says. I'm not getting out of this one, so, to get through quickly, I play Beethoven's "Moonlight Sonata" in super speed time, which sounds pretty off-kilter, but I've completed the duplicitous task of showing him I can play, also giving them the sense I don't want to be the wind-up monkey boy on a leash doing the ivory coast tinkle, ordered to pound out requests for the cheap seats. Now, if he put a few bucks in the brandy sifter placed unassumingly on the old Steinway, we might be in business, but, for now, I should be awarded a sticky gold star for feigning politeness and staying away from being too critical. Because of his son, I give him more leverage than the usual human being, but while their backs are turned, I make a getaway then get back upstairs to write.

Mom comes up after he leaves and says she had a good time. He helped fix the latch on the back door, some company was nice and she gave him some chicken to take home. Before she leaves the room she adds that he'll be eating all alone, which I positively hate to hear. This makes me sick and sad and brings on a special cerebral weakness. Why is it that I'm called in to witnesses and get a whiff of his ballistic isolation? I can now see it as clearly as the soup stain on his yellow tie. Anyway, I wait until she leaves the room to cry. At least I'm feeling, feeling terrible and down that is, but allowed to feel and crying about another's sorrow and not just my own. In any event, that's better right?

It's a rip-off, as we only begin to have a paltry understanding of ourselves and our relationship to the world; and that all comes right around the time that carpet tunnel China syndrome, Alzheimer's and fibroma algae start in on us. These things? We begin to slide when? Mid 50's, 60's? Earlier? What a scam. The friggin' game is rigged. A lack of possibilities in other games of chance Some scientist should come up with at least a couple of other options. Do I feel sorry for this guy (or anyone?) or for myself? It's blurred and there's a moment that doesn't seem to matter either way as it calls mortality to the forefront, makes one look at things differently. Like, how the minor stuff that seems daunting and important is later going to be embarrassingly miniscule on the Darwinian, convoluted, evolutionary scale of things, whenever all that gets weighed.

We take nothing with us.

I think I'd feel more mature if I didn't worry so much about the idiotic, trivial stuff. But I do. And changing is an unbearably tough thing to do - all at once anyway.

I'm so fucking tired of answering, "I don't know" to everything. It could be one psychotically clear thing that's staring me smack-dab in the face, that's continually throwing me and has been for a very long time. I swear to God I don't know. I'd bet my life that most people don't walk around with all this. There's no way.

* * *

32. L i e B u r y

Egomaniacs with inferiority complexes, please apply.

S o i t ' s h e r e . A l l t h i s Christmas, all this death, and there's an outstanding loss of patience all around. I've lost patients before, once in a great while mostly for no other reason than they just drifted off, somnambulently-speaking, they or their insurance companies never to be heard from again. (See tf#2631: Unhelpful Sleepy People.)

Have you ever felt like something really severe and unnerving was about to happen? Like, irreparable? I have that feeling and can't shake it, no matter how many altruistic acts I commit, no matter how much I pray. Walk dogs at the Humane Society, walk that 90-year-old whose mind is tethered so badly I have to introduce myself each time I show up at the retirement residence, poor dear. Nothing works; even if I act all polite, make sure to complete some good deeds each day, be responsible by dealing with matters of importance, organize and prioritize life stuff that's in the mental TO DO basket.

At the starting gate, I already feel too much like The Artful Dodger, wanting, waiting to be chosen by one of the top-ranked teams but not stylish or fit enough; I sit out another bonding game of Dodge Ball and ultimately, the kid with braces, sewn-in toupee, wooden leg and shirt on backwards is chosen ahead of me. How can I ever ask a girl out with this kind of contagious last place mentality? Jaundiced thinking and fuzzy logic can't be the only contributors to this foreboding spook-sense realm, this mother-time. The cuckoo clock chants, "Hey-you, hey-you, hey-you..."

Something's ruthlessly at work; bad luck, bad breaks, bad Karma and demons beavering away... and they're all looking to stick their furry marsupial head out and materialize.

So, what to do? How to shake it? I've become superstitious of late and on a number of nights have left a tiny saucer of milk out for any malevolent spirits who may happen to wander by in search of calcium and better bone structure. (Milking the Devil - a chapter?) I don't like this feeling that someone, or something, is at my heels.

Though many a time I was too sketched-out to listen properly, my friend Frank in Orange County CA has always said that "One should change a losing game, if the one you're playing isn't working for you." Of course. Change this losing game. Okay, so... how is this supposed to work then? He also told me something so simple that I almost fall down in disbelief: bruising my shin (and my ego) on the way down.

Get two pieces of paper; write down just what it is that you want on one, and on another, the steps you'll need to take in order to acquire that thing that you want. Wow. Amazing, this Get It Down On Paper stuff. It's a long way from Simple though. If it were simple, probably a billion or so people would be doing it.

But he does make a good point.

And he means well. Always has. Maybe there's even a chance of me applying it, and getting it to work for me, that is if I don't take its meaning and twist it around by adding my two or three cents to it. Though he is forgetting one thing, and that's to factor in the solar system of unexpected hurdles and baggage, the colossal fears and pulverizing phobias, plaguing issues, never mind the (Bullocks) all over the map finances and responsibilities; then there's my old pals,

Justification and Rationalization, plus a whole slew of other skinned cats that get swung by the tail in this dainty little shop of horrifically cracked china. Excuses have always been a reliable friend to me (unlike the others) and I can't blame Frank for wanting to point me in the right direction, towards something that will inspire.

————————

An awful night, particularly unpleasant, because I'm able to hear Mom off in the other room weeping to herself. This kills me because I'm getting to see (and hear) how truly lost Mom is; and there's not a damn thing in this world I can do to ease her pain. I don't have the power to bring Ron back, and further, I'm pretty certain I wouldn't want to. He wasn't terribly fond of me. Back when the three of us were living together, and that didn't last long, shortly after Dad died, he'd leave little notes around the house, written in what looked like blood, telling me to pick up after myself, to finish things I started. He marked his territory - my mother - and ended up pissing on me? Something I wanted to think was accidental. He disapproved of pretty much all the ways Mom and I interacted, and wasn't much for my manner of living: didn't get it, or me. We never clicked. Eventually, it was left up to me to define our complex relationship, to set him straight, so I began leaving hateful - though whimsical and cryptic - Haikus around the house for him to find:

Step father, step monster, exploding brains on discerning pavement,
big drunken bear meat, canoe paddle overhead,
splintered blister bastard blister.
Smothering, drowning, beneath ice that has frozen us...all
Yoko Yoko, Yuckety yuck-yup. Yoko Oh no, oh no. Yoko, oh no.
Nightmare befalling me. Trap door, Triage, trap door, don't look up.
YOU do the friggen dishes, *mister.*

I've since learned better skills with which to communicate.
Somewhat, but it still isn't getting me where I'd like to go.

* * *

33. Look up the ingredients of snow. I'm melting.

S n o w   r e m i n d s   m e   of my Dad going on his business trips to Montreal and other towns in the province. Also his return home with the just released Fleetwood Mac and KISS records for my birthday. I never quite knew what dad was up to, where he'd stay, who he would see. Did he eat and drink merrily along the way, on the red-eye trains to empty cities of sulk to ply his creative ideas? Was he at all happy when he was there? What scared him? I mean, how did he feel about anything? Did he have joy for our home? Did he look forward to returning? How did he feel about me? Did he root for the Toronto Blue Jays or those Damn Yankees? Or what was it like to be an American living in Canada? Did he have a mistress; a teenage Mensa whore who may have kept his syntax intact? How might I have sensed any of this? In truth, what kind of heart-to-hearts do 12-year-old kids have with their fathers? Is it even healthy to be so intimate with a parent's personal plight, if in fact there's one to speak of? Most kids at that age (the ones that give a shit) aren't usually even given a clue as to what's happening with their parents anyway; minors and pre-teens are kept pretty much at arm's length from whatever disaster or complicated adult stuff is going down. I guess what I'm saying is, even if he didn't die, how desperate would I have been to put the work in to develop an unwaveringly respectful father-son connection?

I wish I had known him better.

There are burdens; concerns split in-between frustrations, internal struggles, but all this I could only imagine. Unanswered questions, predicaments and puzzles; such things now have headed on home here, set up shop and residing in an unspeakably lonely to think of, category;

unverifiable and disturbing enough to have stayed with me all this time.

The worst thing about the whole messy loss has been, and remains, the vacant feeling, the unknown-ness, missing things someone forgot to let me in on. Are these further key ingredients to me not feeling 'a part of'?

At Union station, moments just before hopping a red-eye train bound for who knew where, he may have given a few words of advice or instruction, "You're the man of the house while I'm gone." He'd always buy me these really cool tropical-fruit-flavored LifeSavers: pineapple, wild berry orange, coconut, though I'm guessing dad's trips weren't as exotic or fruitful; such excursions seemed more often than not - desperate, certainly joyless, at the very least, urgent... "All Aboard," a slumped-over, grey-haired conductor would yell out, resonating within the great coliseum of train travel, those seconds from missing the train, these last minute meetings, at the mercy of some large advertising conglomerate, pedaling much too often his terminally ingenious concepts to persons sometimes half his age and sorely lacking in imagination a good chunk of the time: home-run ideas falling on blind eyes and blocked ears, a man alone, returning back to the house. Mom and me waiting. Even at that young age, I began to pick up on his feelings of failure and frustration, to have somehow not provided. I wasn't aware of the cycle until I got a little bit older, when Mom began dropping hints of how off-center things were. I began to see by their interactions with one another, things were on the backward slide. Years after the fact, I thought about this… of him always trying to find that outlet, an avenue, a forum for his creative genius.

There are startling similarities. I truly am my father's son, and everything reminds me of something.

Falling snow also reminds me of walking to girls' homes after school, hating the accumulated snow, making it an absurd Eskimo-stroll with no snow shoes, my almost frost-bitten hands shoved down as far as they could go into my parka. O'er fields après l'ecole to rehearse. "Just get inside and protect my precious hands. I'll need these," I remember thinking. They were 'my bread and butter.' My bread and butter, more often than not, was a less metaphoric, more tasty, toast and margarine offering prepared by doting over-zealous, stay-at-home-yentas that waited for me at these sugary sweet, (though often astonishingly talent-free) girls' homes,

"Doesn't my Anita have a lovely voice?"

"Yes, Miss Kostolano, yes, she does. Now, go on and make yourself scarce; I need some time to work at getting her top off." I may have mumbled this last part so she would think I was too shy to make myself heard.

The irksome eavesdropping from the kitchen, annoying... and inconvenient. The Percodanic pachyderms too often popping their heads in during various stages of rehearsal and undress. Her mom made it almost impossible to get anything done, all the inappropriate breaks into the bellowing chords and melodies.

"Yes, ma'am she's got the music in her. Also, breasts: an astounding and beautiful robust inviting set waiting to be pounced upon... by me, in privacy. Would you mind shoving off, and leaving us be? Oh, and turn down the lights so the atmosphere is soothing and will induce greater affection, and I can play her romantic songs that aren't entirely mine, but I'll say are, so she'll think me sensitive, a tortured talent in need of nurturing, all so I can at least get to zesty first base with her? 'Atta boy. We will now indulge in this smorgasbord of sensuous youth without discerning elders' eyes of impoverished…"

Sorry, did I say that out loud?

That happens sometimes.

* * *

34. A Different Kind of Desperate

M o m   l e a v e s   w h a t   looks to be about 90 cents on the kitchen counter. This will allow me to purchase bread, milk, a stick of butter, maybe some gum - in the year 1934. Who can blame her for this? I can. She is frugal, Scotch, and like my grandmother, from a different time, though I can't help but think that if she's existing in this world and in this present day, why some alterations can't be made. Then again, I only say this in passing, on my way out to the same old street with my pious and pointless currency, off to look for a job, my lot in life, or at very least a part-time position for now. Though more than likely, after rifling through the miniscule classified section at the coffee shop, I'll end up sitting alone in the movie theater for the afternoon, wondering why my own personal muse got off the bus at the wrong stop and is now offering poetic inspiration and wisdom to an unshaven, bulbous-nosed, barely literate trucker who doesn't know what the word MUSE means. I really feel I have no business applying for positions I know I'll depart from scant hours after that first shift of mine begins. It isn't fair to waste the time of peoples' mini-minded ventures with my nonsense. I truly believe this.

"I don't know who you think you are. I can't afford many more trips for you down to the city." Her support - staggering, a frosty comfort. I'm not listening and have turned off even before I've turned on for the day.

And just when I thought I'd gotten away relatively unscathed,

"Do you know why there won't be presents this year?" "Oh, I don't know, Mom, because of me?" She's grabbed me pre-morning coffee, I'm extra agitated.

"Don't be smart, you... well, that's part of it, but..."
Knowing when to leave a party is just as remarkable a skill,
as knowing when to go numb, the glossed over and glazed
kind of numb, like a deer caught with head-lice.

These accumulative little interactions sure can get the
mind feeling pretty unkeen.

I'm concerned that no one's come forward to let me in on
just how we managed to pick up the Millstein family's
Jewish guilt. We lived just down the block, but that was
more than out of reach (I prayed) for catching such a chilly
and disfiguring lifelong affliction, this un-affection and
crazed mode of communiqué? How was I to know such an
ethnic osmosis was set on 'record'? Later to be played back
to whatever immediate family happened to drop by for some
entertainment. Why wasn't I told? Such surprises I can do
without. What other hidden diseases and flaws are
forthcoming, I dread...

———————

So now I've got a new buddy in tow called Ephedrine: it's
white and oddly shaped with a bitter aftertaste, much like a
gal that I shacked up with unsuccessfully in the eighties,
weirdly enough. (Her name, coincidentally, was also
Weirdly.) I crush it up in the garage with a mallet and snort
up the powder; these nifty Ephedrines, and yes; it is
pronounced EpheDREEENE, as in DexedRINE, a
benzodiaze-PEEN, sight un-seen, no one's caught on yet, my
thin veneer, like a racy wintery Dent-yne. Things are
spiraleen. Eeni-meeni-mini. I'm unaware if the result is a
clean high, or just something that comes with the package,
wanting so badly to be out of my head that I just start
bouncing around a little bit more than would be considered
normal.

I don't really want to tell any of my doctors that I've got this new chemistry project, ingesting yet another substance, the reason being they might think I've arrived at a new bottom basement level; a different kind of desperate. But, to further disappoint them, and at Christmas of all times - is a raw deal. So, I'll wait until the New Year, once I'm all behind me. I mean, once it's all behind me.

* * *

35. T e a   T a o

"You are sometimes strange and somber, and often silly,
     but that's in character with ce qu'on appelle genius."
  "What do you call 'genius'?"
       "Well, seeing things others don't see. Or rather the invisible links
between the things."
          "I am speaking, then, of a humble morbid condition which has
             nothing to do with genius."

Vladimir Nabakov
Look at the Harlequins!

I t ' s   a   p r e t t y awful thing, becoming an Earl Grey Tea
addict. I'm in denial because I know that sooner or later - I
pray for later - I'm going to unplaster my skin off the
caffeine asylum wall to straighten up and fly right. A vivid
splendid notion, I see this serene surreal scenario: driving an
old green Jaguar X12 around town, the soundtrack to Oliver
blaring and between stop lights, ripping open tiny bags,
doing 'tea lines' on the hand-crafted arm rest.

At least I don't glamorize the drugs.

We all start off slow: probably herbal; intrigued by the
enormous selection from lands far away, or maybe you're
brought up on a well-defined Red Rose or Clockwork
Orange Pekoe, eventually sneaking that distinctive flavor
and aroma derived from oil extracted from the rind of the
bergamot orange, between classes. Kids start fucking around
with the stuff, their parents blind to them upping the doses
to the danger point. People drift, it just happens. Before you
know it, you've got Lapsang suchong tea on the brain and in
your pockets "just in case," thinking it's all above board, not
realizing those River-dancing munchkin-tea soldiers have
got you cold. The caffeine takes precedence. He is your
president and the vote unanimous; your soul, by now
running far back in the pack. Way Back.

And so, there you are, wandering around the skuzzy railroad districts, dedicating yourself to the clumsy hunt, and now, a new unavoidable sketchy commitment to lower companions who deal in elaborate schemes involving heated beverages. You, now a member at after-hours haunts, diving into pools of tea that just aren't there, your own private hallucinatory hazelnut shell hell, unfresh abodes serving up dilapidated dirty old mugs with over-priced, all too-tough-to-find proper Earl Grey, the real stuff. Rip-off artists abound, sewing in birdseed and crumbs, parsley· and sawdust, devilish duplicators who've made off with your dough before you're good and steeped; an unlucky from-out-of-nowhere harsh and scary sobriety slamming you across the face, leaving you holding your bag; no rest for this woven wickedness that seeps in and stirs unforgiving inside.

Weeks, maybe months later, if I'm able to live through this insane narcotic run, my independent Cabinet of Dr. Caligari footage I've grossly assimilated my living corpse into (to what end?). I'll find myself somewhere in Banff or Baffin Island, maybe Cleveland. They've got me on a kind of syrupy syntax syringe, a type of intravenous methadone for mendacious tea-totaling world-drifters who've lost all hope of regaining a real toe-hold on a purposeful life, aside from designs on knocking over a fuck'in totalitarian Tetley Tea factory. On the lamb and on the nod. And all this talk surrounding Designer tea? Overpriced and unglamorous. I've been around enough to know what's authentic; no one can tell me different.

But oh, those caffeine injections, the rhyming to myself out loud, hallucinations of Oriental opium addicts donning my team outfit; a costumed cape, or the Super-shawl of hooded dementia with my face on it. "The Caffeine Shadow Knows." (The Green Lantern's got nothing on me).

(tf#32) Senior Xiao Wang and his sweatshop underlings toil around the clock packing my personalized scrumptious sachets, but I selfishly still bark down to the basement at them, "Not enough." - having by now picked up (and perfected) my Mom's disapproving tone.

I begin trying all sorts of foreign teas, and other imported beverages and other goods, and justify. I haven't even thought about injecting it right into my veins nor has the idea of snorting, chopping up the tea into lines and freely inhaling, although, now that I'm talking about it, I'm getting more curious. I'm precariously built and in way over my head in this sandbox, digging towards China. Mixing lap-sang-soo-shong, Worcester Sauce and green tea has been known to create bizarre behavior in bug-eyed Belgian Hare rabbits and nosy lab kittens, so I've taken to keeping a steaming kettle in my room under the bed, though I can't imagine what for, but I do know that it comforts me (much in the same way my handy but rarely needed knowledge of 'How Damp Squirrels Manage To Dry Off Unassisted' and 'How Totally Crazy Birds Feel Not Having Arms' does). Boy, the gal who finally lassos me is in for some surprises. (I began merging these two topics in the early 90's into a 13,000-page thesis, with pictures, audio and a stage show from donated puppets - yet have never finished; a work still in progress, a ton of research still to do.)

———————

It's evenings like this when Dad is missed the most, like when there isn't someone older around, who knows about adult stuff, someone who'd have nothing but your total best interest at heart, who'd be there for you to ask questions about things you don't have a clue about, like, mysterious and baffling complex math, geography and recess, not to mention how to begin navigating a romance between humans and how to use words properly in conversation, like Hyperbole or Semantics. Or all this endless hulla-babaloo-crapola with the car... and a job I could really stick at, is there one out there, what's the best way to go about it? So many attempts and so many times it just ends being a scam; all of that can make a guy feel pretty much on his own - again, the thought of regrouping and repacking for the uphill, shadowed, clumsy climb leaves me cold. And damp. Maybe mildewy, nevertheless tired. Damn tired.

I consider myself to be most fatherless on the days in which I'm lost, lacking direction. How about a bloke in my life who's older and taller, or for starters, more virile and manly with some experience, who'd make me feel like he was in my corner (not caring if he's wearing a Hudson's Bay coat or not), just as long as he's not going to split on me when the going gets going. Where might this father person be then? Maybe he'll appear magically when I've burnt all of my bridges and have to settle for a bush in Doheny Harbor for overnight accommodation. I mean, it wasn't that end of the line, it was summertime after all, but being so high, not remembering correct reservation procedures – "How to phone ahead to reserve quality make-shift lodging amidst shrubbery." Maybe Dad might pop up when I was injecting those weird things with those weirder people in the weirdest of places, countless miles from what anyone could ever call a home, post-mortem or pre. I would have chosen anything else if given the fateful shot. God, I hurt.

Typical conversation, near the end.

Me: "Thanks for saving a spot for me guys, sure is nice to have a place in this world."

Drag Queen drug-dealing hookers: "Where's the money you owe us, Pretty Boy?"

Me: "You know, I'm going to have to get you fellas next time, I…"

Drag Queen drug-dealing hookers: "No problem, we know where you live."

Me: "Yes, right now it's in an alley past Broadway, where Hope meets 7th Street: [

Tim: Hope and Spring don't meet, that's why I changed Location, location, location! I always say. It's what it's all about, guys. Girls? I mean, um, well everyone."

You have to find family in whoever is around sometimes.

All this coupled with a wounded widower-hood that seems to pop in and out. I've mostly felt that I haven't deserved, leaving me at the bottom of the hill, while everybody else is at the top, all festive and crisp and Carnivale!-bushy-tailed ready to prance - princes and pals, all of them. A teenage steroid monkey boy stole my ski pass. There's no more hot chocolate, the fire's gone out, the good kindling burned days ago, and try as I may, try as I might, I can't seem to get these crazy screaming twins out of my room. Am I the only one who's taking notice? AND these snowballs in my pocket that I'm saving for a rainy day ain't getting any dryer, either. Nope.

The dope with the rapidly melting snowball,

no great place to get thrown,

left weeping, wet and worn,

a wick dying for light.

Maybe I should have myself glazed?

Then I wouldn't have to pay so much attention, as I'd be so streamlined, too quick even for my off-the-cuff-cemetery-commentary. To be more like the gifted gang now swishing solidly down that enormous bunny slope. Screw 'em. I'll show them all and scratch 'em off my Christmas card list and take the ski-lift. Me, all prepped and ready-to-rock the Luge event, but missing my starting time and a proper uniform, ultimately embarrassed after getting my snowsuit caught in the whiskey chalet smokestack (initially hoping to make a quick $20 for a little rapid cleaning.)

"I've got some tools for this sort of thing in the car, I've done this before, really it'll just take a few minutes." Haggling with the day manager of the Swiss-style ski chalet. It made sense to pack my neighbor's tools, just in case.

"A cheque, eh? Mmm, you know cash would really be better." Remembering that I have the sort of juvenile novice account usually held only by teenagers and prison inmates, the kind where the financial institution has to hold the check for something like five days.

———————

A germ of Dad's image came up when I was brought in to that hospital place last year, all dosed and dazed, not properly framed. He might have had some advice, but all I mustered up in my hallucinatory medicated vision was a disapproving, stern look, an ephemerally lost and misallocated gaze that reeked of, "What's your excuse. You'd better get back out there and get in the game."

I'm a tough kid. I mean, I was, right? If I am, no one taught me how to be that way. He just left, and I was just 16, which is a perfectly wonderful time to lose your father, consequently giving you all the advantages, because you've got it all figured out already, right? So stable and sure-footed.

———————

tf#32: now, Aqua-Man, on the other hand made me completely mental. He made me nervous and suffocated my senses whenever he bounded onto the screen. I felt as if there was much more to him, that he suppressed a lot, always in the shadow of others. I turned off the TV and left the room when he came on.

* * *

37. Another Visitor

I hear Mom ringing what sounds like the dinner bell, so I make my way downstairs expecting to lend a hand organizing the supper situation. But it's not the dinner bell. It's the doorbell. I walk to the foyer/vestibule area and open the door.

It's Jen's father. *What? Why?* I am stunned and must look idiotic. This is going to be uncomfortable. I don't know what to say, but he quickly solves that. "You. I remember you! You son of a bitch," he barks in a kind of Yugoslavian accent that reminds me of some foreign teacher from grade school. He seemed surprised, entwined of course with the intense rage of a Tazmanian divorcee. Just who, I wonder, did he expect to open the door? He who has traveled thousands of miles cross country to ask questions, see the asshole who was face to face with his daughter.

"You're a liar and a fraud, and you call yourself her friend?! You didn't even come to the funeral."

"I've had my fair share of them, thanks," feeling a need to protect myself from his jabs, though quickly realizing it's quite a glib thing to say to the father of a dead girl I was in a hotel doing illegal substances with.

To my astonishment, he punches me in the face and I fall backward into the basket of umbrellas and canes with a thump that knocks me breathless. Too stunned to reply, I stare up at him. He kicks me in the ribs, hard, tossing at me what looks like a promotional flyer for caskets from the local funeral parlor, which seemed symbolic of something, or other. I'm not sure what. (Is this for me?) Then he turns his back, wraps a woolen scarf around himself and trudges brokenly through the drifts of snowy slop that is our sidewalk. I imagine he's off to find his better half to report my whereabouts, maybe finish me off, as she was promised a turn at getting her shots in.

I crawl into the breakfast nook, grab some ice for my eye, then open the crumpled envelope that was flicked at me.

Mom, with her inestimably perfect timing, emerges from the kitchen.

"How did it go at the library?" she asks innocently of her only child.

I look up at her from the floor, stymied, bruised, holding my side. I confess to mom that I received the black eye and limp posture from one of the librarians who added a physical dynamic to her scolding, this, for my screwing with their re-shelving protocol, plus late items still unreturned, not to mention the microfiche manifest now in terrible disarray from my earlier beating by Bernadette. Mom, capable of seeing things only on a selectively protective basis, believed me, and left the room to go knit or do a crossword or take pills or something. I opened up the envelope and it was a letter from Jenny.

Hello, it's me,

If you ever write your stories, promise that a part of me will be in them. You've got some great ones to tell. But you see, things got screwed up, I don't want to go into it.

You, of all people, know I was good once, innocent even, before bitterness barged in, there's some alliteration for you, babe, though that's funny now.

And this is enough for you today, my old friend.

Come find me.

It was kind of tough to read: all smeared, and the ink having run like she'd written the thing while in water or something. But I could make out enough of it to get the gist.

She knew I was headed off on my trip home that morning and couldn't take being left alone again, not wanting to face another day, scared out of her mind.

She somehow wanted to be immortalized in my "Warped and Wonderful" tales, as she used to call them.

I let the letter drop to the floor as I didn't feel too great after that.

* * *

38. Going for Sleep

I can't sleep. Not properly. I drift in and out. A few sentences from a book, five minutes of TV, turn on the lights, turn out the lights, toss and turn. Get up in the night, 1:00 feels the same as 4:00, 4:00 the same as 6:00; grind the beans, put on the coffee, risk a small fire by putting a towel over the coffee maker to deaden the sound and not wake Mom. Some days I don't know if *(Do I play for them or do I have one? Can't bloody well tell, (tf#33) that's how baffled I'm getting. Maybe I sprouted from the Cree Tribe?* If that were true there'd be more literature sent to the house, and certainly I'd be eligible for more exceptions, tax-wise, grants and all. I'm pretty sure I'd know about that.

I should feel entirely lucky that I'm not forced to work at something awful, to have to show up at some coffee house graveyard or rotting asbestos plant, a drone at some defunct factory line, some 24-hour sad and dirty donut store suffering burning retina rays and doughy maple-glazed minds, having to adapt to persnickety-placemat-rules, plus staff meetings dedicated to the most efficient way to stuff sanitary napkins in metal containers. I should feel privileged, fortunate, better off than the average worker bee, that I don't have to partake in any of that marsh-mellow-minded-misery, so why don't I? Spoiled, I feel that alright; tainted, scatterbrained and upside-down. How far off the map am I anyway? Am I unrealistic, thinking I have something special to offer - all this frustration and fragmentation, not even knowing quite what that thing is or how to parlay it into some sort of meaningful existence.

Why don't I feel better?

Breakthrough? Breakdown? Breakaway? Mostly it all feels like some hellish hockey game - forced to play for an untalented amateurish mallard team with no hope of being let off the ice. At today's playoff though, I somehow am able to free myself from the savage pack and manage a breakaway. Skating in a frantic hustle down the Icelandic frost-bitten surface, I'm about to take a shot on goal, a tad panicky how this seems all too easy, unusual that the net appears unattended by anything resembling a goaltender. *(tf#34)* I continue whipping down the ice, amidst the multitudes of screaming fans of all ages unable to control their cheers, "C'mon, c'mon, you've got this!!" My loving teammates (of sorts) warmly egging me on, yelling, "Just put it in the goddamn net, this is your chance, idiot!" Tim, with his newfound tribe, equipped with burlap helmet, a JAWS 2 belt-buckle and slipper-skates, will win, will conquer! Not only win and conquer, but will feel validated, that everything will not be for naught. I'm about to wind up, take the shot, tongue in cheek, flexed just so, teeth grinding, eyebrows raised, cup in place, the crowd cheering, focus, big breath in... wait.

I have no puck.

Wait, oh, no. Shit. This can't be right. It must be in my pants pocket back in the dressing room. Holy crap. It's all flourishing back to me now; it's in there with my half-eaten baked potato, keeping my breakfast burrito company. I was in too much of a hurry to keep it all together, what with all those cock-eyed monster-ish Foot Locker employees dressed as referees, their unconvincing support clearly falsified, barking at me to "Do up your skates and get the hell out there, kid." Man, that was weird. They're in league with something very bad and foul - those Foot Locker wicker-people and their referees. The less said about them the better. They make me nervous, all of them.

The fact remains that we are neither unique, nor important to this world; it will go on just fine without us, no matter how many times we score.

So, why not call in sick and just nap? *(tf#35)* Yes, good point.

Am I really that much further ahead, to carry around with me the knowledge that I'm unspectacular, not special, common currency, unbecoming to a flock, terminally tarred and feathered, ill-advised, far from unique? Someone told me this was a good way to think, but why? So not to feel pressured to stand out with extraordinary measures and passions, maybe to protect and conserve what's left of us, maybe her suggestion, so then, what exactly is the point?

Some days I'm just not up to the rickety cartwheel challenge, nor can I find any good reason to show up much at all, but, I am still looking for reasons, to hope, maybe even putting some work into catching a worthwhile special lady companion, with a boatload of patience, with blistering eyes that can see right through all the muck that's got in my way... That can't be all bad, right?

I'm not obsessed or possessed, and I hope I'm not living too much with one foot in the past and one in the grave, or one in the future and one appendage just left to freely pee on my present. (How many feet is that?)

I'm well on my way to becoming A Spindly Spidery Dude On His Way Out Geezer With Gums Of Disproportionate Vulgarity.

HA!

F i n a l l y , a t i t l e .

All this pontificating is enough to exhaust even me.

"What are you doing in my room?"

"Nothing, Mom, I'm just turning on the nightlight for you and..." She falls back asleep.

I don't think she'll miss a few of these little helpers.

---

tf#33 the Taxi Driver hairstyle though? Such a positively unsocial, intimidating hairdo I can't condone, one reason being, I'd then have to purchase Mowhakian men's ware, which I don't even know exists.

tf#34 I later learn, the goalie was off at his analyst's, wrestling with violence issues and personal concerns: Why people in his masked life are always "Shooting junk at me."

tf#35 Uh, OK, but call in where?

* * *

39. Water's Slip Upside Down

**Our immediate neighbors are not wild beasts but other human beings...
Whatever the inward darkness may have been to which the shamans of
those caves descended in their trances, the same must lie within ourselves,
nightly visited in sleep.**

Joseph Campbell

"The Way of the Animal Powers"

M y m i n d s p e c k l e d a n d wandering, again...
brought on by an agonizing caffeine psychosis, an overdose
from all the tea. Had to be revived by a team of Duracell
Easter Bunnies. I don't know what they are, from what
demonic serpent egg they've sprouted, even what they do in
their time off, when not reviving near dead writers who live
with their mothers. Were they waiting, prepped and on call
down at the station? I am not ready to consider their
gossamer web of self-entertaining downtime. Not yet.

I hear their approach, with strange sirens and German
funeral music announcing the arrival on our front lawn. A
ruby red fire truck covered in polka dots decapitates my
mother's prized azaleas. Rabbits of all ethnicities, sizes and
persuasions hang off the vehicle swinging on the ladders,
sporting very gay but chic aftershave attaches, maybe their
marsupial pouches? A theme from a 60's maudlin-squadron-
cop-show now blasts at an ear bleeding level... none of this

making sense, but I have to tell it like it happened, because, I live the truth. Unfortunately.

Instead of friendly and inviting looks, their faces are menacing, some, missing entirely. Scowling jowls, dirtied quizzical mugs, matted pooh bottoms. There are freakish gurgling noises, verbal Morse code bubbles through pink noses. They are not unlike burrowing rabid chipmunks, disgruntled, vengeful, cast out to the underlying gunk of an inner city. All this, reminiscent of ongoing battles we've all had, with shifty clowns in recovery programs, amusement park carni-folk and mimes with backwards agendas. White faces are disconcerting, painted on smiles, more so. These are not an embraceable people: the bunnies, I mean.

Embrace the discontent, I say.

Like geese that get screwed, fundamentally-fucked and off-track-winged-critters that don't make it south for the winter. The tardier ones never arrive at the foul pool before it freezes over, seeing they missed the boat on flying south; there's nothing like seeing a goose stuck half-below and half-above. It's sad, I know. One - even if one is a bird - must be sure to check those tiny yellow sticky notes placed just so on the ice box, reminders, Important Dates To Remember, like, Packing it in and high-tailing it out of town, triple underlined deadlines to prevent bone chillingly below-sea-level frozen lakes, currents of a cold stream of unconscious. Geese must overcome the impulse to feather their nests with birds of their own flock that simply bring them down and learn instead, to give and take, to interact in beak-peck alphabet. Much attributed to lack of communication, yet again, and not paying attention to immediate concerns. But the bunnies...

They jump with hurried purpose off the rickety Ferris wheel and fall into rescue formation. The windows in the garage are the first to be broken. I yell, "The doors are unlocked. The doors are unlocked!" Stupid rabbits. Tricks are for kids, rabbits strictly for the birds, the frozen ones. I mumble the last part under the little breath I've left while wondering which planet I'm inhabiting today and what minimum level of air is needed in my helium tank to keep me on my feet.

There is a clambering in the kitchen, eight of them: in through the out door, the side one in the garage. Three are left behind in the yard to shovel snow and two to practice boxing on a professional Golden Gloves speed bag in the basement with a punching bag they brought along. Why, is anybody's guess. Perhaps these may be the ultra-violent, ultra-violet squeaky-clean rabbits - I'd heard rumors of their visits - though only bedtime story myths when I'd had teeth knocked out and awaited the crack-cavity fairy who I'd heard was a fox. Not so, it seemed.

Lying on the kitchen floor, still weak and shaky from the Earl Grey, but able still to mutter through clenched teeth, "Wipe your feet, would you?" The bastards have ferret-tea nails that clickety-click, and ruin the lino. Muck is dragged in from the flower beds as I laugh at myself, out loud, while holding my liver in place.

One of them, a darker humorless bunny, hops in seemingly from out of nowhere, and sticks me in my side with his billy club.

Where Mom is through all this, I cannot recall. Wouldn't it be funny if she was at The Humane Society contemplating a pet rabbit for the hutch in the backyard? This though, far from the truth.

An effeminate rabbit attempts mouth-to-mouth on me. It's unnecessary really, but no attention is paid. I guess 'I doth protest too much.' She tongues me... what I'm hoping to God was a she. Wheatgrass-ish. I pause, confused by the recollection of something 'fresh squeezed.'

Three reinvigorated weekend warriors ferociously wrangle me into the manicure position; I'm subdued, weighed down with pretty paperweights with snowy Citizen Kane-like-scenes in them. They say. They are there to get "The Truth," they tell me and I don't know what this means. I, again, swear that in this coming clean, this is my truth, the way it went down.

"My tongue is loosened by champagne," my rabbit says. Good for her/him. Just what I'm supposed to do with that information, I'm at a loss. A huge friggin' loss.

This presents even more stormy concerns as the only audible English I've been able to catch are lines they've recited, word for word, complete with Lithuanian accent, from an Ava Gardner film. And what of their drinking on the job? This, all too much to contend with as my visceral reaction takes hold, my heart pounding from the rabbit tongue-lashing just received.

One rabbit, now indulged in smoking the forbidden fruit of a Cuban cigar, condescendingly jokes with another, while doing a rather elaborate hoity-toity jiggle dance, "He certainly acts high and mighty for a Count, doesn't he, Marvin?" Which, indicated they had entirely the wrong house. And the wrong man; my all-too-identifiable low self-esteem and self-deprecating verbal missives making clear, even to rabbits, I am nothing more than a jester who keeps forgetting where the Kafka castle lies.

Bewildered, grimacing at the foul stench of unprofessionalism. Me, all amuck. One of them whips out a spray paint tin - magenta, and writes on the ice-box,

"...W o r k is d o n e Pl ay Noww...", their call of the wild, I guess. All are assembled now to commence stuffing the silverware from Mom's china hutch into a soggy potato sack. A neon diner-style sign (which I'm pretty sure wasn't there before) flashes "...Evrybo ody Reeporrt to ddiniig Ro oOm ...OnEE ST O Oo P S HO P IN ggg"

"Must clean, must clean." More muttering. A bunny frenzy. At dedicated play, I suppose. Intense was there frantic and maniacal mucus-y giggling. These can't be the rabbits I know from childhood: Fluffy, Bunny, Wingnut and Hoppy. Or are they? I, now in my own private version of La Femme Nikita, a spooky Jean Reno type fellow and his personalized manner of 'cleaning' hoovers over me. A wretched spook-fest occurring right under my whiskers.

Why they are downing all my refrigerator-poetry magnets so hurriedly, I intuit, as 'fuRry friEndss wuRe hear foR fRoliC c .a.ll m e B uNny FoUrlegg'd funn' fUel'. I'd not planned for iambic pentameters or painted prose with furried cotton mouth when I stirred this morning.

One of them wearing a diaper and baseball hat that reads I KNOW WHAT'S MINE begins rubbing himself furiously against the towel rack by the stove. I can only assume he's turned on, deliriously excited, though still baffled at how slow-dripping-honey seeps from a plastic bear's head, with not speckle one of blood spilled. I think a couple of them

'Spray,' but things were sticky by that point. I just wanted it to end.

The excrement excitement is waning. Jaundiced urine, unfluffy bunny tufts have blown into crevices near the recycling carousel as Mom comes in from her shopping excursion. She doesn't seem to be jarred or thrown by the gigantic polka-dot fire truck parked on the lawn, the kitchen in terrible disarray from my "Rescue"; the freshly raked garage, the scattered sweaty-bunny-boxing-gloves, nor the clanging of hundred-year-old forks, knives and salad spoons rattling 'round about in sacks, tossed over burly-festering-furried shoulders. I imagined a furrowed brow. Not even the foul stench of pooh spackled on the chartreuse greeting-mat like jelly reindeer-dispensed brown beans, brought a query from mom. The bunnies pass her as quickly and eerily as they came. An army of fur scuttling off, but not before rifling through her pockets for change, minestrone soup recipes or stray 10 cent stamps.

They clamber through the broken window. One after another, stumbling, falling; not the slick getaway I imagined demonstrated in non-union, rabbit academy training films - the Weekend Sessions – covering 'Rapid in and out Procedures' (also doubling as a racy 'Birds-and-the-Bees' primer for inexperienced pre-pubescent baby bunnies). All this lacking from their protocol. It was peculiar, and colored the experience, as to me they were nothing more than rumpled rodents.

The first winter back home was getting gruesome - grief-wise. Bunny-wise. Mom, consumed with forlorn affliction triggered by witnessing multiple closings of Zeller's stores in the area, and the realization that today is her deceased husband's birthday, the first of many she would now and always spend alone.

Downsizing is sad, lonely and all-consuming.

The rabbits didn't help with replenishing anything. They have their own wave of sadness. They're not friends, and, I don't buy that guff about how they only show up to help me. Domestic turbulence is what they bring and it is also what they leave. I pray they do not return

---

The CAT Thing EXPLAINED...

During my tenure at The Humane Society, I managed to pick up some little known facThe 'Great War of the Humans and the Felines' actually occurred in 1963 between a Martin Salesnick and three tabbies, hardened stone-cold killers but only lasted about four and half minutes, though news spread quickly to the outer provinces. Details are sketchy, at best, and many, '2 leggers' and '4 pawed creatures' prefer their own interpretation. (See footnote-drivallry #273 for a few of the most authentic versions of the historical battle.) This, by no stretch of anyone's amalgamation even on the same world suppository as a musical developed by this 'Lloyd Weber' fellow, entitled, incredibly, 'Cats'. Cats, as a rule, don't dance or wear make-up, or fuck each other at cast parties. Nor do they 'howl in the dead of night' to anyone, musing, "Macavity's a mystery cat, he's called the hidden paw..." That specific fur ball I remember running into when I lived in New York, and yes, he had many cavities, attributed mainly to Big Macs, and sugary treats, this found after a gross but decent cavity search, and his paw might very well have been 'hidden' on occasion, (due to less than pristine cleaning procedures), but he was far from mysterious, and no one ever, ever called him 'the hidden paw'. He was considered a drifter in surrounding Hasidic-kittanic-orthodox communities, always borrowing beyond his vittles in the Tenderloin district, disappearing for days on end, with less than above-board females, plus the 'not changing his litter in admirable fashion thing' just plain stunk. Messy business all around. These words, these lyrics, if you will, are also not to be confused further with the occasions I might have liked a girl, let's say 'a little too much', in countless vain attempts only wanting to 'tuck her in', me, left to hide in her broom closet for days dumb-founded, having to watch her and her new boyfriend endlessly 'neck', the Macavity tune just something I may have sang to them after being discovered, finally, undercover romantic ad-nauseum, (having nausea at the museum) found, me curled up in the laundry basket.

AND

None of this has anything to do with the time I went to Russia on a "talking tour" of the musical CATS. No musicians could be hunted down for such an Communist redundant mounting of what became a tragically tiresome long play. I played the role of Jellylorum while simultaneously understudying for Shimbleshanks, but was sent back to the United States when it was discovered I was selling some of the costume material to half frozen comrades out the back stage door.

* * *

40. Health Fool Store

One of the symptoms of an approaching nervous breakdown is the belief that one's work is terribly important.

Bertrand Russell

T o d a y   w i l l   b e   d e d i c a t e d to the health store, body emporium, or all-natural soul place, whatever they're naming it these days. Okay, no more caffeine. No more Ephedra or Lorazapam. No sniffing Ritalin. No quick trips to the city for my "Treats." I'll get some Echinacea, get really soy and emu-oily and begin making some much-needed repairs.

This Renewal Therapist sort of mystic I'm going to try to be visiting was adamant, saying my body sorely needed some "good-lovin." I managed to piece together that this wasn't the technical term. I'm guessing she dumbed down her diagnosis for me. (Write this down so I can remember to bring it up next time I find myself in Dr. Dave's office). She gave instructions, cleansing-wise, wisen-up-wise and some spiritual suggestions to consider. This sweet old Rinpoche-rogue in sly boots operates under many hats: cranio-sacral, body circuitry, plant energy therapy, quantum leaping, spiritual healing, vibrational testing, discovering past lives through hypnosis, that sort of grift. I could have a field day. If I put some concerted effort, I think, to really mess with her Chi. This doctor-like lady of white witch persuasions, and Caucasian tendencies, would look as comfortable serving homemade baklava (in a balaclava?) as she would awarding her family a provincial pumpkin pie with whipped cream, as she would dancing around this massage table I'm glued to serving up a bottle of herbal tinctures and oils just for me. Face down on her chiropractic chopping block, my energy mucked about with, I'm guessing she was consequently unaware she was crushing my wind pipe, and with her other thick, doughy baker's hand pinching my third vertebrae (which I'm pretty sure I'd be needing). I thought it unfair (she) was able to speak freely, as I could make only muffled warbly grunts and gurgling sounds. I learned: she enjoyed long walks on the beach; how she dug putting crystals and gems in her ears; the laundry detergent she favors; intimate details of her six failed marriages; AND if I'd been listening better, the secret resting place of all the nasty children that beat her up in high school, having captured them for genetic engineering purposes (cloning a new man was on the menu, apparently). She's way past spells and curses.

You'd think with all those talents she'd be eligible for her parole, I mean her own parking spot, steps away from the building's entrance, maybe under a pretty elm tree for shade, but I guess things are tough all over. Just like poet/writer Jim Carroll once let out, "I just want to be pure," whereas Miss Alternative Healer, I imagine, just wants to park closer.

These hearty health store finds all have a similar gigantic marketing scamarama stench about them: perchance it's a more sincere promotional grift… and these companies, who say they want what's best for me (I want to believe them), what will make me prosper in the amazing years to come, or so Rocket Robin Hood's narrator would have had me believe. God, I hope this dandelion-Delilah-shop-keep understands the importance of all this. Why, I'm destined to be a fairly famous and respected kind of Canadian writer! I need clarity. Maybe more muffins. I need to get back to the palatial estate and write about the very, very important trip to the Humane Society; heated exploratory discussions: what to do if bats fly in through the basement window, table manners – at what point does one put certain utensils into action; our adventures in Zeppelin-sized Loblaws-like conglomerates, and their specially built community service rooms that shelter not only AA meetings and classes in Making Gingerbread Houses from Manure, but all sorts of mini-maudlin, weird-ass associations too, so fond and familiar in these obscure towns. The Masons and The Stone Cutters also meet here. And I'm sure I saw a sign reading KLAN FRIENDLY (which may have read SPAM Friendly, but that can't be right?)

Veganism, Vaginarium or was it Veganese? There were times I really felt I could commit to a healthy style of living, and not just for a week or so, but long-term. I didn't think the Vegan thing had all that much to do with eating habits anyway; more like guidelines to pay strict attention to in regards to things such as which trees I could and couldn't cut down or carve sayings into, which bins to toss garbage into, that sort of thing. At any rate, the whole thing turned out to be waaaay too much trouble, so now I eat what I want, even if sometimes it may resemble garbage.

———————

I've got very little on the shekel & drachmas side of things, so I rope Mom into buying me Echinacea tablets, some black Baltic Avenue sea soap and nighty-night organic herbal tea. After a lengthy Spanish Armada-like inquisition by the granola-gone-wild sales lady, I succumb to the items she suggests. Today, I am a testy tea bag sample and yep, I'm cleaning up. I am the milk thistle in some incongruous unrelenting zeitgeist. I hum this a few times over to myself, knowing there's no way it could make much sense, but liking how the words fit perfectly together with that nursery rhyme-like-melody, "Hang down your head, Tom Dooley." Is this a stepping stone across the river (Pick Up) Styx, when you think you sound slick and smart repeating phrases aloud to yourself, but understand less than half the words in those phrases? God, I hope not.

I raise my eyebrows rapidly back and forth and crinkle my nose repeatedly, kind of Bewitched-like (but manly), trying to let her in on a secret, a party game in which I can't use any sounds to tell her she's got the next Farley Mowat in front of her, though, much younger, less furry and without so pronounced a paunch.

Mom storms out of the shop saying that I'll be 'the death of her,' that I'm going to 'break her,' just ruin her altogether (financially, I assume). There's pity from the sales girl as she relinquishes a couple Valium from underneath the counter, saying, "I know how mothers can be," winking at me. My mother uses 'Jewish Guilt' on me, as I call it (she calls it 'just talking'), though I probably couldn't be farther from understanding that truly remarkable faith. I just know this doesn't feel good, interaction-wise, family-wise. "I've dated a lot of Jewish girls," my miserably weak link to that favorite faith of mine, me, still too Hasidically-challenged for my own good. I'm suspecting this won't cut it. (Insert circumcized dancing Moyle joke here.)

Mom waits in the car with the engine running and yells out the window at me, "You know none of this health, natural granola crap is going to help the likes of you; it's your goddamn attitude. You're always glum, you've been neglecting your problems for I don't know how long. I'm confident in telling you that you're sure not going to find any answers in there, mister."

A pretty profound thing for my mother to say. And maybe she's right.

I purchase what I need to from the health food store, return back to the car and say, "I hear what you're saying, really I do." Then I escort my mom out of the car to a nearby tree.

"Okay Mom, help me out here. I've been working on this one. Just step over here, yes that's right, by the big willow tree, now take this huge red apple with you... No no, keep going, the tree over there, the huge willow, that's right. Now, I haven't been practicing maybe as much as I should for a trick like this, but let's give her a whirl, what do you say? Atta girl. Put the apple on top of your head and be very still." I say to mom, calmly and slowly, "NOW DON'T MOVE A MUSCLE." I can do this, just take it slow. Crossbows are wobbly weapons at best, and with these mittens on, and my eyes watering from the cold, maybe I should go over this a few more times in my mind before using a real live human guinea pig.

Ah, fuck it.

"Hey, Mom, c'mon back. Hey, I was only kidding... Mom?"

Weeks from now, I can see driving up from the city to find my mother frosty from the intense mind-numbing, mitten-less below-zero weather, and past terrified as she would have no idea how to survive outside in small-town Ontario in January, huddled up and clutching a dampened refrigerator box, blocks from where the old home still sits; the same one she had to sell, mostly because of me, it seems. Muttering to herself into the lapel of her Goodwill coat, "Why the Echinacea, why the tea? Why weird soap? W e e r d o soap. Minestrone soap would be good... someone... please." She trails off with, "Futures are down... and Kleenex: why so pricey... so, sooo pricey..." And something about pork bellies gone awry or astray - some grand nautical Scotia Bank Depression or something. By this time, I've rolled up the window to tune out the annoying - almost indecipherable

- jabbering, and have soiled her damp and empty appliance box home with muck and slush from my new winter tires, the ones she helped me pay for.

I'm a funny one.

* * *

41. Lessons of Bonding / All Tongues All the Time

Today is shaping up to be 'Mother and Son Day' (though I'm unable to find it on any calendar). It begins with us creating and consuming maple-flavored oatmeal. It's also 'Bird And Gull-Feeding Day.' The moms says there are birds visiting from China who'll be dropping in on a stopover, their seventh inning stretch, I suppose - though not specifically to retrieve her offering of moldy white bread and rotten Romaine lettuce she had me procure from the grocer's back room. I run these and other odd errands because Mom's speech isn't so hot. So, on occasion I'll find myself inquiring after tainted and unsellable leafy roughage, so that Oriental birds can get theirs. It all made sense at the time.

We live a reassuringly obsessive and organized life; and right now, Mom is excited, and for the moment it's all that matters.

Task One: seemed to go down without a hitch.

And when we return, we move on to the changing of Mom's bed: a weekly affair that requires the precision of a Cirque de Soleil telelinguist, whatever that is. It's a religiously precise process that has its feet dipped in sappy elder Anglo-Saxon, Lucy-maudlin arsenic soup-and-lace protocol. It's gooey and complex but it's down in the books somewhere.

Now, there are preoccupations with

The Fitted Sheet:

and its corners, an immediate cause for concern. More on her side - a fretful and worrisome project, plus the plain old concern of the mediocre thread count that will add to everybody's unmendable cause. Remember here, everything is a huge deal of grandiose proportions. During these moments of fabric repair, I can't help but lose all perspective of where all this falls in the grand scheme of importance. (Is there a world on the other side of the window?)

The Flat Sheet:

Absolutely requires tucking in just so. The fact that hers is sort of a 'Rubble-bubble-double-trouble-king size baby'; (no longer produced for multiplicitous reasons, she hastens to recount yet again). It all makes matters worse, and to get from one side of this coffin-ish monstrosity to the other is an obstacle course of entwined questions, glazed in flaming hoops of issues ensconced in a relentless ongoing looped audio track, an all-too-predictable mixed tape pattern (now transferred to CD, a real charm killer). Its effect is to torture me, I'm certain, a familiar response with her so unaware how she turns my fucking insides out; Suggested chapter, "The Complete Unimportance of Unimportant stuff." What was just tucked in, what is about to be tucked in, if I did it with grace, how it could have been improved upon next time, all of that.

The next contender,

The Electric Blanket / Task Two::

and how that must sit just so and... you get the idea. Truthfully, it takes a tidy 18 minutes to complete but feels more like two hours. She times us with the Denmark clock, in preparation for what competition I can't fathom. But it gets done. Even with the horribly disfigured and pathologically avarice Eastern European judge in those inhumane skater tights with untreatable dandruff and B.O that's best described as harshly disrespectful to other humans, we still manage to slide by and push through. OK, so Task Two is down.

The Third Seal: Me, now less than half an extra in a Bergman film. This is where it gets dark.

Time to fetch the Sunday paper. She wants me to go with her, which is nice. She's openly admitting she would like to spend time with me. Or is it she doesn't want to be alone? I can't make out if I'm an extra or an understudy on this surreal set. Either/or, it's the same result, and who am I to question? But before getting in the car, a litany of garden tools must be checked, cleared for possible upcoming emergencies, though I can't imagine just what a 'Gardening Emergency' might be. There's minimal snow and ice accumulation in the driveway, certainly not enough to require ice picks and specialty shovels. Further, it's getting warmer and in stark contrast to my mood, is sunny for some reason, which will be for naught in a few hours, as everyone's melting and I'm feeling too much like Linus, his head in the clouds, freezing my animated ass off in that horrendously bone-chilling pumpkin-patch, my fucking mind coming apart and my disappointment hitting another all-time low as one of my fave childhood Hollywood heroes, The Great Pumpkin, leaves me waiting, again, the fucker. But Mom's on top of it.

"Ron and I used to do this for hours at a time." The elements of bonding that act held, I can only imagine; braving the results of foul northern driveway elements; the risks taken, and having come out winners. Winners, the store. Oh God, how did that find its way in here?

I'm losing my grip, sobbing inside and it's drizzling clearance items.

"Christ ma, would you just get in the friggin' car!" I exclaim.

Today, poor Mom is dressed in purple pants and grey slaughtered fox boots. Her sweater and turtleneck go with it, I guess. I offer her what I feel to be an important proverb that could be applied to this scenario: "The food in this restaurant is terrible," the response: "Yes, but such large portions."

An amusing notion, yes, and I'm hoping the lesson will make the smooth transference over: that just because there is a lot of something, in this case - purple, for example, does not mean that, well... it all falls a tad short. I was hoping this would be a humorous way to get the message across, not hurt her feelings - maybe she'd consider doing away with the purple pantsuit of questionable quality. (It's not enough that the sweater goes with the pants, the turtleneck matches the slacks, or whatever is the case - it's next to impossible to take stock of the obtuse patterns, the freaky pastels, where one is tucked in, where we begin and ultimately end; a baffling ordeal, all of it.)

It's all happening now. Everything is now an insulated out-of-touch, below-board purple pantsuit. The wretched ensemble isn't helping her mood, it just can't be, and it sure is depressing the hell out of me.

But the colors:

That she wears follow designer instructions given to her from off-kilter crack-head fashionista police-ladies, who somehow rack up points, percentages even, when they spot and ticket people wearing such alarming shards of chartreusie-toosie (my name for the color, as it's indescribable). Someone is making something off of this, big-time - benefiting from the pathological benevolence, this unstylish epidemic. It's all out of vogue, out of the question, off the mark and sends the spiritual thermometer way below fuckin' freezing. Mom offers further details in the car about

these extraordinary birds I'm getting all prepped to hook up
with.

The arrival at the bridge:

We arrive at the lake-like-streamy-pond situation and lo
and behold there are gulls, mallards, loons and daffy'd
derelict ducks mincing about, though looking less than
excited to see the likes of us. They peer our way while
conversing in a huddle, seeming to say, "Yeah, we're birds;
we're here hanging out; we have stuff to do. Uh, just what is
it you want? And, please, tell us you're not going to sing any
selections from 42nd Street today. We were actually just
about to take off, anyhow. How's the writing coming along?"
(I may have imagined the last part.) The things with wings
seem less than interested in our burnt offerings (or purple
mama-watoosie-costume.) When I get around to asking how
the Trent Waterway System swishing along in front of us
actually works, I really must have hit some chord, as here is
where the ugliness floats to the surface and washes away
even the remote chance of carefree episodic laughter; I'm
shot to hell in a basket of gangrene limbs.

"What do you mean you don't know, certainly you do... I
don't know what's wrong with you, don't be so stupid."

If there were hungry piranhas and sharks in the stream,
I'm thinking Mom might have nudged me in, just to reduce
some fury going on inside her that she doesn't understand,
brought on by me in spades, her one and only boy. I am
grateful to her for not pushing me into the streaming action,
whatever those complicated emotions were stirring within
her.

The disapproval:

The scowling eyebrows and overall tone of not wanting to
change in any capacity - as change engenders fear I guess (a

cliché I apologize for) - sends the 'Mother and Son-Oatmeal-bed-making-Sunday-paper/petting-zoo-Day' straight down the ovarian inner tube, as well, the preceding lunch far from worked out as we ended up not talking, me, again alone, glued to the TV, hypnotized, rocking back and forth, hands to my chest while The Shining plays. Oddly enough, the visions and voices on the screen line up eerily, more and more, with what's occurring here at home. But it isn't uncommon these days for art to rip off life's heartfelt images and ideas. Not around here, though. I'm spent from interacting with humans, gulls and zombie-like droids who work at the grocery store. I cry heavily during a late night showing of the film Awakenings, when Mom comes in and asks me "What's wrong?" at the precise moment the doctor is telling the mother character that her son has this debilitating disease - again, creepy and spooky just how many moments on the boob tube parallel our paralyzing Lost in Space universe, our transparent tangled cobweb galaxy that I bet all could see, though no audience response was audible. This happens a lot, actually - hangdog humans not paying attention, a crime that doesn't carry a weighty enough punishment, though all guilty parties should be awarded overpoweringly harsh terms, with unpalatable foreign language paragraphs to decipher, rife with dangling participles in storyboard death camps. Don't ask. Rarely is anyone ever called on it; most leave the state and change their names before any sort of felon-pursuing posse could ride in and organize an authentic investigation. Even better, a vigilante group on a worthwhile cause, ready to lynch anybody cerebrally constrained who can't conjure up images to describe what's happening in their own God damn lives. Lackluster and lifeless rhetoric should bring a death sentence. Mediocrity is thriving, climbing the charts and letting nothing stand in its way and is continuously rotten and severely infectious and debilitating to our society: a disease best avoided. It's at the core of feeling unmotivated and kills any get-up-and-go you've ever had. And that can make the soul and heart irreparable if you caress it too long.

Today I am losing it. I am a rotund and ridiculous, plaid-shirt-wearing axe-wielding Jack Nicholson and Mom is Shelly Hack or Duvall or Long, or worse - that Mary Shelly person. (Why is she always visiting?) I haven't heard from her (Mom, not any of those Shelly people) for about an hour. But now I hear knocking around upstairs, so I slink up there to see what the commotion was all about. Seems we can't be apart too long.

Hold on, what fresh hell is this? Before me, the cinematic circumstance is too fantastic. I see before me, painted on the bedroom door:

R e d R U M

Not entirely, but I imagine the worst sometimes. Yes, I sure can.

This time last year I was appearing at Drug Camp. This year, I'm booked in to Grieving Mother and Son Writer's Headquarters Aftercare. Why I'm always in some semblance of kinder-institution is unclear. When I heard the news that I was to be carted off to the YMCA Sadists Training Camp, the only sensibilities that arose were hatefulness and no control. I hated the couple of summers I was forced on to that crowded all-boy-bus. Here we go again. I am The Town Crier, the local Writer in Residence; my friggin Mom's residence.

The times I don't feel like writing are the times I'm most scared. But that's the time to get down to it and trudge forth, they say. That is, if you're planning to merge with anything of substance, to veer infinite miles up and away from mediocrity. I'd rather not delve into the times in Santa Ana, shaking and waking up in the bushes in that park, unbecoming to me (I felt) but what I was becoming, me arriving down in the harbor, after hunting around for suitable streets to park overnight on in Silver Lake. (Not a lake at all). These things, as well as others, all testers. For what? One dares not think what they may actually be prepping you for. Perhaps D R E A D. Things you half-consciously swirl through, that you know can't really be you. You grapple, you have to keep moving. You feel if you stop you'll die.

I don't want to think about the times I'd muster up the courage to call her, then say the wrong thing, then drive at high speeds wailing like a retarded crying baby, trying to convince myself not to turn the car into oncoming traffic, eventually having to park, place a hand inside my shirt where a human heart would normally sit to see if it was in its casing. The hyper-ventilating, the heat and the sorrow... infinite, me not so much with the jesterly attributes anymore... sickly-celled and misplaced, all that.

There's something happening to me. I can feel it. Maybe I'm dying of something, a wrong deed I've done and need to pay for, here on earth or someplace that's waiting, maybe... made up of lining from a cat's unraveled innards. Who knows? A Hecubus-ly-driven devilish red-lit district; written into the asphalt sidewalk, probably when the city was repaving, attempting to make Perdition a better-quality

community to live out one's day in ALL TONGUES TOUT
LE TEMPS. Why it's a mix of English and French I can't
say. Maybe this is wired to the suffering wheel so that a
discussion can be had about Quebec being a different sort of
netherworld to exist in; nothing but the foul stench of
encrusted worn-out thoughts and feelings, ludicrous
relationships and half-assed attempts pissed in vigor live
here, along with the false starts and failures plastered on the
walls dripping with red wine vinegar, it looks like

REDRUM

is scratched haphazardly in red lipstick and I can't find the
mirror to read it backwards so I take it to mean that I
somehow missed my class on drumming exercises.

So now I am to drum for all eternity. Ha Ha. A sweating
Tito Puente mercilessly hulks over me. Tito is relentlessly
cracking a personalized whip with a balsa wood handle. I am
in a hell specifically set aside for me… I plain can't help
myself, and I am R-E-D-R-U-M-M-I-N-G. He screams in a
demented blasphemous Spanish tone, "More little drummer
boy: triplets, paradiddles; now 5/8 time… Ha, ha, ha… You
think you're a good-hearted soul, you are nothing!" I'm left
to march to the sound of a deafeningly dissonant drummer.
Crap. This is sure going to leave a mark. Indelible-wise.
"You with your words and editing, and that's the worst
character development I've ever been privy to witnessing.
YOU'RE GOING TO LEAVE A MARK ALL RIGHT!"

I'm not able to discern whether this is one of my
annihilating eerie dream sequences, or if it's actually
happening. Cause for concern? Lines are really getting
blurred around here. The Dante-esque mass of bodies isn't as
alarming as I figured. At least there are others around to
compare notes and convalesce with. In this special Hades, I

come across all sorts - people who'd lived their time on earth ripping off their fellow man, the ones who'd stolen and hurt innocents, folks who got nailed for returning items they'd stolen earlier that day for cash, the frighteningly less-than-talented pop-star-shams who've taken horrible advantage and even worse, were disrespectful to animals. They were all there, no tongues to speak of, no voice to speak up with, unclear just how they arrived at this inferno. But I've got their number.

I shimmy up to the devil and try to get an assistant's job.

"What is it you're doing there mortal fool?" The devil's accent sounded close to the way people spoke who lived their whole life in Boston.

"Me? Oh, I'm just jotting down stuff, keeping track and all. Just pretend like I'm not even here." So, I plead my case, saying how my time on earth seemed to get pretty messed up, that I wanted to start over again, that's if it was even allowed or possible, and maybe how a position of some kind in this evil spirit's firm might help me feel a part of, something I couldn't make sense of during my days on planet earth.

Whatever the case, I'm almost positive that this life-threatening slice-of-life prominently features a deceased John Ritter playing some peculiar fidgety war vet neighbor with out-the-window, through-the-roof garden concerns, who plagues our streets with disquieting, eerie early morning ride-by wake-up calls on a girls pink bicycle, with punctured tires.

There is symbolism, how things are looked upon, how they can seem bizarre and nonsensical, and then there is just the off-putting. I'm pretty sure this one has all of those.

I need these things - my pain, my memories, my tongue, my father. I'd give anything to see and spend time with my Dad, and for him to have a look over my writings, to see my book. Not many things worked out for him, a sickening drastic cruelty that's transported itself into me.

Add it to the pile.

Maybe avoiding main issues; again, straying from the point by entering into self-created worlds and scenarios is a disease.

That's crazy, but people do it all the time. Even the ones in my fantasies.

* * *

42. H i p n o t i c

Even if I had to rub myself like a cat against every human being I encountered, I was going to get to the bottom of it. Rub long enough and hard enough and the spark will come!

Henry Miller

Tropic of Capricorn

I'm t h a n k f u l t h e r e's no mandatory cavity search prerequisite to hang out in this neighborhood. The Recruitment Board seems to be getting stricter when it comes to reviewing potential applicants, I hear, as only 'top drawer folk' get a shot at fairy-tale-like highbrow living. I'm already embarrassed by the amount of sweets I ingest, and I certainly can do without some lactose-tolerant, dreary lab coat person meddling around my bicuspids and molars, taking inventory of my misbehavior and inappropriate goings-on that the board will certainly frown upon.

And just who do these fussy gadflies think they are, screening the applicants yearning to set up shop in the safer and pretty areas? My Grade 7 French Haiku attached (with bubble gum) to my petition - *"Mon chien est blanc et grand. Bonjour mon ami. Au revoir."* - did little else than reveal a dismal and alarmingly limited knowledge of foreign languages and proper prose. My grant application was returned with the helpful suggestion that if I were indeed retarded, special allotments could be made.

And there's just no escaping the Hip Replacement Chart that sits unassumingly near the bottom corner of, yes, the front page of the local paper, that only seems to report events from the bubble of Lindsay, keeping any events that didn't happen outside. I sense these perversely pretzel-headed regional folk consider the New York Times to be, well, just different clocks hanging in some train station somewhere in a recently built, unnecessarily and daunting super-mega-metropolized place called York. Each time someone partakes in one of these queer and unorthodox procedures, it seems to get mentioned. Big news. The operations, I mean, if that's in fact what they are; as I imagine, some med-student-reject-from-the-dark-side who rips off limbs and hips in the less than greater metropolitan area. To me, it's unbearably funny to think about, but more than likely is not going on.

Just who keeps track of all this, I can't say, and just where those hips, that have been replaced go, is anybody's guess. What comes to mind (mine, I realize) is a field, hidden behind a haunting triage of decrepit barns, maybe out near the leaky rusting water tower, lambs and fowl of varied kinds booting elderly appendages across manure-laden pigpens no farmers have any damn use for. Unless the animals - stay with me here - have turned this mass limb-phallic-field into some kind of Orwellian satellite. Yes, that's it. They are building it. Oh yes, they will come. Maybe not until spring, like the ducks, or the ex-girlfriends with funny foreheads and thick ankles, but they'll come... and in droves, too. Everyone loves a decent satellite built out of seniors.

Overheard at a cocktail party, George Orwell once said that, "Evil begins with the euphemism." Well, I believe that "Goodness begins with a field of hip seniors." Slightly more obscure, granted - abstract, theoretical even, but nonetheless, relevant and coming from a hearty and true place. Seniors are sweet. They're cool. Kind of. Few have ever hurt me, so there. With my luck I'll probably end up as one, which will, of course, be the ultimate cruel joke. If that's all I'm being kept around for, knock me down now; I can do without the predictable and inevitable gum demise. I've had a lifetime of that to draw upon. The doing without part, not the seniors.

Today, a story appeared in that same Daily Post newspaper on some veterans giving cats, and some down dogs, select selective serotonin reuptake inhibitors (SSRI's) to treat their depression.

I recall a time a pet feline suffering from obsessive compulsive grooming, for example, would have required one of those gramophones thrown around its neck. They've done away now with such a bulky apparatus. In retrospect, I believe the old way may still be useful and could perhaps serve me well, so I'm off to search through the Barney rubble in the garage in search of my own medieval-megaphone to wear around my neck.

Some strange looks sure come my way when hiking around town, but who's to dictate fashion, really, these days? It's their sins, yes, their own uncomfortability with themselves at play here. It's their mini-minded jealousy, their hideous embarrassing envy of the big city writer fellow who knows better (or is it, the little rural scribbler who's lost and doesn't know dick?). Queerly (queerly?) enough my hearing is enriched, magnified miraculously and I can't imagine how I've lived with such a low volume audio in my life - that is once I got used to the alarmingly loud echo. People are, perhaps, more wary of me now, as no one wants to set me-a-ringin'. But I'm fairly certain there's no way I could look that threatening wearing my enormous catacomb-like Jabba the Hut ear-piece snuggly around me... but who's to say? The moistened inflatable water wings - part of the designer uniform - seem to bring the most questions, but also add to my acidic isolation.

Similar to the neighborhood feline system, I've begun to lick my fur patches, thus have gone balding in the oddest of places, due to what I'm guessing is either stress, or neglecting to properly change my litter. ("Environment friendly clumping garnish," my ass).

I focus my too fervent attention away from my unsturdy self (impossible at times), *(tf#37)* and begin to furiously groom our cat, keeping him from mostly all its daily duties. Now almost hairless, the little guy plain just konks out, dog-tired after being almost combed to death at our last session, while being held down by those circular, green-felt-bottomed paperweights with pretty flaky scenes of Snowmen giving creepy looks at lusty lasses wearing snug-tight snowsuits sliding down on Rosebud-decal sleds. Slick.

Actually, we don't own a cat, per se, but in theory, doesn't it kind of become your pet by a kind of designated ownership, say, if it magically appears in the house where you live? And, is one not permitted to do things to this jellicle furry four-legger that's made its way in through some side door, this incidental accidental-tourista, *(tf#38)* this brow-moppy-bandito, this perky-eared barista? And haven't I then, in fact, made a step towards marking my territory on that particular kitten through aforementioned brushing sequences? Just to make sure, I take some of my very personally produced emollient (sticky stuff) and dab it behind that chosen cat's ear, just to be sure.

There have been memos and letters from townspeople instructing me legalize-wise, creepy-wise, to stop brushing their pets. The neighbors say that they'll press charges for luring their animals into my house with meow-meow liver snacks and promises of calcium, cured meats and an abundance of cozy spots on the couch in the TV room. (Coincidentally, how I got one of my first girlfriends over). I'm unable to keep a proper tally, can't keep track, have misplaced my good deeds, and fear Alzheimer's has begun to unravel The Inside Me, exposing the most unfragrant behavior I'd prefer not look at. I miscalculate, lose the simplest of things, and can't comprehend too well why the radio station will not change when I flick the lamp switch on and off. The goddamn timers Mom has the infrared lights rigged up to sure don't help my cause either.

---

tf#37: All right. Maybe I do have a lavish array of phobias piling up, but I'm pretty sure I don't have that Auto phobia one, a fear of referencing oneself. Let's move on. (see back of book for a complete list of every kind of fear known to mankind, as of the summer 2015).

tf#38: years later, some literary fame came-a-calling when I was awarded the 'Booker T. Bookman Gillette Track 2' prize for a set of pointless, unhelpful short stories, a self-help pamphlet of sorts, titled "The Purposeful Urinist". It represents mans' starved passion, a longing to travel thwarted by incontinent inappropriate bouts of wild urination in his church and Radio Shack stores which kept him from this dream. Known to be a jaundiced trickling pony, until the narrator takes up with a cat trainer - really his maid - but also a cat trainer, who performs somnambulent surgery, installing a sort of 'kitten catheter' and everyone lived unhappily ever after, the man's passion no longer denied. "Gripping, a rare introspective look into people who like cats but are plagued with going to the bathroom", said The Post. I was proud. Later, William Hurt, Sigourney Weaver and the guy from An American Werewolf in London starred, with Jon Lovitz playing the overly-friendly amputated palsy vet neighbor with an inability to keep his yard tidy.

* * *

43. Ticking for Timing

I am forbidden to turn on any lights, as a good chunk of them are hooked up to these bizzaro taboo timers and inviso alarms. It's voodoo, as they go off at various times and I'm convinced it's part of a botched experiment, a random and arbitrary order - specific to whom, I can't say. I guess Mom. The divergent delicate time zones of the home: the old brown wicker lamp in the den is set to After Eights Swiss Chocolate time, wound and monitored, I imagine, by a contorted fellow named Oluf Bangdenson. Everything's set to go off at precisely the instant some Viking removes his helmet before chowing down on his Salisbury steak supper service for one. Either that or at that moment, the third child of the Seventh sealed sign of Liv Ullman's breasts hops atop an Ikea jungle gym, from lack of oxygen to the brain from gorging on grey shellacked Swedish meatballs, the affixation full-on whilst inattentive parents are precision buying.

Regardless of season; that old summer heat, the dead of winter solstice, daylight spending-time, turning back or jumping ahead of anything, the tiny brass piano lamp magically turns on, every night at 6:10 p.m. That's it, and seems it will forever be this way. And don't think you can get away with monkeying about with any of the dusty golden chords; precariously woven wiring, as grime from certain years (my theory) makes it churn out time a suspicious kind of way. Some things should just not be tampered with. Some time phantom unbeknownst to me has been screwing with that Prime Meridian I keep hearing about, mainly whilst visiting drab cousins in a really Mean area of Greenwich, Connecticut. I never seem to be around when they actually phone to ask for proper directions. Screw 'em, they've probably got GPS. They'll figure something out.

And the kooky chirpy-chimes that beckon from the attic, well, no one knows. Someone should mosey on up there and look into it. Mom and I don't talk about it. It's gone on far too long to begin investigating now. If I recall (recoil?) correctly, there's no actual clock up there, though there is rapid ticking, keeping track of what, I'm sure just the knowledge alone would lessen me somehow.

There is fear in all this muddled time; to come into contact with any of the disproportionately sensitive strange wiring and fragile hands may upset some godly balance in the grand procession of things.

To jump clear of the clockwork may have lent a hand in a freedom I was seeking, but I truly feel to even leave my Mom's house, if only physically, that these things would inevitably catch up to me. I'm tired of running; running from something that I can't put my finger on.

All this, very dismantling.

Comfort = Home? Hmm.

These pens still don't work. Of course they don't - half of them won't - why should this surprise in this mausoleum of mopus writing implements, sustained in a stupor of ad-nauseum-disensability? Same goes for those clocks, which I'm now getting used to, since each of the dozen or so timepieces are either ahead or behind, I'm constantly pretending that I'm in some alternative universe. Mmm.

Now I know what the problem is: a good deal of this house is not set up for the living, but for the much more foreboding construct entitled the dying. It is not a house which can exactly be "used." It's the sort of place that should be rectified under a big glass, in a see-through crystal coffin the size of a biodome out in the backyard of some Caucasian-friendly museum. (Charge admission?) So charming, all these perfectly pledged 100-year-old tapestries and bedspreads, so decorative yet so dysfunctional. To drape something cozy over me while watching TV, would be a real heaven, a blast, snug and sheltered. But it seems more important how all the hand-crafted doilies hang, the ones to be viewed and judged.

There's something to that, and this isn't the first time it's come up.

I did better today as nothing went up my nose or in my arm. None of the Ephedrine. No Lorazepam luncheonette. Only tea. Lots of tea. How did I make it through the day without spinning off the rails and becoming unglued? Well, I took a break just to shut down the system and watched some great intense films, including Awakenings. For starters, the film made me idle, kind of zapped any energy I was thinking about conjuring up to move; it made me emotional, exhausted and far too preoccupied me with the fear of ingesting anything like El-Dopa (what Robin Williams administers to De Niro's character) for fear my head would be lodged permanently to a side angle (like the main character), hence, the idea of putting on any kind of sweater by myself would make for a hell of a chore; even brushing my own set of teeth would require an assistant. The watching and digesting of all that ate up a whole bunch of minutes. A couple hours got dedicated to pondering how gruesome, how badly in need of proper sculpting I'd appear to the opposite sex if I ended up like that poor thick-spectacled sod whose medication initially seemed to get him on the the half-human carousel and then just as hastily up and deserted him - a sluggish drooling hero left a sadly shaking imbecile. A hell of a box-step, though, he ended up being able to handle, but not much on outings, as when it came time for that once-in-a-dog's-age date, that gruff nurse was always in tow, monitoring the medication that temporarily set him in the right direction. This nurse's constant interruptions desecrated any possible romantic atmosphere, and sent south any future feminine companionship as no one wanted to compete with his daily routine (blood work, catheter adjusting, anal probing, etc.) that overshadowed and demolished any chance of spontaneity. His dance card with the fairer sex, lost.

I tried to write. A lot. And I cleaned. Boy, can I clean when I want to. It's a clear start to completing a kind of immediate gratification sort of thing: no bloody Wumpa's World or Puppets-with-hardons-Killing Zoe to get in the way. It's an easily distinguishable project that lies directly in front of me and can't be diddled around with by friends, Mormons or marionette or Mennonite countryside dwellers. I'm in control. And isn't that what I, we, ultimately want? Not the Mormons - but the control part.

* * *

44. Sickness in Motion

I p u r c h a s e d these peppy pills at an authentic 'health food store,' so they can't be bad for me, much in the same way that the printed written word never tells a lie. I met with my doctor friends today: both of them say what I'm holding is Speed: I'm dancing with the devil - haven't got this step quite down - I'm driving dangerous with my own limitless rules. Though my friends in lab coats can't seem to offer any explanation why I hurt myself so, why I tempt fate in the manner to which I am so betrothed.

I get the "You're an addict" thing and "This is just what you do." And sure, these helpful hints are handy to have in the old memory banks, though they won't hold much weight when I'm dead. Always on the lookout for whatever that thing is that's gonna work.

My pals the doctors, two different people who share the exact same "Haven't-we-been-here-before?" look. Just how much pathos is needed in this tremulous doctor-patient interchange? I don't want to lose my audience or my manuscript to my therapist. I tell myself that the real reason for him being there after all is as a Script Supervisor. But he is encouraging and even asks that I make sure to save a part for him. I don't know what this means.

My merry addiction counselor stops me on my way out the door and whispers, "Look, I know a client who's got a production company and, well, we'll see what happens." One thing I'm wondering, "Why is he whispering?"

It is only I who can seduce and rope these busy professionals into listening, advising, even being in on the ongoing ridiculous rhetoric. I sure have missed my calling, though… I can't imagine the field, this, a big part of the problem. These misguided, seemingly manipulative qualities, my coup d'etat sadly too late to power this tugboat. Can my muffled, placating talents aspire to a better French vocabulary, or provide a hand up to me? And nothing produced yet but some approximation of me, appearing out in the sticks at some amateur community theater, some Rice-Krispie square fundraising project that rehearses in a church basement.

———————

Over time, I've managed to maintain ongoing relationships with a litany of doctors who I check in with every so often to make sure they're getting along. They need me - for what, is unclear at press time - but I'm on it, on to them and their agendas. I'm not fooled. They need papa pigs from Papua New Guinea to test the stream of newly-arrived-on-the-market-anti-depressants that dangle the promise of a cure. I have the time, and I'm all for medication as long as it's the right kind, the real good kind, so get out the swabs and surgical mittens and begin prepping, doctor. I'm King of Solving Problems, or am I The Unsolvable Problem? (I can do the Rubik's Cube in like, one day.) I'm all for taming my beasts, as well as whatever is jotted down there on those prescription pads, so let's book an appointment.

My turn for impossible-to-answer questions.

———————

I spoke with Dr. Dave and asked whether these potions and all the immense selection of various vitamins, anti-depressants and mind-juggling substances will have a cumulative condemning effect. He takes some blood and says he'll get back to me. Of course, he won't know, but watching him squirm through leery medical doctrines can be entertaining and takes the pressure off me, momentarily anyway.

Could it be they need me to be depressed? I can't say 100 percent but I get to wondering. Exactly what is my affliction? Is it a disease in itself, the not knowing by this stage quite what the illness is? Do I need my depressive introverted morose moods to complete the persona that I've cultivated? Shit.

What in hell do they think drugs are for anyway?

* * *

45. Up and Out Before it all Gets Going Again

Lady Heroin speaks to me at moments that are convenient for her. "It's clear, we're going to get along...." This eerily familiar voice chants lyrics from musicals when her throat is not obstructed from swallowing the devil's semen. She's grown up, a real lady, but still has a home nestled inside of me. My maddening, hurtful Medusa screams daunting hymns even though she's tone deaf. But to tell her so becomes a drawn out ordeal, so it seems just shutting up and taking part in the drizzle parade is the path of least resistance, and again, I'll show up and make the most of it. This alarming siren has no business singing (her deathly job), because she is out to hurt everyone who comes close to her. Nothing seems able to stop her. If somebody else could just control the volume on her, then maybe I'd have a shot at listening. Because it is kind of beautiful.

It is difficult to imagine how I'd lived through the adversity and chaos, now a muddled confusion I haven't sorted out, on or off drugs; it's chilling to realize there will be much more of this life business to get through. The old haunts, well, that's exactly what they are, assaulting me at each turn - unable to assist with any info about how my hand plays a part in ripping me down.

I know I should really save this money for that movie I've been meaning to see later tonight, but all of that goes out the truncated window when I spot that guy who holds the possibility of well, you know. He doesn't even speak any friggin' English, thus his nickname, 'No English'. He's kind of an old timer, Vietnamese, I think, but with this creepy child-like pansy, sort of Tatum O'Neil-ish skin. Both have the same mole but he's way less cute, and probably doesn't even know who John McEnroe is. I don't understand it, or him, not really. I mean, all that time running around the market, he'd have to pick up at least one word of English in his dealing drugs and living that sort of life? Wouldn't he?

She's still singing.

He motions to me to sit down and gives me his mop to hold. I'm thinking it may have been stolen since it's still in a plastic bag and has a tiny orange price tag. Right off the bat, I am 'Hardware Boy Accomplice.' Between my 14 dollars and whatever we can get for my throwaway camera, my used CDs and DVDs that I was actually getting kind of proud of as a little library of entertainment I was beginning to stockpile. But justifying erases any guilt as those are parting gifts that I can always pick up down the line. The immediacy takes precedence, each and every time. So, with his mop, we could probably be looking at... well, not much of anything. He does say "Fee mini," which comes close to sounding like five minutes (this, or a further fee for a swift game of mini-put). In some capacity, I'm on board, and hoping that magically, by some bizarre happenstance, someone owes him, or he's getting it fronted and I'll be able to partake. The sad thing is I'm busy grasping at irrational and slight possibilities, lying with wait and hope. I thought time would allow me to get past this sort of scrounging around for bills and coins. The personality trait called resourcefulness often makes me feel like a punk.

Still singing.

I should really check in with my friend Michelle. I should really drive back to her house where I've parked my ass for these few days in the city... I should stay on good terms so she doesn't feel like I'm just using her, which come to think of it, I kind of am. But that's a longer, more uninteresting story. So let's get back to how I should be doing a lot of things I'm not.

Eventually, I get up and leave, as sitting in that crappy Chinese mini-mall begins to make me feel swampy and sluggish - and stupid, real stupid. So I bail. I didn't want to, especially with the possibility of a nice smooth morphine sandwich so close by, but it was one of those times when something was telling me to cut my losses before the damage really got going, and someone would end up having to post bail.

There's moments like this one where I really can see and feel and almost touch the gloom and murky Nowhereville of the market. Just whose eyes am I seeing all this stuff through anyway? It's skewed and I know it. But I can't help myself. I'm drawn. Drawn to the sickest hurtful parts of life and don't know why. After a couple arduous hours of self-created brilliant idioms, and that self-defeatist apathy thing creeping in; the ole adage, the 'what's the difference' thing, the pendulum of such importance, feelings of having something true and new to offer to the others, and that just being outweighed by heavy sand on the beach that no one visits anymore. All the things I thought I could do and be lost to, blinding disappointment and heartsickness and an inability to pick myself up at those times that mattered, the times that count. These moments I find myself sauntering through all the nicely stacked fruit and pristine display bins of nuts and raisins and the fresh bakery, so the visiting shoppers will be intrigued; the guitar strumming punks in the park by the kiddie pond, the flowers and granola type denizens of the market, who may have even been harmless... But the hex that grabbed hold of my mind at that second was, "It's all dirty, the same drunks and derelicts are still here and no one's gonna do anything with their lives, no one's gonna move on from this place that smells of flowers but reeks of despair and longing. Too many police on bikes cruising around. Something was about to go down. There's always something going down, you just have to peel back the skin. And a good chunk of the time I don't want to examine the hypocrisy too closely for fear I'll forget the sweet things. Sometimes the things that you want to be special and left untouched just aren't, and there's not a goddamn thing you can do in your own lifetime to switch those lifeless lymph-notes around.

Here, I make a note to pray tonight.

Still, she's singing inside of me, but the voice is a little quieter now. I escaped this time, unscathed but undeniably less wholesome, up and out before it all got going again.

---

*Note: will have to tell Mom not to go down to that room as it will bring despair and what's worse, further questions.

She imagines it to be some sort of 'Jean Luc Picard not-quite-right-un-ready-room-of disarray-for-writers' and so queries come to a halt. She senses something is not quite right, many of the neighborhood's more chipper charismatic six to 10-year-olds are being told to "Put the lotion in the basket," right under her nose. They are kept warm - heated actually - by a specially made incubator manned by a team of tortured palsy squirrels, some stray cats in designer helmets and a crew of mute opium fiends in capes donning my picture. They're also kept content, vehemently stuffing as many bonbons as they can in their mouths at one time, the kids. Also, they're well-moisturized and supple, thanks to ample Chanel samples left behind by girlfriends who after a spell, seemed to care less and less whether I was properly moisturized or not.

If anyone were ever to see their way to actually popping by for a visit, that person is sure going to ask a lot of questions about all of this when (and if) they get here. But I just have to keep moving forward, it'll all work itself out. Things have a way of doing that. On occasion.

Now I feel like the witch in that Bugs Bunny cartoon, the one with all the rusty fallen hair pins and gargantuan, all-too-visible panty lines, melodically chanting, "A cup of tea-ee, a cookie and you-u." I'm besotted and fall into a passionate fog amidst the meticulously embroidered curtains my mom told me never to touch. The little munchkins will be excruciatingly delicious for someone, as the taste of children is just but a silly story, for me to busy myself, no ephemeral Faustian feast here. You just know that while this all makes for murderous material for some twisted Aesopian mopey-dope fable of legendary degree, it'll never see the light of a children's reading room *a la bibliothèque,* due to laws too numerous and uninteresting to mention. All this, again, harmless fun - as long as no one gets hurt.

I've taken to elaborate grifts, the removal, fast and furious of entire children's play areas from McDonalds, Ikea and other crass conglomerates catering to parents in 'spend-mode.' Also, the addition of a petting zoo in mother's basement keeps things moving swiftly. Animals in nearby towns go missing; I pat myself on the back, or have the goat do it for me, as none of this is any easy feat.

Mom hears indistinguishable, strange sounds from downstairs and begins to bark her own questions. In response, I offer up, "Music, Mom, it's for the show." I've regretfully morphed into The Troll of Comedy, starring Jerry Lewis, an even more isolated, less stylish (if that's possible) Rupert Pupkin. It's getting eerie: me now Creepela-like, Grizelda-ish, but more masculine, slightly. Further, I'm the freak boy, as I have little or no contact with adults since they're all spoiled. Not like in too-much-too-soon spoiled, just tainted, soiled, matted, turned and past their prime, their un-delicate Dewey-Decimal due date dashed, they having forgotten where their inner child ends and they begin.

————————

Their awful memory plagues and is handily persistent, as during the ride home, there is no awareness. There's one less person in the car. Their specially selected youngster has found his or her way to 'Timber's Precious Carnivalesque, Bottomless-Bonbon-Pit-Of-Pampered-People-Pets'.
Scrumptious, no? Maybe a more memorable festive kid-friendly carnival park may attract an even higher grade of edible tyke. *Look into this.

* Research: Be sure to rent that movie with Lou Grant, Alive,'where after he crashes into some frozen mountains, he feasts on a delicious smorgasbord of fellow passengers. Question: Now, does he do it with a "Lou Grant-y" editorial slant, or is it just plain survival-limb-feasting? And organize a day where I invite that little girl who lives down the lane, Jodie-something-or-other, and watch all the versions of Hansel & Gretel in one sitting, alone with her in the dark. That'll be sweet. Can't wait.

My best thinking regarding the automobile has resulted in the installation of formal dining chairs, in place of those lumpy-soggy-sunken-in bucket seats, the ones I could never adjust properly. It's really much better now, but in defense of the inquisitive and alarmed officers, it does look a little out of the ordinary - reason enough to hold me back from merrily moving along my way on to sin. Those chairs are quite something to see though: big old brown Philadelphia Chippendale antiques, carved from Virginia walnut - a set of them, the legs sawed down for proper sizing, providing fashionable leg room for all my friends who join me for pleasant Sunday drives. Someday. It makes grand sense, on the ambiguous planets of 'Anything Goes' and 'I Don't

Know' that I seem to inhabit. At least I have more than one planet. Honestly, even I would have to question a lady's sanity if she were to climb into such a vehicle; perhaps this'll be the ultimate test of loyalty, of longevity? Of love?

Anyway, the chairs look smashing, and, I think, make the car run better.

* * *

46. Always the Critic

When visiting others, I try to hold my tongue. What would be the point of making people feel overly self-conscious about profoundly garish drapes, or exhibiting fashion choices that can only be construed as doilies-taped-together-on-plastic-place-mats-for-syrupy-beverages, outfits dancing their way into cobwebbed closets, settling where the costumes and various fun formidable wear hang mischievously in plastic wrap. There's a medieval armor knight suit for serious jousting, a fetishy French Maid burlesque-type get-up, as well as full-on Fireman apparel complete with fog nozzle, breathing apparatus and helmet for the swift and heroic savings of cats in trees. I'm not anybody's idea of the ideal house guest: me often dressing all wrong for the affair: underwear only for tuxedo and gown gatherings, suit and tie for casual parties by the pool, plus putting the dribble glass in play long after the party has peaked; a hoax for pranksters of only the highest professional stock; admittedly, it's been getting entirely too much play. Can't seem to put it down. I'm hyper-aware, a caustic commenter, a dissecting sonneteer riffing off (putting off) everyone, and who wants to be put under my kaleidoscope of extreme scrutiny and terror? And who can blame them?

How about just sticking to the things that I've some control over, like my own actions and attitudes. Others have talked to me about this and I'm now running it over in my head on my own time when I feel like it, but I'm not entirely convinced. If I could just stop being such a harsh judge of other people's character. It's just too embarrassing for me, this jaundiced ineffectiveness, tangling the old tentacles in my core, merged with my self-serving, all-too-self-protective criticism of others, those unwilling and unassuming participants, poor imbecilic sods, shabbily sewn-together-sock-puppets, no distinguishable political power to part with. My own mockery gets the best of me, stirring up the worst. I don't know any other way than to drive right through it.

Keep following the bouncing Clues:

The Mobile Sickness/Some Concerns

I admit there were times that being behind the wheel, in the state I was in, admittedly, may have seemed less than proper. I always thought I had reliable reflexes and all of that, but who really knows, when you're loaded, parading yourself in an eternal drug-nodding-siesta, I bet you don't know as much as you think you do. And just how bloody scattered is someone if they're nothing more than the tally of their own predictable, pleasure-seeking preoccupations? Everyone measures themselves differently.

* * *

47. The Continuous Complex Car Concern

People, in general, do not know how to get the most out of their gas cards. What first began as a lark and occasional necessity, became a kind of a day job, though the desperate hours spent down at the plant (a gas station) were more "inclined to shadows," as Jim Carroll once said. I slipped through oily fingers amidst leering looks from cashiers. The stories I would make up:

"I just can't... get to... any... money, my bank card... not working, it's causing me confusion... and loneliness... I'm at a loss as to how such..." Looking much the disheveled charmer. I must have really poured it on to have anybody even consider responding in my favoillianesque exchange. Various accents emerged and vanished in mid-stream sentence, which must have alarmed and impressed the attendants, enough that they assisted me with the currency required to get me back out and into the race.

On occasion I'd have to whip out a piece of ID to prove it was truly my card, that I didn't steal it, or worse, find it whilst sifting through a public garbage receptacle, equally possible by then. If only they'd known how desperate I was. How cool it would have been to have surveillance videotape of these crazed proceedings. I could have opened with it at my 'Special Advance Screening For Addicts And Street Urchins: Invite Only' *(tf#39)* - I know I'd have been awarded my Screen Actors Guild card right then and there based on some of those stellar performances (Where was that held? Why can't I remember? Some bandshell, somewhere Greek and round, I think).

"My bank? Oh... yes, well you see ma'am (sniffle sniffle), they're closed on this holiday," praying to some god it actually was some holiday, some past president's birthday or anyone's anniversary for someone doing something important, lest I put my foolish foot in my mouth at such a promising juncture in the twisted game. A real live bank account (with something other than Monopoly money in it) seemed way off the board.

"I'd like Garbage Receptacles for 50, Jack. Hey, let's let another 1000 ride on Accents I Don't Know."

"Hey, are you all right? Who are you talking to?" They didn't see my cameras.

There were the times it got so bad that the next stage wasn't too far from out-and-out begging. "I just plum ran out of gas, I can't understand it. Damn American built cars... I've got to get home, you understand." Which quickly deteriorated to, "Could you help me out with just a dollar or two?" (The last request when my special card reached her bouncy limits.) What felt like selling a little piece of the soul immediately justified an imperative, a need based on supply and demand: me needing my supply and acting in a very demanding manner to get it, or demanding my supply in a demeaning, disenfranchised dementia-like manner: Crazed and corrupt either way.

I had a means to an eerie end as an hour of quality subservient pleading could produce a windfall of about $20-$30, enough to score. Well, at least enough to page Pedro, arrange a meeting: "I'll get the rest next time, Colonel, please? C'mon, I'm dying!"

Hiding under a car seemed high-class creativity put to good use, well a kind of use. Hopping out of the vehicle after giving him a rolled up $20 - in place of the requisite $40. I then envisioned myself in an outdated and unfunny Chevy Chase comedy where some fat guy would exit the drugstore, start up the engine, unaware, and just drive over me. That never happened. Luckily. Or not.

Avoiding Pedro, the dealer I took off from, for weeks after took some doing - not easy when everyone's in the same game on the same board, everyone landing on the same spot intermittently. There's the having to switch dealers at least until some time passed, so when I eventually called again, good old Pedro couldn't quite recall if it was me in fact who'd jumped ship (and rolled under the nearby vehicle to avoid paying for my product) or not, and yes, the classic Rubber Nose and Glasses are silly, but disguise still has its place.

Santa Ana *(tf#40)* and Costa Mesa, so comical, the warped sour irony: the proximity to her work, driving back and forth, wearing a path in front of her building, pursuing my infatuation with living that way, the daily pilgrimage to Chevron stations, me fitting the part, tattered and begging, the meet-and-greet with dealers and their hotsy-totsy delivery spots, so unbelievably all too adjacent to the quaint spots we'd meet for lunch… Hoping to God Carrie'd call out to me, put an end to the loneliness, that cut into me enjoying anything much at all. The rescue that never came, leaving me with only the comfort of insanity, but proud to have survived. I don't quite know how I did make it through. Many did not.

"Sir, you can't stand out here."

"Why, I was just holding the door open for hungry customers while I wait for a girlfriend. I mean, my girlfriend."

Spiraling down, no one around to give me a leg up, it seemed less outrageous to stand outside that In-N-Out burger joint and just plain beg for change: another line crossed, more double-faulting. I thought I was too different and special and in multiple ways too well-trained to be in the running in that particular burger hurdle, but I developed a taste for it and rose to the pathetic challenge. I had no association with these people, not in my league in any capacity, those fortunate burger folks wandered into my specific territory of misbehaving. I learned to think fast. Or slow in triplicate. I couldn't tell anymore, everything multiplying backwards, or maybe as well upon us, the teetering skyscraper structures of a lifetime.

You can become the sum of devilish

b e h a v i o r a n d t h e w a r p e d d e s i r e s o f

o t h e r s .

There were some even less glamorous sleepover spots, like the
drafty Salvation Army in Santa Ana where you slumber on a plastic
blue mat on a gymnasium floor. You don't end up in those places
lest you are spinning in some real off-the-cuff, out-of-your-hands,
soul-free dimension. No mask or costume needed here, though it's
quite a play - me, the unrehearsed selfish monster, gestures
indicative of an idiot contracting hardships and misfortunes,
repeating dodgy and precarious, self-sabotaging life choices. I'd been
making plenty of those of late.

In front of me is some rusty, dreadfully mud-soaked Silence of The
Lambs-basted wicked van. No license plates whatsoever, the driver -
patch on one eye, motoring along with inattentive flurried zest,
knees on wheel, hands busied and burnt with barbaric multi-tasking
tokes on his cocaine piping-hot piece. He's driving around all fruit-
loopy, scott-and-fancy-free. Me? I can't seem to crawl out from
under these mind-numbing hurdles, or jump through these flaming
hoops; driving-wise. I'm drowning in protocol.

They say a car is an extension of the man. Well, I think the man is
an extension of the car. This 'mechanic person' presents a deal, but
I'm convinced he's bad news for bears. My new mechanic friend
offers me a thousand bucks and some old piece of shit Granada
Marquee something-or-other from the 1800's in exchange for my
baby, The 1993 Pontiac Sunbird Convertible (with cassette player!).
Images of a brown soiled makeshift water bed, my new home (?),
inescapable. If I did sell him my lovely beast of a machine and accept
his offer for this evil van concern, would I start driving around and
hunting for prey with the proper width-sized-back for my steamy-
hot scrumptious and savory youth stew? Needing a good stirring

every few hours in the gooey cauldron downstairs at headquarters. I can see it now: a black and dark heavy orchestra, playing Mahler, maybe "Dead Can Dance," the music at a blistering volume wafting up from the specially built room for The Pit of Curried Children I hold dear.

Ideally, in a perfect world, I'd be sticking to my own whereabouts and what not's, not frowning over the ridiculous chapeaus and scuba gear of others: I'd go off and wear goggles, goalie masks; carry a sword made from Skittled candy; model an argyle sweater sporting loons and caribou; and T-shirts that scream preposterous statements about Jesus; stick unnerving bumper stickers on that generic-boxy-vehicle that state with pride for procreating, BABIES ON BOARD. Go on and proudly boast about your miniature town, the hamlet that hasn't made it onto a map. I don't care and would prefer not to acknowledge it, but sometimes it's unavoidable. And sometimes it's too goddamn alarming and off-putting.

Inside I'm screaming. I can't help but comment.

It all gets lumped into the same system, swept with the same old broom anyway, or so it seems.

I'm beginning to see that if I'm screaming, wanting some form of respect and attention, well, maybe they do too; maybe they're just going about it differently, me not getting their approach, them not bothering to ask why I have a filing cabinet full of stories tied to me and notes in multiple briefcases in my hands. Or just why I'm yelling high to the heavens (up to editorial offices in the Vanilla Sky) what I believe are well-crafted stories. And I've just discovered I have been yelling up to the wrong enterprise, as they've moved on, warp speed, evacuated and downsized into some short-lived webzine nonsense.

So go to it, I say. You won't hear a peep out of me. Not today. Wear your loons; buy your Tartar sauce, your frumpy shirt and faux-pas-slacks jump suits with KISS ME sewn into the ass. Ladies, go and book an appointment to get one of those Oriental tattoos on your back, shoulder or - the worst - just at the top of your butt crack that you've been told by the tattoo shop owner translates into something poetic about peace or freedom, but any Chinaman worth his salt giggles if he gets a shot at spotting it, knowing full-well the letters symbolize "Low-mein in Parking lot." Consume your wildly overpriced doodles, that seemingly important appliance; yes, that's a fascinating reality show, why don't you TIVO or T-Bo it?; microwave your trans-fat din-din; record the soundtrack from that tragically unoriginal and glossy CD; read the same bad news regurgitated for your consumption; be that continuum of all-too-easily-digestible dreary and dull unchallenging guppy placentas.

You want to make your bed like that? Fold the puppy that way. That monkeyish manner you coil the toothpaste? Fine by me: you comb your hair in that dry queer style, so be it. You see, to me there are bigger things at play here, the surface stuff is just that: surface stuff. If we're all going to act and pretend, let's at least have a seat, chat a while and make light of it even a little, just fucking acknowledge it's about crossing the T's and dotting the 'I's and being in bed early on a school-night at 41, and not spending any money whatsoever on anything, because it's all an extravagance and we're all overdrawn beyond legal tenderness.

You can scar deep where it really counts, as long as it doesn't render you unable to get out of whatever quicksand you might be calling bed that week. What are these language games we play?

I can't afford any of it so what is the point? I'll just stick to myself. Just for today.

Those galoshes are pretty silly

on such a sunny day, though.

I am what I carry around with me,

the whimsical way

  which things appear

  demented in my rear view mirror.

   I am the sum of how absurd it all is,

 how at odds I am with most everything

  I come into

  c o n t a c t   w i t h ,

    that yoga, leafy vegetables and small town book prizes

   I award myself,

    will far from fix.

---

tf#39: Santa Ana winds are a particular class of wind with foen-like or Chinook-like characteristics (terrain effect). APPARENTLY, descending motion heats the air adiabatically, thus further reducing the relative humidity of the already dry desert air. In this case the Santa Ana is also enhanced by the land-sea breeze. A phenomenon that the land cools down at night rather rapidly (due to the high pressure preventing the forming that could shield the outgoing long wave from the surface) and forces the wind blowing offshore. I looked and smelled and listened for any signs of any of this to blow through me just so I know it wasn't a lie. I never felt any of it.

tf#40: that was a weird event, that Special Advance Screening For Addicts And Street Urchins. Invite Only…Where was that held? Why can't I remember. Some band shell or somewhere Greek and round, I think. [Again Tim, I think you've got this same passage already written above. E.g. double mention.]

* * *

48. Head Stone

It's all too big to make a difference, it's all too wrong to make it right.
Everything is too unfair, everything too much to bear.
He doesn't have the strength left for the fight.

The Cure

Numb

This soundtrack of slow suicide possessed me and had me in its grasp when things seemed not so good, in the conventional sense. Brightened only in minuscule fashion, on occasion, by sparkling broadloom and bewildering denial. Feeling excitement for something I told myself I was proud doing. My spectral form was making diminishing appearances at my own show; too damn disorganized to arrange my fragmented self into any sporting position out in there in left field. The parade of usual arts events, that I'd always look forward to, now alljust passing me by, out of my price league; entertainment was hard to come by. To carry a disappointment so entirely, so Thoreau-ly, so incomplete, the cooped-up nincompoop, ramshackled and hitting bottom long before any growth can occur, then shutting down completely, wandering, wonderless, moping about neglected snowy tennis courts and colossal-sized barren hospital parking lots late into the night, a hideous wintry landscape wherever I went, reflecting sentiments causing my heart grief at every corner's turn, stopping occasionally to collapse into phone booths found along the way to warm the old hands. The acoustics of such shelters far surpassing that of the open night air in the park, for harmonizing with myself. Just where has everyone gone? I reached in my back jeans pocket and opened my dog-eared phone book: so many names and addresses crossed out with big black harsh lines, no new contacts written in.

"Congratulations, Mr. Masterson Esquire, you are exactly the same person you were a number of years ago." I imagine this line said with immense condescending sarcasm and dripping with... Oh, I don't know, maybe margarine, or that word that always comes up in crossword puzzles. OLEO. That's it! Or, it could be said with fingers snapping along to the tune of, "Hang down your head, Tom Dooley," in itself a grotesque and off-color musical outing. Why did they have us play that in Grade 1 Music Class, with ukuleles and recorders? Were they trying to kill us?

Holy shit. I just had an image of the final words on my gravestone; an unfinished crossword puzzle. How morbid and crazy is that? Fans (fans?) would visit my grave, just like they still do for Jim Morrison or John Lennon, but have to fill in the blanks. My suspicion: something or someone would come along and mess up something as cool as that. I just know it. An image comes across the screen, people filling in the blank boxes of the computer screen attached to my gravestone. (It will be all the rage in Final funeral postings, even with the depression I'm still a creative and alive soul.) An image comes to me: more fans jotting in the incorrect answers on a crossword stuck to my headstone, and with pen, mind you!

Headstones are gargantuan in price, am I supposed to be saving for such an occasion? Another question: should I have been saving my quarters in that piggy bank on the dresser? When my Dad died, my Mom could only afford a headstone, like those slabs or rocks for fallen men, lying flat on the ground. Will I be a directionless impostor when I die? I'm learning about consequences, and speaking of maturing (Were we speaking of maturing?), as one gets older, trying to become a man (What is a man? Where is the man?), one begins to see the consequences of one's own flagrant behavior. Where images, concepts and ideas passed off as my own blow up in my face. Harder to see are the consequences of the flagrant behavior of others - on my life. What's not clear yet, but felt right here, gents, is the relationship between stealing and the loss of a father, but what would I know?

And doesn't this all just bring us back to that film reel they forced us to view in grade school, between assemblies, some nightmarish video noir along the lines of, 'Baby burning; fire bad. If I do this action, it will have this effect...' A cautionary tale of sorts. Some learn as babies not to touch the stove after burning themselves once; others spend their whole lives poking and playing with the hot pendulum, teasing and being toyed with by the far-side of danger.

"Let me see, if I let this crazy person shoot this into my arm with that syringe... Hmm, well, last time I had to be picked up by paramedics. But, this is supposed to be good stuff. And I do deserve a treat and..."

What I deem a treat, most would think of as death.

Always at odds.

* * *

49. Stuffed Characters and their Sukras

A house has fallen on me and I don't look so hot in sparkly red shoes.

"When alcoholics and addicts stop drinking and using drugs, their subconscious minds still crave them. That craving is still sometimes manifested in dreams that can seem startlingly real and, in a sense, are real. Although you didn't use, some part of your mind did. You'll probably continue to have them for as long as a year."

That'll be fun.

James Frey

A Million Little Pieces

There is still a small child living inside me. One that believes Santa and his sidekick, the Duracell Easter Bunny, deliver babies.

To this day, I get my nursery rhymes, movies and make-believe all muddled. Just plain backwards. I'm guessing this is where a lot of the non-sequitur stuff began, and to make things hazier, maybe that Italian marble table I pulled over on myself totally annihilated and mashed my soft spot, leaving a bump on my noggin' the size of Nebraska for many weeks after. (Further confusion: Don't they keep moving that sweet spot-of-softness around much in the same way Easter and Thanksgiving are never on the same day? Isn't baby just one huge soft spot anyway? How many is the diaper-wearing critter supposed to have? I've never had much of a soft spot for them, to tell you the truth; those selfish, whining droolers.)

"Yes, Mrs. Johnston, I see you had sex some months back, seems you're in that procreation stage like many before you, and are barely surviving, though making a valiant go of it. You now cast a fair depiction of the witchy nag who'll bug this bundle of love until they hit their pre-teen years and begin hating you (more of a drain on your dwindling bank account.) No secret this town is tops as far as teens procreating, popping out miniature humans with mommy welfare checks all ready from their kid's first day out. This ordeal will cause you frantic nights of wondering just where they've decided to lay their heads, or who they have chosen to lay - unfortunately for you, none of your business. So congratulations to you and *bonne chance mon chere*, and let me know how all of that works out. I'll be over here making the world a better place, sleeping through it all." Reproduction is rocky and reality bites; except of course when it's a fantasy which is absolutely worth participating in.

Maybe I'll take a shot at the kissing booth girl when she gets off work: could be good, as rumors around the base are she's a slut, but I'm not that eager to jump on the procreation bandwagon just yet. Many have mucked it up, and to add to what seems to be more of a problem than a solution doesn't build much of a case as far as making smaller updated renditions of me. How would that be helpful for anyone? God help us. At least I don't delude myself into thinking that if I find the *right* girl and have the *right* baby, acquire the right job and live in the *right* suburb, it would make a whole hell of a lot of difference. I'm gonna' ante a guess into the pot that I'd be even more miserable, because I'd look at myself and my situation that I would have no one to blame for except good ole me, and maybe think, "I have it all, so why can't I scoop up any happiness?" Of course, it wouldn't be all, as it's an inside job, all that wake up with a hard-on-for-life stuff.

Not entirely anyway. But I'd kind of like to keep my options open. Not shut the castle door just yet.

If I ever actually do get around to having a son or daughter (are those the only options?) and they approach me stating firmly how they've decided on being some form of

'Artist,' here's what I'll do: I will march them out back, lock them in the tool shed, toss in a copy of *Pride & Prejudice*, a tape recorder to play cassettes of the dreariest of Beethoven, white bread, birdseed and water, and let them out only when their spirit is sunken and depleted and has been hypnotized - even zombified - made bereft of consciousness and self-awareness, yet ambulant and able to respond to surrounding stimuli. They'd have to convince me that any aspirations of doing anything even remotely creative or emotionally taxing (even going against the grain, so to speak) had been numbed by the cold exterior of my frosty parenting skills (and the icy temperature in the shed). If I had no shed to speak of, I would use the neighbors'. If neighbors were not available, I'd hunt some down and ask them to build me one, P.D.Q. and A.S.A.P., so I could house my wannabe creative but clueless offspring. What are neighbors really for, anyway? Who knows? I've never had much use for them. Nor them I. Further, I feel totally justified in rifling through that same tool shed for those flavored marshmallows and Rice-A-Roni treats I'm convinced they stole when I wasn't looking. But that's another court case, and someone mentioned something about sticking to the point. I'm just saying I wouldn't want my kids to go through the greater part of their lives submerged in maddening soul-nullifying careers, that's all. If they could learn at all from my mistakes, rejections and near misses, that would be great.

Genius breeds insanity and poverty breeds creativity. Also a lot more soiled sheets, but what of soiled sheets when such soul-searching through suffering is being strived for? Persons stricken with the oddest of ailments don't seem to have any problem reproducing at an alarming rate; often the production of many children can be a hobby, a production line, if one so chooses. I choose not. For some, I suppose, there isn't a whole lot of other things to do but get production going early with the in-breeding, in those really windy, arid, mountainous territories, the quieter states where it's legal to smoke cannabis and marry your sister - whilst watching reruns of shitty shows everyone knows the drab outcome of. And what of babies with many chins and two heads? Tough to shop for, but I digress and refuse to answer further quips down this line as to such brain-dead, fuchsia-wearing, track-pant treasonous acts against humanity, the lustful but dumpty-shaped sort. That's nothing though. How about 'The Man Who Mistook His Wife for a Hat?' He must have been waaaay fucked up. Is he still at work? Is he ever coming home?

Boy, I bet now you're wishing your first cousin wasn't so flirtatious and frisky, wasn't looking so come-hither, wickedly-white-hot and Kristen Stewart Lolita-like, at that Spring-fling cotillion-barn-dance for the local yodeling yokels. And what of that training film on birth control? Too busy out back smoking bad things with the bad kids to pay any real attention? Oh yes, so now you'll pay. Actually, it's others who'll be paying out their unknowing overalls, some new teen mother tax, ultimately, one more box to check off at the yearly "Choose a Box Behind the Curtain Unfunny Fair," when you give the government half of what you are, by now taxed, only coins left to scrounge together for a good waxing that my gal pal, the bearded lady, sorely needs. It's Food Bank time, Jethro.

Babies are remarkably unfathomable creatures to the actual sperm and egg donors who have produced the bundles in question. Though if you're not directly involved, it's really just something apes and gorillas have been doing, for like a million years. I've seen it on tape and it's not that big a deal.

Just how Saint Nick and the Baby Bunny got compensated and ended up teaming together as partners in kiddy crime, I can't say for sure - but maybe that sort of financial pooling can be learned from. They're making a good deal of cash from it all, don't you worry your mashed potato head about that. It's blurry to me just how a hobby turned into a profession, coincidentally and strangely blended at tax time, to subsidize the freelance biz of their "other" personas - The Cavity Fairy and The Antlered Crusader. I suppose to keep them from going out of their minds with too much free time and all. Both tending to constant pregnancies and nervous anorexic concerns, these super-fly kids still manage to possess the grand magical marsupial pouch, which I've always dug for some reason and am more than eager to get wrapped up in and explore. The mushy front pocket, or sewn-in-basket carrying thing, I guess is mainly to warm the little suckers and carry wrapped presents and smokes, weapons, maybe some baked goods. All the while having the caped ability to fly about expectant neighborhoods, stuffing gifts down chimneys and such. How any of that gobble-dee-goop gets done is amazing to me, a task of Houdini-like proportions.

Then came the early morning crying spells along with the Dreams of Rabbits With Wings, plaguing thoughts of them falling out of the sky, smashing their skulls on fences and walls where this other guy, Humpty Dumpty, sat; a mind severed, never to be put back together again, a debauched rebuilding, very un-Six Million Dollar-ish, Humpty D. awaiting something that I don't think ever came. That sort of thing makes me want to use drugs: The Humpster's loneliness, an isolated fish drowning in its own water, a metastasized mammal. And, what's with all that hanging around time? Were there no crimes for him to solve? If all I was responsible for was sitting on some goddamn wall, rhyming to myself and gushing out limericks, hell, I'd be all over it and wouldn't need any of the king's men to prop me up; alcoholics from ye old country, absentee slum landlords wielding swords and gunny scrotum-sacks with sharpened knives, their furry Queen of England *chapeaus*, all damp and mangy, none of those fuckers ever being there for me when I really needed them, crooked-teeth cretins.

Furthermore, what of this wizard I've been trying to get r some face-time with? Couldn't he assist? Maybe inform on some fawn friends lollygagging on the mellow-brick-code? They know much more than they're telling. And where the hell are these secret Wonka Bars? I've been trying to infiltrate, buying multitudes of chocolates in a valiant attempt to come upon the special golden wrapper, but no one seems to have any information. I can't get anyone to talk; not out of their mouths anyway.

And this Kukla, Fran and Ollie outfit keeps coming up; a malevolent mincing mothballed gang. What, if anything, are they trying to achieve? An even stranger group of misfitted cobwebs, made toys of demented proportions exported over here from East Berlin (or is it Belize?) who go by the name Kulosh, Gronk and Oinkel; haunted deviants, unwanted appendages to the aforementioned trio. These kooky goblins are sharpeners of household items that don't need sharpening, like hi-fi systems and snowsuits. They think they're hilarious but eerily only to each other, these matted puppets, distasteful militant menaces, frightening to all they come in contact with. The cast and crew on the soundstage know they are nothing more than pieces of cloth, taped-together Popsicle sticks, with crude and terrifying sewn-together faces and non-union hands up their asses, blubbering away. The directors and costume ladies alike are still afraid of everything taking on hidden meaning in an all-too-alive paralleled personification.

It was rumored during The War of Oceanites and On-
land Creatures, the fiendish Frolsk placed some rarely used
hex on a child that had refused to eat all his buttered
zucchini. The youngster awoke with no nose and a
propensity to rub sour cream on himself. Parents actually
use the frisky marionettes as a threat, a scare tactic for
Hansel and Grettlish-type toddlers who let's say, might have
other ideas aside from retiring for the night and leaving
parents to do important grown up things (like make more
loud ungrateful children, I suppose). Effectively threatened
with a life of eating sick amounts of coal out of wooden
muck-a-lucks, punishment enough; having those morbid,
woolen prankster charlatans hover over you as you're forced
to do chores and eat vegetables that disgust you in the first
place, I can't think of anything worse. So everyone make
sure they retire early - I know I have.

I'm saying there were times during my sentence as an
adolescent where confusion took precedence, bombarded my
synaptic process and seemed to get in the way of my process.
I embraced my confusion rather than expunge it; a parental
unit should have dragged me to see that Vincent Price fellow
over at The Hilarious House of Frightenstein, to see what
could be done. He would have set me straight. Who was I to
turn to? My heroes - like Doug on The Trouble with Tracy
- lived in a glowing box and were part of an insanely
peculiar television world I felt gipped that I wasn't somehow
linked to through photosynthetic nepotism or osmosis or
something. Further, the absurd mentors I began to respect
were impossible for me to interpret to others; spooky TV
puppets (Pigs in Space?), sometimes with antlers. And
absolutely nobody's mentor has antlers. What about Relic on
The Beachcombers. What category did he fit into?

What I would have given to fly away with that magical
and bewitching Elizabeth Montgomery on one of those

tarps, or muumuus - those lavish housecoats she'd parade around in. Or was that her Aunt Pandora? Maybe it was Endora? "Paging Dr. Bombay, Paging Dr. Bombay." "There's no place like home." Clearly a lost vessel searching for a port that just isn't there. Me, weaned and coddled by a chaotic, fantastical I.V youth-drip, a ship carrying a cargo always at sea, never to reach any real destination; precocious was something the doctors said I may have bouts of; shaving a tremendous capacity to wind myself in endless cyclical thought, a dizzied dyslex-sick, often looking up strange words I just liked the rhythm of, like Perambulator or Marmoset, then challenging myself to see if I could work in any of the crafty critters at the dinner table.

"Say Dad, the roast beef looks to be a choice cut of fowl this evening, really top drawer. It looks maybe even like a baby's head, the way it's all smooth and sinuous, moist and hey, you know if you turn it around a little, like this (I interrupt the electric meat carver momentarily) does it not bear a resemblance to an infant's cranium? My, wouldn't this quality-cut tyke look just fine and dandy in a PERAMBULATOR?" There were stares. Often no response. Sometimes stealth perspiring as well as disapproving facial twitches. Uncles excused themselves, sauntering off into the kitchen for early night caps. Aunts rushed to the verbal field to save the situation and share something that all could understand, in hopes that my sharp satirical satire and blistering ready-for-the-world commentary would just go away. My last-ditch effort to share my new language: "Marmosets live in family groups of three to 15, consisting of one to two breeding females, an unrelated male, their offspring and occasionally extended family members and unrelated individuals. Their mating systems are highly variable and can include monogamy, polygyny and occasionally polyandry. Marmosets, you really have to...um..." Serious concern from the remainder of friends and family team now is up and running, so, before I could get up from my seat at the dining room table to go look up what those last three adult-sounding words that I read from an encyclopedia meant, for the dessert-rationing part of the evening, I found myself whisked-over and demoted to The Little Table, a nifty but drastic offshoot from the main event happening just a few feet away. An immediate little problem-solver created quite cleverly (I'll give 'em that) by the elders. I spent many a meal performing to the butter and leftover rolls who were quite warm, even receptive on occasion, to my use of impressive long words I knew not the true meaning of. So, my drama as a gilded only child began. *(tf#41)* Three stuffed dolls were propped up on kitchen stool chairs around my little eating area, I suspect to look as if I was not dining alone. They tried.

It'd be blasphemous and journalistically irresponsible not to speak of the H.R. Pufnstuf thing. Jesus H. Christ, what was that farcical and impure nonsense? I'd just as soon not upset the balance of Hades or tamper with cookies not marked as mine, but that kiddie character was nothing more than a grim, weirdo-spooka-spooka frightening affair. The only pre-requisite to work on that show was dropping ludes and frequent acid ingestion - clearly. The program was taken off the air when 83 children became suddenly mute for life after being placed too close to the television (proper human babysitting units unable to be tracked down... the idiot box, an all-too-willing and apt teacher set to "Numb" and "Repeat.").

The poor tykes were placed in fosterish group homes for wayward victims of cretinish cartoonists and animators, who'd given no long-term concern to developing minds. Cared for by the state because of Hypnotizin' Contortionist Cartoony Cataclysms. What an ordeal. I suppose I got off lucky.

A nightmare or two still to this day, I can, with remarkable accuracy, summon up being unescorted at some cavernous mall, bouncing atop the knee of a sweating and burly Captain High Liner's, telling him what I wanted for Christmas. Knowing full well at that age, he wasn't even the real Captain High Liner - just a five-dollar-an-hour, rough trade fish-whore dressed up in a less-than-manly sappy sailor's costume, feeding his own addiction. His real job, front desk clerk back at that seedy hotel, "Get these twins out of my room, right now," I pleaded.

I awake Christmas morning all excited, donning warm woolen socks, (my neighbor's) flannel pajamas made by Granny (my own). Sprinting to the living room, I only find my spirally red and white stocking bubbling over with salty Pacific Ocean presents: golden tasty fried squid, fish sticks past their due date, and manta-ray paste. All my presents being 'of the sea:' dried cod wrapped in minty carp esophagus, a goldfish handkerchief knitted by a strange ultra-ethnic aunt I'd never met, the smeared manta-ray placenta paste stench and peppermint pine needle redolence, a wintry burnt offering. There's more, but it gets stiflingly intolerable and even weirder to talk about, even for me. Maybe it will come up later, but I'm praying not.

Years later, in a startling therapy session of cinematic proportions, recalling all too clearly the probing and prodding by this High-Linerish Shitza-hoy Santa with a disjointed walrusy mustache at the mall, teasing me with treats. His goal? Luring me into answering his questions - specifically, what kinds of nanotchka's and knick-knacks my parents had, which drawers were locked, safe combinations and such - odd questions from a fishy Santa. Aren't I supposed to tell him what I wanted? None of these grizzly misfitted presents were on my list; I, not so naughty or nice, just passed out, badly bruised and put off by the season of discontent - far too adult emotions for such a youngster, no? Raised on preservatives, additives, minuses, fishy flavored High Liner Haddock TV dinner-style fish stock, things murky from the get-go, drowning and inconsolable: 'Screwed from the Breech Birth' - *oceanically* speaking... Still trying to put it in the past, waterskiing along a Crustacean cul-de-sac that dogs me to this day. True, I worship the sea. Just not what's in it.

My bible: The Good Book of Bad Beliefs, garnished with tacky Don Ho Grenadine-soaked cocktail inedible umbrellas (found out the hard way), creepy-jeepy cartoons right out of an etch-a-sketchy hell, yellow rain boots that have never, ever fit and an all-you-can-eat surf 'n turf set of ethics and rusty moral barnacle coil that have fallen sadly short. And when I last checked, we're all on the run from the authorities, racking up convictions as we speak.

And what of this Polkaroo character? Green, hefty and indistinguishably bottom-heavy. If I had kids I wouldn't want them near that thing. And don't get me started on that fraudulent purple pedophilic, Grimace guy; greasy glutton-mutton, mute-monster jug-head. If you did some hunting, I bet you'd find he's got a hell of a rap sheet and a jumbo incontinence problem. They're all cut from the same masturbatory agnostic mustard cloth, manufactured from the same misanthropic misfitted Milltown-gulping-muck-a-lucks. I could be wrong, but I don't think I am.

I miss my childhood. Though right now, when I recollect in this manner, I couldn't begin to tell you why.

---

tf#41: TimFoolery Footnote: It's The Drama of the Gifted Child, yes, that's the book. A splendid read, that one.

* * *

50. The World is Out of Order
You have to give up the life you have in order to get to the life that's waiting for you.

Jungian Psychologist

James Hillman

T h e   o n l y   l i v i n g objects stirring when I take my nightly strolls are robbers and squirrels. The two of them sat down and discovered it would be advantageous and best for all parties involved if they pooled their resources and worked together. Now, just how they're going to help each other along with one another's mysterious and complicated struggle, is anybody's guess. But it's kind of fun to think about, no?

I've made it my responsibility to say all things true and clear right here, things others might find tough to say or hard to hear. So, what's said here stays here. Here, here. I'd like to think I have no pretense, or at very least, it's been bled out of me. Nevertheless, I will no longer pop in to those methadone clinics and lounge around where all they give you is juice and a smile for a pint... of blood, that is - not ale. Or was that a blood donor clinic? A lot of those clinical outfits sporting walls full of rules and green paint seem to look alike, especially if one's senses have been fucked about from being a test subject for a brand new narcotic that Pfizer's looking at showering the eager pill-popping public with this spring. I asked once, and they weren't so forthcoming. I need mine, the good blood, and whatever other tissue they're looking at scraping off of me to secretly build whatever it is they're building. I don't have it to spare. Besides, smiles are easy to come by and juice from concentrate is a petty and bedraggled offering.

The   nearby   mall   is   today   dizzy   with   mad Mephistophelean trolls. Luckily, there are coin contraptions that simulate rides on elephants, toy cars and a wide range of other ferocious rodents; all this to keep the vibrant sugar-flooded-youth occupied and not continuously at the heels of well-wishing but worn out parents. Unfortunately, today, it appears they're all out of order. The rides, too. Someone most certainly is dropping the ball here - no one to tend to the needs of bewildered infants. So sad to see what once were streamlined glossier versions of themselves, these contraptions. The rides too. A telling tragedy, these unlucky foundlings with hard-earned quarters prepped to shove in a slot with crud slopped all over it. (Machines to guide boys losing their virginity to ladies with questionable ethics?) A sign hangs around this dumb, untricky pony's neck, "Halt! Out of Order!" What kind of life will these children lead? A world of micromanaged misery and over-compensating mothers, guilt-ridden by rides not taken. Shawls of failure to wear for all eternity, the over self-examining, wondering what's wrong, cloaked in a soon-to-be fragmented existence... Driven by a million forms of self-deception, as he grows older and colder in the world we live, this pint-sized tiger will not be one with himself. He will be, if lucky, a spoon-lift or carnie-ride operator with overt on-the-job, masturbatory tendencies; goggles glued to bikini-clad, wolverine-like wrestling princesses that falsely invite, tossing off into nearby bags of Doritos, though hopefully not all at the same time. Safety first. If he just wears the goggles and gloves... yes, that's safe. Wasn't there a time when safe sex just meant washing afterwards? And what of this Oral Sex, I can't see how it can be just talking? I'm a fragile lost man. All this from not being able to ride a horsie.

And don't worry: many of us end up back at our parents' for a brief stint: changing all or parts of our names at one time or another. And just who polices the police? They are drunk too. I'm trying to remember all the good things she taught me. She told me I was closed up, that I had a lot going on inside me and that I was afraid to let people in. I don't think I'm a hard person to get to know, not really.

I drop further levels of numbness each day, each time it seems believing that it can't get any worse.

She apologizes today, because I think she senses I've almost completely given up, have taken leave of my senses, therefore she'll not be able to get a rise out of me. I'm unable to acknowledge her wildly pointless concerns and pain. I'll be no good to her if she can't get a response out of me. Even in her weakened state, she still knows which of her sick cards to pull out, to keep me at least involved; less adrift in this garbage-strewn sea neither of us are escaping anytime soon. Making *the most of it?* More like making *the least of it!* And just who's paying enough attention to keep score, and what does any of it matter if coming out ahead is a sweltering waste of time, reminds me of *Guess Who's Coming to Dinner?* (Or in this case, *Guess Who's Coming to Lindsay, Ontario?*).

Do other humans joined by blood interact in a similar unhealthy manner?

So what's next? To get up, even a few days in a row and not have to fight, to contend, to quarrel with things around me - to not be down on myself or at odds would be a gift.

Still, none of the fucking pens work here. A spooky overtone flourishes, but flows un-fluidly along with all the clocks that are tick-tocking away, marking time - some of those don't work so hot either.

*Note to self: stop trying to fit in. Things just tend to happen when you let them so don't try so hard. What Step am I on? I'm pretty sure I need more than 12. Talk to a sponsor.

* * *

51. The Drama of The Gilded Truffle

I need to stop railing at the world for my condition.
Humans are weird hybrids, distinguished by these
overdeveloped intellects that incline them to
imagine ideals way beyond the capacities of their
otherwise simple animal nerve-circuits.

Richard Hell

Go Now

I've realized something that should have been realized long ago: it's absolutely imperative I change the way I am with people. The unrealistic expectations bestowed upon them as well as the titanic demands I... leave me wishing I'd not acted that way in the first place. These uneasy interactions everyone ends up in - getting easily inside the door, but rarely knowing the password, draining me - and it's not even their fault. If good intentions were gold, I'd be rich, - though that's not coming into play much.

I should be careful what I put out there; emails, letters, phone messages; how I conduct myself with others who have their show going on (and they do have a show - in which, I suppose, I'm little more than an extra). *(tf#44)* Some humans are more sensitive than others, and I don't think that I know people as well as I think I do. So, with that in mind... I'll look into governing myself accordingly. Maybe I'm over-analyzing, but I don't think so.

What would Freud say? Most likely, "Don't be bothering me with your dribble, I have clients with real issues and frantic concerns. Now pass me that syringe, you idiotic man-child." But who's to say what dead doctors would come up with, advice-wise or addiction-wise, anyway? They served their own sentence long ago and got off easy.

Note: Make sure to read that section, Delusions of Grandiosity from The Drama of the Gifted Child, by Alice Miller.

"The person who is Grandiose is admired everywhere and needs this admiration; indeed, he cannot live without it. He must excel brilliantly in everything he undertakes, which he is surely capable of doing

(otherwise he just does not attempt it)."

I'm befuddled, bemused, intrinsically becoming indelicate and plugged into a mismatched contorted frequency. What's worse, my comforter needs a good washing. I've taken to sleeping in an enormous bird-feeder out back; I need my own domain, in order to keep control, keep track of things. I have begun putting on elaborate shows, organizing fixed-lotteries in Zero Mostel-like fashion, like I'm in the Catskills for Christ sakes, playing to a vacationing Orthodox Hebrew audience that just isn't there *("Stupid putz, you call THAT juggling? Off the stage!!")* My multi-level rationale has taken over, my narratives notorious and often nauseating, with nobody grasping just where it is their seats are. I stick a good chunk of my captured – and now heavily medicated - animal audience in the cheap seats out in the garage. These are only pre-season rehearsals, I tell myself, to take the pressure off. There's no human rejection, no one trouncing mud in the house, no bad reviews. I am my own critic and I'm fabulously entertaining.

I arrive on stage out in the garage, and lo-and-behold there are two blonde pig-tailed twins in lacy pink Sunday doily-dresses rummaging around. I've startled them. They perk up (in unison, of course) and stare at me, armed with garden tools. Can't say at this stage of the game if they (the tools) are for disemboweling, bludgeoning or if they (the twins) are equipped to just do some simple digging; my broken mind splices together multiple scenarios, none of which are self-esteem boosters.

Somewhere along the line, my mother and I have turned into Stiller and Meara, or a drastically over-ripened Martin and Lewis episodic neurotic combo with no audience. The best line of the day from Mom after I announce I'd be taking the car into town, "Just don't park anywhere," she says.

"Um. Okay."

I wait about the amount of time it would take to butter half a crumpet and then say, "Well, I guess then I'm more like my Dad." We both get sullen. She hates things like I do, just differently. Ashamed of her behavior towards me, as much as I am with her, we fall to petty digs which change nothing. I feel and want to say that my family is in the States - Aunt Aggie, Ellie and Rosie, Cousin Chris - they're my family. But that's too easy and not fair as they haven't been in strict attendance with the ongoing agony, haven't been part and parcel to my mauling, and I'd most likely be at odds with them just as much as I am with these people here. I should really call them.

A smart man learns from his mistakes.

A wise man learns from other's mistakes.

A really, really smart man will most likely just stay in bed and take whatever medication he finds on the night table.

---

tf#44: which is a laugh on account of the fact that I see extras as the bottom of the barrel. (Even though I've played that role hundreds of times).

52. Witch Flavored Yogurt

There is no way that I can remake the world.

The world itself is interesting, much more interesting than I who am merely one miniscule capillary in and of it.

We think it's glamorous to assert ourselves when in fact it's only foolish and sad and obviously futile.

Richard Hell

Go Now

M a y b e   i f   I start again from scratch. Or at the very least begin scratching the surface, get back to basics, maybe some of that mercury-busting sweaty-sauna-style yoga stuff that I convinced myself gave me a spiritual leg-up back in California?

Down the block from the house, I learn of a yoga studio growing in popularity; Downward Dog, it is aptly named. Always the rebel, always with the next grift, I ingeniously foresee good times ahead with my patented **PAINTBALL YOGA**, which I'm getting set to introduce. An old Lithuanian man directly across the street is going to pony up the dough and sink some cash into my genius venture. Plus, he'll let me have his smooth hardwood Slovak studio, Byzantine columns and insanely high ceilings just kitty corner cross the way (a good dose of competition is healthy I figure) for like 4000 rubles a month? Or was it shekels, maybe drachmas? (*Drakkar Noir?*) All this makes for a super sweet deal. I've lucked out because due to his Alzheimer's (and an obvious language barrier), he's not quite certain how his currency fares in our unfair city (or why he's resolved to wearing fuzzy bright green ladies bedroom slippers and a Mr. T-style hair piece when he's out for a stroll). All this, a further un-formidable scam, direct from the treasonous trampoline that is my mind. He mumbles, stumbles and signs our contract with a finely sharpened purple crayon fetched out of his moth-eaten maroon dressing gown, and the rest is history. So is he, as it turns out - apparently these doggone downtown warehouse stairwells are precariously built.

Back to work.

My frisky facility will be called **UPWARD KITTY** and it'll cater to the downwardly immobile, lactose-intolerant, urban underground ultra-shady crowd; a hugely untapped market (I've got charts and graphs showing how it'll all go down). My tribe of gangly malcontent pusses, languid scalawags, will don skin-tight-scuba-like-gear to put out the word and it will be tremendously successful.

I'm absolutely convinced that no one in this city wants to be seen as taking themselves too seriously, so many will want to jump on the bandwagon to make light of themselves. Tragically still, underneath it all, they'll think themselves to be ultra-hip, slick Shake 'n Bake Shakiras, because it's tongue-in-cheek. Exactly whose tongue and whose cheek is doing all the posing and pouting, not for me to say. But it's all hugely important, and oh yes, I'm a grand success amidst this swirling kitten crescendo.

I think I'm doing well today, by my standards. (By whose standards should one measure themselves?) The fact that I haven't sliced and diced a barrage of capsules and tablets to sniff and snort away or done anything that wasn't strictly un-ballroomish, well... I'm behaving, for the most part.

* * *

53. Yo yo Mommy, Daddyo

Yo Yo Ma. This year I will name myself after a chewy
plush children's play toy and tour the world with my
instrument. What is it I play again? Oh yes, I am the
illustrious and magical Bassoon Boy and you can call me
'Play-Dope.' I'll be The Eighth Dwarf, because one more was
always needed, I felt. This nutty gnome's special power?
"Alluring candied dishevelment, steeped in morphine-
mopiness and overly placated self-concern." (Elves tend to
turn bad, wordy and tend not make little sense in summer
months). The splendidly whorish Snow White screamed,
"More! More!" Seven wasn't enough. This particular princess
confided in me one day - or maybe it was the girl wearing a
tiara who worked the phones at an escort agency who had to
get some things off her chest? Whichever, she let me in on
some secrets. She could weave a tale, I'll tell you. Shrouded
in mystery, a Forrest Gump of frumpy ridicule, I hugged
some trees and was told to leave before demolition began. I
left without incident. My only purpose really was to hunt
down some dwarfs to see what might be done; dwarfs and
gnomes are known to be good with children and assisting
with the building of time-travel machines, fueled by caffeine
and mother's criticisms.

There are intern worker bees, dronish interns of all
ethnicities, working on plans for my international tour.
During interviews (me screening the press, they unaware), I
will recant of a time when I was raised by wolf-like people in
grass skirts who ate only bark, berries and aluminum siding.
And how one day while out spear fishing, I happened to
come across some floating wreckage washed up on the shore
(which could have only come from a doomed airliner, or a
bizarre and rare, stupidly-taped-together-mammal-fish made
from plankton and airplane cushions). Inside, I discovered a

sea-weeded case with a rusty but playable bassoon; attached to a floating cadaver whose hands I had to unwrap from the case he was clinging to for dear life, this all having gone down when the jerky jet went south. I will tell of trying to play him, but achieving no pleasurable sound, thus having to discard the unmusical carcass, leaving the whole bloody wrecked appendage for some smarter, more musical aquatic creatures to contend with.

I can see it now, confessing to the press and social media an incredulous tale, revealing strictly personal details, of how I was raised on an island south of the Philippines, etched somewhere in the South Pacific. Between people's lazy nature coupled with my foul language and obtuse irritating accent (which I'll have to drum up, properly curate and covet consistently), no one will be the wiser. That's for sure. No one will bother to pick up an atlas; they'll just tell themselves that they'd never choose my area as a travel destination.

While attending one of my massive sold out shows at some American arena, fans' (Again, with the *fans*?) complaints and sneering are overheard during intermission. "Most likely, the tropical shithole is filled with the same kind of uncouth, foul-mouthed indistinguishable bassoon-blowers, why bother? But just maybe we should appreciate this fad now. Shouldn't we?" Yes, yes you should. I have an important message to spread. Just what that is, I can't say, but it's going to be worthwhile and you'll be glad you stuck around.

His instrument, mine, just riding some momentary magic carpet ride, some

'Ashley-MacAissac-Lena-blow-Horne-Dog-Lorna-Luft-like-Ofra-Hanoy-Hilton-Loreena-Mcflavour-of-the-week-constituent' that'll just blow its own candle out after a time -

if it hasn't already, by publishing time - so why pay attention?

This, an immense undertaking as I'm perfectly, harmonically, deathly (and every other 'ly' in relation to wind instruments) sub-par. I mean I've got my piano and I'm pretty passable on guitar when I accompany myself to "My Darlin' Clementine," but wind instruments, you can have 'em. Your lips have to be made of an endurable polyurethane combo-mesh-meld of collagen and plastic from a small Pinky-Tuscadero-ish island, and further, it's a must that such musical mannerisms begin in the crib.

On your way out, please leave your address, folded and placed in the gold-tinted glass receptacle in the lobby, so my people can send out all relative upcoming information, as I may be coming to your town. But more than likely just to nap.

* * *

54. C i n e m a V e r e t e a

"I'm a l l u n d e r the weather today." I catch only a bit of what my mother is saying, as we're playing Upstairs, Downstairs again it seems.

"What? Carl Weathers? What about him?" I'm confused.

"Who?" mom asks.

"Carl Weathers."

"Just who is *Carl Weathers*?" Mom asks.

"I know who he is, the actor Carl Weathers, yeah, what's the deal is this a crossword question?

"Timothy, did you take something?" This spiraling sub-par prize-worthy communication would go on all the time. We were just on different wavelengths.

The black guy from almost all of the *Rocky* movies - I'm sure the one I'm thinking of here is *Rocky 3*, where Sly's manager dies and he has to get back the Eye of something-or-other. Carl Weathers, that's his name! Apollo screams at Rocky, "There is no tomorrow. There is no tomorrow!" I picture some nameless, faceless scuffed-up lesbian lacrosse referee in oversized polka-dot boxer shorts yelling at me, "There is no game tomorrow. There is no game tomorrow!" Why she screams this to me in Farsi while rubbing her belly with a soggy carton of Dad's Oatmeal cookies, downing a flask of Hawaiian Tropical Sun tanning oil, is unclear. I said it was a dream, but even in a dream its weird how you find yourself almost understanding, adhering to, even obeying rules barked by meaty-necked furry lesbos in other languages.

*Note to one of my self's: find something to train for. I just spoke to Ray at the old theater and requested any kind of work at all; parking cars, picking gum off chairs, maybe changing seniors at intermission out of soiled undergarments and into fresh and clean onesie jammy-jumpers so they can catch the whole show (or maybe just move them around); setting grandfather clocks (really just a 90-year-old guy in a propped-up coffin in the lobby who tells you the correct EST time when you poke his tummy; you get to put a quarter in his mouth, kind of like in the movie Big with that Bosom Buddies guy Tom Hanks, where he goes back to being a kid. I can't promise just what type of wish this contraption grants; Ray also asks me if I'm good at vacuuming and I don't know what this could mean.

The next morning, I recount the stellar monsoon interplay.

"I'm all under the weather today," mom whispers from the dining room while I work away in the kitchen.

"Why did you mention him again?"

"Who?"

"Carl Weathers"

"What? I never said that. Is that a friend of yours? Have I met him? He's not into drugs, is he?" This is how another morning starts. The clarity in our spellbinding communique sometimes alarms even me.

I'm taken abruptly by the hand by a tiny person, led into another kind of cinematic wreck room, a continuation of the mousy Munkustrap game of Clue On Acid event I'm consistently - and I feel unfairly - miscast in. These scenarios bring to mind that old German expressionistic silent horror film, *The Cabinet of Dr. Caligari,* or more recently that logic-defying Guy Maddin surreal but claustrophobic offering, *Keyhole*.

Zip.

Ok, now I seem to be appearing in a completely altered scene, a long hallway situation, not unlike the somber decay from *The Shining*, steeped in an *Alice in Wonderland*-like landscape - a black and white tiled floor leads to smaller and smaller doors, but my portals get bigger, infinite, unlit with endless frightful possibilities. It's pouring rain, darkness reigns. Apothecaries of crud can become all too apparent at each turn, if you're in the wrong head space.

I open a door to one of the rooms to find a person sitting at a desk; a plain, brown antique desk with a lamp on it. The lamp is not on, the room lit by a flashlight pointing upwards towards the ceiling. The room itself is thick with blackness, possessed. I still can't make out the shadowy outline of a person lumped in the creaky swivel chair. This cloaked wonder appears to be wearing a kind of smock, or a cloak; it could also be many shawls or wraps all sewn together, perhaps a muumuu or a tarp? Let's say for now it's a cloak. I move my hand up the wall searching for a light switch. I feel around for it, find it and then flick it a couple times to double check. Nothing happens. An eerie, musty smell is now evident in the room. Have I turned on some sort of expired room deodorizer? I smell the indistinguishable lemon scent of Pledge. More than likely though, it's just the fragrance of a false allegiance to a positively unquenchable thirst for challenging mixed metaphors. This could lead to the re-opening of a wound of awful hijinks, though I can't help but stick around to see where this leads; all the other doors I tried previously in this imaginary cinematic hotel are locked or under renovation, unable to assist in telling a worthwhile adventurous fable. I creep slowly about the room, approaching the omnipotent dark figure. All of a sudden, someone - or something - taps me on the shoulder. I turn around to see who it is and there with what looks in one hand like a trident - God, I hope it's not a javelin - and a flashlight in the other is the menacing but fumbly character of Blair's cousin from *The Facts of Life*. She is only inches away from my face and screams at me. It's an ear-bleeding, centrifugal-force scream that shakes my skeleton from her throne - a wooden toilet wheelchair - which she carries on her back.

"There are no edits tomorrow, there are no edits tomorrow!"

See. Sometimes things just happen, with no real reason behind it.

As far as that thing hunched over at the desk?   Some sheets. Just some sheets.

Never assume.

Scarier still, I hear the tinkling of the baby grand downstairs. I've never heard this because there has never been anyone playing in the house except me. I can't imagine who (or what) was making the keys play the dissonant Erik Satie melodies I thought at first I was familiar with, but which began to take all sorts of curvy directions that are not part of the composition. Without making a sound, advancing gently down the thick-carpeted stairs, I headed towards the living room. It was Carl Weathers... All sweaty in boxer shorts and horrific cologne, humming along to his absurdly and now off-key piano playing.

What can we learn from this? Rationalization coupled with justification has always been tantamount to survival . . . my survival. Maybe I should get a guard dog to keep out the creepiest of the worst-case dream scenarios. Would a teacup-sized Chihuahua be intimidating enough? Why always the predictable bullying guard dog? Why not an animal like a nipping ring-tailed lemur with fox-like muzzle?

I've always had a fairly bright idea that it would all come to an end.

I knew in my mind that I'd not only eventually be burning in hell from a creepy karmic debt long overdue, but would also be set on fire and forced to lounge around on fried-up still-burning patio furniture, past the point of melting. Forcibly enlisted to take part in something Uncle Hecubus had dreamt up for little old me, a nifty side project Dante was working on before he passed through and headed south, an inspiring new experiment dubbed, 'The Eternal Hellish Melting Fire for Terribly Bad and Awful Types of Humans.' Though at the time rumors of my death were circulating, only mildly exaggerated, they were working on a catchier title.

This particular occasion - of course, I am not accountable because it was sincerely a dream - I set Blair's cousin on fire because I, well, why not? The high-pitched voice I found incredulous. How it could come from something human, like a child screaming or a sitcom star shooting sparks as she runs around an uneven broken house, all ablaze, nothing to say in her own defense.

I admit, I've had my fair share of poignant moments. Always with the grizzly aftermaths, amidst a buzz of chaos, they have not served me in a complimentary light. Though it makes for engaging listenable tales to express down the line; that's if I get off at the right stop to even be able to recount them.

I wonder where everybody's gone even before they've left? A lot of that gets fairly canceled out when I'm at the whim of whatever hex inside me decides it's time to play with my mind...

Maybe for my delusions to go away, I have to formally say goodbye to them?

That might be a start.

On some days, I'd see if I could still hear anything inside myself. Me, the Fiddle Faddle, falling apart, nothing healthy, all treats all the time, wondering where my panache went - the four food groups too wild and gross to consider. I gave myself an occasional test during the times I'd occasionally catch a glimpse through windows of electronics and stereo good stores while running through everybody's lives, catching scenes from flicks here and there: *Requiem for a Dream, Basketball Diaries;* other tough-to-watch films that'd always muster up my moisture works, extracting mystification, me misty. But these kinds of times, even *The Way We Were* or *When a Man Loves a Woman,* yeah, the sappy ones... nothing. Not a drop. If I was numb enough for my pains, concerns and worries to hold little concern, then other peoples were invisible.

Other people aren't exactly high up on the list when you're self-absorbed to the square root of double digits. I want. I need, and you're far from fit - not coming close to a helpful Timbit of information. Fucked again from 'The Get

'N Gone.' (Is that near The 7-Eleven?) My ability to create a life undercut by the malfunctions of something internal; maybe a neon alarm clock I didn't know how to wind properly. I'd stopped accelerating, and it was no longer clear what any of my passions were, no refuge from sheer sadness and fears. In order to weigh the evidence, one must first have all the evidence. I seem to have missed out on learning how to add everything up.

I know what I am doing.

I am right.

You are wrong.

Are you going to finish that burger?

* * *

55. G r a v e   W o r d s

It's   q u i e t   h e r e, in this place. The sky is grey and dead and unmoving. All these notes and tales add up to a lot of pages, but don't cover a grave the way you'd think they would. These impressions of life, beside this place of eternal slumber of father, of mother... I know they hear me. Parents stay with us in many forms, long after they're gone from this earth. Or so it seems.

I ignore my fears to light a cigarette. Since I've never smoked, I put it out immediately, but derive some small pleasure in knowing I had a power to set things on fire. I sit down at a bench and recast all the interactions I've had with my mom (for better or worse), since I've been back. I haven't moved any of the furniture or anything around much, I guess out of respect for how she would have wanted it. I can't recall just how long she's been gone for. I know it's been more than a year while at the same time, I can still hear her unforgiving tone around the house; scolding, worrying, fretting, questioning, at a loss. At least I feel she's much more at peace, wherever that is.

I kick a Cracker Jack box in the cemetery parking lot, get in the car and return back to the house. This home is haunted, uniforms of youth and league seeming hollow, photos capturing moments long past; better times. I'm talking to myself a lot more these days. Not only does my behavior scare me, but I scare me. I have to talk myself down, talk myself out of doing things.

Some days are more motherless than others, back at this homestead. It's comforting in this place because there are no more lies in my veins. All there seems to be is serenity... and prayer. If I had my choice I'd prefer not to go through the eye of the storm, not drive cross the desperate and impoverished murderous country I've crawled through this time. I'm going to do my best to veer away.

There seem to be places that people just don't come back from.

Home is a big word, any way I slice me.

I still am kept from something…

…what more can be done?

* * *

56. Back to the Airport

I pick up my stuff in the car and leave home the way mom would have wanted it. Just the way she left it.

I feel like going somewhere. I've got to get somewhere that's inviting. So, I figure I'll go hang out at the airport. The possibilities are endless, but are cut immensely short when I realize I've forgotten a passport and any travel funding. (Again?) There are people waiting for me to enrich their lives. I just have to find out who, and where they are hiding themselves.

I have unmatched torn baggage, the kind that calls up flags at airport security. Seams coming unsewn, me unglued, unclaimed, all that.

I arrive at the airport and feel as though it hasn't been that long since I was here last. It feels like… déjà voodoo?

I sit down to watch some sporting event on one of those television monitors, where men are hurriedly running around a field bruising one another (Mennonite Rollerball?), wearing angry faces. Some have their own faces, but all of the faces are rushing around a stadium-sized field, being really mean to one another, knocking each other over and yelling. The commentator has an English accent and they keep handing the ball off to each other - if that's in fact what it is - *horizontally*. Yet no one seems to be making any headway. The crowd is going wild, that is until some muscular smooth-shaven player runs to the goal area, kicking the oval pigskin into the stands. Which freaks out the thousands of spectators. The forum is momentarily silent, then the onlookers storm the field and rip the limbs off of the offending player, leaving only a few bones behind. I forgo putting another coin in this video box, as I've seen enough carnage for a while.

While sitting there cheering for both and neither team, a man in a khaki safari outfit and pith helmet shuffles slowly my way and sits down. I figure he is either a Jungle Trapper of sorts or works at a pathetically themed tropical cinnamon-bun stand. He has a name tag reading HELLO MY NAME IS, but nothing written in the space. He launches into a story of how he just brought back six Ecuadorian Spider-monkeys from the Congo, and was supposed to meet someone here to deliver them. He insists each one is worth at least 50,000 Kronkas, which sounds like a lot, but he will let me have all of them for one thousand Loonies. "A steal, at twice the price!" (Twice the animal?) he hollered, while dribbling some of his Orange Julius shake into his beard. Maybe a pet (or pets) would help me take the focus off of myself, make me feel needed. I began counting out the loonies from my change holster, when he stopped me and said, "No, no, no... I said LOONS!" I thought it over for a moment and still figured it was a hell of deal, so I went to see about hunting down those birds. I first walked over to the airport's holding compound and approached the cages carefully. "Good monkeys, you stay," I whispered. I then pulled the car around to the cargo bay and loaded up, patting myself on the back for such crystalline thinking. I paid the cinnamon-bun-trapper-guy and loaded up my new Spider-monkey friends. They weren't entirely stable sticking out from the trunk, so I did away with the cages and grabbed what bungee cords I had so as to pile these furry and newly landed immigrants on top of one another.

At the time, it made such perfect sense. Though now, looking back, I may have been a tad too rash in my judgment. I mean I hadn't really thought ahead.

* * *

57. Nothing at All

Excommunicated on what felt like the very last day, and all that, what now, came to feel like so much wasted time, the reclining with very little on the plus side in my mind, except escapism, black and white cinematic shots of New York and fields I'd never visited in Europe, came to a halt as I realized I'd never gain garner enough wages to make the trip, basically anywhere: I was a captive to my own disarmed thinking and crestfallen temperament and redundant actions that were catching up to me. I couldn't say with any certainty that this is where I was, together with heart, mind and spirit, they were all locked together in shackles, the farthest thing from fecund, unable to move forward, progress, they must have a name for it, as it is monumental, the crushing blows to ones soul over time accumulated in anguish, even embarrassment. The things that were tangible, and possible, would be none of the things that would be on the menu of salvation. Confusion ran the game board and had nothing else to do but taunt me, laughing at my ways of thinking I knew the world and it's movements. Disarmingly present, boomeranged back to a foggy youth with all its trappings and inabilities of...longing still for consistency and my own rules of unstructured bohemia, but hogtied, shackled to persevering mediocrity at what seemed like every turn.

She scolded me today for taking $20 from inside a notebook she had. Stupidly, I even tried to return it once I was flush and not sporting lint. The hours filled the day with trading at the depressing pawn shop, but she was already on to me and my ways, calling me a thief and asking what was I'm sure, a simple question for her, "What was it you needed so bad that you would steal from your own mother."

I could not answer.

If cracking and keeping from me what sense of independence and self-sovereignty I had was what mom sought, then they all flowed making contagious all failures and further plans not unlike the highways and byways of America that were built with little thought to how they would intersect, haphazardly tossed together like cement tentacles that were pointless and whom nobody took responsibility for.

* * *

58. Pretty Named Streets that Weren't

She comes in to the back room where I'm writing and feels, needs, to get this message to me. "I'm sorry I don't have any respect for you. I've given you too much." How it helps me (or her) is unclear - some pivotal pinnacle, for the most part, pointless.

Should I let it lie or query further? I don't dare get into it. Those sorts of words are different, worse than fighting words. They sound final and they should cut deep, but the truth is I don't know how they cut anymore. Best to leave it alone and let her lie. And if I were to tell anyone about it, they'd probably say, "Well mister, you must have done something pretty bad for her say that."

Best not to arm myself and get on the field. Best to stay in the stables, the sidelines, the bullpen and make notes on players from the dugout, which I can submit later to the proper authorities.

I should really get down to checking on Mom who by now, I'm guessing, has been sitting in the back seat of the car for what must be going on two days. She must need either 'changing' or at very least a hot meal. Though my project with the rings in the bathtub, how they all relate with Saturn's rings, now takes precedence and has truly taken on a life of its own. I've been making detailed notes, at the properly aligned star module times, since mom has been away. Now I've the time to focus on such tasks as keeping fervent notes on just how I, if I leave the tub unattended, scrubbing-after-wise, can recreate with blistering creative will and staggering astronomical ability the exact same lines that orbit so wondrously around Saturn. Who could deny me such an endeavor? What of Pluto and its many moons? There is work to be done. Much work.

Trying always to deaden the space between girls and me, me and me. No one else could take responsibility for the death, even through the haze. Moreover, I hated myself for it. No place in sight to correctively repair, or even just patch it up with super-sealer.

You'd pick your sorry ass up if you could,

if you could muster up something.

a thousand lonely lifetimes in that fucking grimy car.

...getting coagulated in your heart each time you go off anywhere.

"I swear they keep moving the beach, you sure I take this road?"

Hunting for the perfect lavatory situation became a hobby; the flat, smooth, mostly private surfaces (the perfectly sleek symmetrical metal bathroom shelf on an airplane comes to mind on occasion), baby-changing kiosks whilst visiting Starbucks washrooms, men's room floor, that greasy bathroom at the auto repair place downtown (funny escaping with that mechanic's outfit with a nametag belonging to, I guess a mechanic named Sal, it hanging up all clean and pressed back from 'the cleaners'... me, unseen and unclean), the lost angels quickly losing their taste... near Spring, Hope and Hill; pretty named streets that weren't, my own, not so private Nowhere Avenue.

You'd dust yourself off, but you'd find again and again more layers of the same dust and crap engrained and encrusted on you... No proper tools in the toolbox to tend to your own highly stylized mess. So you'd let it sink in and absorb.

The inconsolable grief and irritability get a free ride.

The part and parceled parasitic pals clinging on to your lifeless skeleton, emptiness running rampant, chased by the invisible but violent devil into crazy akimbo dancing in the quicksand, hoping to God to get somewhere, to find something... Someone who'll make a difference, who might tell you how to separate the good and bad, the wrongs and rights and weirded-out turns... The black onyx melting and sapphire dead blue endings.

So I'll speak the things that cover it up, the things I can't even lend the old smarts to, I, turning out to be more maroon than burgundy. There are levels, shades of wrongness; my arms and legs are caught in all of those stupid shredding machines that temps are always waiting to shove pointless documents into, their bored minds elsewhere, in order to shred the wrong bundle of very important papers.

I'd jump in if I could fit, but I might only scar further this time, on the outside.

'Give me some credit for the hell I've paid... Let me show you how... The less I know the more I comprehend..." Some lady's words, but I feel them just as deathly, so aren't they also mine? No. No, they are not.

Then, j u s t w h a t i s m i n e ?

Terribly troubled, my off-kilter antidotes a personal era burdened and too faithful to the snide and darkly ironic, though, through coming clean, I thought it might have helped the old malaise of spirit to confess. Sadly, I've fallen short, cause I kind of feel I haven't done enough, with helping to explain, in assisting with my plight, my cause. My one big toe, jammed into a shoe two sizes too small, I just want to feel whole, to be pure, to feel good about something, get past this unkind of

'not enough', wrong sized

the land of un-right

in and of itself, not helping me…and what of

what I've missed?

Untimely

Relentless

Clawing at me

And the times I have said: more later or to discuss later, there is no more later time.

I'll tell you after, because this is after and this is later

a n d

my time, certainly more than done here. Yes, a completion

in its

own selfish self-right. The need to eject oneself, salvation…somehow, some

pleasing   peaceful   moments

So, tonight I'll go back to the drawing board, even though everyone else is snug at home in their 'each otherness,' being now, far from it all.

Shuffling, stunned down the longest cold hallway, the slippery flux, my certifiable cocoon of damaged charm, maybe still the Hall Monitor… Hands in ripped pockets, but I have to say… w e ' v e h a d f u n …

And hasn't it been just creamy and peach-like sharing all this with you...

　　　Who knows, maybe

I'll see you out there, though you may not recognize me.

　And this leaves us where?

　　We're essentially all alone.

* * *

EPILOGUE

I'm wearing full-on monk garb: heavy brown-woolen-Friar-Tuck apparel, a rope for a belt and Jesus-sandals, laurel wreath atop the old head, the whole deal. Forget that it's blistering three-digit degrees out in this fuckin' corn field where they hold these spiritual talks. Convalescing is the business at hand, yet, I am one big sweat lodge of dispersed logic; the Snowman in those sweaty summer months, melting with a detoxed head of marbles.

It's a self-inflated solitary place, where one of the few acts that makes sense is imagining more ways of expressing yourself and have them really get it. They'd had their shot at sharing in the fascinating details and dreams of my life and had blown it big-time. I'll show 'em. I'll do myself in. But what would I be showing them exactly? My old friend Felony Phil used to say, "Any day above ground is a good day." I think he's right. Seems for so long I've been a guy without a philosophy... This, but a small sin in a wash of greater ones. The only way to survive may be to drink in a new diet of the mind, so now I choose not to indulge certain appetites.

I've taken everybody for granted; lovers and relations alike. And justified it when their predictably disagreeable behavior failed to suit or inspire me. I don't know life. I am a man whose conclusion is uncertain... The things that you take for granted seem to leave you.

When Things Fall Apart and fly off the rails: yes they have, and yes they have. I could call Father Kevin. Or Primo, I'm sure he'd be up at this hour, but that wouldn't help. I can still write, and this place is as quiet and serene a place as any to do it. I keep running into me no matter where I seem to try and plant myself. But all that is so elementary, it makes me feel like just another joker in the maze.

There's a Buddhist-nun-lady here, a sage of sorts. A kind of meditation master (with the weirdest far-out hairdo), she's trying to help me sort through all this mess, teach me some lessons that'll stick, so I'm not walking around all glaring, crazy, relentless, probing. The robes that people wear here sure are funny, too. And I'm still hearing voices within the hectic hustle, all to flow and follow a schedule in the already too scorching day, oriented towards a brief moment of transcendence... Putting more and more distance between me and my hair-brained schemes.

Yes, for my path to change, I have to say goodbye to some things. It hurts all over to walk away from what you know, and there's no closure with something that never fails to feel continually good. I think I'm finally okay with that. I'm trying. I'm addicted to memories, not particularly longing to return to them, just the intensity of the experience, along with the people and how they've shaped me. I somehow miss both. Why does it have to be me that has this morbid reflection affliction? Guess everyone has something. Sometimes it takes a lifetime to figure out what it is you need. *Note: make an earnest attempt to find what that thing is as soon as you can. Breaking free from formality, those predictable and generic human moves. Any image I have of me right now - I agree with them - would be wrong. I have emerged in the aroma of something indescribable, neither fatherly or romantically reliable. I feel untranslatable, and God, don't even start about my presently non-existent procreation plans... Is there really no one? Is that all snipped? How the fuck can that be?

*Note: An absence of affection destroys the soul...everyone needs affection.

Having been universally rejected 'out there', I turn my focus to meeting the group, I thought it best to keep the thing about scalping tickets at The Dalai Lama show to myself - it wouldn't have garnered any Karmic Credit points and certainly wouldn't be a step up in the Making New Friends Department. I've convinced myself to put a hold on the whimsical shock-therapy commentating, in favor of an upcoming bingo night I'm told is just around the O-22 corner.

The ongoing simmering melodies that encompass the group here is calming, all Wyndam Hill-like, though a tad on the new age side, I get their concept. They have spiritual pancake breakfasts here, these extreme creamy marshmallow-laden caramel delights glazed with lime-green food coloring; the kind of deal that looks like it was glued together with cookie dough by some margarine-glazed gals in the kitchen troughs. A skeletal Walter Matthau comes over, saying just above a whisper, "Here you go, Brother." He also hands me the entire front row of his teeth, sharing with me how proud he is of "how accessible they are." I don't know what this means. But I'm here to recover, not judge. He starts to turn away but not before placing in my hand a rolled-up white bread, salmon-head and what looked - and smelled - like a motor oil sandwich, pressed hard and round into a baseball shaped sphere. My line of questioning seemed harmless enough. Why not fuck with him a bit? I had to have some fun, I told myself. "Who sent you? Are the plans inside?" If you're dealing with someone who's off their rocker collapsing through to the dementia basement, then there's not a hell whole lot you can do. He gave me a knowing kind of manly nod and slid off away into some bushes.

If we're studying Buddhism and practicing meditation, we might talk of no self and emptiness, of patience and generosity, of loving kindness and compassion. We might have read something or heard some teachings that turned our usual way of seeing things upside down, but you don't know if you can do it because you've never done it before.

That adage about, "If you want something you've never had, you're going to have to do something you've never done," and "To have the life you've always wanted, you're going to have to leave behind the life you've had." Or was all that just mature-sounding mumbo jumbo to impress girls?

I guess I just always hoped it would make more sense. But in the end, I guess it doesn't. I should go, I think they're calling me… I hope it's one of those candle-lit scripture-study sessions, because I actually catch myself looking forward to those. (It's also a super time for naps).

Great big beautiful things almost always are mixed in with some fear. But the rewards are absolutely priceless.

'CALL SOMEONE YOU LOVE' BREAK, and tell them so.

{And also about this book you've read}

an End

* * *

These two perk ditties were written Christmas morning immediately after the author was ejected from a hospital in Pasadena and alighted in downtown L.A after walking all night, alone.

Haikus for Hooligans / A Gazillion Miles from Kind and Pretty

Two letters I should keep close as I would brass in my pajama pockets.
Found in pocket
Note: Keep these two sonnets, of sorts, my hellish Haikus,
in a designated pants pocket.
Maybe I'll look at them before I decide to use next time –
Decide? The word is obligatory as there's no decision,
it just becomes me.
Always looking for the unequivocal, something or someone to
play the role of Saving Grace.
You, the dummy never learning the eternal lesson,
still looking in the direction of some female to save the day.

The clue of the sonnet / Planets of Regret deep in pockets

A.

Who takes a cab to a soup kitchen?
A couple dozen grown men, a few women, waiting,
milling about, fleas bounce off inconsistent light,
all outside the church and it's Saturday 7:20 A.M,
far too early for anything to be going on, really.
I have been up all night injecting cocaine into
an overworked undecided bloodstream.
Lacking and empty again, so now I look towards

scrambled eggs, a needed nourishment, me needy as usual.

It's sad and wretched   from the start and

here lie the dregs, the outcasts.

The broken ones up this early are desperate;

they haven't found a way,

to hunt, gather or collect properly;

they know they need to rely on something, someone else.

I am given a coupon, a ticket upon entering,

this my cathedral colonic, a weirdo ghost ride,

this fucked up Un-fair, my cleansing an amusement park

of tired sausages and watery coffee

not up to meeting the need, to give anyone energy.

There is fighting, always fighting; words of war over petty things;

bikes tied outside, some dogs not meshing well,

many locked to fences outside, masters missing altogether,

someone looks at someone the wrong way,

wanting to fight so he knows he's still alive,

still has guts, no further reason,

he understands this right now.

A crazy lady with a shopping cart has Delirium Tremens

a result of her own show gone badly,

and it's not helping my appetite,

but it's not hurting it either,

this because I can't feel to begin with.

And someone, is not handling this woman

in a manner she should be handled.

The one thing I am sure of is an

accelerated deathly remorseful nostalgic feeling

creeping up into me at this strange but free breakfast offering.

I have never worn a longer face,

my frown is to the grave. I show none of the teeth I have left.

If one person says one thing to me, or touches my shoulder,

I will start crying.

I will start crying because it would bring up a lot of things,

prompt me, this my triumphant return to this church where I recall

walking hand in hand with Granny to that Sunday school I begged not to

go to. And later not to be thrown out of.

It's not funny, sometimes, things we revisit.

I am crazy alone and it touches everything I am.

No one to share in me. Once more, in a place

where people are at their bottom, a place I don't need to see again,

but seem to choose to be, or so I'm told.

I say this is where I belong but I don't really think so entirely.

A place for me to be at my lowest, no one telling me to cheer up,

to put on a happy face.

I hate that. All this gloom and there's no soup in this soup kitchen and

I'm a thousand lonely lifetimes

and a trillion miles from kind and pretty.

When I get to the window, I give the girl my ticket,

nice unharmful girls, here, volunteering their time,

so they don't end up in selfish mode, pretty girls

I would have flirted with in younger days.

But today I'm painfully shy, even embarrassed,

a sad person with not much hope, all his things behind him,

gross, disheveled, and I'm hoping they don't look right at me.

I take my eggs, white toast on paper plate, on green dirty tray

out to the park bench in front of the church.

We used to get cookies and sandwiches here after, sometimes even tea,

just like the grown-ups.

Now, two homeless people are threatening each other,

loud curse words fly. I am in-between them,

I keep my head down - very down.

Please don't take notice of me,

don't ask me stuff,

to take sides or comment, I'm no good.

Or I was and don't remember.

I'm Johnny Rotten and I have nothing to offer.

It is 7:35 A.M now and I don't know how I came to be here

in this place of endings in this very early morning.

Nothing has gotten going yet.

The used syringes in my pocket are jabbing my leg,

so I get up and find a big blue plastic garbage bin

to get rid of me and dispose my junkie tools.

I am hard-worn. (Hardware?)

Making my way off the too sparse grassy knoll,

I overhear someone is thinking of selling his watch,

another hears of a place to get shoes,

more people prepping their unhelpful artillery,

their talk for the time,

and the day upcoming seems like

another scary daunting monster.

Better get back out on the playing field.

My break is now over...

The second thought if I missed something on the first one.

You Dummy.

B.

A Junkie's Tired Draining Lament
Tired of coming up empty
Tired of not appreciating the moments,
of what and who I have.
This is where the broken parts go
Tired of being afraid of the whole thing
I do not know what's up and I certainly don't know
what to do if I wasn't living where I am.
Who'd kidding who? I'd be dead.
I wish drugs away from me, but they run after me
and stop me from being good. It's their job.
Everyone needs a job.
I'm an impostor but I'd like to have friends
I mostly just feel alone, ya know?
Scratch that. I am very fucking alone and
this makes me feel like death.
Okay, time for a change, I mean a real change
from the style of life which I live,
the kind of change where I don't return to what I was a week later.
No one is coming with me on this ride,
not for long anyway.
I'm tired.
Sick and tired of being sick and tired.
Tired of being so selfish.
Tired of being this scared,
Lonely and scared,
Tired of being chased.
So tired of feeling cheap – that I don't matter.

Tired of being down, my soaring ups and spooky downs and

In the end, Withdrawn. Withnail? Not With.

Tired of lusting after those girls that are,

or might as well be,

imaginary, the 'wonderful shiny and alive unattainable.'

Tired of wishing time that is mine gone.

Tired of trying to hide things.

Tired of being an eyesore to myself and some others

Tired of being tied to looking over the shoulder,

Again with the being chased thing, the "closing in" thing

I've completely exhausted myself.

There was a time when I was good, did better

didn't feel like I do now.

I don't know where or when that was, but it happened

I swear to God it did.

This time, I'm gonna be better. Will I allow myself. Is it fair, fun,

possible, hopeless, hopeful, pathetic? How can I tell anymore.

C.

Running through promises I can't keep.

Running.

Running.

Running.

Howling out loud to myself

suddenly forgetting how important to pay attention,

losses quickly building, marinating into sludge.

I put on that t-shirt - the one with 'Roar-a-saurus' wearing a crown on

the front and 'Rationalization King' on the back...those made-up, mixed-

up, un-animated characters from some un-royal court who don't solve

crimes and aren't upstanding members of any community, just there to cover up scars,
tracks that lead nowhere,
to remind me of who I can't be.

BONUS WORDS

Early On - Somehow Still Relevant

A Bizarre But Entertaining Date I Seem To Have Survived:

*   *   *

(Another Tale from Timber's Dementia Cul De Sac)

*   *   *

Discussed: Hotsy-Totsy-Mamas-On-The-Make, A Sexy Mensa Swim Squad, Gregorian Step Monsters, Warm & Exotic Muffinish Places, A Hypnotic Ricardo Montalban-like Accent, Ma Mere's Den of Menopause, Inedible Playmobile Farm Animals, Masculine Prancing, Something Big And Furry With A Tongue To Pet, A Mammothly Humorless Wonderwall

*   *   *

B O N U S exercise: In the Beginning...
what helped to make me the boy/man that I am today

*   *   *

A Bizarre But Entertaining Tennis Date I Seem To Have
Survived: My Balls in Her Court
(Another Tale from Timber's Dementia Cul De Sac)

Discussed: Hotsy-Totsy-Mamas-On-The-Make, A Sexy Mensa Swim Squad, Gregorian Step Monsters, Warm & Exotic Muffinish Places, A Hypnotic Ricardo Montalban-like Accent, Ma Mere's Den of Menopause, Inedible Playmobile Farm Animals, Masculine Prancing, Something Big And Furry With A Tongue To Pet, A Mammothly Humorless Wonderwall

*   *   *

Every year at this time, I turn into Monsieur Nostalgia. *(tf#1)* Summer is all around us and thoughts of youthful zesty romance can't help but pop up. To this day, I can still can conjure her intoxicating devilish scent; an overwhelming combination of Bob Mackie perfume betwixt poppies and lilacs; a narcotic essence, brilliant and rare, hurdled through me and has stayed with me ever since. Did all hotsy-totsy-mommas-on-the-make smell like this? As I would learn in my intensely puzzling later life, whilst shacking up with country gals who work with horses, had pronounced foreheads and an axe to grind from prior relationships, sadly no. We were destined, it seemed, to get together and mate. Most of the original and alluring scents of the morphine-headed, meaty-necked maidens I got mixed up with quickly took a backseat to a new preoccupation: saddled with the question in fact, of how to tend to my unquenchable, curious thirsts and all-encompassing mopey moods. Poor ladies. But what an introduction to countless bachelor days that first encounter with the fairer sex was for me.

Our tryst began teaching her the game of tennis while simultaneously dreaming of her on some sort of sexy Mensa swim squad, her arriving at our lessons in a white terry-cloth bathrobe, high heels, black Chanel glasses staring at me suggestively, while sucking on a long cigarette and flipping open and shut a silver cigarette case. Her smoke intrigued me. Why, in my vision, she had two Jon Benet Ramsey, Honey Boo Boo–like twins pushing her to the courts in a broken-down golf cart singing selections from Les Miserables is anybody's guess; it was a dreamy affair, after all, so the less time spent feeding my Demented-and-Delusional-Cul-de-sac-of-not-sticking-to-the-Crux-of-The-Story habit, the better.

Just what made Jenny accept an invitation back to my lair; the Weekend Den of Slick Bachelor-Hood, a.k.a. MY Castle, while mom and the Gregorian Step Monster were away at their cottage, I can't say. I could not imagine very well just what this minxish lady with super-hero personality and intimidating I.Q. wanted with the likes of me. Never mind that I was sixteen and she thirty-something.

We shared a passion for playing tennis, though she was astonishingly talent-free, virtually forehandless, and bereft of any recognizable backhand. With years of dedicated practice, she may have been able to manage that tricky task of holding a couple of balls in her cute little pockets while she played, but that's about as far as her professional career would have gone. She was, nevertheless, unbelievably stunning out there on the court.

I took great delight in watching the male population on other nearby courts, unable to focus properly on their game, bewildered, hypnotized by Jenny's wildly spastic yet invitingly sultry form. The obvious lesbian players were clearly perturbed by the boys' recurrent kicking of tennis balls onto our court just to get a closer look. "Please excuse me, sweet miss. Um, a little help please?"

But who could fault them? Embarrassment was a small price to pay, as they were caught gawking, pretending to discuss stocks or boating in an attempt to catch an eyeful of the exotic, erotic, jungle-kitten sweetheart, swinging blindly at balls a good three feet out of the reach of any racquet in this solar system. But she more than made up for it.

Her white silky chiffon dress with ruffles billowing free against tanned skin, was completely adorable. Her pig tails – gorgeous, golden and radiant. To my youthful self, it was a game, set and match I longed to conquer; I imagined club members remorseful about their own unfortunate mistakes –

selecting wives hastily back in the day instead of waiting for a catch like Jenny. But, she was mine, mine to teach and get all dreamy for our forty-five minutes of fitness and boy/girl finesse. Her eyes were on me. I felt like a king.

They imagined (I imagined) Jenny's streamlined body - perfectly slick glutes, buttocks you could bounce a quarter off of and washboard abs - though, this only served to bring an unflattering comparison and grim image of the gentleman's hermunklan snaggletoothed troll, now balloon-thighed and hefty-shouldered counterpart at home, drunk and doddering about, catatonically-scrubbing their laundry on a washboard. Shame.

My hectic hustle during the big day foreshadowed a racy bout in a stellar but all too brief upcoming cuddling session. There's me, prepping for even just a moment of something as yet imagined; a sensed and longed for promise of transcendence. I was setting the stage for an event that would leave an indelible mark on the rest of my romantic life.

While I was cleaning up the family home, carefully placing props here and there for the event, I thought about how very little I really knew about just what went on down there with a woman. Now, I had seen the occasional pop-up picture in biology class, joining in with the typical, locker-room-type chatter concerning women's womby confines that occur in alcoholic, less-than-articulate fashion in guy's gathering places. I believed the femme-fatale-locale-of-intrigue was a warm, exotic place - muffinish and unknown - maybe like Henry Miller's Tropic of Capricorn? My awkward and fruitless fumblings in the backseats of cars at drive-ins and the groping of cousins at family funeral after-parties hardly qualified me to comment. I'd heard tales and dreamt Audrey Hepburn-like cinematic fables; I gathered the whole deal would be an epic

Longing so to be the great Trojan, but dismally no more than a fatally stricken gelding with a stall full of inedible Playmobile farm animals and busted up Lego stables, I was unable in the dim light to make out those notes on the ole Etch-a-sketch, the sands of time and instruction, now cruelly disassembled. The **HOW TO MAKE LOVE TO A LADY** portion, with its sub section **WHAT TO DO IF YOU RUN INTO TROUBLE,** all now a tragic blur. I was stirred and shaken like a bruised and overdone bizarrely-spiced Shake & Bake Chicken, as the evening crashed down around me. Jenny, the wolfette with the red roses, was ready to rock and roll, but I was far from the valiant George-Hamilton-of-Dionysian-love-making that the evening required. There was, alas, nothing close to 'Paradise by The Dashboard night-light'. I was her premature baby.

When I awoke the next morning, Jen had already split the scene. A crumpled note was all that remained, saying she'd see me out on the court, or something. This left me numb and uncertain with a pulverizing hangover – another new taste experience for me – and with Mom's arrival quickly approaching, I began the horrifically depressing task of cleaning up and putting the house back together how mom left it.

After walking through the door from her weekend away, she began to sniff around and stopped me while I was investigating what there was in the fridge to munch on, I hear "Stop right there, mister." Being heavily fatigued and down in the mouth, this is about where I would lose all sight of mind and reason. A fable that might have explained at least some of the misplaced and rearranged items in the home is something that flowed out of my mouth without my arranging it to. Admittedly, it was not my best work.

An innocent yet perplexing interrogation soon followed as she simultaneously surveyed the playing field.

"This wouldn't be your bra under my bed, Timothy?"

"Why does my room smell *funny*?"

"What the hell are these in the sink: cherries soaked in Bailey's Irish Cream?" she asked, "Just what went on here, mister?' I stood motionless and very far from the world of Glee.

Later in the day, the thunderstorms came, clearly washing out my next lesson with lovely Jen.

I gazed out the window, overwhelmed, dumbfounded, disappointed, and unsure which conundrum to address first. I needed a hug, or at least something big and furry with a tongue to pet. After my infamous all too sobering virgin escapade, mom felt she was going to be less inclined to, in the future, leave her fastidious warren in my helpful hands.

I hate to admit it but I may not be the ladies' man I think I am.

TimFoolery #1: Nostalgia, eh? Just what sort of nostalgia does a sixteen-year-old think he has anyway?

TimFoolery #2: thankfully, miles from The Murphy Bed near the brown Basement Bar that screamed Bits and Bites and-unclassy-keggerless-gatherings from-days-past that would have been a mammothly humorless wonderwall, too numerous in comedic snafus that wouldn't have helped with getting to the carnal bliss portion of the twilight.

The following information is vital…to something,
though I can't recall just what right now. Take the data
and use it as a workbook for those willing high school
students, the ones who can string a few words together
and can appreciate some obscure commentary on human
nature. To order workbook, see address
and at front of the novel.
Thanks.

* * *

Animal Group / Collective Names

aardvark: aarmory
albatross: rookery
alligator: congregation
alpaca: flock, herd
ant: colony, nest, army, swarm, bike
antelope: herd, cluster
ape: shrewdness, troop
ass: pace, drove, herd, coffle
auk: colony, flock, raft
baboon: troop, flange, congress, tribe
badger: cete, colony, set, company
barracuda: battery
bass: shoal, fleet
bat: colony, cloud
bear: sleuth, sloth, slought, maul
beaver: family, lodge, colony
bee: colony, grist, hum, swarm, hive, cluster
beetle: swarm
bird (general): fleet, parcel, flight, volery, cast, flock, aviary
bison: herd, troop, gang, thunder
bittern: sedge, flock, siege
bloodhound: sute
boar: singular, sounder, herd
bovine: herd
buffalo: gang, troop, herd, obstinacy
bullfinch: bellowing
bullock: drove
butterfly: rabble, flight, swarm
buzzard: wake, flock
camel: flock, train, caravan, herd
caribou: herd
cat: clowder, clutter, pounce, cluster, colony, glorying, destruction (wild cats)
caterpillar: army, nest

cattle: drove, herd, bow, bunch, draft, drift, mob

cheetah: coalition

chicken: brood, clutch, flock, peep, hatching, battery

chimpanzee: cartload

chinchilla: colony

clam: bed, flaccidity

cockroach: intrusion, swarm

cod: lap, school

colt: rake, rage

coot: cover

cow: herd, drove, pack, team

coyote: pack, rout

crab: cast

crane: sedge, siege, flock, herd

cricket: orchestra

crocodile: bask, nest, congregation, float

crow: murder, horde, parcel, hover, muster

deer: herd, leash, bevy, game, quarry, bunch, mob, parcel

dog: gang, legion, kennel, pack (wild), litter (young)

dolphin: team, school, pod, herd

donkey: drove, herd, pace

dove: dule, duet, flight, troop

duck: brace, flock, gaggle, paddling, team, raft, badling, bunch, waddling

eagle: convocation, brood, aerie

eel: swarm, bed. draft, wisp, knot

elephant: herd, host, flock, parade, memory

elk: gang, herd

falcon: passager, cast

ferret: business, cast

finch: charm, chirm, trembling, trimming

fish (general): school, shoal, draft, nest, cast, draught, run, catch, drift, haul

flamingo: stand, flamboyance

fly: business, hatch, swarm, community, cloud, grist

flying fish: glide

fowl: plump
fox: leash, skulk, earth, troop
frog: army, colony, froggery, knot
gerbil: horde
giraffe: tower, troop, corps, herd, group, stretch
gnat: cloud, horde, swarm, plague
gnu: herd
goat: tribe, trip, flock, herd
goldfinch: charm, chattering, drum, troubling, vein
goldfish: troubling
goose: flock, gaggle, skein, line, wedge, nide
gorilla: band
grasshopper: cloud, cluster
greyhound: gallop, leash
grouse: covey, pack, brace, drumming
guinea pig: group
gull: colony, pack
hamster: horde
hare: down, husk, leap, , leash, flick, kindle, drove, warren
hawk: cast, kettle, boil, leash, mews, aerie
hedgehog: nest, array, prickle
hen: brood, battery, parcel, roost, mews
heron: siege, sedge
herring: army, glean, shoal
hippopotamuses: bloat, pod, herd, huddle
hog: drift, drove, herd
hornet: nest, bike, swarm
horse: harras, herd, pair, team, stud, field, mob, troop
hound: cry, mute, pack, kennel
hummingbird: charm, chattering, drum, hover, troubling
hyena: cackle, clan
impala: herd
jackrabbit: husk
jellyfish: smack, brood, smuth, smuck, fluther
kangaroo: mob, troop, herd
kitten: kindle, kendle, litter, intrigue

lark: ascension, exaltation, bevy, flight
lemur: group
leopard: leap, prowl
lice: flock
lion: pride, tribe, sault, sowse
llama: herd
locust: host, plague, swarm, cloud
louse: colony, infestation, lice
mackerel: school, shoal
magpie: tiding, gulp, murder, charm, tittering, flock
mallard: sord, brace, puddling, flush
manatee: herd
marten: richness
minnow: shoal, steam, swarm
mole: labor, company, movement
monkey: troop, barrel, tribe, cartload
moose: herd
mosquito: scourge, swarm
mouse: nest, colony, harvest, horde, mischief
mule: barren, pack, span, rake
nighthawk: kettle
nightingale: watch, flock, route, match
orangutan: buffoonery
ostrich: flock
otter: romp, bevy, lodge, family, raft
owl: parliament, stare
ox: yoke, team, drove, herd, nye
oyster: bed, hive, cast, culch
parrot: company, flock, prattle
partridge: covey, bew
peacock:muster, ostentation, pride
penguin: colony, rookery, parade, parcel
pheasant: bouquet, nest, nide, nye, brood, covey
pig: drove, litter, drift, flock, hoggery, herd, sounder
pigeon: flight, loft, flock, dropping
plover: congregation, wing, leash

polar bear: aurora, pack
polecat: chine
pony: string
porcupine: prickle, family
porpoise: school, crowd, herd, pod
possum: passel
prairie dog: coterie, town
quail: bevy, covey, drift
rabbit: colony, nest, warren, bevy, bury, drove
raccoon: nursery, mask
raptor: cauldron, kettle
rat: horde, mischief, rabble
raven: unkindness, congress, conspiracy, parliament
reindeer: herd
rhinoceros: crash, herd
rook: building, shoal, congregation, pack, parliament
salmon: run, bind, gib, school, shoal
sardine: family
scorpion: bed, nest, colony
sea horse: herd
seal: pod, herd, school, trip, rookery, harem, team
shark: shiver, school, shoal
sheep: drove, flock, herd, drift, fold, mob, pack, trip
skunk: stench, surfeit
snail: escargatoire, rout, walk
snake: bed, knot, den, pit, nest, slither
snipe: walk, wisp
sparrow: host, flight, quarrel, tribe
spider: cluster, clutter, venom
squirrel: dray, scurry, colony
starling: murmuration, cloud, chattering, clutter
stork: mustering, flight
swallow: flight, rush, swoop
swan: bevy, wedge, flock, game, team, ballet, regatta
swine: drift, sounder, herd
swordfish: flotilla

termite: colony

tiger: streak, ambush, hide. ambush

toad: knot, nest, knob, lump

tortoise: creep

trout: hover, leash, troup

turkey: rafter, posse, gang, dole, flock, raffle

turtle: bale, bevy, nest, dule, turn

turtle dove: pitying

toucan: durante

viper: nest, den

vulture: wake

wallaby: mob

walrus: pod, herd, huddle

wasp: nest, knot, bike, swarm, colony, pail

weasel: pack, gang, sneak

whale: gam, herd, grind, pod, shoal, school, mob

wild boar: sounder

wolf: pack, rout, route, horde

wombat: mob, warren

woodcock: fall, covey, plump

woodpecker: descent, gatling

worm: bed, bunch, clew

wren: herd

yak: herd

zebra: herd, cohorts, crossing, stripe

Animal's Children's Names

aardvark: pup
alligator: hatchling
alpaca: cria
ant: antling, larva
anteater: pup
antelope: calf
ape: baby, infant
armadillo: pup
baboon: infant
badger: cub, kit
barracuda: spet
bat: pup
bear: cub, whelp
beaver: kit, kitten, pup
bee: larva
beetle: grub, mealworm
bird: fledgling, nestling, chick, hatchling
bison: calf
bittern: chick
boar: calf, farrow, piglet
bobcat: cub, kitten
bovine: calf
buffalo: calf
butterfly: caterpillar, chrysalis, larva, pupa
buzzard: chick
camel: calf, colt, foal
cat: kit, kitten, kitty, puss, pussy
cattle: calf, yearling, stirk
cattle (castrated male): steer
cattle (male): bullock
cattle (female): heifer
cheetah: cub
chicken: chick, poult, fryer, pullet
chimpanzee: infant

cicada: nymph
clam: chiton, littleneck
cod: codling, hake, scrod
cockroach: larva, nymph
coot: chick
cougar: cub, kitten
cow: calf, heifer
coyote: pup, whelp
crane: chick, craneling
crocodile: crocklet
crow: chick
deer: fawn, calf, kid
dog: pup, whelp, puppy
dolphin: calf, pup
donkey: colt, foal
dotterel: chick
dove: chick
duck: duckling, flapper
eagle: eaglet, fledgling
eel: fly, elver
elephant: calf
elk: calf
ewe: teg
falcon: cast, chick
ferret: kit
finch: chick
fish: fingerling, fry, alevin
flamingo: chick
fly: grub, maggot
fowl: chick, chicken; flapper
fox: cub, kit, pup, whelp
frog: polliwog, tadpole, froglet
gerbil: pup
giraffe: cub, whelp, calf
gnat: larva
gnu: calf

goat: kid
goldfinch: chick
goose: gosling
goshawk: chick
gorilla: infant
grouse: cheeper, chick
greyhound: pup, puppy, whelp
grouse: cheeper, poult
guinea pig: pup
gull: chick
hamster: pup
hare: leveret
hawk: eyas, brancher
hedgehog: piglet, pup
hen: chick, pullet
heron: chick
herring: brit, sprat
hippopotamus: calf
hog: farrow, shoat, piglet
horse: colt, filly, filt, foal, yearling
hummingbird: chick
hyena: cub, pup
hyrax: bunny
impala: calf
jellyfish: ephyna
kangaroo: joey
koala: joey
lark: chick
lemur: infant
leopard: cub
lion: cub, whelp, lionet, shelp
llama: cria
locust: pupa
louse: nit, nymph
lynx: kitten
mackerel: blinker, spike

magpie: chick
mallard: duckling
manatee: calf
marten: kit
meerkat: pup
mink: cub, kit
mole: pup
monkey: infant, suckling
moose: cub, calf
mosquito: larva, flapper, nymph, wiggler, wriggler
mouse: kitten, pinkie, pup
mule: foal
muskrat: kit
nighthawk: chick
nightingale: chick
opossum: joey
ostrich: chick
otter: pup, whelp
owl: owlet, howlet
ox: calf, stot
oyster: spat, brood
panda: cub
parrot: chick
partridge: cheeper, chick
peafowl: peachick
pelican: chick, nestling
penguin: chick, fledgling
pheasant: chick
pig: piglet, shoat, farrow, suckling
pigeon: squab, squeaker, nestling
pike: fingerling, fry
plover: chick
polar bear: cub
polecat: kit
porcupine: pup
porpoise: calf

possum: joey
quail: cheeper, chick, squealer
rabbit: bunny, kit, kitten, nestling, leveret
raccoon: cub, kit
raven: chick
reindeer: fawn, calf
rhinoceros: calf
rook: chick
rooster: cockerel
salmon: alevin, fry, parr, samlet, skegger, smolt
sandpiper: chick
scorpion: instar
seal: calf, pup, weaner, cub, whelp
sea lion: pup, weaner, cub, whelp
shark: cub, pup
sheep: lamb, lambkin, cosset, hog, yearling
skunk: kit, kitten
snake: snakelet
sow: gilt, piglet
sparrow: chick
spider: spiderling
squirrel: kit, kitten, nestling, pup
stallion: colt
starling: chick
stork: chick
swallow: chick
swan: cygnet, flapper
Tasmanian devil: joey
termite: larva, nymph
tiger: cub, whelp
toad: tadpole
trout: fingerling, fry
turkey: poult, chick
turtle: hatchling
turtle dove: chick
viper: snakelet

wallaby: joey
walrus: pup
wasp: larva
weasel: kit
whale: calf
wild boar: boarlet
wolf: cub, whelp, pup
wombat: joey
woodchuck: cub, kit
woodcock: chick
woodpecker: chick
yak: calf
zebra: foal, colt

Animal Male / Female Names

alligator: bull(M); cow(F)
alpaca: stallion(M)
ant: gyne(F), queen(F)
anteater: male; female
antelope: buck(M); doe(F)
ape: male; female
armadillo: male; female
ass: dicky(M), jack(M), jackass(M); jenny(F), she-ass(F)
baboon: male; female
badger: boar(M); sow(F)
bat: male; female
bear: boar(M); sow(F), ursa(F)
bee: drone(M); queen(F), queen-bee(F), worker(F)
beetle: male; female
bird (general): cock(M); hen(F)
bison: bull(M); cow(F)
bittern: cock(M); hen(F)
boar: boar(M); sow(F)
buffalo: bull(M); cow(F)
butterfly: male; female

buzzard: cock(M); hen(F)

camel: bull(M), stallion(M); cow(F), mare(F)

cat: tom(M), tomcat(M), gib(M), gib-cat(M); puss(F), queen(F), tabby(F)

cattle: bull(M); cow(F)

cheetah: male; female

chicken: cock(M), rooster(M); biddy(F), hen(F)

chimpanzee: male; female

cockroach: male; female

cod: male; female

coot: cock(M); hen(F)

coyote: dog(M); bitch(F), gyp(F)

crane: cock(M); hen(F)

crocodile: bull(M); cow(F)

deer: buck(M), hart(M), stag(M); doe(F), hind(F), roe(F), teg(F)

dog: dog(M); bitch(F)

dolphin: bull(M); cow(F)

donkey: dicky(M), jack(M), jack-ass(M); jennet(F), jenny(F), she-ass(F)

dove: cock(M); hen(F)

duck: drake(M); duck(F)

eagle: male; female

eel: male; female

elephant: bull(M); cow(F), koomkie(F)

elk: bull(M); cow(F)

falcon: tercel(M), terzel(M); falcon(F)

ferret: dog(M), hob(M), buck(M), jack(M); doe(F), jill(F), bitch(F)

finch: cock(M); hen(F)

flamingo: cock(M); hen(F)

fly: male; female

fox: dog(M), reynard(M), vix(M); vixen(F)

frog: male; female

gerbil: buck(M); doe(F)

giraffe: bull(M); cow(F), doe(F)

gnat: male; female

gnu: bull(M); cow(F)

goat: billy(M), buck(M); doe(F), nanny(F)

goldfinch: cock(M); hen(F)

goose: gander(M), steg(M); dame(F), goose(F)

gorilla: male; female

greyhound: dog(M); bitch(F)

grouse: cock(M), gorcock(M); hen(F), gorhen(F)

guinea pig: boar(M), buck(M); doe(F), sow(F)

gull: cock(M); hen(F)

hamster: buck(M); doe(F)

hare: buck(M), jack(M); doe(F), jill(F), puss(F)

hawk: tiercel(M); haggard(F), hen(F)

hedgehog: boar(M); sow(F)

heron: cock(M); hen(F)

hippopotamus: bull(M); cow(F)

hog: boar(M); gilt(F), sow(F)

horse: sire(M), stallion(M), stud(M); dam(F), mare(F)

hummingbird: cock(M); hen(F)

hyena: dog(M); bitch(F)

impala: buck(M); doe(F)

kangaroo: boomer(M), buck(M), jack(M); doe(F), flyer(F), jill(F), roo(

koala: male; female

lark: cock(M); hen(F)

lemur: male; female

leopard: leopard(M); leopardess(F)

lion: lion(M); lioness(F)

llama: male; female

lobster: cock(M); hen(F)

locust: male; female

magpie: cock(M); hen(F)

mallard: drake(M); duck(F)

manatee: bull(M); cow(F)

mink: boar(M); sow(F)

mole: male; female

monkey: male; female

moose: bull(M); cow(F)

mosquito: male; female

mouse: buck(M); doe(F)

mule: jack(M); hinney(F)
nighthawk: cock(M); hen(F)
nightingale: cock(M); hen(F)
opossum: jack(M); jill(F)
ostrich: cock(M); hen(F)
otter: male; female
ox: bull(M), steer(M); cow(F)
panda: boar(M); sow(F)
parrot: cock(M); hen(F)
partridge: cock(M); chantrelle(F), hen(F)
pelican: cock(M); hen(F)
penguin: male; female
pig: barrow(M), boar(M), hog(M); gilt(F), sow(F)
pheasant: cock(M); hen(F)
pigeon: cock(M); hen(F)
polar bear: boar(M); sow(F)
polecat: hob(M); jill(F)
porcupine: boar(M); sow(F)
porpoise: bull(M); cow(F)
possum: jack(M); jill(F)
prairie dog: boar(M); sow(F)
quail: cock(M); hen(F)
rabbit: buck(M); doe(F)
raccoon: boar(M); sow(F)
rat: buck(M); doe(F)
raven: cock(M); hen(F)
reindeer: bull(M); cow(F)
rhinoceros: bull(M); cow(F)
rook: cock(M); hen(F)
salmon: jack(M); hen(F), raun(F)
seal: bull(M); cow(F), matka(F)
sea lion: bull(M); cow(F), matka(F)
shark: bull(M); female(F)
sheep: ram(M), tup(M), wether(M); ewe(F)
skunk: boar(M)
snake: male; female

snipe: cock(M); hen(F)

sparrow: cock(M); hen(F)

spider: male; female

squirrel: buck(M); doe(F)

starling: cock(M); hen(F)

stork: cock(M); hen(F)

swallow: cock(M); hen(F)

swan: cob(M); pen(F)

termite: king(M), male(M); queen(F), female(F)

tiger: tiger(M); tigress(F)

toad: male; female

trout: jack(M); shedder(F)

turkey: gobbler(M), tom(M), jack(M)(young); jen(F), jenny(F)(young)

turtle: male; female

turtle dove: cock(M); hen(F)

viper: male; female

wallaby: jack(M); jill(F)

walrus: bull(M); cow(F)

wasp: drone(M); queen(F), worker(F)

weasel: buck(M), dog(M), hob(M), jack(M); bitch(F), doe(F), jill(F)

whale: bull(M); cow(F)

widgeon: drake(M); duck(F)

wild boar: boar(M); sow(F)

wolf: dog(M), he-wolf(M); bitch(F), she-wolf(F)

wombat: jack(M); jill(F)

woodchuck: he-chuck(M); she-chuck(F)

woodcock: rooster(M); hen(F)

woodpecker: cock(M); hen(F)

wren: jenny(F), jennywren(F)

yak: bull(M); cow(F), dri(F), nak(F)

zebra: stallion(M); mare(F)

Fears. *We have them!*

A-
Ablutophobia- Fear of washing or bathing.
Acarophobia- Fear of itching or of the insects that cause itching.
Acerophobia- Fear of sourness.
Achluophobia- Fear of darkness.
Acousticophobia- Fear of noise.
Acrophobia- Fear of heights.
Aerophobia- Fear of drafts, air swallowing, or airborne noxious substances.
Aeroacrophobia- Fear of open high places.
Aeronausiphobia- Fear of vomiting secondary to airsickness.
Agateophobia- Fear of insanity.
Agliophobia- Fear of pain.
Agoraphobia- Fear of open spaces or of being in crowded, public places like markets. Fear of leaving a safe place.
Agraphobia- Fear of sexual abuse.
Agrizoophobia- Fear of wild animals.
Agyrophobia- Fear of streets or crossing the street.
Aichmophobia- Fear of needles or pointed objects.
Ailurophobia- Fear of cats.
Albuminurophobia- Fear of kidney disease.
Alektorophobia- Fear of chickens.
Algophobia- Fear of pain.
Alliumphobia- Fear of garlic.
Allodoxaphobia- Fear of opinions.
Altophobia- Fear of heights.
Amathophobia- Fear of dust.
Amaxophobia- Fear of riding in a car.
Ambulophobia- Fear of walking.
Amnesiphobia- Fear of amnesia.
Amychophobia- Fear of scratches or being scratched.
Anablephobia- Fear of looking up.
Ancraophobia- Fear of wind. (Anemophobia)

Androphobia- Fear of men.

Anemophobia- Fear of air drafts or wind.(Ancraophobia)

Anginophobia- Fear of angina, choking or narrowness.

Anglophobia- Fear of England or English culture, etc.

Angrophobia - Fear of anger or of becoming angry.

Ankylophobia- Fear of immobility of a joint.

Anthrophobia or Anthophobia- Fear of flowers.

Anthropophobia- Fear of people or society.

Antlophobia- Fear of floods.

Anuptaphobia- Fear of staying single.

Apeirophobia- Fear of infinity.

Aphenphosmphobia- Fear of being touched.

Apiphobia- Fear of bees.

Apotemnophobia- Fear of persons with amputations.

Arachibutyrophobia- Fear of peanut butter sticking to the roof of the mouth.

Arachnephobia or Arachnophobia- Fear of spiders.

Arithmophobia- Fear of numbers.

Arrhenphobia- Fear of men.

Arsonphobia- Fear of fire.

Asthenophobia- Fear of fainting or weakness.

Astraphobia or Astrapophobia- Fear of thunder and lightning. (Ceraunophobia, Keraunophobia)

Astrophobia- Fear of stars or celestial space.

Asymmetriphobia- Fear of asymmetrical things.

Ataxiophobia- Fear of ataxia. (muscular incoordination)

Ataxophobia- Fear of disorder or untidiness.

Atelophobia- Fear of imperfection.

Atephobia- Fear of ruin or ruins.

Athazagoraphobia- Fear of being forgotton or ignored.

Atomosophobia- Fear of atomic explosions.

Atychiphobia- Fear of failure.

Aulophobia- Fear of flutes.

Aurophobia- Fear of gold.

Auroraphobia- Fear of Northern lights.

Autodysomophobia- Fear of one that has a vile odor.

Automatonophobia- Fear of ventriloquist's dummies, animatronic creatures, wax statues - anything that falsly represents a sentient being.

Automysophobia- Fear of being dirty.

Autophobia- Fear of being alone or of oneself.

Aviophobia or Aviatophobia- Fear of flying.

B-

Bacillophobia- Fear of microbes.

Bacteriophobia- Fear of bacteria.

Ballistophobia- Fear of missiles or bullets.

Bolshephobia- Fear of Bolsheviks.

Barophobia- Fear of gravity.

Basophobia or Basiphobia- Inability to stand. Fear of walking or falling.

Bathmophobia- Fear of stairs or steep slopes.

Bathophobia- Fear of depth.

Batophobia- Fear of heights or being close to high buildings.

Batrachophobia- Fear of amphibians, such as frogs, newts, salamanders, etc.

Belonephobia- Fear of pins and needles. (Aichmophobia)

Bibliophobia- Fear of books.

Blennophobia- Fear of slime.

Bogyphobia- Fear of bogeys or the bogeyman.

Botanophobia- Fear of plants.

Bromidrosiphobia or Bromidrophobia- Fear of body smells.

Brontophobia- Fear of thunder and lightning.

Bufonophobia- Fear of toads.

C-

Cacophobia- Fear of ugliness.

Cainophobia or Cainotophobia- Fear of newness, novelty.

Caligynephobia- Fear of beautiful women.

Cancerophobia or Carcinophobia- Fear of cancer.

Cardiophobia- Fear of the heart.

Carnophobia- Fear of meat.

Catagelophobia- Fear of being ridiculed.

Catapedaphobia- Fear of jumping from high and low places.

Cathisophobia- Fear of sitting.

Catoptrophobia- Fear of mirrors.

Cenophobia or Centophobia- Fear of new things or ideas.

Ceraunophobia Fear of thunder and lightning.

Chemophobia- Fear of chemicals or working with chemicals.

Cherophobia- Fear of gaiety.

Chionophobia- Fear of snow.

Chiraptophobia- Fear of being touched.

Chirophobia- Fear of hands.

Chiroptophobia- Fear of bats.

Cholerophobia- Fear of anger or the fear of cholera.

Chorophobia- Fear of dancing.

Chrometophobia or Chrematophobia- Fear of money.

Chromophobia or Chromatophobia- Fear of colors.

Chronophobia- Fear of time.

Chronomentrophobia- Fear of clocks.

Cibophobia- Fear of food.(Sitophobia, Sitiophobia)

Claustrophobia- Fear of confined spaces.

Cleithrophobia- Fear of being locked in an enclosed place.

Cleptophobia- Fear of stealing.

Climacophobia- Fear of stairs, climbing, or of falling downstairs.

Clinophobia- Fear of going to bed.

Clithrophobia or Cleithrophobia- Fear of being enclosed.

Cnidophobia- Fear of stings.

Cometophobia- Fear of comets.

Coimetrophobia- Fear of cemeteries.

Coitophobia- Fear of coitus.

Contreltophobia- Fear of sexual abuse.

Coprastasophobia- Fear of constipation.

Coprophobia- Fear of feces.

Consecotaleophobia- Fear of chopsticks.

Coulrophobia- Fear of clowns.

Counterphobia- The preference by a phobic for fearful situations.

Cremnophobia- Fear of precipices.

Cryophobia- Fear of extreme cold, ice or frost.

Crystallophobia- Fear of crystals or glass.

Cyberphobia- Fear of computers or working on a computer.

Cyclophobia- Fear of bicycles.

Cymophobia Fear of waves or wave like motions.

Cynophobia- Fear of dogs or rabies.

Cypridophobia or Cypriphobia or Cyprianophobia or Cyprinophobia - Fear of prostitutes or venereal disease.

D-

Decidophobia- Fear of making decisions.

Defecaloesiophobia- Fear of painful bowels movements.

Deipnophobia- Fear of dining or dinner conversations.

Dementophobia- Fear of insanity.

Demonophobia or Daemonophobia- Fear of demons.

Demophobia- Fear of crowds. (Agoraphobia)

Dendrophobia- Fear of trees.

Dentophobia- Fear of dentists.

Dermatophobia- Fear of skin lesions.

Dermatosiophobia Fear of skin disease.

Dextrophobia- Fear of objects at the right side of the body.

Diabetophobia- Fear of diabetes.

Didaskaleinophobia- Fear of going to school.

Dikephobia- Fear of justice.

Dinophobia- Fear of dizziness or whirlpools.

Diplophobia- Fear of double vision.

Dipsophobia- Fear of drinking.

Dishabiliophobia- Fear of undressing in front of someone.

Disposophobia- Fear of throwing stuff out. Hoarding.

Domatophobia- Fear of houses or being in a house.(Eicophobia, Oikophobia)

Doraphobia- Fear of fur or skins of animals.

Doxophobia- Fear of expressing opinions or of receiving praise.

Dromophobia- Fear of crossing streets.

Dutchphobia- Fear of the Dutch.

Dysmorphophobia- Fear of deformity.

Dystychiphobia- Fear of accidents.

E-

Ecclesiophobia- Fear of church.

Ecophobia- Fear of home.

Eicophobia- Fear of home surroundings.

Eisoptrophobia- Fear of mirrors or of seeing oneself in a mirror.

Electrophobia- Fear of electricity.

Eleutherophobia- Fear of freedom.

Elurophobia- Fear of cats. (Ailurophobia)

Emetophobia- Fear of vomiting.

Enetophobia- Fear of pins.

Enochlophobia- Fear of crowds.

Enosiophobia or Enissophobia- Fear of having committed an unpardonable sin or of criticism.

Entomophobia- Fear of insects.

Eosophobia- Fear of dawn or daylight.

Ephebiphobia- Fear of teenagers.

Epistaxiophobia- Fear of nosebleeds.

Epistemophobia- Fear of knowledge.

Equinophobia- Fear of horses.

Eremophobia- Fear of being oneself or of lonliness.

Ereuthrophobia- Fear of blushing.

Ergasiophobia- 1) Fear of work or functioning. 2) Surgeon's fear of operating.

Ergophobia- Fear of work.

Erotophobia- Fear of sexual love or sexual questions.

Euphobia- Fear of hearing good news.

Eurotophobia- Fear of female genitalia.

Erythrophobia or Erytophobia or Ereuthophobia- 1) Fear of redlights. 2) Blushing. 3) Red.

F-

Febriphobia or Fibriphobia or Fibriophobia- Fear of fever.

Felinophobia- Fear of cats. (Ailurophobia, Elurophobia, Galeophobia, Gatophobia)

Francophobia- Fear of France or French culture. (Gallophobia, Galiophobia)

Frigophobia- Fear of cold or cold things.(Cheimaphobia, Cheimatophobia, Psychrophobia)

G-

Galeophobia or Gatophobia- Fear of cats.

Gallophobia or Galiophobia- Fear France or French culture. (Francophobia)

Gamophobia- Fear of marriage.

Geliophobia- Fear of laughter.

Gelotophobia- Fear of being laughed at.

Geniophobia- Fear of chins.

Genophobia- Fear of sex.

Genuphobia- Fear of knees.

Gephyrophobia or Gephydrophobia or Gephysrophobia- Fear of crossing bridges.

Germanophobia- Fear of Germany or German culture.

Gerascophobia- Fear of growing old.

Gerontophobia- Fear of old people or of growing old.

Geumaphobia or Geumophobia- Fear of taste.

Glossophobia- Fear of speaking in public or of trying to speak.

Gnosiophobia- Fear of knowledge.

Graphophobia- Fear of writing or handwriting.

Gymnophobia- Fear of nudity.

Gynephobia or Gynophobia- Fear of women. Stigiophobia-

H-

Hadephobia- Fear of hell. Stigiophobia-

Hagiophobia- Fear of saints or holy things.

Hamartophobia- Fear of sinning.

Haphephobia or Haptephobia- Fear of being touched.

Harpaxophobia- Fear of being robbed.

Hedonophobia- Fear of feeling pleasure.

Heliophobia- Fear of the sun.

Hellenologophobia- Fear of Greek terms or complex scientific terminology.

Helminthophobia- Fear of being infested with worms.

Hemophobia or Hemaphobia or Hematophobia- Fear of blood.

Heresyphobia or Hereiophobia- Fear of challenges to official doctrine or of radical deviation.

Herpetophobia- Fear of reptiles or creepy, crawly things.

Heterophobia- Fear of the opposite sex. (Sexophobia)

Hexakosioihexekontahexaphobia- Fear of the number 666.

Hierophobia- Fear of priests or sacred things.

Hippophobia- Fear of horses.

Hippopotomonstrosesquipedaliophobia- Fear of long words.

Hobophobia- Fear of bums or beggars.

Hodophobia- Fear of road travel.

Hormephobia- Fear of shock.

Homichlophobia- Fear of fog.

Homilophobia- Fear of sermons.

Hominophobia- Fear of men.

Homophobia- Fear of sameness, monotony or of homosexuality or of becoming homosexual.

Hoplophobia- Fear of firearms.

Hydrargyophobia- Fear of mercurial medicines.

Hydrophobia- Fear of water or of rabies.

Hydrophobophobia- Fear of rabies.

Hyelophobia or Hyalophobia- Fear of glass.

Hygrophobia- Fear of liquids, dampness, or moisture.

Hylephobia- Fear of materialism or the fear of epilepsy.

Hylophobia- Fear of forests.

Hypengyophobia or Hypegiaphobia- Fear of responsibility.

Hypnophobia- Fear of sleep or of being hypnotized.

Hypsiphobia- Fear of height.

I-

Iatrophobia- Fear of going to the doctor or of doctors.

Ichthyophobia- Fear of fish.
Ideophobia- Fear of ideas.
Illyngophobia- Fear of vertigo or feeling dizzy when looking down.
Iophobia- Fear of poison.
Insectophobia - Fear of insects.
Isolophobia- Fear of solitude, being alone.
Isopterophobia- Fear of termites, insects that eat wood.
Ithyphallophobia- Fear of seeing, thinking about or having an erect penis.

J-
Japanophobia- Fear of Japanese.
Judeophobia- Fear of Jews.

K-
Kainolophobia or Kainophobia- Fear of anything new, novelty.
Kakorrhaphiophobia- Fear of failure or defeat.
Katagelophobia- Fear of ridicule.
Kathisophobia- Fear of sitting down.
Katsaridaphobia- Fear of cockroaches.
Kenophobia- Fear of voids or empty spaces.
Keraunophobia or Ceraunophobia- Fear of thunder and lightning.(Astraphobia, Astrapophobia)
Kinetophobia or Kinesophobia- Fear of movement or motion.
Kleptophobia- Fear of stealing.
Koinoniphobia- Fear of rooms.
Kolpophobia- Fear of genitals, particularly female.
Kopophobia- Fear of fatigue.
Koniophobia- Fear of dust. (Amathophobia)
Kosmikophobia- Fear of cosmic phenomenon.
Kymophobia- Fear of waves. (Cymophobia)
Kynophobia- Fear of rabies.
Kyphophobia- Fear of stooping.

L-

Lachanophobia- Fear of vegetables.

Laliophobia or Lalophobia- Fear of speaking.

Leprophobia or Lepraphobia- Fear of leprosy.

Leukophobia- Fear of the color white.

Levophobia- Fear of things to the left side of the body.

Ligyrophobia- Fear of loud noises.

Lilapsophobia- Fear of tornadoes and hurricanes.

Limnophobia- Fear of lakes.

Linonophobia- Fear of string.

Liticaphobia- Fear of lawsuits.

Lockiophobia- Fear of childbirth.

Logizomechanophobia- Fear of computers.

Logophobia- Fear of words.

Luiphobia- Fear of lues, syphillis.

Lutraphobia- Fear of otters.

Lygophobia- Fear of darkness.

Lyssophobia- Fear of rabies or of becoming mad.

M-

Macrophobia- Fear of long waits.

Mageirocophobia- Fear of cooking.

Maieusiophobia- Fear of childbirth.

Malaxophobia- Fear of love play. (Sarmassophobia)

Maniaphobia- Fear of insanity.

Mastigophobia- Fear of punishment.

Mechanophobia- Fear of machines.

Medomalacuphobia- Fear of losing an erection.

Medorthophobia- Fear of an erect penis.

Megalophobia- Fear of large things.

Melissophobia- Fear of bees.

Melanophobia- Fear of the color black.

Melophobia- Fear or hatred of music.

Meningitophobia- Fear of brain disease.

Menophobia- Fear of menstruation.

Merinthophobia- Fear of being bound or tied up.

Metallophobia- Fear of metal.

Metathesiophobia- Fear of changes.

Meteorophobia- Fear of meteors.

Methyphobia- Fear of alcohol.

Metrophobia- Fear or hatred of poetry.

Microbiophobia- Fear of microbes. (Bacillophobia)

Microphobia- Fear of small things.

Misophobia-Fear of being contaminated with dirt or germs.

Mnemophobia- Fear of memories.

Molysmophobia Fear of dirt or contamination.

Monophobia- Fear of solitude or being alone.

Monopathophobia- Fear of definite disease.

Motorphobia- Fear of automobiles.

Mottephobia- Fear of moths.

Musophobia or Muriphobia- Fear of mice.

Mycophobia- Fear or aversion to mushrooms.

Mycrophobia- Fear of small things.

Myctophobia- Fear of darkness.

Myrmecophobia- Fear of ants.

Mythophobia- Fear of myths or stories or false statements.

Myxophobia- Fear of slime. (Blennophobia)

N-

Nebulaphobia- Fear of fog. (Homichlophobia)

Necrophobia- Fear of death or dead things.

Nelophobia- Fear of glass.

Neopharmaphobia- Fear of new drugs.

Neophobia- Fear of anything new.

Nephophobia- Fear of clouds.

Noctiphobia- Fear of the night.

Nomatophobia- Fear of names.

Nosocomephobia- Fear of hospitals.

Nosophobia or Nosemaphobia- Fear of becoming ill.

Nostophobia- Fear of returning home.

Novercaphobia- Fear of your step-mother.

Nucleomituphobia- Fear of nuclear weapons.

Nudophobia- Fear of nudity.

Numerophobia- Fear of numbers.

Nyctohylophobia- Fear of dark wooded areas or of forests at night

Nyctophobia- Fear of the dark or of night.

O-

Obesophobia- Fear of gaining weight. (Pocrescophobia)

Ochlophobia- Fear of crowds or mobs.

Ochophobia- Fear of vehicles.

Octophobia - Fear of the figure 8.

Odontophobia- Fear of teeth or dental surgery.

Odynophobia or Odynephobia- Fear of pain. (Algophobia)

Oenophobia- Fear of wines.

Oikophobia- Fear of home surroundings, house.(Domatophobia, Eicophobia)

Olfactophobia- Fear of smells.

Ombrophobia- Fear of rain or of being rained on.

Ommetaphobia or Ommatophobia- Fear of eyes.

Omphalophobia- Fear of belly buttons.

Oneirophobia- Fear of dreams.

Oneirogmophobia- Fear of wet dreams.

Onomatophobia- Fear of hearing a certain word or of names.

Ophidiophobia- Fear of snakes. (Snakephobia)

Ophthalmophobia- Fear of being stared at.

Opiophobia- Fear medical doctors experience of prescribing needed pain medications for patients.

Optophobia- Fear of opening one's eyes.

Ornithophobia- Fear of birds.

Orthophobia- Fear of property.

Osmophobia or Osphresiophobia- Fear of smells or odors.

Ostraconophobia- Fear of shellfish.

Ouranophobia or Uranophobia- Fear of heaven.

P-

Pagophobia- Fear of ice or frost.

Panthophobia- Fear of suffering and disease.

Panophobia or Pantophobia- Fear of everything.

Papaphobia- Fear of the Pope.

Papyrophobia- Fear of paper.

Paralipophobia- Fear of neglecting duty or responsibility.

Paraphobia- Fear of sexual perversion.

Parasitophobia- Fear of parasites.

Paraskavedekatriaphobia- Fear of Friday the 13th.

Parthenophobia- Fear of virgins or young girls.

Pathophobia- Fear of disease.

Patroiophobia- Fear of heredity.

Parturiphobia- Fear of childbirth.

Peccatophobia- Fear of sinning or imaginary crimes.

Pediculophobia- Fear of lice.

Pediophobia- Fear of dolls.

Pedophobia- Fear of children.

Peladophobia- Fear of bald people.

Pellagrophobia- Fear of pellagra.

Peniaphobia- Fear of poverty.

Pentheraphobia- Fear of mother-in-law. (Novercaphobia)

Phagophobia- Fear of swallowing or of eating or of being eaten.

Phalacrophobia- Fear of becoming bald.

Phallophobia- Fear of a penis, esp erect.

Pharmacophobia- Fear of taking medicine.

Phasmophobia- Fear of ghosts.

Phengophobia- Fear of daylight or sunshine.

Philemaphobia or Philematophobia- Fear of kissing.

Philophobia- Fear of falling in love or being in love.

Philosophobia- Fear of philosophy.

Phobophobia- Fear of phobias.

Photoaugliaphobia- Fear of glaring lights.

Photophobia- Fear of light.

Phonophobia- Fear of noises or voices or one's own voice; of telephones.

Phronemophobia- Fear of thinking.

Phthiriophobia- Fear of lice. (Pediculophobia)

Phthisiophobia- Fear of tuberculosis.

Placophobia- Fear of tombstones.

Plutophobia- Fear of wealth.

Pluviophobia- Fear of rain or of being rained on.

Pneumatiphobia- Fear of spirits.

Pnigophobia or Pnigerophobia- Fear of choking of being smothered.

Pocrescophobia- Fear of gaining weight. (Obesophobia)

Pogonophobia- Fear of beards.

Poliosophobia- Fear of contracting poliomyelitis.

Politicophobia- Fear or abnormal dislike of politicians.

Polyphobia- Fear of many things.

Poinephobia- Fear of punishment.

Ponophobia- Fear of overworking or of pain.

Porphyrophobia- Fear of the color purple.

Potamophobia- Fear of rivers or running water.

Potophobia- Fear of alcohol.

Pharmacophobia- Fear of drugs.

Proctophobia- Fear of rectums.

Prosophobia- Fear of progress.

Psellismophobia- Fear of stuttering.

Psychophobia- Fear of mind.

Psychrophobia- Fear of cold.

Pteromerhanophobia- Fear of flying.

Pteronophobia- Fear of being tickled by feathers.

Pupaphobia - Fear of puppets.

Pyrexiophobia- Fear of Fever.

Pyrophobia- Fear of fire.

R-

Radiophobia- Fear of radiation, x-rays.

Ranidaphobia- Fear of frogs.

Rectophobia- Fear of rectum or rectal diseases.

Rhabdophobia- Fear of being severely punished or beaten by a rod, or of being severely criticized. Also fear of magic.(wand)

Rhypophobia- Fear of defecation.

Rhytiphobia- Fear of getting wrinkles.

Rupophobia- Fear of dirt.
Russophobia- Fear of Russians.

S-
Samhainophobia: Fear of Halloween.
Sarmassophobia- Fear of love play. (Malaxophobia)
Satanophobia- Fear of Satan.
Scabiophobia- Fear of scabies.
Scatophobia- Fear of fecal matter.
Scelerophibia- Fear of bad men, burglars.
Sciophobia Sciaphobia- Fear of shadows.
Scoleciphobia- Fear of worms.
Scolionophobia- Fear of school.
Scopophobia or Scoptophobia- Fear of being seen or stared at.
Scotomaphobia- Fear of blindness in visual field.
Scotophobia- Fear of darkness. (Achluophobia)
Scriptophobia- Fear of writing in public.
Selachophobia- Fear of sharks.
Selaphobia- Fear of light flashes.
Selenophobia- Fear of the moon.
Seplophobia- Fear of decaying matter.
Sesquipedalophobia- Fear of long words.
Sexophobia- Fear of the opposite sex. (Heterophobia)
Siderodromophobia- Fear of trains, railroads or train travel.
Siderophobia- Fear of stars.
Sinistrophobia- Fear of things to the left or left-handed.
Sinophobia- Fear of Chinese, Chinese culture.
Sitophobia or Sitiophobia- Fear of food or eating. (Cibophobia)
Snakephobia- Fear of snakes. (Ophidiophobia)
Soceraphobia- Fear of parents-in-law.
Sociophobia- Fear of society or people in general.
Somniphobia- Fear of sleep.
Sophophobia- Fear of learning.
Soteriophobia - Fear of dependence on others.
Spacephobia- Fear of outer space.
Spectrophobia- Fear of specters or ghosts.

Spermatophobia or Spermophobia- Fear of germs.

Spheksophobia- Fear of wasps.

Stasibasiphobia or Stasiphobia- Fear of standing or walking. (Ambulophobia)

Staurophobia- Fear of crosses or the crucifix.

Stenophobia- Fear of narrow things or places.

Stygiophobia or Stigiophobia- Fear of hell.

Suriphobia- Fear of mice.

Symbolophobia- Fear of symbolism.

Symmetrophobia- Fear of symmetry.

Syngenesophobia- Fear of relatives.

Syphilophobia- Fear of syphilis.

T-

Tachophobia- Fear of speed.

Taeniophobia or Teniophobia- Fear of tapeworms.

Taphephobia Fear of being buried alive or of cemeteries.

Tapinophobia- Fear of being contagious.

Taurophobia- Fear of bulls.

Technophobia- Fear of technology.

Teleophobia- 1) Fear of definite plans. 2) Religious ceremony.

Telephonophobia- Fear of telephones.

Teratophobia- Fear of bearing a deformed child or fear of monsters or deformed people.

Testophobia- Fear of taking tests.

Tetanophobia- Fear of lockjaw, tetanus.

Teutophobia- Fear of German or German things.

Textophobia- Fear of certain fabrics.

Thaasophobia- Fear of sitting.

Thalassophobia- Fear of the sea.

Thanatophobia or Thantophobia- Fear of death or dying.

Theatrophobia- Fear of theatres.

Theologicophobia- Fear of theology.

Theophobia- Fear of gods or religion.

Thermophobia- Fear of heat.

Tocophobia- Fear of pregnancy or childbirth.

Tomophobia- Fear of surgical operations.

Tonitrophobia- Fear of thunder.

Topophobia- Fear of certain places or situations, such as stage fright.

Toxiphobia or Toxophobia or Toxicophobia- Fear of poison or of being accidently poisoned.

Traumatophobia- Fear of injury.

Tremophobia- Fear of trembling.

Trichinophobia- Fear of trichinosis.

Trichopathophobia or Trichophobia- Fear of hair. (Chaetophobia, Hypertrichophobia)

Triskaidekaphobia- Fear of the number 13.

Tropophobia- Fear of moving or making changes.

Trypanophobia- Fear of injections.

Tuberculophobia- Fear of tuberculosis.

Tyrannophobia- Fear of tyrants.

U-

Uranophobia or Ouranophobia- Fear of heaven.

Urophobia- Fear of urine or urinating.

V-

Vaccinophobia- Fear of vaccination.

Venustraphobia- Fear of beautiful women.

Verbophobia- Fear of words.

Verminophobia- Fear of germs.

Vestiphobia- Fear of clothing.

Virginitiphobia- Fear of rape.

Vitricophobia- Fear of step-father.

W-

Walloonphobia- Fear of the Walloons.

Wiccaphobia: Fear of witches and witchcraft.

X-

Xanthophobia- Fear of the color yellow or the word yellow.

Xenoglossophobia- Fear of foreign languages.

Xenophobia- Fear of strangers or foreigners.

Xerophobia- Fear of dryness.

Xylophobia- 1) Fear of wooden objects. 2) Forests.

Xyrophobia-Fear of razors.

Z-

Zelophobia- Fear of jealousy.

Zeusophobia- Fear of God or gods.

Zemmiphobia- Fear of the great mole rat.

Zoophobia- Fear of animals.

Laissez-faire Quotes, Memoranda and
Other's Words

Every effort has been made to contact copyright holders; in the event of an inadvertent omission or error, please notify the publisher.

1. Henry Miller / *Tropic of Capricorn/ Obelisk Press /1938 /367 pp.*
2. Chuck Spezzano, Ph.D. / *If it Hurts, It Isn't Love / Marlowe & Company / 2000 / 384 pages /*
3. James Frey / A Million Little Pieces / 2003 / Doubleday Books, a division of Random House
4. Elizabeth Wurtzel / Addiction; More, Now, Again; A Memoir of Addiction / 2000 /
5. Joseph Conrad / The Way of the Animal Powers
6. Erich Goode / *Drugs in American Society / Publisher: McGraw-Hill Education;*
7. Albert Camus / *December 1938 -Notebooks 1935-1942 / published 1962 / Paragon House Publishers*
8. Richard Hell / *Go Now / Simon & Schuster; Reprint edition (June 25 1997) /*
9. Mary Oliver / *Long Life: Essays and other Writings*
"...light flung a rainbow through the moisture; softly the mist rose and rained down onto the deck and baptized all of us."
(Also the quote is actually, *"...mischief of the tides had them...")*
10. Vladimir Nabakov / *Look at the Harlequins! /McGraw-Hill Companies/ 1974*
11. The Cure / *"Numb" / track #10 on the album Wild Mood Swings, written by Smith, Mike. Sony /ATV Music Publishing LLC, Universal Music Publishing Group*

12. Bertrand Russell / "One of the symptoms of an approaching nervous breakdown is the belief that one's work is terribly important." *Conquest of Happiness (1930)*

13. Vladimir Lestrovoy / Hangman photo / Pp #267

14. "You have to be wiped out as a human being in order to be born again as an individual." Pg. 65 Henry Miller from Stand still the Hummingbird. (and other chapters in the book) *Henry Miller on Writing*

15. David Foster Wallace Page #89. "…unhampered by rigid traditionalist notions of what's masculine and feminine, and have never felt the need to adapt that male-gusto-elbows-on-table-open-mouth-pose when ingesting food." Straight out of Infinite jest but wildly and inexcusably applicable AND pertinent here. *There are a few spaces in earlier chapters of this novel that parallel, alright, pretty much quote directly from Infinite Jest - wonderfully super-spot-on phrasings from David Foster Wallace – how this happened I can partially attribute it to being very, very late into the wee morning hours of exploring the written word, and we tackle the similar topics/subjects of addiction (both tennis players too) this is tributary to him, not copyright infringement, I loved the man.

16. Jungian Psychologist / James Hillman

17. Shawn Colvin "Trouble" "…Give me some credit for the hell I've paid…Let me show you how…the less I know the more I comprehend…" Pg. 433

18. A.A Milne : Puffin Books / 112 pages / Now We Are Six

"There were Two little Bears who lived in a Wood…

Picture and Music Permissions

Vladimir Lestrovoy / Hangman photo / Pp #267

#1. Fiddle Faddle / Page 347

Fiddle Faddle is candy-coated popcorn produced by ConAgra Foods. Introduced in 1967, the snack is commonly found in discount and drug stores. Fiddle Faddle consists of popped popcorn covered with either caramel or butter toffee and mixed with peanuts.

#2. H R Pufinstuff Page 245 / *Sid and Marty Krofft* / *CBS Television Distribution* /

H.R. Pufnstuf is a children's television series produced by Sid and Marty Krofft in the United States. It was the first Krofft live-action, life-size puppet program. The seventeen episodes were originally broadcast from September 6, 1969 to December 27, 1969. The broadcasts were successful enough that NBC kept it on the Saturday morning schedule until August 1972. The show was shot in Paramount Studios and its opening was shot in Big Bear Lake, California. Reruns of the show aired on ABC Saturday morning from September 2, 1972 to September 8, 1973 and on Sunday mornings in some markets from September 16, 1973 to September 8, 1974. It was syndicated by itself from 1974 to 1978 and in a package with six other Kroft series under the banner Krofft Superstars from 1978 to 1985. The show currently runs on MeTV at 7a.m every Saturday morning.

After creating costumes for characters in the live-action portion of The Banana Splits Adventure Hour, Sid and Marty Krofft were asked to develop their own Saturday morning children's series for NBC. The plot was recycled from Kaleidoscope, a live puppet show the Kroffts had staged in the Coca-Cola pavilion of the HemisFair '68 world's fair in 1968, including several key characters from this show, such as Luther the dragon and a silly witch. Other ideas were cultivated from Sid's life. As a child, he'd charged friends buttons, not pennies, to view puppet shows in his back yard; buttons were standard currency on Living Island. Sid and Marty had toured with their puppets as the opening act for Judy Garland, and they based Judy the Frog on her. Ludicrous Lion bears more than a passing resemblance to Irving, the eponymous lion in a pilot they had made in 1957 called Here's Irving.

Sid's friend, Lionel Bart, asked him to view a rough cut of the movie adaptation of Oliver. Sid took notice of young actor Jack Wild and immediately decided that was the kid he wanted to play the lead in his television series. Only two actresses auditioned to play Witchiepoo. The first was then unknown Penny Marshall, but it was felt that she was not right for the part. Stage veteran Billie Hayes came in next, set into a maniacal cackle and hopped up on a desk. She was given the part on the spot.

For Marty Kofft, the production was a particular headache. Marty accepted guardianship of Jack Wild while the teenage boy was in the United States filming the show. He later described bringing Wild into his home as a mistake.

Like most children's television shows of the era, H.R. Pufnstuf contained a laugh track, the inclusion of which the Kroffts were initially against. Sid Krofft commented "We were sort of against that, but Si Rose—being in sitcoms—he felt that when the show was put together that the children would not know when to laugh." Marty Krofft added "the bottom line—it's sad—you gotta tell them when it's funny. And the laugh track, [Si] was right. It was necessary, as much as we were always looking to have a real laugh track, a real audience. In comedies, if you don't have them [laugh track], you're in big trouble, because if you don't hear a laugh track, it's not funny. And that's the way the audience [at home] was programmed to view these shows."

Witchiepoo later appeared in the Lidsville episode "Have I Got a Girl For Hoo Doo" where she was lands a date with Horatio J.

Hoodoo. H.R. Pufnstuf appeared in a segment of Sigmund and the Sea Monsters. The Krofft Superstar Hour also involved characters in two segments The Lost Island (which H.R. Pufnstuf was in) and Horror Hotel (which Witchiepoo, Orson Vulture, Seymour Spider, and Stupid Bat are featured with Hoodoo). from Wikipedia

---

#3 Hangman's Rope by nighthawk101stock

#4 the "...elbows on table male gusto..." segment is sinisterly close to page 134 in DFW's **Infinite Jest,** but made perfect sense for this chapter.

#5

"We Are Soldiers In The Army"
Men's Day Celebration/Men's Mass Choir Mr. Golden Skipper and Mr. Johnnie Payne

---

Page#160 reference material words from Wikipedia Encyclopedia.

Rocket Robin Hood leads his "Merry Men", including the strong, dimwitted, and likeable Little John, consummate overeater Friar Tuck (who designs all the Merry Men's weaponry), Robin's two-fisted, red-headed cousin Will Scarlet, Robin's plucky girlfriend Maid Marian, his sharp-witted right-hand man Alan-a-Dale, the scrawny, feisty camp cook Giles (a reformed crook and Gabby Hayes type), and other characters from the classic story of Robin Hood. They live in "the astonishing year 3000" on New Sherwood Forest Asteroid, and are determined to foil the despotic plans of Prince John and his bumbling lackey, the Sheriff of N.O.T.T. (National Outer-space Terrestrial Territories), and other villains such as Dr. Medulla, Manta, Nocturne, and the Warlord of Saturn. Rocket Robin Hood and his people fly in spaceships and use weapons such as "electro-quarterstaffs."

All episodes also feature short vignettes of the various characters.

The drawing and movement styles closely resemble early Filmation productions.

Rocket Robin Hood was animated and voiced by Trillium Productions, an animation studio that was part of the Guest Group—a creative group of companies owned by producer Al Guest. One of the key animators was Jean Mathieson, one of the first female animators, who later formed Rainbow Animation in Canada and Magic Shadows Inc. in the U.S. with Al Guest, where they continued to produce animated TV programming.

Background designer Richard H. Thomas joined the group late in the second season and brought a dark, almost psychedelic feel to the production under director Ralph Bakshi, who would later become a well-known animation producer and would be responsible for, among other things, the animated versions of Fritz the Cat and The Lord of the Rings. Third-season episodes were animated at Ralph's Spot in New York City, although voices continued to be recorded in Toronto.

Bernard Cowan was the narrator of the show and Paul Kligman, who played J. Jonah Jameson in the animated version of Spider-Man, was the voice of Friar Tuck. Len Birman, who appeared in the movies Silver Streak (1976) and Bayo (1985), was the voice of Rocket Robin Hood. Len Carlson subbed in place of Len Birman for Rocket Robin Hood in some of the third season episodes. Carl Banas provided the voice of Little John. Chris Wiggins was the voice of Will Scarlet. There was also a French version titled Robin Fusée, broadcast on French Canadian TV.

This send-off message contains information from Timber Masterson - a simple garden-variety male-type human - that may be proprietary, confidential and/or privileged. This said information is intended only for you, the individual who's got designs around getting into this body of work. Any disclosure, copying, distribution or use of the contents of the information in or attached here in this here laid-out parchment is prohibited...unless, of course, you'd sincerely like to pass on some of these words and/or information to your friends and/or colleagues, as long as it would be for the sole purpose of goodness and myrrh. If you have received this in error, I imagine you're somewhat put-off, maybe even spiritually thrown by these words set oh-so gingerly forth here today, bordering-on-inappropriate-manner in which this sender is, well, sending this thing. We here at the Timber Media offices offer our deepest heartfelt apologies in advance for anything that might seem harsh, hurried through, insensitive, disloyal, insincere, non-sensical, forced, long in the tooth, waste of paper and/or just plain pointless and unhelpful to the intendee i.e. You. Further, Madison MacArthur Knee Braces edible helmet wear and Chiropractic's is in compliance with the Personal Information Protection and Electronic Documents Act (PIPEDA) and we here at Timber Media Enterprises - especially the rather outstanding and ultra-cute temp girl in cubicle #6 - are committed to protecting the privacy and personal information of our predominantly Wingding transcribers, a tattered and misunderstood bunch.

ABOUT THE AUTHOR

The character of Tim Masterson was born on a frosty Toronto winter's eve during the Nixon administration even though he put up a good fight. Little is known about his early years. In another life, he taught tennis at Club Med in the French West Indies, played piano at the Roosevelt Hotel and guitar at The Viper Room in Los Angeles, has thrown wild after-hours underground warehouse jams in Toronto and New York, toured an original Canadian play throughout one of the worst Newfoundland winters on record and has wrote ads for Aaron Spelling's TV website while living in Dana Point, California.

At 17, Masterson began to see himself as a bit of an adventurer and found himself hired on as an usher for the Toronto production of CATS at the Elgin Theatre. ("Yes, sir, your jigs are wildly entertaining, and yes it is mysterious how "Macavity's a mystery cat who's called the hidden paw"...I know, I've seen it - a lot. Now, would you please put your goddamn pants on and return to your seat?!")

Timber got a taste for performing in New York City (living the life of a "club kid,") and in Orange County, CA (living the life of a beach boy and Bikram Yogi enthusiast) but has seemed to keep returning to a home in Toronto, Canada, he's still not sure is there or not.

He co-produced and hosted Toronto's first interactive literary series at The Drake Hotel, bringing innovative American and respected Canadian authors to read and discuss their latest work.

There's been interviews, stories, essays, reviews, arguments, columns and performances. Over the years Tim has been a regular contributor to CIUT's 89.5 FM's talk radio show, HOWL, with Nik Beat and has written for many periodicals and online salons such as *Word Riot*, *Roadside Fiction*, *Akashic Books*, *Fresh Yarn Salon*, *Gadfly Online*, *Pie Magazine*, *Bitchin' Kitsch*, *Unlikely 2.0*, *Yankee Pot Roast*, *Zest Literary Journal*, *Open Book Toronto*, *Flare Magazine*, *Tribe Magazine*, *The Wyre xyyz*, *Milk Magazine*, *Noo Journal*, *3am Magazine*, *Aaron Spelling Prods.*, the *National Post*, the *Montréal Gazette*, *O.C. Metro*, *City Life Magazine*, *Now Magazine*, *Tchad Magazine*, *The Lindsay Post*, *Numb Magazine*, *Wonkavision Magazine*, the *Toronto Special*, *Pages Magazine*, *Chic Magazine*, *The Loop Magazine*, *Purple Prose* and *Onset Magazine*.

He's appeared on stage, screen and the TV shows The Firm, My Babysitter's a Vampire, Reign, Perfect Storms and others, as well as the odd commercial for products he would never use himself. He wrote/produced/hosted segments for a Vancouver-based entertainment program "Metro Café" and a self-styled show, "Life on Timber Street." These are now referred to as The Lost VHS Tapes.

A collection of new and published essays is in the works, *Tales from the Dementia Cul-de-Sac: An Entertaining Life I Seem to Have Survived* which will find its way onto Amazon, Create Space - the usual online suspects and various odd bookstores, and from Tim directly...a recipient of Toronto and Ontario Arts Council Grants towards this non-linear personal adventurist memoir that you caress gingerly before you, now has the Gaul to begin turning this colossal word joust into a screenplay. You can find him on Social Media reporting Timber Talk dispatches from various locals.

Timber Masterson is now a 40-something dandy bachelor and remains just north of Toronto where he volunteers at the Humane Society as a dog walker. No one knows what the future holds for him.

"I see myself as the ridiculous man, the lonely
soul, the wanderer, the restless frustrated artist,
the boy in love with love, always in search of the
absolute and always seeking the unattainable."
(Henry Miller)

Dear
Thompson,
You are a great
support and a
superior sweaterer —
Really hope you
enjoy this.

Timber
Masters